MW01092772

WASHINGTON'S
MARINES

The Origins of the Corps
and the American Revolution, 1775–1777

Major General
Jason Q. Bohm, USMC

SB

Savas Beatie
California

© 2023 Major General Jason Q. Bohm, USMC

All rights reserved. No part of this publication may be reproduced, stored in a retrieval system, or transmitted, in any form or by any means, electronic, mechanical, photocopying, recording, or otherwise, without the prior written permission of the publisher.

First edition, first printing

ISBN-13: 978-1-61121-626-4 (hardcover)
ISBN-13: 978-1-61121-627-1 (ebook)

Library of Congress Cataloging-in-Publication Data

Names: Bohm, Jason Q. author.
Title: Washington's Marines : the origins of the Corps and the American
    Revolution, 1775-1777 / Major General Jason Q. Bohm, USMC.
Description: El Dorado Hills, CA : Savas Beatie LLC, [2023] | Includes
    bibliographical references and index. | Summary: "Washington's Marines
    describes the origin of the United States Marines. It tells the parallel
    stories of the creation and early operations of the Continental Marines,
    Navy, and Army during the American Revolution that culminates in the
    Battles of Trenton, Assunpink Creek, and Princeton"-- Provided by
    publisher.
Identifiers: LCCN 2023006366 | ISBN 9781611216264 (hardcover) | ISBN
    9781611216271 (ebook)
Subjects: LCSH: United States. Marine Corps--History--Revolution,
    1775-1783. | United States--History--Revolution, 1775-1783--Naval
    operations.
Classification: LCC E271 .B646 2023 | DDC 973.3/5--dc23/eng/20230214
LC record available at https://lccn.loc.gov/2023006366

SB

Savas Beatie
989 Governor Drive, Suite 102
El Dorado Hills, CA 95762
916-941-6896 / sales@savasbeatie.com / www.savasbeatie.com

All of our titles are available at special discount rates for bulk purchases in the United States. Contact us for information.

Proudly published, printed, and warehoused in the United States of America.

This book is dedicated to those who fought for America's independence and freedom, and the men and women who defend those freedoms today.

TABLE OF CONTENTS

LIST OF MAPS

Photos have been placed throughout the text for the convenience of the reader.

Note: The views expressed in this publication are those of the author
and do not necessarily reflect the official policy or position of the
Department of Defense or the U.S. Government.

LIST OF ABBREVIATIONS

AA	*American Archives*
AAM	*Almost a Miracle: The American Victory in the War of Independence*
ALID	*A Leap in the Dark: The Struggle to Create the American Republic*
BTP	*The Battles of Trenton and Princeton*
CHS	Connecticut Historical Society
CL	Congressional Library
FONA	*Founders Online*, National Archives
HSP	Historical Society of Philadelphia
GWRWS	*The Papers of George Washington, Revolutionary War Series*
JCC	*Journals of the Continental Congress*
LC	Library of Congress
MCHD	Marine Corps History Division
MCWL	Marine Corps Warfighting Lab
MHS	Massachusetts Historical Society
MIR	*Marines in the Revolution*
MOG	*The Marine Officer's Guide*
NDAR	Naval Documents of the American Revolution
NHD	Navy History Division
PAH	Pennsylvania Archives, Harrisburg
PAP	Pennsylvania Archives, Philadelphia
PB	*Patriot Battles: How the War of Independence was Won*
PCC	Papers of the Continental Congress
PHS	Pennsylvania Historical Society
PMHB	Pennsylvania Magazine of History and Biography
PRR	*Paul Revere's Ride*
RR	*Rebels and Redcoats*
SF	*Semper Fidelis: The History of the United States Marine Corps*
SSAR	*Ships and Seamen of the American Revolution*
SSS	*The Spirit of Seventy-Six: The Story of the American Revolution as Told by its Participants*
TDIO	*The Day is Ours! An Inside View of the Battles of Trenton and Princeton, November 1776-January 1777*
TGC	*The Glorious Cause: The American Revolution, 1763-1789*
TWGW	*The Writings of George Washington*
TWOR	*The War of the Revolution*
WC	*Washington's Crossing*

General George Washington expertly led the Continental Army and many attachments, including the Continental Marines, during the "Ten Crucial Days" between December 25, 1776, and January 3, 1777, to defeat a combined British and Hessian force, saving the nascent United States in the process. *Wikimedia*

Acknowledgments

$\mathcal{I}$ have many people to thank for this book's inspiration, contribution, and improvement. As a student of history, I am grateful to those who made it their mission to preserve America's past and that of the organizations that preserve our great nation. This book has been a labor of love as it allowed a greater depth of knowledge and understanding about two subjects for which I am passionate—American history and the United States Marine Corps.

I am grateful to the authors of three works that were particularly informative and helpful in shaping the drafting of this book. In 1975, Colonel Charles Smith, USMC (Retired), published *Marines in the Revolution*. His definitive and well-researched book takes readers on a journey from the creation of the Continental Marines through the formative years of the American Revolution in which they transformed into the United States Marines. In 1898, William Stryker published a comprehensive history of *The Battles of Trenton and Princeton*, in which the Continental Marines took part. In 2004, historian David Hackett Fisher built on Stryker's good work with a modern telling of the "ten crucial days" that helped turn the tide of war to the Americans' advantage in *Washington's Crossing*.

Several other primary and secondary sources augmented this book. I am thankful to Edward Nevgloski, Director of the Marine Corps History Division, and his archivists, research assistants, and editors, including Dr. Jim Ginther, Mr. John Lyles, and Ms. Annette Amerman. They helped focus my research and provided sound editorial feedback. I am indebted to editors and organizations who have compiled several primary sources into comprehensive works that save researchers countless hours to find these sources individually. Henry Steele Commager and Richard Morris collected several first-hand accounts that effectively tell the story of the American Revolution in their book, *The Spirit of Seventy-Six*. William Clark and William Morgan published a multivolume work on *Naval Documents of The American Revolution.* The National Archives provides electronic access to Philander Chase's *The Papers of George Washington, Revolutionary War Series* through its website, *Founders Online.* I am also thankful to Joan Thomas, Senior Curator of Art at the National Museum of the Marine Corps, for her assistance in including the great work of artist and Marine Colonel Charles Waterhouse, USMC (Retired) in this book.

I must thank Ted Savas and the editorial staff at Savas Beatie for accepting my work for publication, but more importantly, for helping to preserve America's military history. I particularly want to thank Rebecca Hill, editor, and proofreader Joel Manuel for making my work more concise and enjoyable to read.

Cartographer Edward Alexander enhanced this book by producing excellent maps to help readers visualize the battles and actions depicted in this work.

Two other gentlemen who have done much to preserve our nation's history are Dr. Williamson "Wick" Murray and Dr. Charles Neimeyer. Dr. Murray is a historian, professor emeritus of history at Ohio State University, and the author of over 25 books, several articles, and other writings. Dr. Neimeyer is a retired Marine, former Director of the Marine Corps History Division, and the published author of many works. Both gentlemen provided encouragement and mentorship as I was publishing my first book, *From the Cold War to ISIL.* They continue to be an inspiration today.

I am grateful to Dr. Wick Murray, Dr. David Hackett Fisher, Major General James Lukeman, USMC (ret.), and Roger Williams for graciously offering advance praise for this work.

I must thank my wife, Sonja. She has stood by me through over 30 years of service as a Marine Corps family. We have lost count of the many moves, deployments, and new adventures that we have shared together. She remains my rock, and I love her dearly.

Finally, I am thankful to God. The more I mature in life, the more I realize that I owe all that I have and all that I am to Him.

Prologue

*P*atches of frost and snow cover the New Jersey landscape on the cold and peaceful morning of January 3, 1777. The silence is broken by the crunching of hundreds of feet traversing the frozen ground. Small clouds, created by the heavy breathing of Continental soldiers and Marines, rose from a long column snaking its way down a sunken road along the Stony Brook. All is going according to plan, but the element of surprise is lost as American scouts unexpectedly encounter a British unit on the hills outside of Princeton.

At first, both sides are uncertain as to the other's loyalties. Any doubts quickly vanish as the Americans' front ranks observe supply wagons turn and race back toward Princeton. Soldiers in their distinct red coats, with the morning sun glinting off their muskets, rush to gain positions on the nearby high ground. The troops belong to the British 4th Brigade, commanded by Lt. Col. Charles Mawhood, and consist of the 17th, 40th, and 55th Regiments supported by three troops of dragoons. Mawhood had been guarding Princeton but was ordered to reinforce Lord Charles Cornwallis, who had been soundly defeated by Gen. George Washington the previous day in the battle of Assunpink Creek outside Trenton.

Cornwallis believes the rebel army remains positioned just across the creek from his force. Once Mawhood's reinforcements arrive, he intends to traverse the creek and finally crush Washington's troops, ending the rebellion. Using deception and guise, however, Washington's force had vanished undetected, traveling eleven miles farther north throughout the night to capture the isolated British position at Princeton at dawn.

After marching all night, Washington and his troops were exhausted, but their spirits remained high. Following a chain of defeats that began in August 1776, the Continental Army had been forced to surrender New York and New Jersey. It was sitting on the verge of extinction due to casualties, sickness, desertions, and enlistments scheduled to end within weeks. These were desperate times. Washington's army of nearly 20,000 had been reduced to around 2,500, while the British and their Hessian allies remained poised to cross the Delaware River and capture Philadelphia. Responding to Washington's pleas for assistance, Congress called for the New Jersey and Pennsylvania militias and directed the raising of a battalion of Marines. The latter would be detached from the Navy to support the army in its time of need.

Major Samuel Nicholas had successfully led the Marines's first amphibious assault, capturing British weapons and ammunition in New Providence, Bahamas, earlier in the year, which helped supply the army. Now, they were rushing to Washington's aid. Nicholas combined Marine detachments assigned to three Continental frigates under construction in Philadelphia to create a 120-man battalion. Washington assigned the battalion to a brigade of Philadelphia militia referred to as "the Associators."

The Associators and Marines had provided support at the battle of Trenton ten days ago, then reinforced the Continental line to defeat Cornwallis the previous day at Assunpink Creek. They were now following Brig. Gen. Hugh Mercer's brigade as part of Gen. Nathaniel Greene's Division of Washington's army.

Concealed in the low ground of a sunken road, the Marines become aware of a sudden battle to their front, hearing artillery and musket fire break the morning silence. They can tell by the sound of the guns that battle lines are shifting as they receive orders to move forward quickly. Explosions erupt around them, and enemy fire whizzes past as they crest the high ground and enter a chaotic scene.

Brigadier General John Cadwalader, commanding the Philadelphia Associators, sees Mercer's brigade beginning to break. He rushes his men forward with the Marines in trace, forming his troops from the right by divisions. Nicholas maneuvers his Marines to the Associators' right as the mass of troops begins to advance toward the enemy. It does not go well.

With General Mercer down as a casualty, his brigade begins to retreat. The men turn and run head-on into the Associators and Marines, who are attempting to form and advance while under enemy fire. The momentum of the withdrawing soldiers proves too much, and the American line begins to disintegrate. Victory is within Mawhood's grasp, but then George Washington arrives.

Washington's presence and bravery galvanized the soldiers and Marines. The general rallies his men, shouting for them to follow as he charges toward the enemy. Washington's leadership has the desired effect. It inspires the soldiers and Marines to reform and assault the oncoming British, resulting in a rout. The Americans chase the fleeing British for miles, securing their third victory in 10 days.

In 1975, during the bicentennial of the beginning of the American Revolution, Charles R. Smith published the definitive *Marines in the Revolution*.[1] This well-researched

---

1   Charles Smith, Marines in the Revolution: *A History of the Continental Marines in the American Revolution, 1775–1783* (Washington, D.C., 1975). Hereafter cited as *MIR*.

text is a comprehensive history of the creation and contribution of Continental Marines—the predecessors of the United States Marines—in America's first war as a new nation. In it, Smith admitted that primary sources concerning the establishment of the U.S. Navy, and particularly the Marine Corps, are scattered and few. Technological advances in today's interconnected world, however, provide greater access to information than that experienced by Smith and earlier historians. Taking advantage of this access, I have built upon Smith's research, providing another view of the United States Marines's humble beginning and their small, albeit important, contribution to creating and preserving a great nation.

America is a maritime nation. In the eighteenth century, colonists used its vast eastern coastline and abundant lakes and rivers as highways for commerce and lines of communication during military operations. England, France, and Spain validated the need for men who fought on land and sea as they did battle on the waterways to gain control of the North American continent. Each nation employed marines to obtain their national objectives, with American colonists fighting on the side of the British. The Seven Years' War (1756–63) placed Britain in firm control of America's 13 colonies, but it came at a high cost. As a result, the British wanted the colonists to cover the expenses of the war and their enduring defense. The colonists rejected paying increased taxes without proper representation in the government. This conflict led to the American Revolution.

The colonists found themselves at war with a global military power. Thirteen independent colonies needed to unify to break from the mother country. Representatives from each colony formed the Continental Congress in Philadelphia, laying the groundwork to declare independence and establish the United States of America. First, the Americans needed to defeat their British oppressors. Experience had demonstrated the need for a balanced military force that possessed the ability to fight and win on both water and land.

Congress first prioritized the creation of an army to address the hostilities around Boston. George Washington was appointed as commander-in-chief of a force that existed in name only when the war commenced. Washington assumed command of the New England militia units holding the British under siege in Boston following the battles of Lexington and Concord. Slowly, they were molded into a cohesive warfighting organization, but Washington knew more was needed. He pressed Congress to create a permanent national army, but many were opposed to the idea, fearing a standing army could overthrow the government in the future. Instead, Congress opted for state militias that would mobilize only in a time of need.

Debates on the future of the American military continued as hostilities grew between the colonies and England. Washington and his generals prosecuted the war with what forces they received while creating ad hoc organizations to meet operational needs. The early stages of the war found Washington and Benedict Arnold using soldiers to perform the functions of sailors and Marines out of necessity to check the British on the waterways. Different colonies also created their own navies, equipped with marines, to defend their people and property until the Continental Congress provided these forces.

Continued enemy action on the seas compelled Congress to create a navy and marines. Realizing the colonies could never match the Royal Navy ship-for-ship or man and equip large men-of-war and ships-of-the-line, American leaders decided to center their fleet on mid-sized frigates. Congress authorized the construction of 13 frigates and established a marine detachment for each ship but lacked the necessary resources to achieve its goals. Like the army, the navy and marines did not wait for final solutions and began to fight the war with what they had available. They converted merchant ships into combatants and put them to sea to raid British commerce to support the army with captured weapons, gunpowder, and other supplies while also denying them to the enemy. Congress soon called on them to do more.

Washington's army found itself outgunned and outmaneuvered by British regulars, their Hessian mercenaries, and loyalist militia in the war's opening months. In 1776, they suffered one defeat after another in the New York campaign. The British pursued the retreating army across New Jersey, forcing Washington south into Pennsylvania. The Delaware River was the only remaining barrier separating the Americans from their on-rushing adversaries. Washington's force of nearly 20,000 soldiers had been decimated after months of sustained combat, disease, and desertion, and it was facing the loss of thousands more to terminating enlistments. The very survival of the fledging country was at risk. The loss of the army meant the loss of the nation.

By late 1776, the newly formed United States faced a crisis, and the fledgling Congress lacked the power and authority to address the situation adequately. It did have the Continental Marines, however. Created on November 10, 1775, for service with the fleet, the Marines assisted ships' captains in maintaining good order and discipline with their crews. They fought from the top masts of sailing ships, manned ships' guns, sniped the leadership of opposing forces, and led boarding parties to capture enemy vessels. Marines also formed landing parties to conduct raids, defeat enemy forces, and capture limited objectives as part of larger naval campaigns. Though they never ventured far from their assigned ships to whose captains they answered, the army's dire situation now required the employment of marines in a non-traditional role: that of fighting a sustained land campaign. Congress directed the Continental Marines to detach from the Navy to join Washington and the Continental Army in defending the nation.

Major Samuel Nicholas, the Continental Marines's senior officer at the time, combined the detachments from frigates under construction in Philadelphia to form a battalion of marines for service with the army. They were assigned to a brigade of Philadelphia militia known as the Associators that was first formed by Benjamin Franklin and were joined by several state marine units. The Continental and state marines—Washington's Marines—spent the following months crossing rivers, hiking countless miles, and engaging enemy forces beside their army brethren. In the coming days, the Marines participated in three key battles: Trenton, Assunpink Creek, and Princeton, which proved to be a turning point in the war. In Frederick the Great's view, "the achievements of Washington and his little band of compatriots between the 25th of December [1776] and the 4th of

January [1777], a space of ten days, were the most brilliant of any recorded in the annals of military achievements."[2]

The Marines contributed in other ways. Marines and sailors at sea captured critical supplies necessary to sustain the army during the trying winter months, and Nicholas' Marines helped avert another manpower crisis in the army. Following the battle of Princeton, Washington moved his army to Morristown in the New Jersey highlands, where he engaged in a forage war. His small force of 4,000 troops effectively held 27,000 British and Hessian soldiers in check; however, terminating enlistments again reached crisis proportions. The American artillery, under the capable leadership of Brig. Gen. Henry Knox, had more guns than men to work them. Recognizing the Marines's versatility and their experience with the naval guns on ships, Knox requested that they be assigned to the Army Artillery Corps, until they were required to return to their ships. Washington granted Knox's request, and the Marines served in this role for several months before departing for the fleet, marking the end of the Marines's first land campaign.

The following chapters take the reader on a journey that explores the factors that led to America's fight for independence. They also document the parallel stories of the Continental Army, Navy, and Marines, whose paths intersected when most needed to preserve the nascent nation's struggle for survival and freedom. The Goldwater-Nichols Department of Defense Reorganization Act of 1986 codified the armed forces' approach to "joint operations," which the services excel at today. America's first joint operations, however, occurred in 1775–76.[3] This book provides insights into the actions, characters, and challenges of these operations. It is an extraordinary story of virtue, commitment, and sacrifice. The work concludes by describing the evolution of the Marine Corps' roles and missions over the 247 years of its existence.

The further removed our citizens become from the trying and uncertain days of the American Revolution, the less they appreciate the sacrifice, dedication, and perseverance required to continue maintaining these freedoms. By sharing this story of America's heroic forefathers, I hope to help close this gap. I hope you enjoy it.

God Bless and *Semper Fidelis*,
Jason Q. Bohm

---

2   J. F. C. Fuller, *Decisive Battles of the U.S.A., 1776–1918* (Lincoln, NE, 1942), 33.

3   Joint Publication 1, *Doctrine for the Armed Forces of the United States* defines "joint operations" as connoting activities, operations, organizations, etc., in which elements of two or more military departments participate. Martin Dempsey, *Joint Publication 1, Doctrine for the Armed Forces of the United States: 25 March 2013, Incorporating Change 1, 12 July 2017* (Washington, D.C., 2017), GL-8.

Chapter One

Enter the Marines

"Some people spend an entire lifetime wondering if they made a difference in the world. But the Marines don't have that problem."

— President Ronald Reagan[1]

*A*ny person acquainted with United States Marines knows that no matter where they may be in the world, during peace or war, Marines dutifully celebrate the birth of their Corps every year. The Marine Corps' official birthday is November 10, 1775; it is thus older than the nation it serves. The Marines jealously guard the history and traditions that earned them a reputation as one of the world's finest fighting organizations.

One such tradition is the reading at every Marine Corps birthday celebration of Article 38, *Marine Corps Manual*, published in 1921 by John A. Lejeune, the 13th Commandant of the Marine Corps. It states, in part, "On November 10, 1775, a Corps of Marines was created by a resolution of the Continental Congress . . . In memory of them it is fitting that we who are Marines should commemorate the birthday of our Corps by calling to mind the glories of its long and illustrious history." Lejeune's message serves as a reminder of battles won, stating that, "From the battle of Trenton to the Argonne, Marines have won foremost honors in war, and in the long eras of tranquility at home generation after generation of Marines have grown gray in war in both hemispheres, and in every corner of the seven seas, that our country and its citizens might enjoy peace and security."[2]

---

1 Department of Defense, *Deputy Secretary of Defense Speech as Delivered by Deputy Secretary of Defense Gordon R. England, Washington, D.C., Saturday, November 08, 2008*, http://archive.defense. gov/Speeches/Speech.aspx?SpeechID=1321, accessed July 4, 2019.

2 Kenneth W. Estes, *The Marine Officer's Guide*, 5th ed. (Annapolis, 1989), 500. Hereafter cited as *MOG*. See Appendix A for General Lejeune's full birthday message.

Written following the end of World War I, General Lejeune's words are still true today. The United States should be justifiably proud of its Corps of Marines. For 247 years, Marines have demonstrated their willingness to sacrifice all for the greater good. This ethos is manifested in the Marine Corps motto, *Semper Fidelis*—"Always Faithful" to their God, their Country, and their Corps. The Marines' strong sense of selfless service to others is forged in a warfighting culture of shared hardship and an unwavering commitment to always placing one's mission before self.

Marines possess a naval character. Created to serve with the fleet and organized as part of the Department of the Navy, Marines continue to serve on ships as the nation's expeditionary force in readiness. The 82nd Congress wrote into law that the Marine Corps will always be "the most ready, when the nation is least ready."[3] This charter drives Marines to be prepared in "every clime and place" and every warfighting domain, as articulated in the first verse of the Marines' hymn:

> From the halls of Montezuma
> To the shores of Tripoli
> We will fight our country's battles
> In the air, on land, and sea
> First to fight for right and freedom
> And to keep our honor clean
> We are proud to claim the title of United States Marines[4]

Today's Marines operate far beyond the domains of air, land, and sea. Cyberspace and information are new areas Marines must successfully navigate in order to achieve victory on twenty-first-century battlefields.

This concept is often difficult to grasp. Marines have come under attack throughout history by some of our nation's senior leaders, both civilian and military. They questioned the need for a Marine Corps, a special force fighting in all domains, when it has an Army, Navy, and Air Force that excel in these areas. Lieutenant General Victor Krulak attempted to answer that very question in 1957 when Gen. Randolph Pate, the Commandant of the Marine Corps at the time, asked, "Why does the U.S. need a Marine Corps?"[5] Krulak asserted that the nation did not "need" a Marine Corps, it "wanted" a Marine Corps. This desire hails from the nation's belief that Marines are men and women of honor, succeeding at

3 James Kraska & Raul Pedrozo, *International Maritime Security Law* (Leiden, Netherlands, 2013), 41.

4 Estes, *MOG*, 481.

5 Victor Krulak, *First to Fight: An Inside View of the U.S. Marine Corps* (New York, 1984), xvii.

everything they do. The nation understands that Marines live by higher standards and will always remain *Semper Fidelis*.

This reputation was not established overnight. It began in November 1775, as 13 independent British colonies struggled to become a free, united, and independent nation. American colonists resisted the actions of an oppressive British government and determined to throw off the shackles of the motherland. Great Britain, however, was not willing to release its subjects. Americans would have to fight for their independence. Conducting a war in the eighteenth century required an army, navy, and marines, which the colonists lacked as hostilities commenced. The newly formed Continental Congress struggled to keep up with the fast-moving events of the opening years of the Revolution. General George Washington adopted local militias to form the Continental Army as Congress created the Continental Navy and Marines to fight on the sea. Marines would prove their worth in the opening year of the war, but circumstances quickly required more.

Washington's army experienced multiple defeats in 1776. It was forced out of New York and was driven through New Jersey as numbers dwindled due to casualties, capture, sickness, desertions, and the termination of enlistments. December 1776 was a low point for the army and the infant nation. Washington needed help, and Marines answered the call. Although created to fight on the sea and conduct short raids ashore, Marines and sailors demonstrated their versatility in fighting a prolonged land campaign. The Corps' senior officer, Maj. Samuel Nicholas, organized and led a battalion of Marines under Washington's command in the battles of Trenton and Princeton. It was the first of many land campaigns assigned to Marines in defense of the country throughout its history.

This was a new concept to Marines, as they were not trained for prolonged land campaigns or operating onshore beyond the support of naval guns. In the winter of 1776, Marines knew more about running a spar or handling ships' lines than the field craft needed to prosecute a winter campaign like that of Trenton and Princeton. Members of the congressional committee who recommended establishing "American Marines," however, believed they would be "of the Utmost service, being capable of serving either by sea or Land."[6] By the time Marines joined Washington's forces, they were well-equipped and led by officers who had been bloodied in earlier naval battles and land-based skirmishes. They possessed a high state of training and discipline, learning the importance of instant obedience to orders and understanding that failure could result in death and the loss of their ships. Following their early successes when they joined Washington outside

---

6 William Bell Clark, ed., *Naval Documents of The American Revolution*, 12 vols. (Washington, D.C., 1966), 2:957, hereafter cited as *NDAR*; Smith, *MIR*, 8.

Trenton, confidence and morale rose among the Marines, bringing new energy to the tired and weary Army.

The battles of Trenton and Princeton provided one of the first examples of the Marines' ability to adapt to meet the nation's needs. Samuel Nicholas's Marines possessed the skills to fight on land and sea. Trained in the basic disciplines, standards, and tactics of infantrymen, they also brought unique skills required of the naval service. Marines could operate heavy shipboard cannons that could be placed on land carriages and employed ashore. This valuable skill was used at Trenton and Princeton, resulting in some Marines joining the Army's artillery permanently due to a critical shortfall of trained personnel during the 1776-77 winter campaign. Marines also possessed the sharpshooter skills needed to snipe enemy officers while fighting from the high riggings of their ships during sea battles. These skills and many others made Marines valuable partners to their brothers in the Army, and the Marines have exhibited them in all American wars and military actions to the present day.

Marines came in many forms during the opening stages of the Revolutionary War. The Continental Marines, sanctioned by Congress, were joined by state Marines and privateers performing Marine functions. Some soldiers also received the task of performing the duties of Marines to meet local requirements. These different groups often worked independently, performing well together during the battles of Trenton and Princeton. Regardless, the Marines played an essential role in the defeat of the British and the birth of a new nation.

Before delving further into the contribution of America's Marines, one must first understand the origin of marines and their role in history. "Marine" is defined as "of or relating to the sea." No one can clearly identify the first Marines. Men have been fighting on the sea since the beginning of civilization. In 480 BC, the Greek warrior Themistocles employed "Epibataes," or "heavy-armed sea soldiers," to defeat the Persians under Xerxes at Salamis.[7] During the First Punic War (264 to 241 BC), the Romans effectively employed soldiers for sea combat to defeat the Carthaginians. Roman legionaries exploited their superior ground fighting skills by employing long planks with spikes called "corvus" to latch onto enemy ships, allowing their soldiers to board and defeat enemy vessels. In 1203, Venice organized the first formal Corps of Marines to assist in the defeat of the Byzantine Empire during the Fourth Crusade. 1537 saw the creation of the Spanish "Infantería de Armada" (navy infantry) to serve with its Mediterranean galley squadrons.

The modern origin of Marines can be traced to the European powers during the seventeenth century. The French and Dutch formed naval infantry units by training sailors for ground combat. In 1644, the British were the first to establish a dedicated group of soldiers to serve the Admiralty. The Duke of York and Albany's Maritime Regiment of Foot, also known as the Lord High Admiral's Regiment, served in the Dutch and French wars, disbanding in 1688.[8] Regiments of Royal Marines took part in the War of the Spanish Succession (1702-13), the War of Jenkins's Ear (1739-41), in which a regiment of American colonists, including George Washington's brother Lawrence, served; the War of the Austrian Succession (1744-48); and the Seven Years' War, also known as the French and Indian War (1756-63). During the latter conflict, the British Parliament authorized the establishment of a body of Royal Marines that endures today.

The early Royal Marines performed a variety of tasks. While at sea, they ensured good order and discipline of ships' crews, enforced ships' regulations concerning thievery, living conditions and misconduct, and punished offenders. Additionally, they protected officers from possible mutiny. During combat, Marines employed muskets against enemy officers and gun crews, repelled borders or provided boarding parties to capture enemy ships, and manned their own ships' guns beside their Navy counterparts. Ships' captains employed detachments of Marines as landing parties to conduct raids and other expeditions essential to naval campaigns. The close association between Royal Marines and the American colonists who served within their ranks before the Revolution contributed to the Royal Marines later being used as the model for creating the United States Marines.

The United States is a maritime nation. The 13 original colonies relied heavily on the sea for their livelihood due to their location along the eastern seaboard. Each colony grew and prospered through seaport cities that became focal points for trade. Homespun goods and crops produced in the colonies were sold and traded for international products that originated in places like the West Indies, France, Netherlands, and the colonies' largest trade partner, England. Coastal towns also made their livings by fishing and other profitable maritime industries. Major cities such as Philadelphia, New York, Boston, and Charleston became hubs of international trade and were connected to road, river, and canal networks that projected into the interior of the colonies. These factors made the seas and major seaports strategically crucial to both the colonists and the British during the American Revolution.

The British had enormous logistical challenges to overcome during the Revolution. George Washington and the Continental forces possessed strategic interior lines of communication that allowed them to quickly transfer personnel, weapons, and equipment across the colonies. The British held exterior lines that

8 Cyril Field, *Britain's Sea Soldiers*, 2 vols. (Liverpool, UK, 1924), 1:14-25.

required greater travel distances to reinforce and support their land and sea forces fighting in the American campaign. Washington could be reinforced and draw supplies from any of the colonies in which he was operating. At the same time, the British often had to transport reinforcements and supplies over 3,000 miles across the Atlantic Ocean before distribution. Britain's problem was exacerbated by the necessity of protecting its many other holdings and the sea lines of communication connecting them across the world. But this apparent weakness of the British also provided a great advantage. They maintained naval superiority in the colonies until the French entered the war and exploited this advantage by effectively employing the seas and rivers as maneuver space, which the colonists could not match until the days leading up to the battle of Trenton. For these reasons, Britain maintained a large fleet and Royal Marines.

An analysis of British and Continental naval forces at the start of the Revolution is telling. The British North American Squadron, commanded by Vice Admiral Samuel Graves on January 1, 1775, consisted of 24 ships, ranging from HMS *Gaspee*, manning six guns with a crew of 30, to HMS *Boyne*, manning 70 guns with a crew of 520.[9] These ships were based out of major port cities from Florida to Maine and crewed by officers, seamen, and Marines with years of experience.

The number of British ships, seamen, and Marines dramatically increased once hostilities commenced. For example, over 500 transports and 70 British warships sailed into New York Harbor in June 1776 in preparation for operations to capture that city.[10] By the war's end, the Royal Navy consisted of 174 ships of the line (60-100 guns), 198 two-deckers and frigates (20-56 guns), 85 sloops of war (8-18 guns), and many smaller vessels.[11] The ranks of Royal Marines grew to 19,000 during the war to man these vessels and operate ashore.

The Continental Navy and Marines did not yet exist. The colonists would have to build a fleet of warships and man them with sailors and Marines, requiring resources and time. They employed privateers as a stopgap until Congress could establish a professional naval force. Privateers employed privately and state-owned armed merchant vessels to capture or destroy British merchantmen attempting to resupply their forces in the colonies.[12] Generals George Washington and Benedict Arnold also used small personal fleets manned by soldiers to confront British forces

9   Jack Coggins, *Ships and Seamen of the American Revolution* (Harrisburg, PA, 1969), 20. Hereafter cited as *SSAR*.

10   Patrick K. O'Donnell, *Washington's Immortals: The Untold Story of an Elite Regiment Who Changed the Course of the Revolution* (New York, 2016), 37.

11   Coggins, *SSAR*, 22.

12   Robert H. Patton, *Patriot Pirates: The Privateer War for Freedom and Fortune in the American Revolution* (New York, 2009).

at Boston and Lake Champlain in upstate New York. While these local navies and privateers achieved some success, more needed to be done. Fortunately, the colonies possessed shipyards and artisans skilled in naval construction. Colonial ship designers gained a reputation for building larger and faster vessels of the same type as their British counterparts. In examining the *Hancock* after its capture during the war, one British naval officer described her as "the finest and fastest frigate in the world."[13]

The colonists' advantage with frigates later helped to shape the Continental Congress's and the Navy's strategy for prosecuting a naval war against the British. Congress understood that it could not match the British ship-for-ship, so it made a conscious decision to designate mid-weight frigates as the capital ships of the American fleet. The Americans lacked the resources and crews to operate large men-of-war, or ships of the line, like their British and European counterparts. This decision drove them to avoid large fleet battles, choosing to pursue one-on-one naval encounters and focusing on attacking British commerce and resupply efforts. Later, they relied on the French and Spanish to conduct fleet-sized actions against the British on their behalf.

Congress authorized the construction of 13 frigates in December 1775; all of these were launched between 1776-77 and later destroyed or captured by the British. The remainder of the Navy consisted of a hodge-podge of frigates and smaller ships that were either built, purchased, captured, or lent to the colonies ranging from small eight-gun schooners to frigates manning 28 to 36 guns.[14] The Americans built one 74-gun ship of the line in 1782, the *America*, but she never saw service during the war and was later given to France.[15] The decision to equip the Navy with smaller ships helped regulate the numbers needed to fill the ranks of sailors and Marines the fleet required, allowing the masses to enlist in the Army.

The Continental Navy was officially established on October 13, 1775. Initially lacking the resources to establish a national navy, the Continental Congress tasked the individual colonies with providing naval armaments and defenses, just as it had called for establishing local militias. Pressure from the colonies and operational requirements forced Congress to establish a committee addressing the naval aspects

---

13 Ibid., 21. The use of the prefix "USS or U.S.S.," meaning "United States Ship," did not begin until President Theodore Roosevelt signed Executive Order 549 on January 8, 1907 which stated, "In order that there shall be uniformity in the matter of designating naval vessels, it is hereby directed that the official designation of vessels of war, and other vessels of the Navy of the United States, shall be the name of such vessel, preceded by the words, United States Ship, or the letters U.S.S., and by no other words or letters." "Ship Naming in the United States Navy," https://web.archive.org/web/20150103224426/http://www.history.navy.mil/faqs/faq63-1.htm, accessed 12 July 2019.

14 Coggins, *SSAR*, 203-204.

15 Ibid., 205; Samuel Eliot Morison, *John Paul Jones* (New York, 1959), 329-331.

of war; this was done on October 5, 1775. The Naval (later Marine) Committee made its recommendations, and on October 13, Congress resolved to "fit out two sailing vessels, armed with ten carriage guns, as well as swivel guns, and manned by crews of eighty, and to send them out on a cruise of three months to intercept transports carrying munitions and stores to the British Army in America."[16] In November, Congress purchased five additional merchant vessels, converting them into warships and appointing the Navy's first admiral to command the fleet. It had not, however, formally established the Continental Marines. That oversight was short-lived, as the Continental Congress soon received a petition from the Passamaquoddy, Nova Scotia Committee of Safety that would change the course of history.

The people of Passamaquoddy sought an association with the "North Americans, for the preservation of their rights and liberties."[17] This request energized Congress into developing courses of action to welcome Nova Scotia to the fight against British aggression and secure the naval facilities, ships, and provisions at nearby Halifax. The operation was designed as a naval campaign that required marines. As such, on November 10, 1775, the Continental Congress resolved "[t]hat two Battalions of marines be raised" and that . . . "no persons be appointed to office, or Inlisted in to said Battalions, but such as are good seamen, or so acquainted with maritime affairs as to be able to serve to advantage by sea." Congress intended for the Marines "to serve for and during the present war between Great Britain and the colonies, unless dismissed by order of Congress" and further directed that "they be distinguished by the names of the first and second battalion of American Marines." The resolution concluded by ordering Washington to pull select soldiers from the army outside Boston to form the Marine battalions.[18]

16 Stephen Howarth, *To Shining Sea: A History of the United States Navy 1775-1991* (New York, 1991), 6-7; Kenneth Hagan, *This People's Navy: The Making of American Sea Power* (New York, 1991), 1-4; "The Birth of the Navy of the United States," https://www.history.navy.mil/browse-by-topic/commemorations-toolkits/navy-birthday/OriginsNavy/the-birth-of-the-navy-of-the-united-states.html, accessed 4 July 2019.

17 M. St. Clair & Peter Force, *American Archives*, series 4, vol. 3, (Washington, D.C.: 1840), 1904, hereafter cited as *AA*; Smith, *MIR*, 7.

18 The full resolution reads: "That two Battalions of marines be raised, consisting of one Colonel, two Lieutenant Colonels, two Majors, and other officers as usual in other regiments; and that they consist of an equal number of privates with other battalions; that particular care be taken, that no persons be appointed to office, or Inlisted in to said Battalions, but such as are good seamen, or so acquainted with maritime affairs as to be able to serve to advantage by sea when required; that they be Inlisted and commissioned to serve for and during the present war between Great Britain and the colonies, unless dismissed by order of Congress; that they be distinguished by the names of the first and second battalion of American Marines, and that they be considered as part of the number which the continental Army before Boston is ordered to consist of." *Journals of the Continental Congress*, 1774-1789, vol. 3-1775, (Washington, D.C., 1905), 348, hereafter cited as *JCC*; Smith, *MIR*, 10.

General Washington did not support this effort. He wrote to John Hancock, "it will be impossible to get the Men to inlist for the Continuance of the war, which will be an insuperable obstruction to the formation of the two Battallions of Marines."[19] Washington was already short-handed in holding the British under siege in Boston while attempting to reorganize and professionalize his developing army. He hoped to avoid the added burden of drawing troops from his already depleted ranks to form two battalions of Marines. He further lacked the resources to mount successful operations into Nova Scotia.[20] Washington explained to Hancock that "it is next to an impossibility, to attempt any thing there [Nova Scotia], in the present unsettled & precarious State of the Army."[21] On December 8, Hancock responded, "The Congress also have relieved your difficulties with respect to the two battalions of marines, having ordered that the raising them out of the army be suspended. It is the desire of Congress that such a body of forces may be raised, but their meaning is that it be in addition to the army voted."[22] Congress still intended to establish a formal body of Marines on its own to serve in other capacities.[23]

On November 5, 1775, Congress commissioned Samuel Nicholas as the first American Marine officer, making him the senior ranking official in the Continental Marines.[24] Over the years, many have traditionally recognized Nicholas as the first Commandant of the Marine Corps, although this title was not formally bestowed to the Commandant until 1798.[25] Nicholas's appointment became official on November 28 when John Hancock signed his commission.[26]

19 "Founders Online," National Archives, "From George Washington to John Hancock, 28 November 1775," https://founders.archives.gov/documents/Washington/03-02-02-0404, accessed Dec. 31, 2019 [Original source: Philander D. Chase, ed., *The Papers of George Washington, Revolutionary War Series, vol. 2, September 16, 1775-December 31, 1775* (Charlottesville, VA, 1987), 444-448], hereafter cited as *FONA*.

20 Smith, *MIR*, 12.

21 *FONA*, "From George Washington to John Hancock, 28 November 1775."

22 *FONA*, "To George Washington from John Hancock, 8 December 1775," https://founders.archives.gov/documents/Washington/03-02-02-0465, accessed Dec. 31, 2019 [Original source: Chase, ed., *Washington Papers*, 513-515].

23 Clark, ed., *NDAR*, 2:957.

24 Estes, *MOG*, 90; Allan Millet, *Semper Fidelis: The History of the United States Marine Corps* (New York, 1980), 8, hereafter cited as *SF*; Avery Chenoweth & Brooke Nihart, *Semper Fi: The Definitive Illustrative History of the U.S. Marines* (New York, 2005), 35; Smith, MIR, 12-13.

25 The title "Commandant" was not formally assigned to the senior Marine officer until it was given to William Ward Burrows in 1798. See Allan Millett & Jack Shulimson, eds., *Commandants of the Marine Corps* (Annapolis, MD, 2004) for a full history of the Commandants of the Marine Corps.

26 The commission reads, "We reposing especial Trust and Confidence in your Patriotism, Valour, Conduct and Fidelity, DO by these Presents, constitute and appoint you to be Captain of Marines

Major Samuel Nicholas was the first Continental Marine (1775-83). Nicholas led the Continental Marines in conducting their first amphibious operation in New Providence, Bahamas. He later formed a battalion using Marines from three ships' detachments to reinforce Gen. George Washington and the Continental Army. Nicholas is traditionally known as the first United States Marine Corps Commandant, but this position was not formally established until after his retirement. *Author*

Thirty-one-year-old Nicholas was a prominent figure in Philadelphia.[27] He was a Quaker by birth and the only son in his family. Nicholas's father passed away when he was seven years old, after which he attended the Academy of Philadelphia (later the University of Pennsylvania). Graduating at 16, Nicholas was admitted to the Schuylkill Fishing Company, an exclusive gentlemen's club. In 1766, he co-founded the Gloucester Fox Hunting Club, whose members came from Philadelphia's leading families. These associations introduced Nicholas to some of the city's most prominent citizens. Scant information has been found regarding his employment, but it's believed that Nicholas may have been a merchant and later as the proprietor of a popular local tavern called The Conestoga Wagon.[28] Nicholas faithfully served as the senior Marine officer from 1775 to 1783, never attaining the rank of colonel as called for in the original resolution that established the Continental Marines.

Nicholas's first task was recruiting additional Marines to serve in detachments with the newly formed fleet, as opposed to manning the battalions that were envisioned to invade Nova Scotia. In late November, Nicholas's friend from the Fox Hunting Club, Joseph Shoemaker, received a commission as a captain, while local master carpenter Isaac Craig was commissioned as a lieutenant.[29] Captain John

in the service of the Thirteen United Colonies of North-America, fitted out for the defence of American Liberty, and for repelling every hostile Invasion thereof." For a photo of the original commission see Smith, *MIR*, 13.

27 See Smith, *MIR*, 459-460, for a description Nicholas's life and service in the Marines.

28 "Samuel Nicholas," https://pabook.libraries.psu.edu/literary-cultural-heritage-map-pa/bios/Nicholas__Samuel, accessed July 7, 2019; Smith, *MIR*, 13.

29 Melissah Pawlikowski, "From the Bottom up: Isaac Craig and the Process of Social and Economic Mobility During the Revolutionary era," (Master's thesis, Duquesne University, 2007), https://dsc.duq.edu/etd/1028, accessed July 14, 2019.

Lieutenant Matthew Parke served under Capt. Samuel Nicholas on the Continental flagship *Alfred*. He participated in the amphibious raid at New Providence and was later promoted to captain to command the Marine detachment on the *Columbus*. He subsequently served under John Paul Jones on the *Ranger* and later transferred to the *Alliance*, on which he served until the war's end. *Wikimedia*

Welsh and Lts. John Fitzpatrick, Robert Cummings, John Hood Wilson, Henry Dayton, Matthew Parke, and a Lt. Miller later joined Nicholas and the others. Little is known about the early lives of these first officers, other than Isaac Craig and 29-year-old Matthew Parke, the latter of whom had immigrated to America with his grandfather from Ipswich, England.[30]

Recruitment of the first enlisted Marines was conducted by Capts. Nicholas, Shoemaker, and Welsh and Lts. Craig and Wilson. Drummer boys marched through Philadelphia streets, playing drums adorned with decorative paintings to draw potential recruits into the public meeting houses. One such instrument had a painting of a coiled rattlesnake with the phrase "Don't Tread on Me" etched below it.[31] On the day of his appointment, Capt. Robert Mullan, the owner of the popular Tun Tavern, enlisted two brothers to be his drummer and fifer, hoping to use their music to draw potential recruits into his establishment. Tun Tavern, on the east side of Philadelphia's South Walnut Street, became a focal point of Marine recruitment; it has gone down in history as the accepted birthplace of the United States Marine Corps.[32]

By December 22, Lieutenant Craig had enlisted 40 men to serve as the Marine company assigned to the brig *Andrew Doria*. A view of Lieutenant Craig's company provides insight into the composition of the Marine Corps at this early stage. Few of Craig's Marines were born in America. They were immigrants from

30 Smith, *MIR*, 13-14; Millett, *SF*, 8.

31 Smith, *MIR*, 14.

32 Chenoweth & Nihart, *Semper Fi*, 34; Millett, *SF*, 13; Estes, *MOG*, 90. Nihart asserts that although it is commonly accepted that Tun Tavern is the "birthplace" of the Marine Corps, Captain Mullan recruited his company at Tun Tavern in 1776, rather than in 1775 when the Marines were established. He further asserts, however, that the tavern could still be considered the birthplace of the Corps, because Congressman John Adams and the other members of the congressionally appointed Naval Committee met at Tun Tavern when they decided to form the Continental Navy and Marines.

Tun Tavern, Philadelphia, is the accepted birthplace of the United States Marine Corps. Captain Robert Mullan, the tavern owner, commanded the Marine detachment on the frigate *Delaware*. Mullan and his detachment joined Samuel Nicholas in forming the Marine battalion that served under Gen. George Washington in the battles of Trenton and Princeton. *Wikimedia*

Great Britain, Ireland, Holland, Switzerland, and Germany. All but one enlisted from Philadelphia. Their average age was 25 1/2 years old, with the youngest being 18 and the oldest 40. Their average height was five feet six inches, with the shortest Marine only being five feet three and one-half inches and the tallest six feet. The men who joined Craig's company brought diverse skills to the unit. They were carpenters, masons, barbers, bakers, cabinet makers, coopers, jewelers, brass founders, tailors, butchers, painters, weavers, wool combers, millers, laborers, servants, and one doctor.[33]

The reasons each Marine chose to voluntarily enlist in these early years were as diverse as their backgrounds. Some older men may have joined to support their families and livelihood. The artisans no doubt watched with trepidation as the British continued to impose taxes on the colonies without representation and the economic strangle the British placed on those in Boston who opposed such measures. Some may have wanted to settle scores against American Loyalists or

33 Clark, ed., *NDAR*, 3:175-176; "Muster-Rolls of Marines and Artillery Commanded by Capt. Isaac Craig, of Pennsylvania, in 1775 and 1778," *Pennsylvania Magazine of History and Biography*, vol. 13 (October 1, 1888), 351, https://archive.org/details/jstor-20083274/page/n1, accessed July 7, 2019; Smith, *MIR*, 417.

The First Recruits, December 1775. Painting by Col. Charles H. Waterhouse, USMCR. Captain Samuel Nicholas and Lt. Matthew Parke observe a sergeant forming two ranks of new recruits behind the stern of the *Alfred* in port, Philadelphia. *Art Collection, National Museum of the Marine Corps, Triangle, Virginia*

royal appointees who may have done them wrong. The younger men may have joined for the promise of adventure and financial gain from prize money collected from the sale of captured ships and goods.

The revolutionary fervor and hope for independence gaining momentum across the colonies undoubtedly affected Marines of all ages. By war's end, 231 officers and approximately 2,000 enlisted men had served honorably as Continental Marines, with many more serving as state and soldier-Marines. Forty-nine Continental Marines gave their lives in service to their country, and another 70 were wounded in action. Regardless of their reasons for joining, all Marines would contribute to America gaining its independence.[34]

Captain Nicholas organized the newly formed Continental Marines into five companies to serve on the first ships acquired by the Continental Navy. He immediately embarked on a plan to equip and train them for their first duties. The Continental Congress did not have the means to supply the Marines, so the Pennsylvania Committee of Safety provided muskets, bayonets, scabbards, ramrods, cartridge boxes, and belts. Nicholas attempted to obtain uniforms for the

34 Edwin N. McClellan, *Personal Collection*, Archives Branch, Marine Corps History Division, Quantico, VA, reprinted from the *United States Institute Proceedings*, vol. 49, no. 11, whole No. 249 (November 1923).

Marines, but all available clothing was being diverted to the Continental Army. The first Marines deployed with the clothes they acquired on their own or had captured from the enemy. Nicholas also began to drill the Marines in their duties and indoctrinate them through newly published naval regulations.

Although the Continental Congress was short on resources, it devised ample rules and regulations for its infant naval force. Congress published 44 separate articles concerning the conduct of Marines and sailors in the "Rules for the Regulations of the Navy of the United Colonies."[35] The Marines were responsible for personally adhering to these rules as well as assisting the ships' officers in enforcing the rules among the sailors. The reach of the regulations was broad. Ship commanders received guidance on how to "show themselves a good example of honor and virtue to their officers and men" while suppressing "all dissolute, immoral, and disorderly practices." Congress directed that "devine service be performed twice a day on board," and that anyone "heard to swear, curse, or blaspheme the name of God" be caused to "wear a wooden collar, or some other shameful badge of distinction." Drunken seamen or Marines were to be placed in irons until sober and drunk officers forfeited two days' pay. Commanders had the authority to impose punishment, including "twelve lashes upon his bare back with a cat of nine tails."

The new regulations also directed commanders to maintain copious notes. They were to record enlistments, service, pay, prizes taken and distributed, and deaths. Congress directed strict adherence to the supply of provisions for the crew, including food and lodging. It specifically laid out the daily proportion of provisions each crew member was entitled to on the individual days of the week. For example, on Saturdays, each crew member received one pound of bread, a pound of pork, half a pint of peas, and four ounces of cheese. Each man also received half a pint of rum per day. Marine captains were the second-highest paid members of the crew, below the ships' captains. Navy captains or commanders received thirty-two dollars per month, while Marine captains received twenty-six and two-thirds dollars per month. Their equivalent in the Navy, lieutenants, only received twenty dollars each month. Marine lieutenants received eighteen dollars, sergeants received eight dollars, corporals eight dollars, fifers and drummers seven and one-third dollars, and privates six and two-thirds dollars, which is what able seamen received.

The regulations also addressed expectations for conduct in combat and good order and discipline of the crew. It tasked commanders with heartening and

---

35 The information concerning the "Rules and Regulations of the Navy of the United Colonies" in these three paragraphs is derived from the *Journals of the Continental Congress, Philadelphia, 28 November 1775*, as found in Clark, ed., *NDAR*, 3:1174-1178; Coggins, *SSAR*, 207, 209-211.

The *Alfred*. Painting by William Nowland Van Powell. *Alfred* was a converted merchantman that served as the United States fleet's first flagship. Captain Samuel Nicholas commanded the Marine detachment and Lt. John Paul Jones served as first lieutenant on the newly commissioned ship's maiden voyage to New Providence, Bahamas, where she participated in the Navy's and Marine Corps' first amphibious operation. *U.S. Naval History and Heritage Command Photography Collection*

encouraging "the inferior officers and men to fight courageously, and not to behave themselves faintly or cry for quarters, on pain of such punishment as the offense shall appear to deserve." This rule stipulated that deserters and mutineers could be put to death and addressed other offenses that the Marines would help enforce. Having indoctrinated his Marines, Nicholas tasked each company with guarding the Navy's newly acquired ships at the Philadelphia wharves as sailors prepared them for action. The stage was set for another historic event.

On January 4, 1776, the first Continental fleet set sail for the open seas. Fifty-seven-year-old Rhode Islander Commodore Esek Hopkins received command of the small armada of six converted merchant ships, five of which possessed Marine detachments. Captain Nicholas, Lieutenants Parke and Fitzpatrick, and approximately 60 Marines received orders to serve on the Commodore's flagship, the *Alfred* (24 guns). Captain Shoemaker, Lieutenants Dickenson and Cummings, and around 60 Marines were assigned to the *Columbus* (20 guns). Captain Welsh and Lieutenant Wilson led their 40 Marines to the *Cabot* (14 guns), and Lieutenant Craig and 38 members of his company joined the *Andrew Doria* (14 guns). The *Providence* (12 guns) received 14 Marines raised by Lieutenant Wilson and six of Lieutenant Craig's men. They were all placed under the command of Lt. Henry Dayton, and the schooner *Fly* (8 guns) departed with no Marines on board. The sloop *Hornet* (10 guns) with Lt. John Strobagh, but no Marines, and the schooner *Wasp* (8 guns) with Lt. William Huddle and five Marines, later joined this assemblage. In all, 234 Marines deployed with the first Continental fleet.[36]

Thus began the Continental Marines' first wartime operation. Although Congress's original vision of two battalions of Marines for use as a credible, cohesive landing force was never achieved during the Revolutionary War, Marines still served a valuable role. Operational requirements and limited resources caused Marines to organize into ships' companies for fleet service. These companies could combine to form larger task-organized units under the command of a senior Marine or Navy officer, performing specific duties ashore when directed. This was a practice that continued until the formation of the Fleet Marine Force in the 1930s. In the early winter of 1776, newly promoted Maj. Samuel Nicholas created such a unit to answer a desperate call for assistance from General Washington. This helped set the stage for a vital stroke—the battles of Trenton and Princeton—which served to preserve the fledgling nation and the army established for her defense.

---

36 William Morgan, ed., *NDAR*, 12 vols. (Washington, D.C., 1972), 6:702-705; Smith, *MIR*, 45.

Chapter Two

The Path to Rebellion

"Don't fire unless fired upon, but if they mean to have a war, let it begin here."

— Capt. John Parker, Lexington, Massachusetts[1]

The end of the global war between the European powers in 1763 triggered a sequence of events leading to the American Revolution, which in turn gave birth to a new nation and the military organizations that would defend her.

The Seven Years' War, also known as the French and Indian War, began in 1756 following France's expansion into the Ohio River Valley, which was a British-held territory. Conflicts in the backwoods of the American wilderness exploded. Spain sided with France in the struggle against Britain in this worldwide conflict. Some Native American tribes, angered at British expansion into their western territories, sided with the French, which fueled years of fighting far beyond the Revolutionary War. British citizens who fought for the crown during the French and Indian War gained valuable experience, later used by both British regulars and the colonists.

The British victory in the French and Indian War changed the landscape of America. Britain gained territory from the French and Spanish, expanding its control from Canada to Florida in North America. But the management, development, and defense of this newly acquired land came at a high cost.[2]

Great Britain believed it was time for their loyal American subjects to assume greater responsibility in covering the expense of their protection. Seven years of conflict against two world powers was a costly affair. England's national debt doubled to 140 million pounds due to the war. Nearly 5/8 of its budget went

---

1 Theodore Savas & David Dameron, *The New American Revolution Handbook* (El Dorado Hills, CA 2010), 2.

2 For more information on the French and Indian War, see Fred Anderson, *Crucible of War: The Seven Years' War and the Fate of the Empire in British North America, 1754-1766* (New York, 2000).

toward paying interest alone. Yet, American colonists paid only 1/20 of the taxes being paid by the British.[3] Britain's costs continued to grow, funding a standing army of 10,000 soldiers in America. They needed to protect their citizens and investments from hostile Native Americans and European powers looking to regain influence in the western hemisphere. In 1765, the British Parliament decided to impose a tax in the form of the Stamp Act.[4]

The Stamp Act required the colonists to pay a tax on every piece of printed paper, including newspapers, legal documents, licenses, and even playing cards. Americans were furious. They viewed the Act as a veiled effort to raise money without the approval of colonial legislatures and feared that if this action were not checked, it would result in additional forms of taxation.

Heated debates about the Stamp Act ensued on both sides of the Atlantic. Merchants and manufacturers in England and America lost revenue as colonists boycotted British goods in protest. Americans openly demonstrated against the Act, and the Parliament began to use terms like "treason" and "rebellion" when referencing the colonists.[5] In Boston, a group of political dissidents formed an organization, the Sons of Liberty, whose efforts to protect the colonists' rights and fight taxation quickly spread.[6] Many people in both camps called for the repeal of the Stamp Act. The British, however, feared this would establish a precedent of usurping England's authority to govern its colonies. Parliamentarian George Grenville argued, "Protection and obedience are reciprocal. Great Britain protects America; America is bound to yield obedience. If not, tell me when the Americans were emancipated?"[7] Wiser heads eventually prevailed. The British repealed the Stamp Act in February 1766, but not before passing the Declaratory Act, affirming Parliament's authority to tax Americans just as it did its citizens in Great Britain. Deep-rooted animosities remained on both sides.

---

3 Jan Eloranta & Jeremy Land, "Hollow Victory? Britain's Public Debt and the Seven Years War," *Essays in Economic & Business History*, vol. 29 (2011); see also chapter six of Thomas Landenburg, *The Causes of the American Revolution*, Social Science Education Consortium American History Series, May 1989.

4 For a comprehensive explanation of the effects of the Stamp Act in America, see John Ferling, *A Leap in the Dark: The Struggle to Create the American Republic* (New York, 2003), 32-40; hereafter cited as *ALID*.

5 Mary Nesnay, "The Stamp Act: A Brief History," *Journal of the American Revolution*, July 29, 2014, https://allthingsliberty.com/2014/07/the-stamp-act-a-brief-history/, accessed Jul. 15, 2019.

6 Rebecca Beatrice Brooks, "The Sons of Liberty: Who Were They and What Did They Do?," November 24, 2014, https://historyofmassachusetts.org/the-sons-of-liberty-who-were-they-and-what-did-they-do/, accessed Jul. 14, 2019.

7 "George Grenville's Speech in the House of Commons, January 14, 1766," in Cobbett, comp., *Parliamentary History*, 16:97, quoted in Robert Middlekauff, *The Glorious Cause* (New York, 2005), 116; hereafter cited as *TGC*.

St—p!   ſt—p!   ſt—p!   No:

Tueſday-Morning, December 17, 1765.

THE True-born Sons of Li-
berty, are defired to meet under LIBERTY-
TREE, at XII o'Clock, THIS DAY, to hear the
the public Refignation, under Oath, of ANDREW
OLIVER, Efq; Diftributor of Stamps for the Province
of the *Maſſachuſetts-Bay.*

A Refignation ? YES.

Sons of Liberty broadside. The Sons of Liberty was a group of political dissidents established in Boston to protect the rights of the American colonists and to fight taxation without representation. Their numbers swelled across the colonies as British oppression and taxes increased. The Sons of Liberty met under "Liberty Poles" and "Liberty Trees" to share information and build support. Their forceful actions resulted in the resignation of many Royal tax collectors. *Wikimedia*

The lull did not last long before the British once again taxed the colonists. In 1767, Charles Townshend, Chancellor of the Exchequer, introduced the Townshend Acts, which imposed duties on glass, lead, paints, paper, and tea imported to America.[8] These acts were also seen as abuses of power against British subjects, resulting in further boycotts on British goods and limitations on imports to the colonies. Colonists harassed and sometimes tarred and feathered custom agents who were attempting to collect taxes. The British responded by posting four regiments of troops in Boston. Their presence was a constant reminder of the colonists' subservience to the crown, leading to clashes in the streets.

Tensions came to a head in March 1770, when British soldiers killed five Bostonians after being harassed by a boisterous crowd that members of the Sons of Liberty may have incited. The incident became known as the "Boston Massacre."[9] Like the Stamp Act, Parliament also repealed the Townsend Acts, but taxation

8   John Miller, *Origins of the American Revolution* (Boston, 1943), 249-251, 255-260.

9   Robert Middlekauff provides a compelling account of the circumstances surrounding the Boston Massacre in *TGC*, 209-214. Middlekauff reconstructed the incident by researching John Adams's legal papers. Adams had successfully defended the British soldiers involved in the incident.

The Bostonians Paying the Excise-Man, or Tarring & Feathering. Taxation without representation was considered an abuse of power against British subjects, resulting in the American boycott of British goods and limiting imports to the colonies. Colonists in Boston harassed, and in some cases tarred and feathered, custom agents attempting to collect taxes, resulting in the British posting four regiments of troops in Boston. Their presence constantly reminded the colonists of their subservience to the crown. *Wikimedia*

on tea continued, setting the stage for another showdown.

The Tea Act of 1773 imposed yet another restrictive measure upon the Americans.[10] Parliament designed the Act to bolster the failing East India Company—a key contributor to the British economy. The Act granted the company a monopoly on importing and selling tea in the colonies, further angering American merchants, and fueling resentment toward the practice of taxation without representation.

In December 1773, the Sons of Liberty took matters into their own hands, staging a raid on three British merchant ships carrying tea at the Boston wharves. Colonists loosely disguised as Native Americans boarded the ships, dumping 342 crates of tea into the bay; this was the famous "Boston Tea Party."[11] The British were not amused and, in 1774, the government reacted with a barrage of measures called the Coercive Acts—referred to as the "Intolerable Acts" by colonists.

The Coercive Acts consisted of four separate statutes meant to punish Boston for its role in the Boston Tea Party, setting the example of actions that could be taken against the colonies if they attempted to defy the crown.[12] Britain's concerns ran deeper, for if she allowed the Americans to challenge her authority to rule openly, this could spark similar disobedience across the various other colonies and territories under Britain's domain. William Lee provided insight into the British government's thinking when writing to his brother Richard Henry Lee. "You are personally obnoxious to the King and his Junto, as having shown more spirit in

---

10 Harlow Giles Unger, *American Tempest: How the Boston Tea Party Sparked a Revolution* (Cambridge, MA, 2011), 158-160.

11 Ibid.

12 Miller, *Origins of the American Revolution*, 369-376; Ferling, *ALID*, 107-108.

support of your rights than the people of this country [England] . . . Therefore, every nerve will be exerted to subdue your spirit, and make you first bow your necks to the yoke, which will prove a useful example to the people at home."[13] Richard Lee later made the motion in the Second Continental Congress calling for the colonies' independence from Great Britain.

Britain's first order of business was to punish Boston. The Boston Port Act effectively closed the port to any commerce until colonists paid for damages from the Tea Party.[14] Parliament's strong feelings on the matter are evident in comments made during debates on the issue. Lord North voiced his frustration when he stated, "It was impossible for our commerce to be safe whilst it continued in the harbour of Boston."[15] He thought the Bostonians deserved punishment, but Mr. Van's opinions ran deeper, "The town of Boston ought to be knocked about their ears and destroyed. *Delenda est Carthago.* ["Carthage must be destroyed," spoken by a Roman Senator during the 3rd Punic War] . . . I am of [the] opinion you will never meet with that proper obedience to the laws of this country [England] until you have destroyed that nest of locusts."[16]

The Massachusetts Government Act further diminished the colony's freedoms.[17] It restricted Massachusetts from holding democratic town meetings and turned the British-appointed Governor's Council into an established body. In March 1774, Lord George Germain, who served as the Secretary of State for America in Lord North's cabinet during the American Revolution, argued to end the colonist's town meetings, and not to further trouble themselves with daily governance.[18]

This feeling was prevalent among many parliamentarians. They wanted Americans to humbly continue producing and trading goods, generating revenue for England without any thought of governing their affairs.

13 Ford, ed., *Letters of William Lee*, 1:87-90, quoted in Henry Steele Commager & Richard Morris, eds., *The Spirit of Seventy-Six* (New York, 2002), 16; hereafter cited as *SSS*.

14 This was also referred to as the Boston Port Bill. Derek Beck, *Igniting The American Revolution, 1773-1775* (Naperville, IL, 2015), 29-32.

15 Peter Force & M. St. Clair Clarke, eds., *American Archives*, 4th Series, (Washington D.C., 1837), 87; hereafter cited as *AA*.

16 "Debate in the British Commons on the Boston Port Bill, March 23, 1774," in Cobbett, *Parliamentary History of England*, vol. 17, 1163-1165, 1178, quoted in Commager & Morris, *SSS*, 12.

17 Miller, *Origins of the American Revolution*, 369-370.

18 "Debate in the British Commons on the bill regulating the government of Massachusetts Bay, March 28, 1774," in Cobbett, *Parliamentary History of England*, 1195-1196, as quoted in Commager & Morris, *SSS*, 13. Lord Germain wanted to "put an end to their town meetings. I would not have men of a mercantile cast every day collecting themselves together and debating about political matters; I would have them follow their occupations as merchants, and not consider themselves as minsters of that country [America] . . . if they had the least prudence, to follow their mercantile employment and not trouble themselves with politics and government, which they do not understand."

The May 1774 Administration of Justice Act provided immunity to British officials from criminal prosecution in Massachusetts. It authorized the British-appointed governor to move trials of royal officials accused of committing capital offenses to other colonies or Great Britain in order to receive a fair trial.[19] The Act offended the citizens of Massachusetts, who called it "The Murder Act."[20] The other colonies watched with trepidation as the crown continued to suppress their neighbors' freedoms and independence, but the worst was still to come.

The Quartering Act of 1774 was the final coercive decree established to punish Boston. A version of this act was first implemented in 1765 following the French and Indian War.[21] It required colonial families from all 13 colonies to provide provisions and housing to British soldiers stationed in America, including shelter, food, bedding, beer, candles, salt, cider, firewood, and eating utensils. Pennsylvania was the only colony to fully obey the provisions of the 1765 act. Many Americans willingly housed British soldiers during the French and Indian War but believed this was asking too much during peacetime. Following the Boston Tea Party, Parliament reenacted the 1765 act, adding that the governor, not the colonial assembly, had the authority to enforce it. By design, the Coercive Acts were intended to segregate and stifle Massachusetts's rebellious tendencies, but they had the opposite effect.

The other 12 colonies rallied around Massachusetts as she withstood the mistreatment imposed by Britain. An outpouring of defiance against the British emerged as each colony contemplated the possibility of their citizens facing similar hardships under the royal yoke. Popular support for Boston was evident along the entire eastern seaboard. The city received food, blankets, and household items from the colonies. Patriots designated liberty trees and poles in city squares and town centers as gathering places to protest British aggression, building support for a growing call for independence. Responding to the Boston Port Act, over 1,000 Farmington, Connecticut citizens gathered in May 1774 around a forty-five-foot liberty pole they called a "shrine of liberty" to protest British actions. They read aloud the words of the Boston Port Act, flinging copies into a raging fire. The leaders of the group drafted a resolution that stated, in part,

19 Administration of Justice Act, May 20, 1774, http://www.americanhistorycentral.com/entries/administration-of-justice-act/, accessed Jul 18, 2019. "In the present disordered state ... and to the re-establishment of lawful authority that neither the magistrates acting in support of the laws ... in the suppression of riots and tumults, raised in opposition to the execution of the laws and statutes of this realm, should be discouraged from the proper discharge of their duty . . . before persons who do not acknowledge the validity of the laws . . ."

20 Ibid.

21 Page Smith, *A New Age Now Begins: A People's History of the American Revolution* (New York, 1976), 264-267; Middlekauff, *TGC*, 150-151.

2D. That the present ministry, being instigated by the devil and led on by their wicked and corrupt hearts have a design to take away our liberties and properties and to enslave us forever.

3D. That the late Act which their malice hath caused to be passed in Parliament, for clocking up the port of Boston, is unjust, illegal and oppressive; and that we and every American are sharers in the insults proffered to the town of Boston.

4D. That those pimps and parasites who dared to advise their masters to such detestable measures be held in utter abhorrence by us and every American, and their names loaded with the curses of all succeeding generations.[22]

Other colonies voiced their support. South Carolina resolved that "the whole continent must be animated with one great soul and all Americans must resolve to stand by one another unto the position of death."[23] The Virginia House of Burgesses agreed, declaring, "An attack on one colony was an attack on all." This was followed by declaring June 1, 1774, as a "Day of Fasting, Humiliation, and Prayer, devoutly to implore the divine Interposition for averting the heavy Calamity, which threatens Destruction to our civil Rights, and the Evils of civil war."[24]

The colonies called for unification in their efforts. Thomas Jefferson and fellow Virginians resolved that they "will ever be ready to join with our fellow-subjects . . . in executing all those rightful powers which God has given us, for the re-establishment and guaranteeing such their constitutional rights, when, where, and by whomsoever invaded."[25] Later, similar language would find its way into the Declaration of Independence, the Constitution, and the Bill of Rights.

Many hoped for reconciliation with the mother country, but time was running out, and stronger language began to be used. Samuel Adams, a Boston citizen and member of the Sons of Liberty, responded to the Boston Port Act stating, "For us to reason against such an Act would be idleness. Our business is to find means to evade its malignant design. The inhabitants view it not with astonishment, but with indignation."[26] Farmer, politician, and soldier George Washington agreed

22 "Proceedings of Farmington, Connecticut, on the Boston Port Act, May 19, 1774," Force, *AA*, 1:336, quoted in Commager & Morris, *SSS*, 21.

23 Richard Engler, Jr., *The Challenge of Diversity* (New York, 1964), 58.

24 "Resolution of the House of Burgess, Tuesday, May 24, 1774," in Boyd, ed., *Papers of Thomas Jefferson*, 1:105-106.

25 "Resolutions of freeholders of Albermarle County, Virginia, July 26, 1774," in Ford, ed., *Writings of Jefferson*, 1:418, as quoted in Commager & Morris, *SSS*, 23.

26 Samuel Adams to Arthur Lee, Boston, May 18, 1774, in Force, *AA*, 1:332-333, as quoted in Commager & Morris, *SSS*, 20.

when he asked, "Shall we supinely sit and see one province after another fall a prey to despotism?"[27] He further stated that "the crisis is arrived when we must assert our rights, or submit to every imposition that can be heaped on us."[28]

City leaders in Philadelphia, the largest city and future capital of America, watched Britain's handling of Boston with disgust. They met in June 1774, declaring British actions to be "unconstitutional, oppressive to the inhabitants, and dangerous to the liberties of the British colonies . . . we consider our brethren, at Boston, as suffering in the common cause of America."[29] They went a step further, calling for a "congress of deputies from the several colonies in North America . . . procuring relief for our suffering brethren, obtaining redress of American grievances, securing our rights and liberties."[30] The conditions were set for the First Continental Congress.

The colonists were ready to remove the shackles of oppression by either reconciling with King George III or taking more extreme measures if necessary. Three days after the arrival of the Coercive Acts in Massachusetts, Samuel Adams had fellow Sons of Liberty member Paul Revere deliver requests for other colonies to join boycotts of British goods. Some refused until a national assembly of representatives from the 13 colonies met and agreed to a common way forward. Earlier, similar experiences failed when some colonies attempted to boycott the British. Their sister colonies ignored the embargo, winning contracts away from those who had boycotted. This was an all-or-none proposition for many.

On September 5, 1774, 55 delegates from 12 of the 13 colonies met at Carpenter Hall in Philadelphia, forming the First Continental Congress.[31] Georgia chose not to attend as it was seeking Britain's assistance in defending itself against Native American attacks. Many notable founding fathers did participate, including John Adams and Samuel Adams from Massachusetts, John Jay from New York, and Patrick Henry and George Washington from Virginia. The delegates quickly established procedural rules, gravitating toward one of two factions. One faction

27 John Fitzpatrick, ed., *The Writings of George Washington: From the Original Manuscript Sources, 1745-1799*, vol. 3 (Washington D.C., 1931), 232-233, hereafter cited as *TWGW*.

28 Ibid., 240-242.

29 "Pennsylvania Resolutions on the Boston Port Act, Philadelphia, June 20, 1774," from Hezekiah Niles, ed., *Principles and acts of the Revolution in America: or An attempt to collect and preserve some of the speeches, orations, & proceedings, with sketches and remarks on men and things, and other fugitive or neglected pieces, belonging to the men of the revolutionary period in the United States which happily terminated in the establishment of their liberties* (Baltimore, 1822), 179.

30 Ibid.

31 Gaillard Hunt, ed., *Journals of the Continental Congress, 1774-1789*, 34 vols. (Washington, D.C., 1904-37), provides the full proceedings of the First and Second Continental Congresses. Hereafter cited as *JCC*.

led by the delegates from Massachusetts and Virginia were considered more radical, believing the colonies should join in a total embargo against Britain. Some considered independence but were not ready to voice this option openly. The other faction, led by the delegates from Pennsylvania and New York, were conservative in their approach, hoping to take a more moderate and conciliatory stance with Britain.

Debate ensued, and delegates began to take sides.[32] The radicals leaned on past successes in getting the British to acquiesce following boycotts against its products, while the moderates argued that Great Britain had reached a point of frustration with the Americans where any embargo would inevitably lead to war. They added that the Americans would likely lose such a conflict due to their unpreparedness for war.

Joseph Galloway of Pennsylvania proposed a plan to maintain the union with Britain that offered the Americans greater representation in the government.[33] Galloway recommended the creation of an American national government, or Colonial Parliament, with equal representation from each colony and a president-general appointed by the king. He hoped to provide the colonies with their own representatives while remaining loyal to England. This plan was rejected when the conservative faction offered a more drastic proposal.

Dr. Joseph Warren of Massachusetts, a leading member of the Sons of Liberty, proposed the Suffolk Resolves in response to British actions.[34] This plan called for open protests against the Intolerable Acts and further actions to prod the British into meeting colonists' demands. Warren recommended stockpiling military supplies, operating an independent government, boycotting British goods, and denouncing any allegiance to a king who failed to treat his subjects fairly.

The radicals ultimately prevailed, and on September 17, 1774, Congress accepted the Suffolk Resolves with some concessions and modifications. Rather than a full embargo, the southern colonies requested and received a block on imports only. They preserved the right to export goods, supporting their agrarian economy, as they were actively harvesting that year's crops. They agreed, however, to include exports the following year if matters with Britain had not been resolved. Congress denounced taxation without representation and the quartering of British troops in the colonies without their consent. Additionally, it published a declaration of the rights due to every citizen, including life, liberty, property,

---

32 See Ferling's, *ALID*, 112-122, and Page Smith, *John Adams, Vol. 1: 1735-1784* (Garden City, NJ, 1962), 171-187, for good descriptions of the debates in the First Continental Congress.

33 The text of the resolution presented by Joseph Galloway can be found in Ford, ed., *JCC*, 1:49-51.

34 Ford, ed., *JCC*, 1:31-36, quoted from Commager & Morris, *SSS*, 53-54.

assembly, and trial by jury. Finally, it renounced and called for the revocation of the Coercive Acts.

Historian John Ferling argues that the actions of the First Continental Congress had important consequences.[35] First, the adoption of the Continental Association, the name given to the embargo, resulted in the election of 7,000 committeemen, ensuring the proper conduct of boycotts across the colonies. This provided many Americans with their first taste of true representative government. But it also had the unintended consequence of separating Americans into two camps: The Tories, known as Loyalists, remained faithful to the crown; and the Whigs, or radicals, sought concessions or independence from Britain. These groups clashed throughout the American Revolution, causing some to refer to the conflict as the "First American Civil War."[36]

The second significant consequence of the First Continental Congress was its efforts to put the colonies on "a proper footing" in preparation for a possible war with Great Britain.[37] Planning, organizing, equipping, and training local militias took on a renewed sense of urgency. But Congress did not establish a national standing army, navy, or marines; it did not want to provoke Britain, intending to leave the door open for reconciliation. Regardless, a rebellious fervor spread across the colonies and resulted in armed conflict less than a year later.

British frustrations with the rebellious colonists and fears of the Americans' efforts to arm and prepare themselves led to more forceful actions being taken against them. Soldiers quartered in Boston began to disarm Americans, seizing gunpowder and other implements of war from local communities. War almost erupted in September 1774 when British regulars confiscated colonial gunpowder from Charlestown, across the Charles River from Boston. Thousands of armed colonists, known as "minutemen" since they were prepared to respond to British aggression within minutes of notification, flocked to Cambridge and areas surrounding Boston with plans to oust the British.[38] Boston citizen John Andrews recalled, "about ten thousand men are in arms, and are continually coming down from the country back." He shared how his fellow Patriots intended to "collect about forty or fifty thousand by night (which they are sure of accomplishing) when they intend to fling in about fifteen thousand by the way of the Neck [the Boston

35 Ferling, *ALID*, 121-122.

36 Henry Belcher, *The First American Civil War: First Period 1775-1778*, 2 vols. (London, 1911); Leslie Francis Stokes Upton, *Revolutionary Versus Loyalist: The First American Civil War, 1774-1784* (Waltham, MA, 1968).

37 Ferling, *ALID*, 121.

38 A. J. Langguth, *Patriots: The Men Who Started the American Revolution* (New York, 1988), 217; Richard Ketchum, ed., *The American Heritage Book of The Revolution* (New York, 1958), 99.

Neck, a stretch of land connecting Boston to the mainland]." The remainder would follow using ferries "to come in like locusts and rid the town of every [British] soldier."[39] The conditions for war were not yet ripe, and local officials asked the Minutemen to stand down and return home.

Although conflict was averted for the time being, tensions continued to brew. Frustrated, George III wrote Lord North on November 18, 1774, "The New England governments are in a state of rebellion, blows must decide whether they are to be subject to this country or independent."[40] Eleven regiments of British regulars now operated from Boston, and their commanding general, Thomas Gage, was appointed acting governor of Massachusetts. The fifty-four-year-old Gage's long history of service in North America began in 1754. He rose through the ranks during the French and Indian War and, in 1763, was assigned as the commander-in-chief of all British forces in America. Gage exhibited patience and tact in diplomacy, trade, communication, relations with the Native Americans, and the western boundaries. He would fail, however, to quell the building resentment of the colonists toward England.[41]

Colonists raced to gather gunpowder and weapons before they could be seized by the British. In December 1774, Paul Revere rode across the border into New Hampshire with instructions for local militias to confiscate barrels of gunpowder, cannons, and small arms from the Castle of William and Mary at Portsmouth. Governor John Wentworth of New Hampshire accused the militia of treason and rebellion, calling for their arrest. Similar acts occurred throughout the region, and frustrations manifested in physical confrontations.

On January 21, 1775, riots again resulted in bloodshed in Boston. An American watchman on post that evening reportedly insulted a British officer in passing as they walked down King Street. Friends and peers of the watchman and British officer quickly came to their colleagues' aid, and a riot ensued. The watchman and friends brandished hooks and other weapons, and the British countered by drawing their swords. Both sides struck, and participants from both parties were injured. One watchman lost a nose, another lost a thumb, and many others received puncture wounds from swords and other sharp objects. Officials ordered

39 John Andrews, "Letters," *Massachusetts Historical Society. Proceedings.*, 8:327-396 *passim*, quoted in Commager & Morris, *SSS*, 31; hereafter cited as *MHS*.

40 The King to Lord North, Queens House, Nov. 18, 1774, in Donne, ed., *Correspondence of George III with Lord North*, 1:214-215, as quoted in Commager & Morris, *SSS*, 61.

41 See John Alden, General *Gage in America: Being principally a history of his role in the American Revolution* (New York, 1948), for a comprehensive description of Gage's actions during the Revolutionary War.

a court of inquiry, but nothing of note came from it other than the further stoking of hatred between the "Rebels" and "Red Coats," as they called one another.[42]

General Gage was determined to maintain dominance over the colonists, routinely tasking soldiers to travel to outlying towns that local loyalists identified as hiding weapons. On February 26, he ordered Lt. Col. Alexander Leslie and 240 soldiers of the 64th Regiment to sail to Salem, Massachusetts, and capture 19 cannons the militia had prepared.[43] The Americans sounded the alarm as the British marched toward the town, with musicians playing "Yankee Doodle" to mock the rebels. The joke, however, was on the British.

The Americans stopped Leslie as he approached the North Bridge on the way to the foundry, where he believed the rebel cannons were located. Captain John Felt of the Salem Militia established a blocking position, raising the northern leaf of the draw bridge. Simultaneously, Col. David Mason of the Massachusetts Committee of Safety ordered the cannons hidden. Leslie demanded the bridge be lowered and that he be permitted to proceed. Felt refused even after Leslie threatened to fire on the rebels on the far side of the bridge. After a heated debate, the local pastor moderated an agreement, allowing Leslie to save face while permitting the militia to keep their weapons.

Although Leslie had a mission to perform, he erred on the side of prudence. Both parties agreed that Leslie and his men could cross the bridge, traveling no more than fifty rods (825 feet), the distance to the foundry from which the weapons had been removed, before turning and marching out of Salem empty-handed. Leslie could report back to General Gage that he had crossed the bridge but could not find the weapons. This saved Leslie and his men from running through a gauntlet of rebel fire that the hundreds of militiamen who had gathered to assist Salem would have delivered. A local nurse, Sarah Tarrant, rubbed salt in the wounds of British humiliation as she yelled out the window of her home as they marched by, "Go home and tell your master he has sent you on a fool's errand, and broken the peace of our Sabbath."[44] No longer defiant, the British musicians performed "The World Turned Upside Down." They would play this song again seven years later after surrendering after the battle of Yorktown. Although embarrassing for Leslie, the incident at Salem, which became known as "Leslie's Retreat," could very well

---

42 George Scheer & Hugh Rankin, *Rebels and Redcoats* (New York, 1957), hereafter cited as *RR*.

43 Christopher Ward, *The War of the Revolution* (New York, 1952), 21, hereafter cited as *TWOR*.

44 "Leslie's Retreat, or how the Revolutionary War almost began in Salem: February 26, 1775," https://historicipswich.org/2014/07/05/leslies-retreat-or-how-the-revolutionary-war-almost-began-in-salem/, accessed Jul. 26, 2019.

have been the impetus for the start of the Revolutionary War if it had been handled differently.[45] General Gage was not deterred.

On March 30, 1775, Gage sent the British 1st Brigade on a show of force into the countryside to demonstrate and preserve the army's freedom of movement throughout the region. He would not let a bunch of upstarts dictate where and when his soldiers could march. The colonists were unsure of the brigade's intent, so express riders once again scurried across the hills and country roads to alert the Minutemen. Militia near Watertown, nine miles outside the city, responded by positioning two cannons at a bridge to block the 1st Brigade's progress. They fled before engaging their would-be enemy, leaving the two loaded cannons for capture. On the outskirts of Cambridge, other militia destroyed a bridge to impede British movement; but the action had little impact. The brigade returned to Boston without further incident after five hours. Such forays to confiscate arms were becoming common, but they were dangerous and sure to result in armed conflict. This would ensue in the following month.

On April 14, 1775, Gage received orders that would change the history of the world.[46] The British secretary of state, the Earl of Dartmouth, instructed him to disarm the rebels and imprison their leaders. Gage deployed Tory spies and army scouts to gather information on the rebels. He determined that the Massachusetts provincial government led by John Hancock and Samuel Adams had fled Boston, meeting instead in the village of Concord, where rebel weapons might be stored. He further determined that Hancock and Adams were staying with relatives in Lexington Village.

Gage devised a plan to deploy approximately 700 soldiers from the light infantry, grenadiers, and Royal Marines under the command of 52-year-old Lt. Col. Francis Smith, commander of the 10th Regiment of Foot, with 53-year-old Royal Marine Maj. John Pitcairn serving as his executive officer. Both men possessed years of military experience. They were ordered to capture Hancock and Adams and confiscate or destroy the weapons at Concord. Gage had no intention of repeating the debacle in Salem. The light infantry, grenadiers, and Marines were among the best troops the British possessed, and he was sending them out in a large enough force to handle any hostile actions from the rebels.

---

45 See Charles Endicott, *Account of Leslie's retreat at the North Bridge in Salem, on Sunday Feb'y 26, 1775* (Salem, 1856) for more on this incident.

46 For more on the battles of Lexington and Concord, see Arthur Tourtellot, *Lexington and Concord: The Beginning of the War of the American Revolution* (New York, 1959); Michael Stephenson, *Patriot Battles: How the War of Independence was Fought* (New York. 2007); Beck, *Igniting The American Revolution*, 145-156.

The Continentals had been preparing for this day. Local militias were manned, trained, and equipped (although crudely) following the Intolerable Acts, and an extensive intelligence-gathering apparatus had been established. Paul Revere belonged to a group of approximately 30 Patriots who met regularly at the Green Dragon Tavern in Boston, collecting intelligence on British troop and Tory movements.[47] Other patriot spies informed them of Dartmouth's instructions to Gage, and they set out to warn the Minutemen to be ready to move in short order. Revere and others also established a signaling system as a backup to notify local militia of British movements. On April 16, Revere directed two lanterns to be displayed in Boston's North Church steeple if the British moved by sea toward Charlestown and one lantern if they advanced by land across Boston Neck.[48] These signals were a redundant means of communicating British intentions if Revere and other riders failed to evade British pickets, rousing the Minutemen once the Redcoats initiated operations. These timely acts proved beneficial. Gage secretly planned his operation to commence at midnight on April 18.

At midnight, the British lowered boats from their ships to transport Smith's troops across the Charles River to a landing point east of Cambridge. Patriot leader Dr. Joseph Warren preempted Gage, dispatching William Dawes across the Boston Neck, and Paul Revere by boat to Charlestown, spreading the word through the countryside that "the Regulars are coming."[49] The British took nearly two hours to get everyone ashore and organized before beginning what became a momentous day. Revere arrived in Lexington before the British, sounding the alarm and helping Hancock and Adams escape. Forty-six-year-old Capt. John Parker of the Lexington militia rallied his men.

Between 1:00 and 1:30 a.m. on April 19, 1775, approximately 70 Minutemen assembled on Lexington Common—a two-acre triangular patch that separated the main road on which the British were traveling. Their excitement quickly waned as they determined the British were still miles away. Many gathered at the Buckman Tavern to await their arrival as Revere and other dispatch riders continued sounding the alarm toward Concord six miles away. The first signs of daylight appeared around 4:00 a.m., quickly followed by the distinct sound of hundreds of feet pounding on the ground. Parker ordered 16-year-old drummer William Diamond to sound "call to arms" as the militia reformed on the Common.

47 Paul Revere, "Letter," *MHS*, 16: 371-374, quoted in Commager & Morris, *SSS*, 69.

48 For a full account of the action surrounding Paul Revere's involvement in the events leading to Lexington and Concord, see David Fischer, *Paul Revere's Ride* (New York, 1994), hereafter cited as *PRR*. Esther Forbes, in *Paul Revere and The World He Lived In* (New York, 1942), 448, provides Revere's personal account of these events.

49 Fischer, *PRR*, 138-148.

Major Pitcairn led an advanced guard of six companies of light infantry and Royal Marines into Lexington. Approaching the village green, they spotted two thin lines of between 30 and 70 armed men in a mixture of civilian attire armed with muskets. The Minutemen looked nervous as a British officer, believed to be Pitcairn, rode forward, and insisted, "Lay down your arms, you damned rebels."[50] Knowing he was greatly outnumbered, Parker turned toward his men, ordering them to disperse. The facts concerning what occurred next are still contested today. But one thing is certain: Someone fired a weapon, triggering an eight-year struggle that would change the world.[51] That shot was followed by two more, and mayhem quickly ensued.

The British held the advantage in the action. Months of pent-up frustration exploded, but the entire incident lasted only thirty to forty seconds. Most of the militiamen broke and ran, but not before eight were killed and another nine wounded. One British soldier was injured. The British quickly secured the village, searching in vain for Hancock and Adams. It was approximately 9:00 a.m. before the British were ready to move again. Many officers recommended to Smith that they return to Boston now that the countryside was aroused and blood had been shed, but he refused. They continued to Concord.

Concord's citizens were ready, and soon they were joined by many of their neighbors.[52] Smith's force moved aggressively, quickly overwhelming the village. He split his unit into smaller teams, searching for weapons in the surrounding areas. Forewarned patriots had moved or hidden most of their arsenal, but the British found three cannons, several gun carriages, and 100 barrels of flour. Separate detachments reported rebel groups swarming on the high ground outside the village. Colonel James Barrett, a 64-year-old miller, commanded Concord's militia. He kept his citizen soldiers at arms' length from the British due to the Americans' inferiority in numbers but quickly changed his mind when he saw smoke rising from the village center. The British had torched a pile of destroyed gun carriages,

---

50 Ibid., 191.

51 Ian Barnes, *The Historical Atlas of the American Revolution* (New York, 2000), 64-76; William Pencak, *Pennsylvania's Revolution* (University Park, PA, 2010), 144; William Bennett & John Cribb, *The American Patriot's Almanac: Daily Readings on America* (Nashville, 2008), 134. Some believe that this first shot on Lexington Green is known as "the shot heard around the world," but that is incorrect. The term "shot heard around the world" first appeared in an 1837 poem by Ralph Waldo Emerson describing the events that occurred at the North Bridge in Concord following the skirmish at Lexington. Emerson wrote "Concord Hymn" to present at the dedication of an obelisk monument commemorating the Battle of Concord.

52 See Commager & Morris, *SSS*, 84-85, for a first-hand account of the actions at Concord from William Emerson of the Concord militia.

The Battle of Lexington, 19th April 1775. Painting by William Barns Wollen. Captain John Parker of the Lexington Militia led a small group of American Minutemen to meet an advancing unit of 700 British light infantry, grenadiers, and Royal Marines on Lexington Common. In that tense moment, someone fired a weapon, starting a war that would change the world. The Americans sustained eight killed and nine wounded in this first battle of the American Revolution. *Wikimedia*

but Barrett and others thought they intended to burn their village. He ordered his men to load their weapons and approached the North Bridge outside town.

A group of 100 British infantrymen had posted themselves at the bridge, blocking rebel movements into the village. Alarmed by the fast-approaching rebels outnumbering their isolated unit, one British soldier fired, followed by others, and eventually, their officer ordered the rest of the troops to open on the militia. Barrett had the militiamen hold their fire until the British volleys began to inflict casualties on the Americans. A firefight ensued, with the militia having the advantage. Twelve British soldiers were hit, three fatally. It was the Redcoats' time to turn and run. The militia was emboldened, continuing to gather strength as more neighbors from other local militias began arriving from Marblehead, Salem, and other areas over 30 miles away.

Colonel Smith gathered his forces and commenced a treacherous 18-mile trek back to Boston along the same route he had taken to Concord. The Continentals did not intend to let the Redcoats depart without paying for the destruction and needless killing they had inflicted that morning. Individuals, militia groups, and

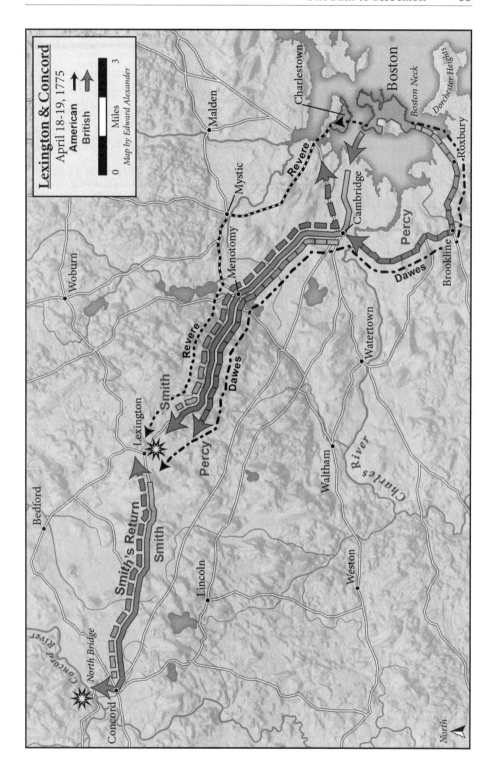

Lexington & Concord
April 18-19, 1775
American
British

0   Miles   3

Map by Edward Alexander

private citizens numbering over 1,000 fired indiscriminately at the British the entire length of their movement home. Thirty-eight-year-old Brig. Gen. William Heath of the Massachusetts State Militia arrived on the scene. He took command of the colonials, organizing ambushes and other limited attacks against the British from behind trees, rock walls, and buildings, employing a style of warfare for which the British were unaccustomed and found dishonorable. The patriots had learned their lessons well during the French and Indian War and in fighting Native Americans to protect their families and property in the wilderness. This American style of fighting and the determination displayed by the colonists resulted in a newfound respect for the once belittled British subjects, as is evident in Brig. Gen. Hugh Early Percy's comments following the battle. "Whoever looks upon them as an irregular mob will find himself much mistaken. They have men amongst them who know very well what they are about, having been employed as Rangers against the Indians and Canadians, and this country being much covered with wood and hilly is very advantageous for their method of fighting."[53]

As the battle progressed, Gage sent General Percy to reinforce Smith, and the two forces linked up during Smith's return trip through Lexington. Thirty-three-year-old Percy joined the army in 1759 and had achieved the rank of captain by the time he was 17, thanks in part to his aristocratic family. He assumed overall command of the British force and pushed Smith with the light infantry, grenadiers, and Royal Marines forward while his brigade provided a rear guard against the rebels. Percy later reported to Gage, "We retired for 15 miles under incessant fire all around us, till we arrived at Charlestown between 7 and 8 in the even, very much fatigued with a march of above 30 miles, and having expended almost all our ammunition." He reported that his troops behaved with intrepidity and spirit, but "[n]or were they a little exasperated at the cruelty and barbarity of the Rebels who scalped and cut off the ears of some of the wounded men who fell into their hands."[54]

The battles of Lexington and Concord were bloody affairs that would unite a people and lead to war. As darkness fell on April 19, 1775, 94 colonists lay dead, wounded, or missing. The British suffered between 65 and 73 killed and over 207 wounded or missing.[55] The die had been cast. Although many still hoped for

---

53 Charles Bolton, ed., *Letters of Hugh, Earl Percy, from Boston and New York, 1774-1776* (Boston, 1902), 52-53.

54 Ibid., 49-51.

55 John Ferling, *Almost a Miracle: The American Victory in the War of Independence* (New York, 2007), 32, hereafter cited as *AAM*; "Lexington and Concord," https://www.battlefields.org/learn/revolutionary-war/battles/lexington-and-concord, accessed Jul 27, 2019.

reconciliation between the colonies and England, there was no turning back. The Massachusetts Committee of Safety quickly released an appeal for help.[56]

Massachusetts's neighbors and fellow colonists responded from far and wide. Great Britain's attempt to isolate and punish Boston and the people of New England had backfired. As the British settled back into a secure Boston following a harrowing day, they could see hundreds of American campfires burning throughout the countryside surrounding the city. Many believed the rebels would vanish into the night as they had done so many times before, but they were mistaken. Captain Parker's company of fewer than 100 Minutemen that first gathered on Lexington Green had grown to approximately 16,000 militiamen from four different colonies within days.[57]

This motley crew of patriotic volunteers had no idea what they were in for or what they would do when they reached Boston. They merely knew that the long-awaited day of open aggression by the Redcoats against the colonists had finally arrived. The Massachusetts Provincial Congress attempted to instill order out of the chaos. Its key leaders—John Hancock, Samuel Adams, and John Adams—departed to join the Second Continental Congress forming in Philadelphia, leaving 34-year-old Dr. Joseph Warren in charge of what became the siege of Boston.

Warren had been actively defying the British and organizing resistance against them for some time. Lord Rawdon of the British army called him "the greatest incendiary in all America."[58] Warren waited for the opportunity to strike at the Redcoats and is reported to have said that he would like to die fighting them in "blood up to his knees."[59] Less than a month later, his wish was realized as he humbly picked up a rifle to fight as a "volunteer" and was shot in the head during the battle of Bunker Hill. Warren's top subordinate responsible for organizing and leading the forming army was Gen. Artemas Ward.

The Provincial Congress had appointed Ward as the senior military official for Massachusetts the previous February. The 47-year-old Ward was a French and Indian War veteran and a graduate of Harvard College. He taught, farmed, and served twenty years in the Massachusetts Assembly before assuming command of

56 The appeal reads: "The barbarous murders committed on our innocent brethren on Wednesday the 19th instant have made it absolutely necessary that we immediately raise an army to defend our wives and children from the butchering hands of an inhuman soldiery, who, incensed at the obstacles they met with in their bloody progress, and enraged at being repulsed from the field of slaughter, will, without doubt, take the first opportunity in their power to ravage this devoted country with fire and sword." Force, ed., *AA*, 2:433, quoted in Commager & Morris, *SSS*, 92.

57 Richard Frothingham, *History of the Siege of Boston* (Boston, 1849), 101; Allen French, *The Siege of Boston* (New York, 1911), 217; John Ferling, *AAM*, 34.

58 Richard M. Ketchum, *Decisive Day: The Battle for Bunker Hill* (New York, 1962), 177.

59 Ibid.

this amateur army. His first order of business was to feed the thousands of men who had dropped what they were doing and rushed toward the sound of the guns when the alarm sounded. He quickly organized groups to gather livestock, bread, and other items and established a kitchen at Harvard that would feed the masses. With this basic necessity addressed, Ward began the enormous task of turning his disorganized force into a cohesive fighting organization, prepared to defend itself if necessary and attack if desired.

Although some referred to this force as the "Grand American Army," nothing could be further from the truth.[60] While the citizen-soldiers who gathered outside Boston possessed a fighting spirit and thirst for liberty, not one of them was a professional soldier. Many older men had some experience fighting in the French and Indian War, but most had never heard a shot fired in anger prior to Lexington and Concord. These would-be soldiers were farmers, merchants, artisans, and laborers, representing every other occupation in the colonies. The men's ages spanned from the teens to the sixties. Some were rich while many were poor, but regardless of their position in life, all openly defied British rule.

The army consisted of groups that hailed from the four New England colonies: Massachusetts, New Hampshire, Rhode Island, and later Connecticut. These colonies, including Virginia and South Carolina, were the only ones to heed the First Continental Congress's recommendation to prepare militia forces for possible conflict. Post riders were dispersed to the other colonies following Lexington and Concord with requests for further assistance. One such rider, Israel Bissel, averaged 60 miles a day in the saddle over five days in carrying his message from Boston to Philadelphia.[61] The Second Continental Congress later recommended that the remaining seven colonies join the original six in organizing their militias to present a unified front against Great Britain.

Ward, like Congress, had no authority to order any actions. Each colony independently manned, trained, equipped, and led its military forces. They nevertheless agreed to follow Ward's direction since Massachusetts provided the preponderance of the force and the fight was on its territory. Ward held a council of war with leaders from the other colonies, and a priority of work was agreed upon. The members swore an oath to join against their common enemy and went about their tasks. Ward dispatched work details to bury the dead from Lexington and Concord and sent others to reconnoiter the area for the best terrain on which to erect breastworks and other defensive positions. Leaders established guard

---

60 Terry Mays, *Historical Dictionary of the American Revolution*, 2nd edition, (Lanham, MD, 2010), 126.

61 Middlekauff, *TGC*, 280.

posts and agreed on the distribution and disposition of forces to place the British under siege.

The colonial army eventually occupied a 50-mile-long perimeter outside Boston. It started in the town of Chelsea in the north, expanded west toward Cambridge, and terminated in Roxbury to the south, forming a semi-circle of outposts caging the British in the city. Ward and his nascent army had the Redcoats surrounded by land with their backs to the sea. Yet the colonies had no navy or marines to isolate the British from reinforcements and support coming from the water. This proved to be a major shortfall that would later need to be addressed, but the colonists first had to focus their limited resources on creating an army to hold the enemy under siege at Boston.

The Massachusetts Provincial Government hoped to build a 30,000-man army to sustain the siege, but this goal was never achieved. Its strength fluctuated between 16,000 and 27,000 men in those early months, with troops often coming and going as they pleased. Inadequate manning continued to plague the Continental Army once it officially formed. It only achieved an end-strength of 46,891 during its peak year of 1776 and systematically dwindled from that year until the war's end.[62] This limited force was responsible for protecting the vast expanse of territory from Canada to Florida. George Washington was never able to amass more than 19,000 soldiers, Marines, and sailors for any battle, and his army possessed far fewer than this at Trenton, Princeton, and most other battles.

Raising and sustaining an armed force was expensive, as the British had learned during the French and Indian War. No single colony had the revenue to fund a large army, navy, or marines, and the newly created Congress had no authority to tax the citizens of the individual colonies to generate the required funds. The military needed food, horses, uniforms, blankets, tents, muskets, ships, cannons, gunpowder, and more. Each colony was responsible for supporting its troops. The units from the different colonies also chose their leaders, often leading to prominent or popular citizens being selected for key leadership positions regardless of their ability to lead effectively. The ad hoc army created outside Boston possessed no standard regulations, operating procedures, or warfighting doctrine with which to challenge a global military power.

These issues were exacerbated by varying terms of enlistment. Some soldiers, sailors, and marines enlisted for the duration of the war. Others signed on for limited periods ranging from six months to three years. Others never enlisted but simply showed up with a rifle in hand after hearing of a coming battle. It was common for some men to reenlist multiple times following the termination of

---

62 Savas & Dameron, *New American Revolution Handbook*, 17.

their previous enlistments, or in some cases, to enlist multiple times while still under one contract to collect enlistment bonuses for others. Some shifted from one unit to another, depending on which branch provided the best opportunity for personal gain.

Washington never knew precisely how many troops he possessed at any time or what he could rely on to prosecute future operations. Estimates compiled after the war showed that while there had been 232,000 enlistments in the Continental forces throughout the eight years of the war, this only represented between 100,000-150,000 men due to reenlistments and other factors as described above.[63] The termination of enlistments at the most inopportune times later proved to be a constant thorn in the sides of the Continental Army, Navy, and Marines, and one that almost resulted in the loss of the war.

Despite these challenges, the colonists leaped into the abyss, unaware of the future. One thing was certain, however: the colonies needed more than the group of amateurs who had assembled outside of Boston. It needed a professional army, navy, and marines if it were to have any chance of defeating the British. The Second Continental Congress soon gathered to discuss this very issue.

---

63 James Strokesbury, *A Short History of the American Revolution* (New York, 1991), 69.

Chapter Three

A Humble Beginning

"The Military Chest is totally exhausted. The Paymaster has not a single Dollar in Hand. The Commissary General assures me he has strained his Credit to the utmost for the Subsistence of the Army. The Quartermaster General is precisely in the same situation: And the greater part of the Army in a State not far from mutiny."

— General George Washington[1]

$\mathcal{W}$hen news of Lexington and Concord arrived, the Continental Congress was preparing for its upcoming May 10 session. The battles and Massachusetts's plea for help created an increased sense of urgency. Many original members returned, with John Hancock, Benjamin Franklin, Thomas Jefferson, and others joining the assembly at the Pennsylvania State House in Philadelphia. The outbreak of hostilities thrust an unprepared people into war. It fell on Congress to unify the colonies into a cohesive nation as the emerging conflict took on new momentum.

Congress began working to establish enduring institutions in order to advance their common interests. Its members faced many challenges in assuming control of fast-paced events occurring outside their control. Early actions by Congress focused on building consensus, pooling resources, and guiding the American people as they determined how to address hostilities with Britain. Lacking a formal central government unable to generate revenue and direct action proved to be an obstacle to Congress's progress. Although a humble beginning, its efforts would ultimately create the most powerful country in the world.

Congress faced an onerous task in establishing a powerful unified nation out of 13 independent colonies. As with the first Congress, two factions remained. One group hoped for reconciliation, while the other focused on preparations for war. Jefferson recognized the futility of reconciliation following Lexington

---

1 *FONA*, https://founders.archives.gov/documents/Washington/03-02-02-0025, accessed Aug. 1, 2019.

and Concord writing that the "last hopes of reconciliation" had been severed. A "phrenzy of revenge seems to have seized all ranks of people."[2] Samuel Adams and his cousin John Adams agreed, hoping for independence.[3] Dr. Joseph Warren, the president of the Massachusetts Provincial Congress, drafted a letter to Congress in which he sought direction and assistance while calling for an army "as the only means left to stem the rapid Progress of a tyrannical Ministry."[4] He believed that "[w]ithout a force, superior to our Enemies, we must reasonably expect to become the Victims of their relentless fury: With such a force, we may still have hopes of seeing an immediate End put to the inhuman Ravages of mercenary Troops in America."[5] Warren did not wait for the slow-moving Congress, but began planning operations as that body settled into Philadelphia.

Around this time, Dr. Warren and others devised a plan to capture the strategically located British position at Fort Ticonderoga, New York. Originally named Fort Carillon by the French in 1755, Ticonderoga guarded the portage between Lakes George and Champlain, a traditional invasion route to and from Canada. The Massachusetts Committee of Safety tasked 34-year-old Benedict Arnold with capturing the fort and its weapons.[6] Ticonderoga housed approximately 80 heavy British cannons, 20 brass guns, 10-12 large mortars, and other armaments.[7] The New England militia holding the British under siege in Boston direly needed these weapons. Arnold embarked on his mission and was surprised by 37-year-old Ethan Allen, a giant of a man who led a group from the

---

2 *Thomas Jefferson Papers*, 1:165, quoted form Middlekauff, *TGC*, 281.

3 See David McCullough, *John Adams* (New York, 2001), 116-117, for a description of the establishment of the relationship between Thomas Jefferson and John Adams and their common quest for American independence.

4 "Letter from Massachusetts Provincial Congress, 3 May 1775," quoted from *The journals of each Provincial congress of Massachusetts in 1774 and 1775, and of the Committee of safety, with an appendix, containing the proceedings of the county conventions—narratives of the events of the nineteenth of April, 1775—papers relating to Ticonderoga and Crown Point, and other documents, illustrative of the early history of the American revolution. Pub. agreeably to a resolve passed March 10, 1837, under the supervision of William Lincoln, 188*, found at https://archive.org/stream/journalsofeachpr00massuoft/journalsofeachpr00massuoft_djvu.txt, accessed Jul. 28, 2019.

5 Ibid.

6 Arnold arrived in the American camp outside Boston in command of a group of Connecticut volunteers eight days after Lexington and Concord. The professionalism of his unit led to his introduction to the Massachusetts Committee of Safety, a commission as a colonel in the Massachusetts militia, and orders to lead the expedition to capture Fort Ticonderoga. See Willard Randall, *Benedict Arnold: Patriot and Traitor* (New York, 1990), 85-88; Arthur Lefkowitz, *Benedict Arnold in the Company of Heroes* (El Dorado Hills, CA, 2012), 11-13.

7 Scheer & Rankin, *RR*, 48; A.J. Languth, *Patriots: The Men who Started the American Revolution* (New York, 1988), 262.

New Hampshire Grants [Vermont] known as the "Green Mountain Boys," which was on the same mission from his colony's government.[8]

Unbeknownst to Congress, Allen and Arnold first met outside Ticonderoga on May 10, each claiming command of the expedition. After a short squabble, they agreed to capture the fort, conducting a surprise attack jointly, and achieved their objective without sustaining any casualties. With Ticonderoga secured, the victorious leaders immediately began forming plans to assume control of Lake Champlain and invade Canada.

As Allen and Arnold consolidated their gains, Congress continued its duties. Much had transpired since Congress last met. Colonies had seized weapons and armaments, ousted royal officials, bloodied the British army, and were currently holding the British under siege in Boston. Thousands of patriotic Americans ran toward "the sound of the guns" with little direction, ammunition, provisions, and no thought to the future. The colonies continued to accept Artemas Ward of Massachusetts as overall commander of the militiamen outside Boston. This was a temporary measure until Congress could appoint a commander acceptable to all 13 colonies, but it was a slow process.[9]

Congress had been establishing committees to address other issues.[10] It recommended defensive measures for the colonies, assessing how to provide ammunition and military stores, establishing a postal service, issuing paper currency, and determining the cost of waging war while exploring ways to borrow funds. It spent over a month pursuing these issues, delaying the question of adopting the militiamen around Boston, creating a national army, and determining who would command it.

As Congress pondered, General Gage requested 20,000 reinforcements from England for operations around Boston.[11] On May 25, HMS *Cerberus* arrived with six infantry regiments, a unit of light dragoons, a detachment of 600 Royal Marines, and three major generals: William Howe, who replaced Gage as commander-in-chief of all British forces in North America; Henry Clinton who would eventually replace Howe; and John Burgoyne, who would attack the colonies from Canada,

---

8 See Randall, *Ethan Allen*, 304-320, and Lefkowitz, *Benedict Arnold in the Company of Heroes*, 11-24 for descriptions of Arnold's and Allen's combined operation to capture Fort Ticonderoga.

9 See Charles Martyn, *The Life of Artemas Ward: The First Commander-In-Chief of the American Revolution* (New York, 1921) for more on Ward's life and contributions to the American Revolution.

10 For an account of the measures taken by the first session of the Second Continental Congress, see Esbon Marsh, "The First Session of the Second Continental Congress," *The Historian*, vol. 3, no. 2 (Spring 1941), 181-194.

11 Matthew Muehlbauer & David Ulbrich, *Ways of War: American Military History from the Colonial Era to the Twenty-First Century* (New York, 2013), 71; Jack Greene & J. R. Pole, *A Companion to the American Revolution* (Oxford, UK, 2000), 236.

would be defeated in the battle of Saratoga.[12] All three officers possessed years of military experience, came from aristocratic backgrounds, and served in Parliament. Later, they would all suffer defeat at the hands of American troops.

Britain's position in America was precarious but not dire. Although Americans surrounded Boston from land, the British maintained control of the sea, which provided the means for supplies and reinforcements to arrive. Yet they lacked sufficient materials and manpower for conducting offensive operations outside the city.[13] Lexington and Concord demonstrated the challenges of attempting such actions.

The American position was not much better.[14] The Continentals also lacked the manpower and proper resources to conduct offensive operations effectively. While the colonies supplied troops to assist in the siege, they also maintained large numbers at home to protect their territories. The colonies also lacked any naval forces to challenge the British at sea. Additionally, Americans had no heavy artillery with which to destroy British fortifications, support infantry attacks, and place British ships in local waters at risk. While the capture of Fort Ticonderoga provided the heavy guns needed, the cannons were located over 300 miles from Boston, requiring monumental effort and time to retrieve. The American ranks' lack of organization and discipline further exacerbated their problems. The opposing sides settled in for a long siege, contemplating ways in which they could tip the scales to their advantage. Simultaneously, other confrontations between them played out elsewhere.

From June 11-12, 1775, an event occurred on the waters off Machias, Maine, 316 miles from Boston, that author James Fenimore Cooper called "the Lexington of the sea."[15] General Gage and Adm. Samuel Graves, in command of the British fleet, were working to keep the forces in Boston supplied. They were leveraging their Tory connections among the coastal towns throughout New England, minimizing the need to transport supplies 3,000 miles from the British Isles. As part of these efforts, Graves authorized Tory merchant Ichabod Jones to sail two merchant vessels loaded with flour and other food supplies to Machias in exchange

---

12 Commager & Morris, *SSS*, 116; Ferling, *AAM*, 126; Ward, *TWOR*, 59; Robert Leckie, *George Washington's War: The Saga of the American Revolution* (New York, 1992), 145.

13 Fortsecue, ed. *Correspondence of King George III*, 215-216, quoted in Commager & Morris, *SSS*, 118-119.

14 For a description of the challenges facing the Continental forces outside Boston, see Edward Lengel, *General George Washington: A Military Life* (New York, 2005), 102-127, and North Callahan, *George Washington: Soldier and Man* (New York, 1972), 34-41.

15 James Fenimore Cooper, *History of the Navy of the United States of America* (New York, 1856), 37-39.

for lumber. He sent Midshipman James Moore's armed schooner HMS *Margaretta* (4 guns) to escort and protect these vessels.

On June 2, Machias' citizens faced the unwelcome arrival of Moore's small flotilla. They did not appreciate the threat posed by armed vessels in their home waters. With tensions increasing, the local militia jumped into action when Jones threatened to destroy the town using the *Margaretta*'s guns after the townsmen refused to trade. The militia held a secret meeting in a forest with others from nearby villages, agreeing to capture the intruders along with their supplies and ships. During church services on Sunday, June 11, locals attempted to apprehend Jones and Moore, but the men escaped. The *Margaretta* sailed away, but the militia captured two merchant vessels still docked at the port. Militiamen with muskets, pitchforks, and axes boarded two small armed ships and pursued the *Margaretta*. The Americans won the ensuing fight, and the battle of the *Margaretta* became the first naval engagement of the Revolutionary War.[16]

As local hostilities continued in places like Machias, Congressional moderates delayed decisions to adopt the army and appoint a commander. They were still hoping for reconciliation with Britain. On June 12, 1775, Governor Gage provided the moderates some hope when he issued a proclamation offering pardons to those who would cease their rebellious activities, "excepting only from the benefit of such pardon *Samuel Adams* and *John Hancock*, whose offenses are too flagitious a nature to admit of any consideration than that of condign punishment."[17] Gage was asking Congress to give up two members as the cost for reconciliation, and his proposal was rejected.

John Adams grew frustrated by the slow progress of his fellow congressmen and the many ongoing motions, debates, and appointments of committees that addressed trivial matters while slowing the move toward independence. He voiced his frustration, describing how the militia outside Boston was "left without munitions of war, without arms, clothing, pay, or even countenance and encouragement."[18] Adams needed an issue with which he could build a consensus to focus Congress on preparing for a war that had already begun. He found his answer in a warrior-politician from Virginia. On June 14, 1775, he informed his cousin Samuel Adams that he was "determined this morning to make a direct

16 Charles Daughan, *If By Sea: The Forging of the American Navy–From the Revolution to the War of 1812* (New York, 2008), 22-26.

17 "Proclamation by Governor Gage, June 12, 1775," in Force & Clarke, *AA*, 2:967-970.

18 Charles Adams, ed., *The Works of John Adams, Second President of the United States: With a Life of the Author, Notes, and Illustrations* (Boston, 1850), 2:415.

motion that Congress should adopt the army before Boston and appoint Colonel Washington commander of it."[19]

A congressman and colonel of the Virginia militia, George Washington came from an affluent Virginian family and possessed many favorable traits.[20] He spent his early years as a surveyor, gaining an appreciation for terrain and living in the wilderness. In 1752, Washington was commissioned a major in the Virginia militia, achieving the rank of colonel by the time he was 23.[21] He fought bravely beside his British allies through the French and Indian War, but never received the regular commission that he sought in the British army.

Following months of hard campaigning against Native Americans at the head of the Virginia militia, Washington became a politician. He served in the Virginia House of Burgesses before being appointed a Virginia representative to the Continental Congress. Washington attended each congressional session in uniform, reminding his colleagues that he possessed the military experience they sought in a commander-in-chief. Throughout the war, Washington remembered the lessons he had learned as a soldier and politician, assisting in the monumental task of leading and sustaining the Continental Army, which later included sailors and a battalion of Continental Marines.

Regardless of experience, several disagreed with the choice of Washington to lead the army. Some preferred former British officer Charles Lee, but others felt he was still too closely tied to his former comrades.[22] Congressional President John Hancock sought the position for himself, but he had other duties to attend to and lacked adequate military experience. After years of British aggression, colonists from New England believed the commander should come from their ranks. They wanted Artemas Ward to remain in command; however, he had health issues. Others favored French and Indian War veteran Israel Putnam from Connecticut,

---

19 Ibid., 416.

20 See Ron Chernow, *Washington: A Life* (New York, 2010); Edward G. Lengel, *General George Washington: A Military Life* (New York, 2005), and Leckie's *George Washington's War* for Washington's life story and his actions during the American Revolution.

21 See David Clary, *George Washington's First War: His Early Military Adventures* (New York, 2011) for a chronicle of Washington's military service leading up to the Revolution.

22 Although Lee resigned his regular commission in the British army to fight on the side of the Americans in the Revolution and was the second highest ranking officer below Washington in the Continental Army, he proved vain and performed poorly in the opening years of the war. Members of Congress, and indeed historians today, have mixed feelings about Lee's accomplishments. See *Washington Papers: Correspondence between Major General Charles Lee and George Washington, June 1778*, at http://gwpapers.virginia.edu/resources/topics/major-general-charles-lee/, for links to several letters between Washington and Lee that will give the readers a sense of Lee's shortcomings, which eventually led to his court martial following the battle of Monmouth in 1778 (accessed Aug.14, 2019).

Colonel George Washington. George Washington served several years in the Virginia militia before becoming a member of the Continental Congress. He attended all sessions of Congress wearing his militia uniform, reminding others that he possessed the military experience they sought in a commander-in-chief. *Wikimedia*

but he was fifty-seven years-old, and there were doubts that he could withstand the rigors of field life.[23]

John Adams and his radical cousin Samuel were more politically astute than many in Congress. They realized the importance of southern support, especially in Virginia, to achieve their goal of a unified nation. Forty-three-year-old George

23 For several resources concerning the life of Israel Putnam, see "Israel Putnam," https:// connecticuthistory.org/people/israel-putnam/, accessed Aug. 14, 2019.

Washington fit their needs. John made the nomination, Samuel seconded it, and Congress unanimously agreed to adopt the army, with Washington at its head. Lee, Ward, Putnam, and Philip Schuyler of New York received appointments as major generals, while Hancock continued as President of Congress. The Continental Army was born, and it had a commander.[24]

On June 16, 1775, Hancock called Congress to order, informed Washington of his appointment, and expressed that body's hope that he would accept. Washington bowed and read a prepared statement he pulled from his pocket, claiming "that my abilities and military experience may not be equal to the extensive and important trust. However, as the Congress desire, I will enter upon the momentous duty, and exert every power I possess in their service, and for the support of the glorious cause." Washington concluded by stating, "I do not think myself equal to the command I am honored with."[25] While humble, these words were not inspiring coming from the man whom Congress had just entrusted with the future of its country.

Over the next several months many Americans would agree that Washington's "military experience may not be equal to the extensive and important trust." Repeated defeats in the war's early campaigns may have reinforced Washington's feelings of inadequacy for the task at hand. He was, however, a fighter who learned from his mistakes and possessed an unmatched determination and grit. He relied on God and the "glorious cause" for which he was fighting to persevere and sustain himself throughout the war, leading the nascent army through its numerous challenges. His first task was to assume command and organize the rabble outside Boston.

Washington and Congress faced enormous challenges in raising a national army. Washington first transitioned the temporary militiamen from the New England colonies into full-time regulars, while Congress expanded its recruiting efforts across the other colonies. The first regular troops recruited by Congress formed rifle companies from Pennsylvania, Virginia, and Maryland. These units quickly moved to join their brothers outside of Boston. By the end of 1776, Congress made plans to raise 104 regiments of soldiers with accompanying cavalry and artillery.[26] While this looked good on paper, the goal proved challenging to

---

24 Smith, *John Adams: Volume I, 1735-1784*, 199-201; Chernow, *Washington: A Life*, 186; T. J. Stiles, ed., *The American Revolution: First-Person Accounts by the Men Who Shaped Our Nation* (New York, 1999), 84-85.

25 Fitzpatrick, ed., *TWGW*, 292-293, quoted in Commager & Morris, *SSS*, 142; Ralph Andrist, ed., *The Founding Father: George Washington, A Biography in His Own Words* (New York, 1972), 101.

26 James Strokesbury, *A Short History of the American Revolution* (New York, 1991), 69; Chadwick, *The First American Army*, 42-45.

achieve. Congress apportioned each colony a fair-share number of soldiers to raise based on population but lacked the authority to hold the colonies accountable for delivering troops.

Although the immediate crisis at Boston convinced Congress of the need to establish an army quickly, it had no intention of immediately addressing the need for a continental navy and marines. Congress decided to postpone discussions on creating a naval force, even though it had a vested interest in the sea until resources and higher priorities demanded such an action. For now, Congress relied on the colonies to independently form naval defenses for their security.

While Washington and Congressional members struggled to organize, the British moved to seize the initiative. As HMS *Cerberus*, carrying three British generals, entered Boston Harbor, General Burgoyne was informed that "10,000 country people" held the Boston garrison under siege.[27] He responded, "What? Ten thousand peasants keep five thousand of the King's troops shut up? Well, let us get in, and we'll soon find elbow room."[28] This comment typified the hubris of the British and their contempt for Americans throughout the war. Washington and the Americans exploited this arrogance several times, much to the dismay of the British. Upon landing, the generals assessed their position. They recommended to Gage that His Majesty's troops seize the high ground at Charlestown, across the Charles River northwest of the city, and at Dorchester Heights south of the city. American control of these key terrain features would make the British position in Boston untenable.

The Americans, learning of enemy plans to occupy both areas, preempted British movements. On June 16, 1775, as Washington was appointed commander-in-chief, Ward ordered 49-year-old Col. William Prescott, a veteran of King Edward's War in 1745 and the French and Indian War, to defend the Charlestown peninsula with a 1,000-1,600-man force and two cannons.[29] President Samuel Langdon of Harvard College led prayer services for Prescott's men before they marched off to fortify Breed's Hill, just north of Charlestown. Although Bunker Hill was the prominent hill and the ground that the Continentals intended to defend, engineers mistakenly staked out a position on the shorter Breed Hill.

27 Richard Frothingham, *The Centennial: The Battle of Bunker Hill* (New York, 1875), 8; Richard Ketchum, *Decisive Day: The Battle for Bunker Hill* (New York, 1962), 2; Christopher Ward, *TWOR*, 73; Nathaniel Philbrick, *Bunker Hill: A City, A Siege, A Revolution* (New York, 2013), 189.

28 *Congressional Record: Proceedings and Debate of the 90th Congress*, 2nd Session, vol. 114, part 23, Oct. 4-10, 1968, (Washington, D.C., 1968), 29952.

29 Diary of Amos Farnsworth, a corporal in the Massachusetts militia, quoted in Commager & Morris, *SSS*, 122; James Nelson, *Fire and Sword: The Battle of Bunker Hill and the Beginning of the American Revolution* (New York, 2011), 221-223. For more on William Prescott, see "William Prescott," https://militaryhallofhonor.com/honoree-record.php?id=2976, accessed Aug. 14, 2019.

Prescott sent approximately 60 men into Charlestown to watch British movements and took the remaining men to the top of Breed's Hill to construct fortifications. Peter Brown, a clerk in Prescott's regiment, wrote his mother, "[W] e entrenched, and made a fort of about ten rod [165 feet] long and eight [132 feet] wide, with a breast work of about 8 more."[30] In a war council the day before, General Putnam reportedly said, "The Americans are not at all afraid of their heads, though they are very much afraid of their shins; if you cover these, they will fight forever."[31]

The Americans intended to fight a defensive battle using protective works. Conventional wisdom states that an attacking force requires a 3:1 force superiority to capture prepared defensive positions successfully.[32] The Americans, preparing to fight against one of the world's most powerful armed forces, needed every advantage they could get. Their position was on a peninsula, surrounded on three sides by water that British warships and gunboats could use to bombard their works. The Americans learned the importance of controlling local waterways to support ground operations during this battle, wisely applying it in later engagements. Fortunately, the British remained unaware that the colonists were also dramatically short on ammunition at Charleston. The eleven available drums of gunpowder would not last long in battle.

The Americans dug all night. Though the British received reports of this activity, they were surprised at the fortified American position on Breed's Hill the following morning. The redoubt was only half complete but provided cover from hostile fire. The Americans continued digging as the sun rose. British artillery soon opened fire on them from Copp's Hill across the river in Boston, while the HMS *Falcon* (14 guns), HMS *Vulture* (14 guns), HMS *Lively* (20 guns), and gunboats on the Charles and Mystic rivers assisted.[33] The fire continued sporadically throughout the day, intensifying around 3:00 p.m. as British grenadiers, light infantry, and

30 "Peter Brown to his mother," Cambridge, 28 June 1775, in Franklin Dexter, ed., *The Literary Diary of Ezra Stiles, D.D., L.L.D.* (New York, 1901), 1:595, derived from Commager & Morris, *SSS*, 123-124.

31 Frothingham, *The Battle of Bunker Hill*, 10.

32 "Force Ratios and the 3:1 Rule Debate," http://www.twcenter.net/forums/showthread. php?746807-Force-Ratios-and-the-3-1-Rule-Debate (accessed Aug. 8, 2019), provides the results of a 1986 study of 600 land battles from 1600 to 1973 by the U.S. Army Concepts Analysis Agency. The study found that an invading force succeeded 74% of the time when achieving a 3:1 advantage over a defending force. See also Shawn Woodford, *Comparing the RAND Version of the 3:1 Rule to Real-World Data*, posted 5 March 2018 on "Mystics & Statistics: A blog on quantitative historical analysis hosted by The Dupuy Institute," http://www.dupuyinstitute.org/blog/?s=3%3A1&submit=Search, accessed Aug. 8, 2019.

33 Commager & Morris, *SSS*, 123; *FONA*, https://founders.archives.gov/documents/ Adams/06-03-02-0070, accessed Apr. 11, 2019; Nelson, *With Fire and Sword*, 232-234.

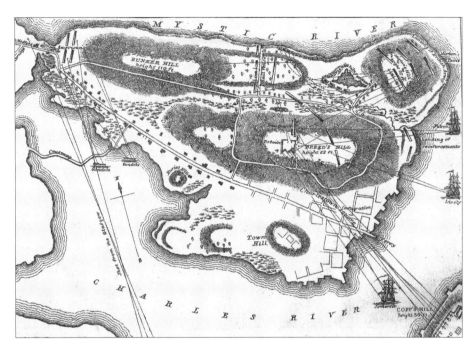

The Charleston Peninsula. Although the battle fought on this terrain is known as the battle of Bunker Hill, the Americans fought from the more prominent Breed's Hill. British cannons from Boston, ships in the river, and forces ashore converged their fire on the shallow American position atop Breed's Hill. *Wikimedia*

Royal Marines boarded barges to cross the Charles. They took around an hour after landing to form and begin their assault, as the peninsula offered little space to maneuver. Charlestown blocked advances on the American position from the south, and Breed's Hill sloped down to the water's edge to the north.

The British formed a broad front, hoping to maneuver and outflank the American position from either side. Sharpshooters killed Royal Marine Maj. John Pitcairn as the Marines approached Charlestown to the south. The British burned the town in retaliation, forcing their troops to move toward the center of the peninsula as the Americans withdrew to their defenses atop Breed's Hill.[34] Additional British troops attempted a flanking movement from the north, but 47-year-old Gen. John Stark of New Hampshire arrived, blocking their progress.[35] He joined the Connecticut troops under 35-year-old Capt. Thomas Knowlton on

34 Commager & Morris, *SSS*, 133.

35 For more on John Stark, see Clifton LaBree, *New Hampshire's General John Stark: Live Free or Die: Death Is Not the Worst of Evils* (New Boston, NH, 2014).

his right, spreading his unit down to the waterline. There they stacked rocks for cover, forming three lines to await the enemy.[36]

The British had no choice but to attempt a frontal assault, marching into American fire three times. The colonists, low on ammunition, were ordered to wait until the Redcoats marched to within 10-30 yards of their position before firing, leading to devastating results.[37] Hundreds of British troops died on that blood-soaked hill. The Americans repulsed the first two assaults, but, low on ammunition, they found themselves under attack on three sides. Falling back into the fort, with one final volley fired as the British attempted their third assault, the battle then transitioned into a hand-to-hand brawl.

The British held the advantage, as few Americans had bayonets, using their muskets as clubs instead.[38] Colonel Preston was seen parrying multiple bayonet thrusts with his ceremonial sword. He gave the order to withdraw as Redcoats poured into the American position. Dr. Joseph Warren, the Provincial President who had come forward as a volunteer rifleman, received a fatal gunshot wound in the mêlée as the Americans withdrew.[39] Peter Brown was also in the thick of the battle. He recalled, "I was in the fort till the Regulars came in and I jumped over the walls, and ran for about half a mile where balls flew like hailstones and cannons roared like thunder."[40]

The British won the battle, but at a high cost. Of the approximately 2,500 British troops who fought, about 1,150 (46%) became casualties. The Americans lost approximately 400 (25%) of their 1,600 troops.[41] More importantly, the British casualties amounted to 18 percent of their force in Boston. They could not afford to win many more victories at such a high cost. In frustration, one British officer wrote, "But from an absurd and destructive confidence, carelessness

---

36 Ketchum, *Decisive Day*, 142-146. Philbrick, *Bunker Hill*, 213-214. For more on Thomas Knowlton see, "Thomas Knowlton: A Small Town's National Hero," https://connecticuthistory.org/thomas-knowlton-a-small-towns-national-hero/, accessed Aug. 14, 2019.

37 Commager & Morris, *SSS*, 126; *FONA*, https://founders.archives.gov/documents/Adams/06-03-02-0070, accessed Apr. 11, 2019.

38 "The Americans are driven from their redoubts: Peter Thacher," found in Commager & Morris, *SSS*, 126-128, is an eyewitness narrative prepared approximately two weeks after the battle of Bunker Hill. *Proceedings of the Massachusetts Historical Society*, 3rd Series, vol. 59 (Oct. 1925-Jun. 1926), 35-42, provides an analysis of the facts concerning Thacher's account.

39 Nelson, *With Fire and Sword*, 301-302; Ketchum, *Decisive Day*, 177, 194-195.

40 Dexter, ed., *The Literary Diary of Ezra Stiles*, 596; Commager & Morris, *SSS*, 124.

41 Frothingham, *The Centennial: The Battle of Bunker Hill*, 106-108, quotes General Ward's orderly book that identified American killed at 115 and wounded at 305. It also quotes British accounts of 226 killed and 827 wounded. See also Nelson, *With Fire and Sword*, 306-312; Philbrick, *Bunker Hill*, 230; "Letter from a British Officer, Boston 5 July 1775," quoted in Commager & Morris, *SSS*, 135.

The Battle of Bunker Hill. Painting by Howard Pyle. The Americans dug in atop Breed's Hill and held their fire until the British were within 10-12 feet of their positions. The devastating result left hundreds of dead British soldiers on the blood-soaked hillside. The British forced the Americans off the hill on their third attempt, winning the battle; but victory came at a high cost. *Wikimedia*

or ignorance, we have lost a thousand of our best men and officers and have given the rebels great matter of triumph by showing them what mischief they can do us."[42] On June 26, General Gage wrote to Lord Barrington, Secretary of State for War, about the folly of maintaining such a strategy. "The loss we have sustained is greater than we can bear. . . . I have before wrote . . . that a large army must at length be employed to reduce these people, as mentioned the hiring of foreign troops." Gage continued, "I fear it must come to that. . . . I think if this army was in New York, that we should find many friends, and be able to raise forces in that province on the side of Government."[43]

Gage's letter made three crucial points. First, he identified Britain's weakness—the cost and difficulty of sustaining an army and navy in America. Second, he recognized the need to rely on foreign troops, leading to hired Hessian troops joining their British partners in America. Third, he acknowledged the belief that American loyalists would aid in conducting war against the rebels. These factors

42 "Letter of a British Officer, Boston, July 5, 1775"; *Detail and conduct of the American War*, 13-15, quoted in Commager & Morris, *SSS*, 135.

43 Carter, ed., *Correspondence of Gage*, 2:686-687, quoted in Commager & Morris, *SSS*, 134-135.

were essential in how the American Revolution developed in the coming months, later contributing to Continental Marines being assigned to Washington to assist the army in the battles of Trenton and Princeton.

On June 23, Washington bid farewell to Congress, leaving Philadelphia for Boston. Accompanying him were Generals Charles Lee, Philip Schuyler, and Thomas Mifflin, as well as Washington's aide, Joseph Reed. Patriotic citizens along the way cheered as they passed. The group stopped in New York, where Washington detached Schuyler to assume command of the Army's newly formed Northern Department, consisting of Continental forces around Fort Ticonderoga, Lake Champlain, Lake George, and other parts of upstate New York.[44]

The Massachusetts Provincial Congress met the party in Watertown, around five miles outside Cambridge. One can only imagine what Washington thought as they addressed him almost apologetically when describing the force he now commanded. "The greatest part of them have not before seen service. And altho' naturally brave and of good understanding, yet for want of Experience in military Life, have but little knowledge of divers things most essential to the preservation of Health, and even Life."[45]

The description is as relevant today as it was in 1775. Recruits must complete basic training before earning the title of soldier, sailor, airman, or marine. Each branch conducts a transformation, with entry-level schools ensuring that civilians with "want of experience" are converted into professional fighters. Sadly, no such institutions existed at the time, and Washington was not pleased with what awaited him on his arrival at Cambridge.

Washington's army was as diverse as the colonies from which its soldiers came. He wrote to his brother, "I found a mixed multitude of People here, under very little discipline, order, or Government. . . . Confusion and Disorder reigned in every Department."[46] Always the optimist, Reverend William Emerson wrote vivid descriptions of the camps around Boston, finding beauty in the diversity of people and structures in the camps.[47]

---

44 Callahan, *George Washington: Soldier and Man*, 18-19; Chernow, *Washington: A Life*, 189-193.

45 "Address from the Massachusetts Provincial Congress, 3 July 1775," *FONA*, https://founders. archives.gov/documents/Washington/03-01-02-0026, accessed Apr. 11, 2019.

46 Fitzpatrick, ed., *TWGW*, 3: 371-373.

47 Emerson provided the following insights into the camps: "Tis also very diverting to walk among ye camps. They are as different in their form as ye owners are in their dress; and every tent is a portraiture of ye temper and taste of ye persons that camp in it. Some are made of boards, some of sail-cloth, and some partly of one partly of ye other. Others are made of stone and turf, and others again of Birch and other brush. . . . I think that ye great variety of ye American camp is upon ye whole rather a beauty than a blemish to ye army." Ward, *TWOR*, 103; Scheer & Rankin, *RR*, 83.

Washington disagreed with Emerson's views. He was horrified by the unsanitary conditions of the camps, the lack of professionalism, and inadequate defensive postures. Immediately, several changes were implemented, and new policies were issued to improve the army's performance overall. Within a few short weeks of assuming command, his efforts were showing positive results.[48] In a letter to General Schuyler, Washington wrote, "We mend every day and I flatter myself that in a little Time, we shall work up these raw Materials into good stuff."[49]

Washington began gaining an appreciation for his nascent army as he toured its lines. While he understood that much had to be done, he saw rays of hope. On July 5, he met 25-year-old Henry Knox outside Cambridge.[50] Knox was a self-made, self-taught man. His patriotic fervor was fueled when he found himself caught up in the Boston Massacre in 1770. In 1772 he co-founded a local militia company called the Boston Grenadier Corps. Knox possessed an insatiable appetite for reading about military art and science and augmented his military lessons before the war by questioning British officers who frequented his bookstore about the topics he read. Knox was appointed captain of an artillery position on the southern end of the American lines during the siege of Boston. Washington was impressed with the young officer's professionalism and detailed defensive preparations, and he relied on Knox over the coming months. Knox was appointed to lead the Continental artillery, and later was briefly given command of the Continental Marines as artillerymen when a shortfall of soldiers required fighting men with expertise in firing cannons.

As spring turned to summer, Washington and the British skirmished around Boston as its residents suffered. The city's population decreased from 17,000 to less than 7,000 during the siege.[51] Some remaining were loyalists, while others were protecting their property from the British, had nowhere to go, or remained for personal or professional reasons.[52] Shortages of food, fuel [wood], and other supplies were common. The British took what they wanted, and American forces constantly bombarded the city. Deacon Timothy Newell, who maintained a journal throughout the siege, noted that "provincials last night attacked the centinels at the lines, and burnt Brown's shop . . . have been imprisoned some time past—

48 *FONA*, https://founders.archives.gov/documents/Washington/03-01-02-0115, accessed Aug. 11, 2019; Leckie, *George Washington's War*, 177-179.

49 *FONA*, https://founders.archives.gov/documents/Washington/03-01-02-0118, accessed Aug. 11, 2019.

50 See Mark Puls, *Henry Knox: Visionary General of the American Revolution* (New York, 2008) for more on Henry Knox; Scheer & Rankin, *RR*, 79-80.

51 Commager & Morris, *SSS*, 146.

52 Ibid.

all they know why it is so is they are charged with free speaking. . . . This day invited two gentlemen to dine upon rats . . . " He added, "Cannonade from both lines. . . . Cannonade again. . . . The spacious Old South Meeting House taken possession by the Light Horse . . . in the most savage manner . . . and destined for a riding school."[53]

On July 6, 1775, Congress approved the "Declaration of Causes and Necessity of Taking Up Arms," which provided a rationale for why the colonists had armed themselves while wanting to avoid a full-scale war with England.[54] On July 8, Congress extended the "Olive Branch Petition" as a final attempt at reconciliation.[55] The colonies were unaware that George III had already given up on them. On July 1, he wrote to Lord Sandwich, "I am of this opinion that when once these rebels have felt a smart blow, they will submit; and no situation can ever change my fixed resolution, either to bring the colonies to a due obedience to the legislature of the mother country or to cast them off!"[56] The king, however, was unaware that his troops in America lacked the resources to administer the "smart blow" he wanted, or that the Americans would eventually cast him off.

The Americans and British were at an impasse, as neither possessed the strength to take the offensive. Washington's army averaged between 13,000-14,000 fit men during the early summer, but they lacked training while still guarding an extended line. On July 17, Rev. William Emerson wrote, "thousands are at work every day from four to eleven o'clock in the morning" improving fortifications.[57] The army did not have the heavy artillery necessary to destroy British works, remaining critically short on gunpowder and other ammunitions; August reports reflected 9,937 pounds of powder and "not more than 9 Cartridges a Man" on hand.[58] For comparison, the British kept their soldiers supplied with 60 cartridges per man.[59]

53 Excerpts from the journal of Deacon Timothy Newell, quoted in Commager & Morris, *SSS*, 147-148.

54 "Editorial Note: Declaration of the Causes and Necessity for Taking Up Arms," *FONA*, https://founders.archives.gov/documents/Jefferson/01-01-02-0113-0001, accessed Aug. 11, 2019.

55 For the full text of the Olive Branch Petition see "The Olive Branch Petition," https://www.constitution.org/primarysources/olive.html, (accessed Aug. 11, 2019).

56 Barnes & Owens, eds., *Private Papers of Earl of Sandwich*, 1:63.

57 Louise Lovell, *Israel Angell, Colonel of the 2nd Rhode Island Regiment* (New York, 1921), 82, https://archive.org/stream/israelangellcolo00love/israelangellcolo00love_djvu.txt, accessed Aug. 11, 2019.

58 *FONA*, https://founders.archives.gov/documents/Washington/03-01-02-0150, accessed Aug. 11, 2019.

59 Ward, *TWOR*, 108.

The British averaged around 5,000-6,000 men fit for duty.[60] They weighted efforts by strengthening positions on both flanks, hoping to prevent assaults on Boston. Bunker Hill was heavily fortified following its capture, leading Washington to opine, "Twenty thousand men could not have carried it against one thousand had that work been well defended."[61] The British erected another strong position on Boston Neck, leaving little to no troops to conduct offensive operations.[62] The British were wary of costly victories, which put them in a precarious position.

As the stalemate continued, both sides increased naval activities. The British navy served two primary purposes at this stage of the war. First, it protected the communication lines required to transport reinforcements and supplies to its ground forces.[63] Unarmed and lightly armed commercial vessels hauled fresh provisions and supplies from the southern colonies, West Indies, and local areas while carrying reinforcements and articles needed for war 3,000 miles from England. The fleet further assumed responsibility for blockading ports along the eastern seaboard, blocking supplies intended for the rebels and strangling the Americans economically.[64] Admiral Graves lacked the warships to perform both functions, providing ample opportunities for the colonists. Without a fleet, Congress could no longer delay a decision on naval matters. It resolved on July 18 that each colony, at its expense, should provide for the protection of its harbors and coastal towns, and also sanctioned the practice of privateering.[65]

Privateering is a legal form of piracy.[66] European governments commonly used the practice to harass enemies, and withhold supplies, as well as for financial gain. Governments issued "letters of marque and reprisal," legitimizing privately outfitted men-of-war to attack and seize enemy vessels.[67] Admiralty courts approved such seizures, earning a percentage of revenue from the sale of captured ships

---

60 Scheer & Rankin, *RR*, 90.

61 Michael Newton, *Angry Mobs and Founding Fathers: The Fight for Control of the American Revolution* (Phoenix, 2011), 63.

62 Scheer & Rankin, *RR*, 90.

63 Kenneth Hagan, *This People's Navy: The Making of American Seapower* (New York, 1991), 2-3.

64 Barbara Tuchman, *The First Salute: A View of the American Revolution* (New York, 1988), 8-10; George Trevelyan, *The American Revolution* (New York, 1964), 305; Coggins, *SSAR*, 19; Ferling, *AAM*, 67.

65 Bruce Elleman & S. C. M. Paine, eds., *Commerce Raiding: Historical Case Studies, 1755-2009* (Newport, 2013), 32; Force, *TWGW*, 3:263-266, 354; Ward, *TWOR*, 113.

66 See Robert Patton, *Patriot Pirates: The Privateer War for Freedom and Fortune in the American Revolution* (New York, 2009).

67 John Frayler, "Privateers in the American Revolution," https://www.nps.gov/revwar/about_the_revolution/privateers.html, accessed Aug. 11, 2019.

and cargoes with ship owners and crews. The Americans granted roughly 1,700 letters of marque during the Revolution, resulting in nearly 800 privateer vessels being employed.[68]

American privateers, which consisted of citizen sailors and marines, quickly proved their worth by capturing 342 British vessels in 1776 and around 600 by the war's end.[69] While not decisive, privateers provided critical provisions to the Continental Army. In response, Parliament passed the "Pirate Act" in 1777, which denied privateers the legal rights granted to prisoners of war, allowing them to be held without trial or prospect of exchange.[70]

George Washington appreciated the value offered by privateers and formal naval forces. He knew that if the British controlled the seas, they could reinforce and resupply their forces indefinitely. Washington needed what America lacked, a professional navy and marines. He decided to fill the void, creating a personal navy until Congress could meet his demands, and looked to the army to find his sailors and marines.[71] Luckily, candidates were available in the regiments from Massachusetts's coastal towns.

These men were experienced seafarers, with years of experience operating on the Atlantic as fishermen and merchants. They also held intimate knowledge of the waters around Boston. Their leader was 43-year-old Col. John Glover, who had worked his way up from fisherman to owning a fleet of fishing vessels as hostilities began.[72] In 1759, Glover joined the Marblehead militia, eventually becoming its colonel. He led his regiment to Boston following Lexington and Concord, providing Washington with his first ship, the schooner *Hannah*, named after Glover's wife.[73] Glover's regiment, later designated the 14th Massachusetts, provided valuable services to Washington and the Continental Army in future battles, but it was in no hurry to join Washington's new navy.

Those familiar with the dangers of operating on the open waters were slow to volunteer. Washington enticed soldiers into joining the naval force, offering a portion of any captured non-military prizes as an inducement. Glover recruited 50

---

68 Ibid.

69 James Fenimore Cooper, *The History of the Navy of the United States of America* (New York, 1853), 76.

70 Patton, *Patriot Pirates*, 34.

71 Smith, *MIR*, 32-36; Leckie, *George Washington's War*, 218-219; Hagan, *This People's Navy*, 2-3.

72 See George Billias, *General John Glover and his Marblehead Mariners* (New York, 1960) for more on John Glover.

73 Stephen Howarth, *To Shining Sea: A History of the United States Navy, 1775-1991* (New York, 1991), 6-7; James Nelson, *George Washington's Great Gamble and the Sea Battle that Won the American Revolution* (New York, 2010), 17-18.

officers, sailors, and marines by August, setting sail in September on the *Hannah* with explicit orders to seek any vessels entering or exiting Boston in support of the British army "and to take and seize all such vessels laden with soldiers, arms, ammunition or provisions, for or from said Army, or which you shall have a good reason to suspect are in such service."[74]

Early results were encouraging. Two days after departing on her first cruise, *Hannah* captured the British commercial vessel *Unity*, which was loaded with naval stores and lumber. Soon, Washington expanded his fleet to six ships, achieving mixed results. The fleet's most significant victory was capturing the British ordnance brig *Nancy* at the entrance of Boston Harbor. She carried 2,000 muskets, 100,000 flints, 30,000 round shots, 30 tons of musket balls, and a 13-inch mortar, which were immensely valuable to the Continental Army.[75] American soldiers were so excited by the catch that "Old Put [General Putnam] mounted on the large mortar . . . [and] with a bottle of rum in his hand" christened the mortar the *Congress*.[76] Though it captured additional vessels, the fleet could not effectively isolate the British in Boston.

Long days of inaction, cold northern winds, and a lack of proper supplies resulted in near mutiny on some ships. One of Washington's agents reported, "The people on board the Brigantine *Washington* are in general discontent, & have agreed to do no Duty on board s[ai]d vessel, & Say that they Inlisted to Serve in the Army & not as Marines."[77] Washington grew impatient and unhappy with his ad hoc navy. He penned his frustration to John Hancock, writing, "The plague, trouble and vexation I have had with the Crews of all the armed Vessels is inexpressible; I do believe there is not on Earth a more disorderly set; every time they come into Port, we hear of nothing but mutinous Complaints." His letter added the dismal news, "the Crews of *Washington* and *Harrison* have Actually deserted them."[78]

Washington was experiencing the challenges of performing the essential functions of a navy and marines with improvised organizations. Although performing as seamen and marines, those in his navy were soldiers, governed by army regulations. The Continentals needed a professional navy and marines, trained, manned, and equipped to perform the special duties of those who fought

---

74 "George Washington's Instructions to Nicholson Broughton, 2 September 1775," in *TWGW*, 3:467-469, as quoted in Smith, *MIR*, 33.

75 Ferling, *AAM*, 103-104; Ward, *TWOR*, 114.

76 Patton, *Patriot Pirates*, 35-39; Ward, *TWOR*, 114.

77 Smith, *MIR*, 34.

78 *FONA*, https://founders.archives.gov/documents/Washington/03-02-02-0437, accessed Aug. 11, 2019.

on the seas. The colonies were also impatient with Congress's failure to protect coastal towns and American merchant shipping.

Unsatisfied with the direction Congress was taking, especially with the requirement that colonies supply their own fleets, the Rhode Island General Assembly led the way on August 26, 1775, calling for a national navy. It resolved that "the assembly is persuaded that the building and equipping [of] an American fleet, as soon as possible, would greatly and essentially conduce to the preservation of the lives, liberty and property of the good people of these colonies."[79] Rhode Island further directed its congressional representatives to use their influence to ensure the fleet was built "at the Continental expense."[80] John Adams recalled how some of his colleagues claimed that this "represented as the most wild, visionary, mad project that ever had been imagined."[81] While some feared such a move, enemy operations soon forced Congress to act.

Congress received intelligence on October 5 that two British ships loaded with military stores needed by the army were traveling unescorted to Quebec, Canada. The news was the catalyst needed by Congress, which quickly formed a committee to devise a plan to intercept the vessels.[82] Committee members John Adams, Silas Deane, and John Langdon directed Washington to secure two armed vessels from Massachusetts with support from Connecticut and Rhode Island.[83] By encouraging the enlistments of seamen and marines, Congress finally acknowledged the need for a force of Marines.[84] As Congress finally began to act, the pace quickened. On October 13, a second committee agreed to outfit Washington's two armed vessels, establishing the birth of the United States Navy.[85] Within two weeks, Congress increased the number of ships to four, appointing four additional members to the Naval (later renamed Marine) Committee.

Initially, Congress directed the New England colonies to purchase vessels for commissioning and arming as Continental warships. Upon finding none, however, they turned to Philadelphia, converting merchant ships for war. Adams described the initial members of the American fleet.

---

79 "Journal of the Rhode Island General Assembly, 26 August 1775," quoted from Clark, ed., *NDAR*, 1:1236.

80 Ibid.

81 John Adams, *Works of John Adams,* III, 7-12, quoted in Commager & Morris, *SSS*, 915.

82 *FONA*, https://founders.archives.gov/documents/Washington/03-02-02-0099, accessed Aug. 11, 2019.

83 Ibid.

84 Smith, *MIR*, 10-11.

85 "*JCC*, Philadelphia, 13 October 1775," quoted from Clark, ed., *NDAR*, 2:441-442.

"The first we named *Alfred* [24 guns], in honor of the founder of the greatest navy that ever existed. The second, *Columbus* [20 guns], after the discoverer of this quarter of the globe. The third, *Cabot* [14 guns], for the discoverer of this northern part of the continent. The fourth, *Andrew Doria* [14 guns], in memory of the great Genoese Admiral, and the fifth, *Providence* [12 guns], for the town where she was purchased."[86]

Esek Hopkins became the fleet's commander-in-chief. Fifty-seven-year-old Hopkins was a sea captain from Providence who had been a privateer commander during the French and Indian War. Perhaps his best command qualification was that his brother, Stephen, was a member of the Naval Committee.[87] Hopkins's son John received command of the *Cabot*.

Congress's actions to create a navy did not come soon enough. Admiral Graves had orders to make the colonists pay for their rebellious acts by assaulting New England coastal towns and harass American shipping.[88] These directives served two purposes. First, by attacking the coasts, the British hoped militias would stay close to home instead of reinforcing the troops around Boston. Secondly, they wanted to prevent the proliferation of privateering vessels, which had begun to have a distressing effect on British shipping. Graves placed four ships under Lt. Henry Mowat's command on October 13, with explicit instructions to carry out his plan.[89]

Mowat wasted no time, appearing with his squadron in Falmouth, Massachusetts (modern-day Maine) on October 17 to execute his orders. He sent word to the townspeople that he intended to begin firing on their homes in two hours.[90] Town leaders pleaded for time, but Mowat began a bombardment at 9:30 a.m. as citizens clamored to escape. Fires spread, engulfing a third of Falmouth by noon. Mowat escalated the attack at 3:00 p.m., sending a landing party ashore to torch buildings not already burning. Driving his point home, Mowat fired on the

---

86 Adams, *Works of John Adams*, 7-12, as quoted in Commager & Morris, *SSS*, 918; Coggins, *SSAR*, 26; Smith, *MIR*, 11.

87 Howarth, *To Shining Sea*, 18; Hagan, *This People's Navy*, 4.

88 Clark, ed., *NDAR*, 2:701-702.

89 Graves shared with Mowat, "My design is to chastise Marblehead, Salem, Newburyport, Cape Anne Harbor, Portsmouth, Ipswich, Saco, Falmouth in Casco Bay, and particularly Machias, where the *Margaretta* was taken . . . and where the Diligent schooner was seized and the officers and crew carried prisoners. . . . You are to go to all or as many of the above named places as you can, and make the most vigorous efforts to burn the town, and destroy the shipping in the harbors," George Daughan, *If By Sea: The Forging of the American Navy-From the Revolution to the War of 1812* (New York, 2008), 44.

90 Commager & Morris, *SSS*, 172.

town once again as the landing party departed.[91] Colonial citizens were enraged when they heard of the destruction experienced by Falmouth's citizens.

Washington devised a plan to strike by land as the British gained the initiative on the seas. With the continuing stalemate in Boston, He intended to preemptively attack Canada, cutting off Sir Guy Carleton's planned attack south from Canada.[92] The 51-year-old Carleton was serving dual roles as governor of the Quebec Province and commander of British forces in the area. Washington intended to launch a two-pronged spoiling attack from the newly captured Fort Ticonderoga and Cambridge. He tasked General Schuyler, commander of the Northern Department, with attacking north from Ticonderoga to capture Montreal via Lake Champlain. Benedict Arnold, departing Cambridge, would attack Quebec via a land route through the wilderness of Maine.[93]

On November 13, Gen. Richard Montgomery assumed command and successfully captured Montreal after Schuyler fell ill.[94] Montgomery, 37, was a former British soldier who settled in America and chose to fight for his adopted country. After capturing Montreal, Montgomery left 800 soldiers in the city, advancing with 300 men up the St. Lawrence River toward Quebec. He was moving to assist Arnold's approximately 650-man force, which was facing challenges in advancing across Maine's treacherous terrain.[95] On December 31, both forces converged, attacking Quebec during a blinding snowstorm. The attack failed, leaving Montgomery dead and Arnold with a severe wound to his leg. With Carleton in pursuit and anticipating British reinforcements, Arnold led his and Montgomery's troops back into New York via Lake Champlain.

As fighting raged on one side of Canada, affairs in another set the conditions for the birth of the Continental Marines. As previously mentioned, not all Canadians were sympathetic to the British. Passamaquoddy, Nova Scotia, had requested to join the Americans. Congress considered the opportunity of gaining Canada as an

---

91 "Report by the Selectmen of Falmouth on the Destruction of their town, 15 January 1776," in Commager & Morris, *SSS*, 172-173.

92 For more on Carleton see "Guy Carleton," http://www.canadahistory.com/sections/eras/british%20america/Carleton.html (accessed Aug. 15, 2019).

93 Dave Palmer, *George Washington and Benedict Arnold: A Tale of Two Patriots* (Washington, D.C., 2006), 113-114, 116-120; Willard Randall, *Benedict Arnold: Patriot and Traitor* (New York, 1990), 135-201; Lefkowitz, *Benedict Arnold in the Company of Heroes*, 37-61. Note: Maine did not become a state until 1820. This area was still part of Massachusetts at the time of Arnold's expedition.

94 "Major Richard Montgomery," https://armyhistory.org/major-general-richard-montgomery/, accessed Aug. 15, 2019.

95 See Commager & Morris, *SSS*, 192-201 for first-hand accounts of Arnold's expedition from the journals of Abner Stocking, a private in Arnold's army, and Dr. Isaac Senter, who accompanied Arnold.

ally and developed a plan to assist the Nova Scotians. The resulting scheme was a naval campaign in the north, and the Congress resolved to form two battalions of marines from the troops under Washington's command at Boston to conduct the operation.

Washington did not support this initiative, informing Hancock that "the Resolve to raise two Battallions of marines will (if practicable in this Army) entirely derange what has been done."[96] He claimed pulling troops from the army would "break thro' the whole System which has Cost us So much time anxiety and pains to bring into any tollerable form."[97] Washington explained that he was reorganizing the army, and his troops would balk at enlisting for the war's duration as the resolution called for, forcing him to hand-pick select soldiers from the ranks to meet the requirements of enlisting those "acquainted with maritime affairs."[98] As Washington was already short on the troops needed to contain Boston, he suggested that Congress look to New York or Philadelphia to find their marines. He also averred that he did not have enough manpower for an operation in Nova Scotia.

On November 30, Congress acquiesced, relieving Washington of the responsibility of raising the marine battalions while indefinitely postponing the Nova Scotia mission. Realizing the value of marines, Congress decided to raise them as separate branch, taking more time as hostilities continued to rage.

As Congress continued deliberating on the best way to form the marines, Washington continued reorganizing his army. Replacing popular or politically appointed officers with more capable individuals was part of this effort, leading to one of the most important tasks: finding an officer to lead the artillery. Washington settled on the young, enterprising Henry Knox, who had earlier impressed him outside Boston.[99] At the time, the artillery was comprised of a single regiment of just over 600 soldiers and about 12 cannons. Complicating matters further, the colonies did not have the means to produce their own guns.

The army needed to acquire cannons from elsewhere until foundries were established in America. While many in Boston disregarded the guns at Fort Ticonderoga due to the fact that they were 300 miles away across rugged terrain, Washington and Knox thought differently. On November 16, Washington

---

96 *FONA*, https://founders.archives.gov/documents/Washington/03-02-02-0367, accessed Aug. 12, 2019.

97 Ibid.

98 Ibid.

99 See Mark Puls, Henry Knox, *Visionary General of the American Revolution* (New York, 2008) for details of Knox's service in the American Revolution.

ordered Knox to Fort Ticonderoga and other areas, gathering as many cannons and munitions as possible, stating, "the want of them is so great, that no trouble or expence must be spared to obtain them."[100] Knox departed for New York as hostilities expanded south.

Any hope of reconciliation diminished once the British allowed the violence to move into the southern colonies. American militiamen, British regulars, and loyalists under Royal Governor Lord Dunmore raced to gather the weapons and powder available in Virginia. Several clashes ensued, resulting in the governor taking refuge on a British warship near Norfolk. Dunmore ordered his troops to clear the American rebels guarding an area known as Great Bridge. The resulting battle was over in 25 minutes, resulting in 60-100 British casualties, while the Americans only had one man slightly injured. On December 15, *Purdie's Virginia Gazette* reported, "This was a second Bunker's Hill affair, in miniature; with this difference, that we kept our post, and had only one man wounded in the hand."[101]

Lord Dunmore ordered a naval bombardment of Norfolk, resulting in its fiery destruction. In response, Washington wrote to his aide, Joseph Reed, "A Few more of such flaming arguments, as were exhibited at Falmouth and Norfolk, added to the sound doctrine and unanswerable reasoning contained in the pamphlet *Common Sense*, will not leave numbers at a loss to decide upon the propriety of a separation [with Great Britain]."[102]

Washington was referring to a document that fueled revolutionary fervor across America. In January 1776, 38-year-old Thomas Paine, a British-born political activist who had arrived in America only months before, published *Common Sense*.[103] Paine's work was the first openly published piece calling for America's independence from Great Britain. It provided compelling arguments using plain language easily understood by the masses. Paine asserted that "the period for debate is closed. Arms, as the last resource, must decide the contest." He added, "The sun never shone on a cause of greater worth." For Paine, "Now is the seedtime of continental union, faith, and honor."

Common Sense made clear and concise arguments, debunking claims calling for reconciliation. Paine argued that "America would have flourished as much, and probably much more, had no European power had anything to do with her."

100 *FONA*, https://founders.archives.gov/documents/Washington/03-02-02-0351, accessed Aug. 12, 2019.

101 "The Battle of Great Bridge," https://www.historyisfun.org/blog/the-battle-of-great-bridge/, accessed Aug. 11, 2019.

102 Force & Clarke, eds., *AA*, 899.

103 See Commager & Morris, *SSS*, 285-291 for the full text of Thomas Paine's *Common Sense*. The quotes from *Common Sense* used here are derived from this source.

He also alleged that Great Britain "did not protect us from our enemies on our account but from her enemies on her own account." According to Paine, "even brutes do not devour their young, nor savages make war upon their families."

Paine attempted to draw distance between the colonies and what some considered the motherland: "Europe, and not England, is the parent country of America." Paine challenged "the warmest advocate for reconciliation to show a single advantage that this continent can reap by being connected to Britain." He asserted that "reconciliation is now a fallacious dream . . . tell me whether you can hereafter love, honor, and faithfully serve the power that has carried fire and sword into your hand." Following his own advice, Paine joined the Continental Army, serving as General Greene's aide, and experiencing some of the Army's most trying days.

The British had overplayed their hand by imposing bitter oppression, violence, and death on the colonies. *Common Sense* gave a voice to the feelings of many Americans. The time had come to cut ties with Great Britain permanently, but this would not be an easy undertaking. Although the Americans would achieve minor victories in the coming months, a major crisis was brewing.

Chapter Four

Early Victories

"There is a time for all things, a time to preach and a time to pray, but those times have passed away. There is a time to fight, and that time has now come."

— Rev. Peter Muhlenberg[1]

The year 1776 started decently for the Americans, as they achieved some early victories. Creating a nation while sustaining the armed forces needed to secure its freedoms, however, was proving an insurmountable task. As the British juggernaut assumed the initiative, Americans faced difficulties slowing the momentum. They began to suffer one defeat after another at the hands of a stronger, better trained, and better equipped enemy. As the year progressed, the new nation faced a growing crisis that nearly resulted in a British victory.

On January 24, 1776, Col. Henry Knox rode into Cambridge, reporting to General Washington that 53 cannons, 16 mortars, and two howitzers would be arriving at their camp from Fort Ticonderoga.[2] Knox had accomplished an incredible feat by hauling approximately 120,000 pounds of weapons and ordnance over 300 miles. He used gondolas, scows, canoes, 42 sleds, and 160 oxen to move matériel across snow-covered mountains and frozen lakes.[3] Though Knox's efforts provided Washington with the weapons needed to turn the tide at Boston, the army still lacked the required gunpowder.

Washington wrote to Congress and the colonies again requesting assistance in providing the powder. He notified John Hancock, "the great want of powder

---

1 *Congressional Record: Proceedings and Debates of the 76th Congress*, First Session, vol. 84, part 13, (Washington, D.C., 1939), 2379.

2 *FONA*, "Enclosure: Inventory of Artillery, 17 December 1775," https://founders.archives.gov/documents/Washington/03-02-02-0521-0002, accessed Aug. 25, 2019.

3 Puls, *Henry Knox*, 39.

is what the Attention of Congress Should be particularly applied to, I dare not attempt anything Offensive, Let the temptation or advantage be ever So great, as I have Not more of that most essential article than will be absolutely necessary to defend our Lines."[4]

On Christmas Day 1775, Washington wrote to Congressman Joseph Hewes, a member of the Naval Committee, that "Our want of powder is inconceivable."[5] Earlier, intelligence reports shared with the Committee showed large quantities of gunpowder stowed by the British on New Providence Island, Bahamas.[6] They undoubtedly informed Commodore Hopkins, identifying New Providence as a possible future objective, creating the catalyst for the first amphibious operation to be conducted by sailors and marines. The burning of Norfolk and British harassment of the coastal towns, however, resulted in Hopkins receiving a higher priority mission.

Hopkins arrived at his flagship, the *Alfred*, on a cold January 4, 1776. A boatswain's mate piped him aboard as officers, including Continental Marine Capt. Samuel Nicholas, stood on the quarterdeck to greet him. Thousands reportedly crowded Philadelphia's Willing and Morris Wharf to watch *Alfred* and *Columbus* cast off. More gathered at James Cuthbert's Wharf down river to bid farewell to *Andrew Doria* and *Cabot* on their historic cruise.[7] First Lieutenant of the *Alfred* and future Navy legend John Paul Jones hoisted the first colors raised on an American warship.[8] *London's Public Advertiser* reported, "The Colours of the American Fleet were striped under the Union with 13 Strokes, called the Thirteen United Colonies and their Standard a Rattle Snake, Motto, 'Don't tread upon me.'"[9]

As Hopkins settled into his cabin, he reviewed two letters of instruction provided by Congress.[10] The first addressed expectations for the conduct of the fleet during the Continental Navy's and Marines' first deployment. It covered topics ranging from the good order and discipline of the crews to the treatment of prisoners by Marines. The second letter identified Hopkins's mission. The burning

---

4 *FONA*, "From George Washington to John Hancock, 4 December 1775," accessed Aug. 16, 2019.

5 Fitzpatrick, ed., *Writings of Washington*, 4:185.

6 The intelligence report was delivered to the Secret Committee of Congress in Nov. 1774, resulting in the Committee recommending that it "take measures for securing and bring[ing] away the said powder," Smith, *MIR*, 44.

7 *Alfred* mounted 24 cannons, *Columbus* 20, *Andrew Doria* 14, and *Cabot* 14.

8 For a short history of the first American flag flown on a naval vessel see Barbara Tuchman, *The First Salute: A view of the American Revolution* (New York, 1988), 47-48.

9 Morgan, ed., *NDAR*, 6:477.

10 Smith, *MIR*, 42.

of Norfolk and pressure from southern Congressional delegates resulted in orders for the fleet to proceed immediately, "if the Winds and Weather will possibly to admit of it," to Virginia's Chesapeake Bay.[11] At that point, "If . . . you find they are not greatly superior to your own you are immediately to Enter the said bay search out and attack, take, or destroy all Naval forces of our Enemies that you may find there." This done, Hopkins should "proceed immediately to the Southward and make yourself Master of such forces as the Enemy may have both in North and South Carolina." The fleet would then "proceed Northward directly to Rhode Island, and attack, take and destroy all the Enemies Naval force that you may find there." Finally, Hopkins would "seize and make prize of all such Transport Ships and other vessels as may be found carrying Supplies of any kind to or any way aiding or assisting our Enemies." These were ambitious demands for a fleet's maiden voyage. Unfortunately, Hopkins faced steep challenges in accomplishing *any* of these tasks.

Ice was forming on the Delaware River as the fleet departed the wharves. The four-ship armada pushed down the river to avoid getting iced-in, laying anchor off Liberty Island to gather provisions and allow missing crew members to return. The time was well spent, as many Marines still lacked weapons. As Congress could not fulfill all the requests for arms, it sought the assistance of the Pennsylvania Committee of Safety. On January 5, the Committee delivered 67 muskets, 60 bayonets, 50 scabbards, and 200 pounds of musket balls to Captain Nicholas on the *Alfred*, and 37 muskets and 136 bayonets to Lieutenant Craig on the *Andrew Doria*.[12] Additionally, Nicholas received "a large supply of brilliantly colored hussar uniforms which included caps, coats, waistcoats, and trousers."[13] While this was not the standard uniform the Marines would wear, any uniforms were welcome during the cold winter season. Nicholas requested additional assistance from the Committee of Safety, as he was still short on weapons. On January 9, it responded, ordering the commissary to "apply to Colo. Cadwalader for all the Muskets he has to spare, and deliver them to Capt. Nicholas."[14] Colonel John Cadwalader commanded a group of Philadelphia militia referred to as the "Associators," with whom Nicholas and his Marines became intimately familiar in the coming months.

11 All quotes in this paragraph are derived from Library of Congress, *JCC 1774-1789*, IV-1776 (Washington, D.C., 1906), 335-336.

12 *Minutes of the Provincial Council of Pennsylvania, From the Organization to the Termination of the Proprietary Government*, vol. 10 (Harrisburg, 1852), 447; Smith, *MIR*, 43.

13 Hussars are traditional light cavalry forces.

14 *Minutes of the Provincial Council of Pennsylvania*, vol. 10, 452; Smith, *MIR*, 43.

On January 17, thinning ice enabled the fleet, now joined by the sloop *Providence* and schooner *Fly*, to continue.[15] The growing armada only got as far as Reedy Island before winter temperatures forced it to remain anchored for four more weeks. The monotony of hard work, standing watch, sickness, poor food, and the bitter cold took a toll on the ships' crews, and at least one Marine. Just as had occurred with Washington's Navy off Boston, many began to desert. Captain John Welsh, the Marine commander on the *Cabot*, purchased an ad in the *Pennsylvania Evening Post* concerning a deserter from his detachment:

TWO DOLLARS REWARD. DESERTED the third Inst. From Captain John Welsh's company of marines, PETER M'TEGART, born Ireland, about thirty years of age, five feet seven inches high, smooth faced, brownish complexion, short dark brown hair. Had on a light brown coat, white cloth jacket and breeches, blue stockings and new shoes. Whoever delivers said deserter to James Guthrie, at the corner of South and Walnut street, shall have the above reward.[16]

As the fleet idled in the Delaware River, North Carolina's Governor Josiah Martin received notification from London, approving his plan to restore royal authority in that colony. Martin set several actions in motion, resulting in the battle of Moore's Creek Bridge, the first battle of the Revolution to take place in North Carolina.[17]

British plans called for separate units of regulars moving by sea under the commands of Lord Charles Cornwallis and Sir Henry Clinton to converge on the Lower Cape Fear River near Brunswick Town, North Carolina. Local loyalists received orders to join the regulars to assist in putting down the rebellion, led by the North Carolina militia. By mid-February 1776, 1,600 American-Scottish Highlanders and others commenced movements to unite with the British troops.

The North Carolina militia wisely chose a natural chokepoint created by swamplands at Moore's Creek Bridge to do battle. On February 26, the militiamen created solid defensive positions along the high ground overlooking the crossing. They also removed bridge planks, greased its girders, and positioned artillery to cover the area.

The resulting battle, which lasted just three minutes, was a massacre. With bagpipes playing in the background, nearly 1,000 militiamen held their fire until

15 *Providence* mounted 12 cannons and *Fly* 8.

16 *Pennsylvania Evening Post*, Jan. 9, 1776; repeated Jan. 13, 18, and 20, 1776, as quoted in Smith, *MIR*, 383.

17 Richard Ketchum, ed., *The American Heritage Book of The Revolution* (New York, 1958), 126-127; David Russell, *The American Revolution in the Southern Colonies* (Jefferson, NC, 2000), 80-83.

500 broadsword-wielding Highlanders stormed the bridge screaming, "King George and broadswords!"[18] Very few made it. As the smoke cleared, about 70 Highlanders lay dead or wounded. The militiamen counterattacked, capturing approximately 850 of the remaining loyalists and their commanding general, as well as 150 swords, 1,500 muskets, and £15,000 in gold. The militia only lost one man, who died from his wounds four days later. The "Lexington and Concord of the South" proved significant, ending any hope Governor Martin had in regaining control of the colony.[19] The British could not accomplish the area's objectives, leading North Carolina to instruct its Congressional delegates to vote for independence.

Meanwhile, the weather finally improved, allowing the fleet to continue down the Delaware River. On February 11, the small armada anchored off Cape Henlopen, Pennsylvania. They were awaiting the sloop *Hornet* and schooner *Wasp*, which Congress ordered to join the fleet from Baltimore.[20] Both arrived two days later, bringing the fleet to 680 sailors and 234 Marines, with 110 cannons ranging from small 2-pounders on the *Wasp*, to larger 9-pounders on the *Alfred* and *Columbus*.[21] On that same day, Midshipman John Trevett of the *Providence* received a promotion to first lieutenant of Marines and transferred to the *Columbus*.[22]

The weather delays gave Hopkins time to ponder his situation and orders. The task from Congress was to engage the world's most powerful Navy with only a handful of converted merchant ships. These were outfitted with low-caliber guns and inexperienced crews, and Hopkins was concerned about his chances of success. Instead of driving the British from the coasts of Virginia, North Carolina, and Rhode Island, Hopkins decided to leverage a clause in his directive that stated, "if bad Winds or Stormy Weather, or any other unforeseen accident or disaster disabled you so to do You are then to follow such Course as your Best Judgement shall Suggest."[23] This directive gave him the out he needed, and he relied on his

---

18 "Moore's Creek National Battlefield," https://www.nationalparks.org/explore-parks/moores-creek-national-battlefield, accessed Aug. 17, 2019.

19 "Battle of Moore's Creek Bridge, 1776," https://www.ncdcr.gov/blog/2014/02/27/battle-of-moores-creek-bridge-1776, accessed Aug. 17, 2019.

20 *Hornet* mounted 10 cannons and *Wasp* 8.

21 Smith, *MIR*, 45.

22 Diary of John Trevett, captain of Marines, quoted in Smith, *MIR*, 325. Trevett continued his service with the fleet following this first cruise. He was later transferred to the *Andrew Doria* and *Providence*. In 1778 he led a landing party back to New Providence to capture Forts Montagu and Nassau a second time. He later served aboard various other Continental and privateer ships for the remainder of the war. He died at the age of 76 in Newport, Rhode Island in 1823.

23 Library of Congress, *JCC 1774-1789*, IV-1776, 336; Coggins, *SSAR*, 27.

better judgment and chose not to confront the stronger British navy. He opted to sail south, capturing the gunpowder over 1,000 miles away on New Providence Island. Hopkins was later criticized and investigated for this decision. But with the current situation, he believed his best course of action was to capture what cannons and powder he could in order to assist Washington and the Continental Army.[24]

During the 1740s, the royal governor of the Bahamas boasted that New Providence was "the strongest possession in British America"; 30 years later, it was a different story.[25] Although heavily armed, Fort Nassau, with 40 cannons guarding the western entrance to Nassau Harbor, and Fort Montagu, with 17 guns protecting the eastern harbor entrance, were in disrepair.[26] General Gage had weakened the island by moving a detachment of the British 14th Regiment to America, leaving only one small schooner, *St. John*, for protection. Governor Montfort Browne established a 300-man militia force under the command of Maj. Robert Sterling, but half of this force was always at sea on fishing expeditions.[27]

The American fleet entered the Atlantic Ocean on February 17. Hopkins had ordered his captains to rendezvous south of Great Abaco Island in the Bahamas if they separated from the rest of the armada. They were to wait 14 days before continuing if they had not rejoined the fleet. This direction proved timely, as the *Hornet* and *Fly* lost contact with the fleet, colliding during a severe storm. Unbeknownst to Hopkins, *Hornet* returned to port, and *Fly* reduced speed to make repairs. Hopkins led the fleet's remainder toward Great Abaco, informing Captain Nicholas on February 27 of his intent to have the Marine officer lead a landing party to capture the forts at New Providence.[28]

On March 1, 1776, the fleet captured the sloop *Endeavor* and another ship within sight of Great Abaco Island, approximately 50 miles north of New Providence.[29] The armada weighed anchor, making final preparations for the New Providence operation. Hopkins intended to deceive his enemy, consolidating the

---

24 See Thomas Jefferson's "Notes on Commodore Esek Hopkin's Defense from a hearing held in Philadelphia in Aug 1783" concerning "The Commodore'[s] excuse for not going to Southern colonies agreeable to orders." Quoted in Morgan, ed., *NDAR*, 6:195-198.

25 Peter Bruce, *Memoirs of Peter Henry Bruce a military officer in the services of Prussia, Russia, and Great Britain* (Dublin, Ireland, 1783), 471; Sir Bede Edmund Clifford, *Historic Forts of Nassau in the Bahamas* (Nassau, 1952), 27, quoted in Smith, *MIR*, 49.

26 Jeff Dacus, "Gunpowder, The Bahamas, and the First Marine Killed in Action," *Journal of the American Revolution*, https://allthingsliberty.com/2019/05/gunpowder-the-bahamas-and-the-first-marine-killed-in-action/, accessed Aug. 18, 2019; Smith, *MIR*, 48-49, 381.

27 *St. John* mounted 4 cannons; Robert L. Tonsetic, *Special Operations During the American Revolution* (Philadelphia, 2013), 53-54.

28 Morgan, ed., *NDAR*, 6:197.

29 Ibid., 6:17.

Marines on board the two captured ships and the *Providence*. The Marines were to hide below decks as the ships approached New Providence, conducting a surprise landing as the fleet's remainder staged out of sight over the horizon.[30] The landing force was to sail into the harbor at dawn, and once they "got in Close to the Fort . . . [were] to land Instantly & take possession before the island could be Alarmed."[31]

Governor Browne, however, was already aware of the fleet's existence. General Gage had forewarned him months earlier that the Americans had readied ships for action, asserting that they intended to "take Advantage of the State of the Island of Providence and make an attempt to Seize His Majestys Property there."[32] Gage also offered to retrieve the weapons and ammunition stored at New Providence. But Browne believed this would open him to attacks from the Spanish and French while also risking a slave uprising. On February 25, Capt. Andrew Law of the British army arrived in New Providence, warning the governor of a "considerable squadron" whose destination was "against this island."[33] Captain George Dorsett reported to Browne on March 1 that during a whaling cruise, he had spotted a fleet of seven vessels "standing in toward the Land from the North East."[34] For reasons unknown, Governor Browne did nothing to increase the island's preparations for a pending attack.

On March 3, 1776, Hopkins's ships assembled nine miles north of Nassau, but strong winds inadvertently exposed his fleet. The harbor pilot spotted the Americans and quickly woke Gov. Browne, who immediately assembled the provincial council. Still in his nightgown, he ordered a cannon to fire three times, alerting locals and drummers to beat the call to arms. Fewer than 30 of the island's 300 militiamen arrived.

Regardless, by 9:00 a.m., Browne moved the force to Fort Montagu's defense, beyond which the American ships had sailed. The winds caused Hopkins's fleet to shift, delaying the landing and providing Browne more time to prepare. Losing the element of surprise, Hopkins reinforced the Marines with 50 sailors under the command of the *Cabot*'s Lt. Thomas Weaver and assigned the *Wasp* to escort and protect the ships carrying the landing force. At 10:00 a.m., Hopkins's fleet anchored six miles from Nassau, out of range of the island's guns.

---

30 Tim McGrath, *Give Me a Fast Ship: The Continental Navy and America's Revolution at Sea* (New York, 2014), 52-55; Morison, *John Paul Jones*, 42-44.

31 Morgan, ed., *NDAR*, 4:815.

32 Smith, *MIR*, 46.

33 Ibid.; Tonsetic, *Special Operations*, 53.

34 Smith, *MIR*, 48; Tonsetic, *Special Operations*, 53.

Between 12:00-2:00 p.m., Captain Nicholas led the 270-man landing force ashore two miles east of Fort Montagu, near the village of New Guinea, becoming the first amphibious landing in Navy and Marine Corps history.[35] The local population was unsure of the invaders' origins; they feared the Spaniards, who presented a graver threat than the Americans in this region. The British at Fort Montagu sent a scouting party forward to "reconnoitre and if possible prevent their landing," but it was too late.[36] The Marines had already landed and were preparing to move on the fort. Seeing that he was outnumbered, the British commander sent a man forward under a flag of truce to determine their intent. Lieutenant Trevett, assigned as a company commander for the operation, provided Nicholas's response: the Americans had been "sent by the Congress of the United Colonies in order to possess themselves of the Powder and Stores belonging to His Majesty."[37] Knowing there was little he could do to stop the Marines, the British commander returned to Nassau to inform Browne.

As the Marines moved ashore, Governor Browne gathered additional militiamen in Nassau and led them to join in defending Fort Montagu four miles to the east. On arriving, he sent another detachment to join the scouting party that had earlier moved toward the Marines. The hastily retreating scouts quickly met this group as the Marines maneuvered to capture the fort. Hearing of the Marines' rapid advance, Browne lost heart; he ordered an evacuation and that all but three of the fort's cannons be spiked before mounting a horse and speeding toward Nassau.[38] Before departing, he ordered two men to fire one round from the three unspiked cannons in defiance before evacuating. They accomplished their task with no casualties to the Marines.

The cannon fire caused Captain Nicholas to halt until he could assess the situation. Nicholas sent Trevett forward to determine the British intent. Approaching the fort, Trevett met a militia officer who, on orders from Governor Browne, would "wait on the Commanding Officer of the Enemy to know his Errand and on what Account he had landed his troops."[39] Nicholas briefed the officer, stating that he would see Browne in the morning. He then "marched and

---

35 The number "270" comes from a letter written by Samuel Nicholas on April 10, 1776, quoted in Smith, *MIR*, 381; Edwin Simmons & Robert Moskin, eds., *The Marines* (Quantico, VA, 1998), 35; Chenoweth & Nihart, *Semper Fi*, 37.

36 Smith, *MIR*, 50.

37 Ibid.

38 Spiking was a method for temporarily rendering a cannon inoperable by hammering a spike or nail into the touch hole of a cannon from which the gunpowder that would hurl a cannon ball could be ignited.

39 Clark, *NDAR*, 4:465; Smith, *MIR*, 52.

Landing at New Providence, 3 March 1776. Painting by Col. Charles H. Waterhouse, USMCR. Captain Samuel Nicholas led a force of Marines and sailors ashore in the Bahamas to capture cannons and gunpowder to support Gen. George Washington and the Continental Army. This was the first amphibious operation for the newly formed Continental Navy and Marines. *Art Collection, National Museum of the Marine Corps, Triangle, Virginia*

took possession of it [Fort Montagu], in which were found seventeen pieces of cannon, (thirty-two, eighteen, and twelve pounders,) and not much damaged; they were spiked . . . which were easily taken out."[40]

The Marines had achieved their first objective without firing a shot. Instead of pushing forward to attack Fort Nassau, however, Nicholas decided to rest his men since they had been hidden below decks "on board the small vessels, not having a convenience either to sleep or cook in" before landing.[41] Governor Browne used this time to make hasty improvements to the defenses at Fort Nassau. As the American Marines and sailors settled in for the evening, Nicholas sent a courier to Hopkins with the day's report. With Nicholas's early success, Hopkins issued a manifesto to the New Providence citizens, hoping to achieve a similar success in capturing Fort Nassau.[42]

40 Smith, *MIR*, 381.

41 Ibid.

42 The manifesto read: "To the Gentlemen Freeman and Inhabitants of the Island of New Providence. The Reasons of my landing an armed force on the Island is in Order to take possession of the Powder and Warlike Stores belonging to the Crown and if I am not Opposed in putting my design in Execution the Persons and Property of the Inhabitants Shall be Safe, Neither shall they be Suffered to be hurt in Case they make no Resistance. Given under my hand on board the Ship Alfred

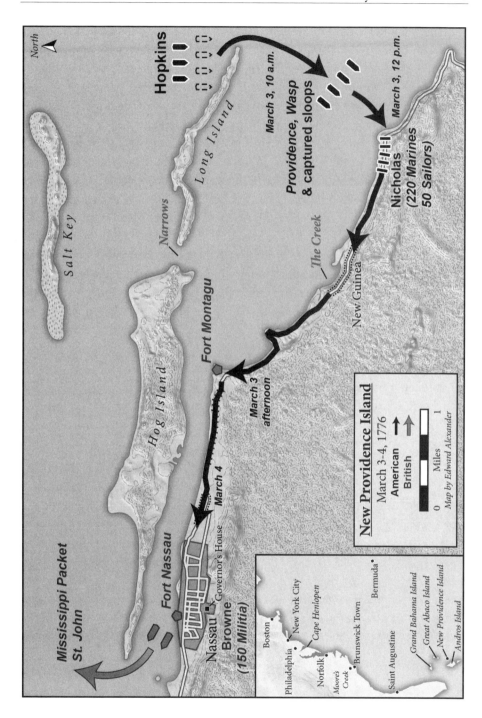

North

Hopkins

March 3, 10 a.m.

Providence, Wasp & captured sloops

Nicholas (220 Marines 50 Sailors)

March 3, 12 p.m.

Long Island

Narrows

The Creek

New Guinea

Salt Key

Hog Island

Fort Montagu

March 3 afternoon

March 4

Mississippi Packet

St. John

Fort Nassau

Nassau

Governor's House

Browne (150 Militia)

New Providence Island
March 3–4, 1776

American
British

0   Miles   1

Map by Edward Alexander

Boston

New York City

Cape Henlopen

Bermuda

Philadelphia

Norfolk

Moore's Creek

Brunswick Town

Saint Augustine

Grand Bahama Island

Great Abaco Island

New Providence Island

Andros Island

The manifesto had the desired effect, as many militiamen refused to defend Fort Nassau and deserted their posts. Governor Browne, on the other hand, removed most of the powder from the area. He and the local council agreed to surrender the fort without a fight, shipping the bulk of Nassau's powder elsewhere and preventing its capture by the Americans. Browne wanted all the powder removed but feared that "sending away the whole of it might enrage a disappointed enemy, and induce them to burn the Town, and commit other depredations."[43] Citizens loaded 119 of the 200 barrels of the garrison's gunpowder onto the British merchant vessel *Mississippi Packet* and another 43 barrels onto the schooner *St. John*.[44] The ships sailed that evening, slipping past the American fleet as they headed toward St. Augustine to deliver the powder to the governor of East Florida.

Unfortunately, Nicholas's failure to capture Fort Nassau and Hopkins's failure to prevent the gunpowder from escaping did not justify the admiral's operational rationale for ignoring his original orders. John Paul Jones later admitted that the powder loss "was foreseen and might have been prevented, by sending the two brigantines [*Cabot* and *Andrew Doria*] to be off the bar."[45] Congress would investigate, questioning Hopkins on this perceived misstep following the fleet's return.

As the *Mississippi Packet* and *St. John* escaped, the British abandoned Fort Nassau. Some citizens criticized Browne for failing to take more aggressive action against the Marines. William Taylor, a local merchant, was critical of mistakes made by the Americans that the governor failed to exploit, and he detailed his feelings in a letter to Lord Germain.[46] The Marines still had much to learn about planning and executing successful amphibious operations. Fortunately, they faced an accommodating enemy who allowed them to learn these valuable lessons in a semi-permissive environment.

March 3rd, 1776." Esek Hopkins, Manifesto, Mar. 3, 1776, quoted in *The letter book of Esek Hopkins, commander-in-chief of the United States navy, 1775-1777* (Providence, 1932), 44; Smith, *MIR*, 53.

43 Smith, *MIR*, 53.

44 Thomas Siefring, *United States Marines* (Secaucus, NJ, 1979), 13; Tuchman, *The First Salute*, 49; Morison, *John Paul Jones*, 44; Smith, *Marines in the Revolution*, 53.

45 "Journal Prepared for the King of France by John Paul Jones," in Robert Sands, ed., *Life and correspondence of John Paul Jones, including his narrative of the campaign of the Liman* (New York, 1880), 36; Smith, *MIR*, 53.

46 Taylor wrote, "My Lord if you had seen the miserable figure the Enemies did cut . . . for they had not so much as one field piece, let alone Battering Cannon, nor a scaling Ladder, nor so much as an Ax to have made a gap in our Pallisades in order to have got under our great Guns, not one armed vessel had they steering along shore to cover them, and to seal the Woods in Case we had fired upon them, nor had they so much as Boats rowing along shoar to take them off if routed, tho' the path was not above a Stone's throw from the sea side all the way they had to March, indeed they came more like Sheep to the Slaughter then men to fight." Smith, *MIR*, 51.

Following a quiet night, Nicholas roused his men early, arriving at the outskirts of Nassau by daybreak. Before capturing the fort, he intended to "take possession of the Governor's house, which stands on an eminence, with two four-pounders, which commands the garrison [Fort Nassau] and town."[47] Governor Browne dispatched another emissary as the Marines approached the town gate. Nicholas gave the same response, to which the emissary responded, "the Western Garrison [Fort Nassau] was ready for his [Nicholas] reception, and that he might march his Force in as Soon as he Pleased."[48] Nicholas assembled a guard, marching toward the governor's house to demand the fort's keys, which were surrendered. The Marines took possession of Fort Nassau without a fight, finding "forty cannon mounted and well located for our reception, with round, langridge [iron rods], and canister shot" that could have caused severe casualties if the British had chosen to resist.[49] The Marines quickly lowered the British colors, raising the "Grand Flag of the United Colonies" in its place.[50]

With the fort secured, Nicholas informed Hopkins that the fleet could safely enter the harbor. As they waited, Lieutenant Trevett and Capt. Henry Dayton, who commanded the other company in the landing party, observed Governor Browne and other officials preparing horses for a possible escape. With Nicholas's approval, the Marine officers took the governor prisoner by the force of arms. Though he complained, Browne yielded to Trevett and 32 of his Marines and was placed under arrest in the Government House. Browne claimed the Marines enjoyed their duty, as they "used at discretion all my wines and other liquors as they did everything else they had occasion for."[51]

The governor was not as accommodating four days later when Hopkins ordered him taken to the *Alfred*. Browne resisted, forcing the Marines to seize, collar, and drag him away "like a felon to the Gallows in the presence of a Dear wife and an aged Aunt . . . who were treated with such abuse, and such language." When Browne asked about the crime for which he was being detained, Cdre. Hopkins replied, "for presuming to fire upon . . . [my] troops from Fort Montague." Also

---

47 Ibid., 381.

48 Clark, ed., *NDAR*, 4:817.

49 Smith, *MIR*, 381.

50 Ibid., 54; The "Grand Union" flag was the precursor to the "Stars and Stripes" that the Continental Congress officially adopted in June 1777. The Grand Union consisted of 13 red and white stripes, representing the original colonies, with the combined crosses of St. Andrew and St. George from the British Union Jack in the upper left quadrant of the flag (later replaced by the blue field and stars). See Tuchman, *The First Salute*, 48.

51 The next three quotes attributed to "Montfort Browne to Lord Germain, Nov. 5, 1776," *PHMB*, vol. 49 (October 1925), 354, quoted in Smith, *MIR*, 55.

detained were the governor's secretary, James Babbidge, and Thomas Irvin, "a Counsellor and Collector of his Majestys Quit-Rents in South Carolina" and inspector general of British customs in North America. The Americans would later use the three men in a prisoner exchange.[52]

By March 16, Hopkins was ready to sail with his captured goods before a British fleet could arrive and turn a limited victory into total defeat. While Browne had successfully removed most of the gunpowder Hopkins sought, the expedition still yielded significant prizes. The Marines captured 88 cannons, 15 mortars, 24 barrels of gunpowder, and thousands of shells, shot, and other munitions needed by the Continental Army, Navy, and Marines.[53] The Marines captured so much matériel that the fleet could not carry it all. Although the *Fly* had rejoined the fleet, Hopkins needed more space, so he impressed the local sloop *Endeavor* with a promise for payment and the ship's return to her owner once she delivered her cargo.[54]

Strategically, this first amphibious operation achieved another unintended consequence, expanding the war beyond the 13 colonies and forced the British to employ their naval forces over a broader area in order to protect its other holdings. Although limited, the fleet's victory also began to change British perceptions of the war. Exaggerated reports began to appear in Great Britain. The London *Public Advertiser* wrote, "a British fleet was totally defeated by Admiral Hopkins . . . after a dreadful slaughter on both sides."[55]

Hopkins had other matters on his mind, as tropical climates had worsened some of the men's medical conditions. He later reported, "When I put to Sea the 17th Febry. from Cape Henlopen [Pennsylvania] we had many Sick and four of the Vessels had a large number onboard with the Small Pox."[56] By March 16, Hopkins had restocked the fleet's provisions and ordered it to set sail for the open

---

52 Browne was later exchanged for American General William Alexander (Lord Stirling), who had been captured in the battle of Long Island. He returned to Nassau in July 1776. Browne subsequently assumed command of the Prince of Wales American Regiment, a loyalist unit, and served in Rhode Island before again returning to his duty as governor of the Bahamas.

53 Tonsetic, *Special Operations*, 62-63; Dacus, "Gunpowder, The Bahamas, and the First Marine Killed in Action," *Journal of the American Revolution*. See Smith, *MIR*, 56 for a photocopy of the original list of prizes taken at New Providence.

54 The Continental Congress reimbursed Charles Walker, the owner of the *Endeavor*, $2,000 for the services she rendered and restored the sloop and her original cargo. The Connecticut Council of Safety purchased the *Endeavor* from Walker for conversion into an armed brigantine in August 1776. She was refitted and renamed the *Defence* and was manned by Marines and sailors.

55 Morgan, ed., *NDAR*, 6:428; Patton, *Patriot Pirates*, 92.

56 Rhode Island Historical Society, *Esek Hopkins letter book*, 49.

seas. The ships were not leaving soon enough. Fevers and smallpox soon killed several men, requiring more than 140 to be hospitalized over the next few weeks.[57]

Meanwhile, far to the north, the situation was changing rapidly. While Hopkins had not delivered the gun powder needed by Washington at Boston, Connecticut sent 3,000 pounds of powder to the Continental Army. Colonel Knox informed Washington that this was enough powder to force the British from the city. On March 2, Knox ordered his artillery to fire on Boston from three directions. Cannons blazed from Lechmere's Point in the north, Cobble Hill from the west, and Roxbury from the south. The British responded in kind. Knox's actions, however, were a diversion.

Washington's and Knox's main objective was to position heavy cannons on Dorchester Heights, which would allow the Americans to control Boston while also putting British ships in Boston Harbor at risk. On the evening of March 4, as Marines captured Fort Nassau, Washington gave the mission of occupying Dorchester Heights to 52-year-old Brig. Gen. John Thomas of Massachusetts.[58]

Thomas organized his force into two parts. An 800-man covering party moved on the Heights first to establish security, with half facing Boston and the other half covering Castle William, located on an island in Boston Harbor. Thomas himself followed with 1,200 men, "a train of more than 300 carts loaded with fascines, presst hay, in bundles of seven or eight hundred," and Knox's cannons.[59] The ground was frozen up to a foot deep, requiring soldiers to use the fascines and pressed hay bales to build protective emplacements above ground level. Others used picks and shovels to dig the frozen ground, installing the cannons. One participant recorded "that by ten o'clock at night, they had got two forts, one upon each hill, sufficient to defend them from small arms and grape shot."[60] The workers continued digging unhindered until 3:00 a.m.

The British awoke to find their position in Boston had become untenable, as American artillery now dominated both the city and harbor. Washington enthusiastically wrote Congress that his army's efforts were "equal to our most sanguine expectations."[61] General Howe, who had assumed command from Gage, was reported "to scratch his head and heard to say by those that were about him

---

57 Smith, *MIR*, 57.

58 Thomas was promoted to major general following the siege of Boston and was ordered to capture Canada, but he died from smallpox in June 1776 before accomplishing his task.

59 Commager & Morris, *SSS*, 178. Fascines are bundles of sticks or wood bound together for use in building earthworks and barriers to provide protection from enemy fire.

60 Ibid.

61 *FONA*, https://founders.archives.gov/documents/Washington/03-03-02-0309, accessed Aug. 25, 2019; Puls, *Henry Knox*, 44.

that he did not know what he should do, that the provincials had done more work in one night than his whole army would have done in six months."[62] Howe understood the dangerous position in which the Americans had placed the British, and he decided to recapture the Heights. He sent roughly 3,000 troops under Lord Percy to Castle William to stage an attack as Washington strengthened American positions and bombarded the city. High winds and rough seas caused the British to abandon their assault, leading Howe to a fateful decision: "I could promise myself little success by attacking them under such disadvantages I had to encounter; wherefore I judged it most advisable to prepare for the evacuation of the town."[63]

Howe evacuated Boston on March 17, 1776. Agreeing not to burn the city if Washington would allow an unopposed evacuation by sea, Howe led 9,000 regulars, 1,200 women and children, 1,100 Tory loyalists, and 30 captive Whigs on board the HMS *Chatham*, HMS *Fowey*, and other transports.[64] He defended his decision, stating, "The importance of preserving this force, when it could no longer act to advantage, did not leave any room to doubt to the propriety of its removal."[65] British defenses and provisions that could not be carried were destroyed as Howe set sail with his army for Nova Scotia to fight another day.

After eight years of British occupation and 11 months under siege, Boston was again free. One citizen rejoiced, "Thus was this unhappy distressed town (through a manifest interposition of divine providence) relieved from a set of men whose unparalleled wickedness, profanity, debauchery and cruelty is inexpressible."[66] Taking little time to bask in his victory, Washington contemplated his next move. As early as March 13, he advised Congress that the enemy would next strike New York and began shifting forces under Gen. Charles Lee's command to that city. Now that the Americans had secured Boston, Washington assigned Gen. Israel Putnam and 2,000 troops to remain there, defending the city as he led the army's main body toward Lee in New York.

During this time, Congress undertook steps to strengthen the Continental Navy and Marines. On March 27, HMS *Roebuck* appeared on the Delaware River, intent on destroying the navigational obstacles on the river protecting Philadelphia—home to the Continental Congress. This new threat spurred

62 Commager & Morris, *SSS*, 178.

63 Ibid., 180.

64 *Chatham* mounted 50 cannons and *Fowey* 24. Ibid., 181; A. J., Langguth, *Patriots: The Men Who Started the American Revolution* (New York, 1988), 329; Michael Stephenson, *Patriot Battles: How the War of Independence was Fought* (New York, 2007), 53; Leckie, *George Washington's War*, 241.

65 Puls, *Henry Knox*, 45; Ward, *TWOR*, 133.

66 Timothy Newell, *Journal of Timothy Newell, a selectman from Boston*, Massachusetts Historical Society Collection, 4th Series, 1:274-276.

the congressmen into action. With the help of the Philadelphia and Baltimore Committees of Safety, they purchased two additional merchantmen, converting them into the newly commissioned *Lexington* and *Reprisal*, as recruiters found new sailors and Marines to man the vessels.[67] Abraham Boyce was commissioned captain to lead the Marine detachment on the *Lexington*, and Capt. Miles Pennington and Lt. John Elliot received commissions to head the Marine detachments on *Reprisal*.[68] John Martin or "Keto" became the first African American Marine in April 1776 when he enlisted on the *Reprisal*, along with at least two sergeants and twenty-four other privates as part of the Marine detachment.[69]

While crews outfitted new ships in Philadelphia, Hopkins's Continental Fleet continued north. The commodore gave orders to proceed to Block Island off the coast of Rhode Island. While en route, lookouts spotted distant sails, and *Andrew Doria* and *Fly* gave chase. The Americans identified the unknown vessel as a French schooner carrying the welcome news of Boston's liberation. Unfortunately, smallpox continued to plague the men, causing frequent deaths. On April 3, Marine Sgt. Thomas Vernon Turner of the *Andrew Doria* succumbed to the disease.[70]

On arriving off Block Island, the fleet found a target-rich environment. It captured HMS *Hawke* on April 4 and HMS *Bolton*, a bomb brig carrying 48 sailors and Royal Marines, on April 5.[71] Several smaller vessels also fell prey to the Americans.[72] Despite these successes, the fleet was about to confront a much stronger adversary.[73]

Just after midnight on April 6, the American armada spotted two unidentified sails. Hopkins ordered all hands to quarters on the 12 ships comprising his fleet. Captain Nicholas and 2nd Lt. John Fitzpatrick staged on the quarterdeck of the *Alfred* with half of their company of Marines, while Lt. Matthew Parke boarded the barge on *Alfred*'s main deck with the other half. The Marines on all vessels were battle ready, prepared to either repel borders or assault the other ship if ordered.

---

67 *Roebuck* mounted 44 cannons, *Lexington* 14, and *Reprisal* 16. Coggins, *SSAR*, 203.

68 No comprehensive history of these officers is available. Charles Smith, however, cited references to them in documents from the 18th Century, placing them on the identified ships and other areas throughout the war. See Smith, *MIR*, 433, 441, 464 for abridged biographies of all three officers.

69 Smith, *MIR*, 63. Martin was listed as the "property" of William Marshall of Delaware. He died in October 1777 when the *Reprisal* foundered off Newfoundland Banks.

70 Smith, *MIR*, 71.

71 *Hawke* mounted six cannons and *Bolton* eight.

72 Morgan, ed., *NDAR*, 6:416, 804.

73 *Hopkins letter book*, 50.

The *Cabot* assumed the lead as the Americans maneuvered toward the two unknown vessels. Tensions ran high as both sides cautiously approached the other in the dark, hoping to be the first to identify the other. The silence was broken when a voice from the unknown ship identified her as the British frigate HMS *Glasgow* and her tender, and demanding the other party's identity.[74] A Marine high atop the *Cabot*'s mainmast answered by throwing an explosive grenade onto the deck of the *Glasgow* as Americans jockeyed for positions to engage the British with their cannons. The *Cabot* fired first, a broadside with her six-pounders, but *Glasgow* responded quickly with two volleys from her nine-pounders. Captain Nicholas reported that *Glasgow*'s heavier guns "damaged her [*Cabot*] so much in her hul and rigging, as obliged her to retire."[75] The *Cabot*'s master, Sinclair Seymour, and two Marines, Patrick Kaine and George Kennedy, died in the mêlée.[76]

As the *Cabot* limped off, *Alfred* joined the fray. *Alfred* and *Glasgow* exchanged broadsides as Marines fired their muskets at the enemy. Nicholas described how during "the first broadside she [*Glasgow*] fired, my second lieutenant fell dead close by my side; he was shot by a musket-ball through the head." When speaking of Lieutenant Fitzpatrick, Nicholas later wrote, "in him I have lost a worthy officer, sincere friend and companion, that was beloved by all the ship's company."[77] In the hot exchange, *Glasgow* shot off *Alfred*'s wheel block, making it difficult to steer the ship and causing her to drop out of the fight. As she withdrew, the *Andrew Doria* joined, but she too was soon forced to withdraw due to hull and rigging damage.

Ninety minutes after it began, *Columbus* joined the battle. *Glasgow*'s captain feared the Marines would board his ship and threw official dispatches overboard to prevent their capture. He frantically maneuvered, attempting to break contact and escape pending defeat. *Alfred*, *Columbus*, and *Andrew Doria* maintained pressure on *Glasgow* but could not catch her because of the added weight of the munitions they had captured in New Providence. After three and a half hours, Hopkins broke off the pursuit, fearing the British fleet in Newport could reinforce the *Glasgow*.

The battle was fierce, but casualties were light. The *Glasgow* sustained one man killed and three wounded—all by American Marine musketry.[78] The minor casualties were attributed to the Americans aiming their cannons at *Glasgow*'s sails, riggings, and mast to slow her. Though in a shambles, the damage did not prevent

---

74 *Glasgow* mounted 24 cannons. *London Chronicle*, Thursday, June 6 to Saturday June 8, 1776, in Morgan, ed., *NDAR*, 6:410-411.

75 Smith, *MIR*, 381.

76 Ibid., 72.

77 Ibid., 381.

78 Ibid., 72.

A Marine Lieutenant Dies, 6 April 1776. Painting by Col. Charles H. Waterhouse, USMCR. Lieutenant John Fitzpatrick of the Marine Detachment on the *Alfred* died when a musket ball struck him in the head in a battle against HMS *Glasgow* off Rhode Island. *Art Collection, National Museum of the Marine Corps, Triangle, Virginia*

her escape.[79] Upon entering Newport, one observer described the ship as "under all the sail she could set, yelping from the mouths of her cannon (like a broken leg'd dog) in token of her being sadly wounded."[80] The Americans suffered nine killed and 16 wounded. Nicholas described how, on *Alfred*, "I lost three of my people out of twelve that were on the quarter-deck, and two others who were in the barge, were slightly wounded."[81] All the Americans gained from this battle was the capture of *Glasgow*'s tender.

The *London Chronicle* praised the captain of the *Glasgow*. It recalled how "she [*Glasgow*] made shift to fight against, and get clear from, six vessels, who had above 600 men, and 104 guns, while the poor *Glasgow* had but 24 guns, and 125 men."[82] The Americans were unimpressed with Commodore Hopkins's performance. According to one report, the new American fleet was unaccustomed to fleet maneuvers and fought "a typical privateering operation—that is, every

79 Morgan, ed., *NDAR*, 6:415.

80 *The Newport Mercury*, April 8, 1776; Tuchman, *The First Salute*, 49.

81 Smith, *MIR*, 382.

82 Morgan, ed., *NDAR*, 6:411.

man for himself."[83] Thomas Jefferson later wrote how Hopkins's "management of engagement with *Glasgow* shews he wanted skill & activity."[84] John Hancock initially congratulated Hopkins on his expedition's success, but later changed his tone following the action against *Glasgow*. One could argue that the fleet's performance in this battle justified Hopkins's rationale for not engaging the British fleet off the coasts of Virginia, the Carolinas, and Rhode Island, as originally directed. But Hopkins must bear the blame for not properly training his fleet to fight cohesively in the time he had before the battle. The controversy surrounding Hopkins's performance continued until he was suspended the following year.

Following the engagement, Hopkins directed the fleet to reassemble and make for New London, Connecticut. He intended to offload his prizes from New Providence and turn over the captured vessels on arrival. Although successful, it would be some time before the Marines and sailors received any prize money from their sale. Lieutenant Trevett recalled, "after 2 or 3 years we were ordered to be paid in Continental money. When we wished to spend it, it would about pay for 1 pair of Shoes, a grand cruise and I am glad it ended so well."[85]

Although the cruise failed in gaining gunpowder for the army, the captured cannons would be extremely useful. The Americans disseminated them across New England to protect ports and harbors, while several were delivered to Henry Knox. Hopkins wrote to General Washington, "I am Order'd by the Marine Committee to get the Valuation of the Stores that I brought from New Providence, and as part of them was sent to New York by your Order should be glad you would Order Mr Knox, or some other of your Officers to put a Value on them, and order them to transmit such Valuation to me as soon as Convenient."[86]

The three-month cruise was rough on the first Continental fleet. Aside from the battle casualties, 202 sailors and Marines were deemed "not fit for duty." They were hospitalized in New London on April 8, due to "some New Malignant Fever."[87] Additionally, resignations and desertions depleted the crews, shifting sailors and Marines around to fill some of them. Hopkins attempted to recruit new members, but privateering efforts proved more lucrative. His situation was so dire that 200 men were requested from General Washington. Washington temporarily provided

83 Hagan, *The People's Navy*, 6.

84 Morgan, ed., *NDAR*, 6:197.

85 Diary of John Trevett, Captain of Marines, in Smith, *MIR*, 326.

86 Morgan, ed., *NDAR*, 6:650

87 Ibid., 4:1358.

170 troops, and on April 24, the fleet ventured out to sea, but it was soon forced back due to inclement weather.[88]

Arriving back in port, Hopkins learned that Washington had directed the return of his soldiers. The commodore wrote to Washington, "I am very much obliged to you for the Use of your Men, and shall dispatch them to New York immediately in the Sloop Providence," now under the command of Captain John Paul Jones. Hopkins closed by adding, "it will be impossible to go to Sea with the Fleet, before we get recruited with hands which will not easily be done."[89] The departure of Washington's soldier-sailors and continued sicknesses among the crews was the *coup-de-grâce* for Hopkins's fleet. It never sailed again as a cohesive force. In the following months, Hopkins could only muster enough crew members to send small one- or two-ship armadas to sea. It was an inconspicuous ending to this historic cruise.

George Washington, meanwhile, was preparing for battle in New York. Arriving on Manhattan Island on April 13, he quickly assessed the situation. New York was America's second-largest city, with 25,000 inhabitants, and occupied the southern tip of Manhattan Island. Henry Knox described its character to his wife as "a place where I think in general the houses are better built than in Boston. They are generally of brick and three stories high. . . . Their churches are grand; their colleges, workhouse, and hospital most excellently situated." He concluded by adding, "The people—why, the people are magnificent."[90]

Though New York also possessed an excellent harbor and port, it was a hotbed of loyalists. Outside the city, the island consisted of country roads, rolling hills, marshes, and farmlands stretching twelve miles to the north, where a bridge connected it to the New York mainland. Long Island lay beyond the East River to the east, Staten Island to the south, and New Jersey to the west across the Hudson River.

New York's geography also posed a disadvantage for Washington, as the open access to the ocean and the numerous waterways around the city would favor the British. Washington understood that the enemy could maneuver quickly, shifting forces and striking at unexpected locations, cutting off any line of retreat. The British could also shift heavy firepower from their ships' guns to locations of their choosing.

---

88 Ibid.

89 *FONA*, https://founders.archives.gov/documents/Washington/03-04-02-0148, accessed Aug. 30, 2019.

90 The Gilder Lehrman Institute of American History, https://www.gilderlehrman.org/collection/glc0243700237, accessed Aug. 30, 2019.

Washington considered finding a more defensible position outside the city after discussions with his commanders and staff, but political pressure kept him from doing so. He recalled an earlier conversation with John Adams in which Adams stated, "That Colony is a Post of such vast Importance, that no Effort to secure it should be neglected."[91] Adams explained that New York was "the Nexus of the Northern and Southern Colonies, as a Kind of Key to the whole Continent, as it is a Passage to Canada to the Great Lakes and to all the Indian Nations. No Effort to secure it ought to be omitted."[92] Washington knew the New York delegates to the Continental Congress would not give up their city without a fight, leaving him little choice. He would have to spread his troops and limited resources over a vast area susceptible to naval attacks.

During the first week of May 1776, Congress braced for a naval attack on Philadelphia. Henry Fisher, a lighthouse watch station operator at the mouth of the Delaware River, reported HMS *Liverpool* and three tenders joining HMS *Roebuck* making their way upriver.[93] The Continental Navy's *Lexington* had just returned from sea under Capt. John Barry's command. As it required some repairs, the Continental Navy and Marines would join forces with elements of the Pennsylvania State Navy and Marines to stop the British advance.

The Pennsylvania Navy included an eclectic group of 48 vessels of varying sizes and designs, and received its orders from the Pennsylvania Committee of Safety.[94] The fleet's flagship *Montgomery* carried fourteen 18-pounders and a detachment of Marines, while many smaller galleys only mounted a single cannon. The fleet also possessed two floating batteries, *Arnold* and *Putnam*, each carrying around a dozen 18-pounders, manned by Pennsylvania Marines.[95]

On May 8, 13 small American galleys, a floating battery, and a sloop "fitted as a fire ship" bravely confronted two British frigates and their escorts.[96] Captain Barry was given overall command of the operation, using his sailors and Marines

---

91 *FONA*, https://founders.archives.gov/documents/Washington/03-03-02-0023, accessed Aug. 30, 2019.

92 Ibid.

93 *Liverpool* mounted 28 cannons and *Roebuck* 44. Jeffery Dowart, *Invasion and Insurrection: Security, Defense, and War in the Delaware Valley, 1621-1815* (Newark, 2008), 123; Smith, *MIR*, 63.

94 Kennard Wiggins, Jr., *America's Anchor: A Naval History of the Delaware River and Bay, Cradle of The United States Navy* (Jefferson, NC, 2019), 23; "The Pennsylvania State Navy," http://www.ushistory.org/march/other/pennnavy.htm, accessed Aug. 31, 2019.

95 "Minutes of the Pennsylvania Committee of Safety and Lieutenant John Hennessy to the Pennsylvania Committee of Safety, Philadelphia, 22 August 1776," Morgan, *NDAR*, 6:287, 393.

96 Dowart, *Invasion and Insurrection*, 123-124; Smith, *MIR*, 64-68.

from *Lexington* to supplement the fleet.[97] Marine Capt. Miles Pennington led a detachment of two sergeants and 24 Marines from the *Reprisal* to reinforce this small fleet.

Captain Andrew Hamond of HMS *Roebuck* commanded the British force. He recalled, "I took the *Liverpool* with me and sailed up the River within a few miles of the Chevaux de frizzes, as they call them, which are immense frames of thick wood, sunk with Ballast in a narrow part of the River." He described American defenses as including "batterys on each side, and a floating one in the middle; together with 13 Row Galleys, each carrying one Gun, from a thirty two pounder, to an eighteen pounder, and from Seventy to fifty men."[98]

The galleys opened the engagement with their single cannons against HMS *Roebuck* and her imposing 44 guns. The boats swarmed the larger ship, challenging her in unexpected ways. Captain Hamond recounted how the British "lay under the disadvantage of being obliged to engage them at the distance they chose to fix on, which was scarcely within point blank shot: and being such low objects on the water, it was with some difficulty that we could strike them."[99] Taking advantage of the situation, the galleys fired on *Roebuck* from several directions and ran her aground, although neither side sustained severe damage. *Reprisal* and *Montgomery* remained upriver as a secondary line of defense.

The galleys disengaged as darkness fell, and the British, preparing for the next battle, were able to refloat *Roebuck* with the rising tide. The following day, they headed toward more maneuverable waters, drawing the Americans out as the galleys again started their attack. The Americans gave chase and continued firing until approximately 10:00 p.m., when they broke off the engagement.

The Americans got the better of the British in the second day's engagement. HMS *Roebuck* sustained several piercing hull shots above the waterline on both sides and her stern. One 18-pound round entered a port window, destroying a nine-pound gun, killing one sailor, and injuring two more, and *Roebuck*'s riggings, sails, and spars were in shambles. HMS *Liverpool* did not fare much better, with one crewmember recording, "Several Shot through our Sails, some few in our Hull, and one in our bowsprit."[100]

The Americans suffered only minor damage, and achieved a decisive victory, as the British decided to disengage and head back to the open seas. The Americans' small, outgunned freshwater fleet had defeated a decisively stronger

97 Martin Griffin, *Catholics and the American Revolution* (Philadelphia, 1909), 11.

98 Morgan, ed., *NDAR*, 6:69-70.

99 Ibid.

100 *Pennsylvania Evening Post*, June 29, 1776, quoted in Smith, *MIR*, 63.

British force, maintaining control of the Delaware River. This proved invaluable to Washington later in the year, with the operation demonstrating the benefit of Continental sailors and Marines working beside state navy and marine forces. Similarly, combined operations would be invaluable in the forthcoming battles of Trenton and Princeton.

As Washington assumed command over New York, General Lee, working on defensive positions, was free to be assigned elsewhere. Congress directed him to assume command of the newly formed Southern Department, responsible for protecting the colonies in that section. The southern royal governors had convinced King George that loyalists would rush to the defense of the Crown with the backing of British regulars. Their first attempt in February had failed, as the North Carolina militia were victorious at the battle of Moore's Creek Bridge. The British focus now shifted to Charleston, South Carolina, the most important port south of Philadelphia.[101] The South Carolinians began defensive preparations immediately upon hearing that Charleston was the British army's next target.

Like New York, Charleston's location is at the tip of a peninsula formed by the confluence of two rivers. The Ashley and Cooper rivers flowed on either side, emptying into a harbor with two key islands: Sullivan Island to the east and James Island to the west. South Carolina militia under the command of 46-year-old Colonel William Moultrie centered the defense of Charleston on these islands. He led the construction of Fort Sullivan on Sullivan Island and Fort Johnson on James Island, blocking access to any invading army from the sea.

Moultrie, outspoken and confident, had gained experience fighting Cherokee Indians on the Carolina frontier. On June 1, he grew concerned as he watched 50 British vessels arriving outside Charleston Harbor. Fortunately, General Lee arrived later that week with 1,300 Virginia and 700 North Carolina troops, joining the nearly 1,000 men Moultrie had assembled at Fort Sullivan.

Lee was unhappy with what he found at Fort Sullivan, as it was only partially completed. Moultrie recalled Lee's concerns: "He said there was no way to retreat, that the garrison would be sacrificed, nay, he called it a 'slaughter pen' and wished to withdraw the garrison and give up the post. But President [of South Carolina John] Rutledge insisted that it should not be given up." Moultrie continued, "Then General Lee said it was 'absolutely necessary to have a bridge of boats for a retreat.' But boats enough could not be had, the distance over being at least a mile." Moultrie confidently added, "For my part, I never was uneasy on not having a retreat because I never imagined that the enemy could force me to that necessity."[102]

---

101 Commager & Morris, *SSS*, 1063.

102 William Moultrie, *Memoirs*, 1:140-144, quoted in Commager & Morris, *SSS*, 1064-1065.

Moultrie remained convinced that he could hold if attacked and conveyed these feelings during an inspection by a naval officer just before the battle. They observed the British fleet through a gun embrasure as they walked among the fort's 26 cannons mounted on gun platforms, reinforced with the trunks of palm trees and earth. The officer asked, "Colonel, what do you think of it now?" Moultrie responded that he would "beat them." "Sir," the officer said, "when those ships . . . come to lay alongside of your fort, they will knock it down in half an hour," to which Moultrie responded, "Then we will lay behind the ruins and prevent their men from landing."[103] Lee left Moultrie to defend Fort Sullivan as he focused on improving the defenses of Charleston.

After days of unfavorable winds, the British finally entered the harbor, commencing their attack on June 28. Their plan called for a classic pincer attack, where Maj. Gen. Henry Clinton would conduct an amphibious landing on Long Island to Fort Sullivan's rear, attacking from the landward side of a small body of shallow water. At the same time, Sir Peter Parker would attack with the fleet from the seaward side.

Things did not go according to plan, however, as Clinton took eight days to land and prepare his force, only to be stopped by the unexpected water depth at the crossing site. Insufficient boats and a determined American rear guard blocked Clinton's advance. Between 10:00 and 11:00 a.m., Moultrie observed the enemy fleet loose its sails, beginning its advance on the fort. He wrote, "We had scarcely manned our guns when . . . ships of war came sailing up as if in confidence of victory. As soon as they came within the reach of our guns we began to fire."[104]

The battle commenced with the bomb-ketch HMS *Thunder* launching mortar rounds into the fort, covering the warship's advances. Moultrie recalled, "we had a morass in the middle [of Fort Sullivan] that swallowed them [mortar rounds] up instantly, and those that fell in the sand and in and about the fort were immediately buried so that very few of them bursted amongst us."[105] The remainder of the fleet rapidly approached Fort Sullivan with the intent of overwhelming it with superior firepower. The frigates HMS *Acteon*, HMS *Bristol*, HMS *Experiment*, HMS *Solebay*, HMS *Syren*, HMS *Sphynx*, and HMS *Friendship*—with 226 guns in all—rapidly closed to within "less than half-musket shot from the fort" and commenced a duel against the Americans' scant 26 cannons.[106]

---

103 Ibid.; Scheer & Rankin, *RR*, 135.

104 Moultrie, *Memoirs*, quoted in Commager & Morris, *SSS*, 1068.

105 Ibid.

106 *Acteon* mounted 28 cannons, *Bristol* 50, *Experiment* 50, *Solebay* 28, *Syren* 28, *Sphynx* 20, and *Friendship* 22; Commager & Morris, *SSS*, 1067.

Initially, the Americans only had enough powder to fire 28 rounds per cannon and 20 per musket, but they held.[107] The battle raged for nearly ten hours, and supplies arrived during the day. The *Syren*, *Sphynx*, and *Acteon* were ordered to maneuver to "the Westward, to prevent the Fireships, or other Vessels from annoying the ships engaged, & to cut off the Retreat of the Rebels when driven from their Works."[108] Unfortunately, all three ships became fouled and ran aground. The *Syren* and *Sphynx* escaped, and the British set fire to *Acteon*, preventing her capture.

The battle continued until the injured warships limped away into the dark. Vastly outgunned, the patriots manning Fort Sullivan only sustained ten killed and 24 wounded. British casualties totaled over 100 killed and 66 wounded.[109] The captains of HMS *Experiment* and HMS *Bristol* both lost arms, and "one shot from the fort, took off three midshipmen's heads."[110] For the time being, the Americans had rebuffed British attempts to conquer the south. Realizing their fruitless efforts, Parker and Clinton led their soldiers and fleet back to New York.

British actions in the south contributed to more Congressmen shifting toward declaring full independence. Many representatives had no authority to take such actions, and reluctant colonial governments would need convincing first.

On May 10, 1776, Congress addressed the colonies' hesitancy to break from Great Britain, passing a resolution recommending they form independent governments to, "in the opinion of the Representatives of the people, best conduce to the happiness and safety of their constituents in particular, and *America* in general."[111] The strong moderate faction led by John Dickinson of Pennsylvania prevented Congress from going further until May 15, when Dickinson took a leave of absence from the proceedings.

John Adams exploited the opportunity, drafting a preamble, later passed by Congress, that more assertively recommended that each colony establish governments free of royal authority or control. The movement gained momentum, and on June 7, Richard Henry Lee of Virginia introduced a resolution, "That these United Colonies are, and of right ought to be, free and independent States, that they are absolved from all allegiance to the British Crown, and that all political

---

107 Moultrie, *Memoirs*, quoted in Commager & Morris, *SSS*, 1069.

108 *Precis Prepared for George III of Events Leading to the Expedition Against the Southern Colonies*, London, Aug. 21-22, 1776, quoted in Morgan, *NDAR*, 6:563.

109 Commager & Morris, *SSS*, 1067-1068; "The Revolutionary War In Mount Pleasant, South Carolina," http://scbattlegroundtrust.org/rwmountpleasant/fort-sullivan-(circa-1776).html, accessed Sept. 1, 2019.

110 "Extract of a Letter from Philadelphia, 3 Aug. 1776," published in the *Constitutional Gazette*, Aug. 7, 1776, quoted from Morgan, *NDAR*, 6:42; Commager & Morris, *SSS*, 1067-1068.

111 Force, ed., *AA*, 4th Series, vol. 6 (Washington, D.C., 1846), 847.

connection between them and the State of Great Britain is, and ought to be totally dissolved."[112] Lee called for forming foreign alliances and establishing a confederation of states.

Congress established committees to further these aims. One group worked on drafting articles for establishing a confederation while defining the authorities of the Continental Congress. Another committee came up with a declaration identifying the colonies as free and independent states. John Adams asserted, "It is now universally acknowledged that we are and must be independent. But still, objections are made to a declaration of it."[113] Discussions continued for weeks before Congress finally approved a resolution for independence on July 2, 1776. It took two additional days to approve a formal explanation—the United States Declaration of Independence. Following its approval on July 4, 1776, express riders distributed the printed declaration across the country.

On July 6, George Washington received one of the first copies of the Declaration. Congress directed that he "have it proclaimed at the Head of the Army in the way you shall think it most proper."[114] Washington's general orders to the army on July 9, 1776, stated, "[T]he Continental Congress, impelled by the dictates of duty, policy and necessity, having been pleased to dissolve the Connection which subsisted between this Country, and Great Britain, and to declare the United Colonies of North America, free and independent STATES."

In celebration, he ordered that "[t]he several brigades are to be drawn up this evening on their respective Parades, at six OClock, when the declaration of Congress, shewing the grounds & reasons of this measure, is to be read with an audible voice."[115] While troops cheered, hearing the words of freedom, Washington likely contemplated Benjamin Franklin's words of wisdom, "We must now all hang together, or we shall most assuredly all hang separately."[116]

---

112 Ibid., 1731; "The Continental Congress Declared Independence from Great Britain," https://history.house.gov/Historical-Highlights/1700s/The-Continental-Congress-agreed-to-declare-independence-from-Great-Britain/, accessed Sept. 1, 2019.

113 John Adams, *Works of John Adams: Second President of the United States*, vol. 9 (Boston, 1854), 409.

114 Joseph Ellis, *Revolutionary Summer: The Birth of American Independence* (New York, 2013), 71; Fischer, *Washington's Crossing*, 29.

115 *FONA*, "General Orders, 9 July 1776," https://founders.archives.gov/documents/Washington/03-05-02-0176, accessed Sept. 1, 2019.

116 There is some debate as to whether Franklin actually made this quote, yet it continues to be attributed to him. See Milton Meltzer, *Benjamin Franklin: The New American* (New York, 1988), 230; Thomas Fleming, ed., *The Founding Fathers: Benjamin Franklin, A Biography in His Own Words*, vol. 2 (New York, 1972), 274.

Britain had failed to quell the American rebellion, and it was time for new strategies and leadership, prompting the king to turn to a team of brothers. In early 1776, 47-year-old Gen. William Howe, with 30 years of experience, assumed command of the British army in North America.[117] He had followed his two older brothers into military service, distinguishing himself during the War of the Austrian Succession, and the French and Indian War at the battles of Carillon (Fort Ticonderoga) and Quebec. Howe also led British forces during the battle of Bunker Hill, where he learned the danger of frontally assaulting American troops defending fortified positions.

William Howe's older brother, 50-year-old Adm. Richard Howe, assumed command of the British fleet in North America.[118] Richard entered naval service when he was 14 and gained distinction in the War of the Austrian Succession and the French and Indian War. Richard's expertise in amphibious operations against the French in these earlier conflicts would be useful during the American Revolution.

Both brothers served in Parliament and were sympathetic to the Americans' concerns that led to the war. They maintained strong connections to America following their service during the French and Indian War, where their older brother was killed fighting near Fort Ticonderoga. The General Court of Massachusetts honored their brother, touching both men, by establishing a memorial in his name at Westminster Abbey. Before the Revolution, Richard became acquainted with Benjamin Franklin during his stay in England.[119]

The Howes wanted peace but willingly returned to the service at the war's beginning. Though agreeing to serve, they insisted on being granted dual roles as military commanders and peace commissioners. They hoped to negotiate with America's leaders, granting amnesty and pardons to those who swore oaths of allegiance to King George.[120]

The Howe brothers devised a plan to divide and conquer the colonies. They asked Lord Germain to heavily reinforce their numbers in America, enabling a phased approach to defeat the rebellion. They first planned to seize New York City, using it as their base of operations, while a smaller force from Canada under Sir Guy Carleton attacked south into upstate New York. Carleton intended to recapture Fort Ticonderoga, maneuvering in the waterways, as another British

---

117 "William Howe," https://www.battlefields.org/learn/biographies/william-howe?, accessed Sept. 1, 2019.

118 "Richard Howe," https://www.battlefields.org/learn/biographies/richard-howe, accessed Sept. 1, 2019.

119 Middlekauff, *The Glorious Cause*, 344.

120 Ibid.; Miller, *Origins of the American Revolution*, 475; Commager & Morris, *SSS*, 426.

force from New York City attacked north up the Hudson River, joining Carleton around Albany. The operation would effectively cut off the seat of rebellion in New England from the rest of the country. Once New York was secure, the Howes would move to attack Rhode Island and New Jersey, winning back each colony with offers of amnesty and pardons. Although conceptually logical, the plan's execution would prove challenging.

General Washington and the newly designated United States military provided significant obstacles to the Howes' plans. Washington, however, had other troubles, and remained perplexed about how to defend New York without a credible naval force. General Lee shared these concerns. "What to do with the City, I own puzzles me, it is so encircle'd with deep navigable water, that whoever commands the Sea must command the Town."[121]

Washington continued to make what preparations he could, including reorganizing his army. Breaking his force into ten brigades, he deployed them in defense of potential British landing sites, mostly in lower Manhattan. Two brigades were placed on Long Island, two along the East River, two regiments on Governor's Island, one brigade outside of town in reserve, one remained in the village, and two brigades defended forts while blocking access up the Hudson River.

Washington ordered the construction of two forts on either side of the Hudson connected by a *chevaux-de-frise*, which would block access to the north.[122] In July 1776, soldiers began construction on Fort Constitution (renamed Ft. Lee that September) on the New Jersey side, while Fort Washington was built on the New York side. A ferry provided a supply line and was the only link between the two works.

The forts and the troops positioned along the East River were all Washington could do to control the waterways without a proper fleet to challenge the British. Unfortunately, by attempting to defend areas from static positions, Washington violated one of the basic principles of war: By attempting to strengthen each area, he ensured that he was strong in none. He soon learned that spreading out his forces rather than concentrating them permitted the British to lock him in while they massed their troops to systematically defeat each isolated American position.

The embarrassment at Boston reinforced the belief of the British that they needed to increase their military presence significantly in order to quell the rebellion. By October 1775, they agreed to enlarge the army by 55,000 men and

---

121 *FONA*, https://founders.archives.gov/documents/Washington/03-03-02-0242, accessed Sept. 1, 2019.

122 A *chevaux-de-frise* is an obstacle consisting of a chain of projecting, long iron or wooden spikes or spears.

the navy by 12,000.[123] Recruiting teams searched the English, Irish, and Scottish countrysides but fell short of the numbers needed. The Duke of Brunswick, Prince of Waldeck, and the Landgrave of Hesse-Kassel (modern Germany) became willing partners of the British. Lacking abundant natural resources in their land-locked homelands, these leaders raised citizens as hardened warriors for hire, called "Soldaten-handel," or "soldier-trade."[124] Initially, the British hired around 18,000 German mercenaries; these numbers reached nearly 30,000 by the war's end.[125] Although the Germans came from six separate principalities, the Americans collectively referred to them as "Hessians."

On June 25, General Howe arrived in lower New York Bay with three warships and an advance party that had been rearming and refitting after withdrawing from Boston. By June 29, Howe's force grew to 130 warships and transports carrying 9,300 British regulars to Staten Island. Arriving from England, Admiral Howe brought 150 ships and transports loaded with reinforcements. Admiral Sir Peter Parker joined the Howes with nine warships and 30 transports carrying 2,500 men under Generals Clinton and Cornwallis, returning from their defeat at Charleston. A final armada of six warships and 28 transports disembarked an additional 2,600 British regulars and 8,000 Hessians on August 12. By mid-August, the British committed two-thirds of their army and half of their navy to the American theater.[126] They also controlled the waters, and 32,000 troops lay poised, ready to attack the Americans.

As Howe arrived in New York, Congress appointed a new batch of officers to recruit and lead Marine detachments on board the original 13 frigates authorized by Congress in December 1775. To speed construction, Congress spread contracts for building the new warships between the states possessing the best shipyards. Men from New Hampshire built the *Raleigh*, which carried ninety Marines. Bostonians built the *Boston* and *Hancock*. Rhode Island was responsible for the *Providence* and *Warren*, and Connecticut built the *Trumbull*. The *Virginia* was built in Baltimore, and New York began constructing the *Montgomery* and *Congress*. Shipyards in Philadelphia built the *Delaware*, *Effingham*, *Randolph*, and *Washington*.[127] Captain

---

123 Ward, *TWOR*, 208.

124 David Fischer, *Washington's Crossing* (New York, 2004), 52, hereafter cited as *WC*.

125 Stokesbury, *A Short History of the American Revolution*, 72; Savas & Dameron, *The New American Revolution Handbook*, 37-38.

126 Fischer, *WC*, 33; Commager & Morris, *SSS*, 231.

127 *Raleigh* mounted 32 cannons, *Boston* 24, *Hancock* 32, *Providence* 28, *Warren* 32, *Trumbull* 28, *Virginia* 28, *Montgomery* 28, *Congress* 24, *Delaware* 24, *Effingham* 28, *Randolph* 32, and *Washington* 32.

Samuel Nicholas was tasked with organizing the "four Companies of Men [Marines] being then raised for the Frigates on the Stocks" in Philadelphia.[128]

Nicholas intended to remain in command of the Marines on the *Alfred* in Rhode Island, but Congress had other plans. Commodore Hopkins granted Nicholas a personal leave of absence to temporarily return to Philadelphia, tasking him with reporting the fleet's daily activities to Congress. Nicholas asked to return to the fleet after appearing before the Marine Committee, but Congress reassigned him. As the senior Continental Marine officer, Congress ordered Nicholas to form and organize the Marine detachments for the four new frigates in Philadelphia.

Recruiting efforts commenced immediately to find Marines for the four companies.[129] Captain Robert Mullan, *Tun Tavern*'s proprietor, was one of the first to receive a commission, and Nicholas tasked him with leading the recruiting efforts. First Lieutenant David Love and 2nd Lt. Hugh Montgomery filled the remaining officer positions on the *Delaware*. Using *Tun Tavern* as their operations base, the three officers vigorously assumed their task. Mullan quickly enlisted two brothers, Collin and Peter York, as the company's drummer and fifer, helping draw recruits to the tavern. Mullan also recruited two African Americans, Isaac Walker and "Orange Negro," who performed the same duties and collected the same pay and allowance as the other Marines.[130] The *Delaware*'s detachment grew to include four sergeants, four corporals, and 75 Marines by the time Mullan was finished.

Captain Andrew Porter received command of the *Effingham*'s Marine detachment, and was soon joined by 1st Lt. Daniel Henderson and 2nd Lt. James McClure. Porter was a schoolmaster from Philadelphia, and many of his recruits are believed to have been former students. But he was no push-over. Later in the war, Porter transferred to the Army as an artillery officer and had a confrontation with another officer who chided him about his background. Major Eustace commented, "He is nothing but a d____d schoolmaster." Porter responded, "I have been a schoolmaster, Sir, and have not forgotten my vocation."[131] Drawing his sword, he struck Major Eustace's shoulder with its backend, signifying a challenge to a duel. The two officers met at the southeast corner of 9th and Arch streets in Philadelphia. Porter won, shooting Eustace through the heart. He was later court-

---

128 "Samuel Nicholas to the President of the Congress, 10 August 1781," *Papers of the Continental Congress*, 78, 28:301-304, quoted from Smith, *MIR*, 87, hereafter cited as *PCC*; Bud Hannings, *Chronology of the American Revolution: Military and Political Actions Day by Day* (Jefferson, NC, 2008), 112.

129 Smith, *MIR*, 87-88 provides a comprehensive listing of the officers commissioned to lead the Marine detachments formed to join the four frigates in Philadelphia.

130 Smith, *MIR*, 88.

131 Thomas Marshall Green, *Historic Families of Kentucky* (Cincinnati, 1899), 273.

Captain Andrew Porter commanded the Marine Detachment on the frigate *Effingham* before being assigned as company commander in the Marine Battalion formed by Samuel Nicholas to support Gen. George Washington in the battles of Trenton and Princeton. Porter later resigned his Marine commission to join the Army as an artillery officer. *Wikimedia*

martialed but acquitted and promoted to major to fill the position left vacant by Eustace's demise.

On June 25, Philadelphia natives Benjamin Dean and Samuel Shaw also received commissions as captains. Dean assumed command of the Marines on the *Washington*. First Lieutenant Peregrine Brown and 2nd Lt. Abel Morgan joined him. All three later fought under Nicholas's command while attached to General Washington at Trenton and Princeton. Shaw assumed command of the *Randolph*'s Marine detachment. First Lieutenant Franklin Reed and 2nd Lt. Panatiere de la Falconniere from the French West Indies joined Shaw's detachment. The men of the *Randolph* would not join Nicholas at Trenton and Princeton, as he would choose to hold them back as *Randolph* was nearing completion. Congress wanted *Randolph* to put to sea as soon as possible. Falconniere was later arrested for misconduct and ceremoniously discharged when a group of six naval officers signed a petition asking for his relief. The *Randolph*'s service came to a tragic end off the coast of Barbados in March 1778 during a battle against HMS *Yarmouth*. *Randolph* was reportedly winning when she suddenly exploded, killing all but four of her crew.[132]

On July 12, 1776, Admiral Howe directed HMS *Phoenix*, HMS *Rose*, and three tenders to force a passage up the Hudson River, testing American defenses and intercepting provisions meant for the rebels.[133] American shore batteries and the guns of Forts Constitution and Washington barraged the ships, achieving several hits. Undeterred, the British returned fire and continued upriver. The ships' easy passage by what many believed were impassable positions and their firing into urban areas behind American positions caused hysteria. Washington observed, "When the men of war passed up the River, the shrieks and cries of

132 *Yarmouth* mounted 74 cannons.

133 *Phoenix* mounted 40 guns and *Rose* 20.

these poor creatures, running every way with their children, was truly distressing, and I fear will have an unhappy effect on the ears and minds of our young and inexperienced soldiery."[134] Washington would not forget this valuable lesson. Controlling the rivers facilitated the success of land campaigns, and he would use this knowledge at Trenton.

Generals Horatio Gates and Benedict Arnold of the Northern Department also learned lessons about controlling rivers and lakes in order to support land operations. Following their defeat in Canada, Arnold's American forces retreated to Fort Ticonderoga. Intelligence indicated that Sir Guy Carlton planned a southern attack through Lake Champlain to Lake George. He would eventually move on the northern reaches of the Hudson, joining General Howe, who was attacking north, upriver from New York City. Immediately, the Americans began constructing a fleet on Lake Champlain to block Carlton. By late July, they had commissioned the schooners *Royal Savage*, *Revenge*, and *Liberty*, the sloop *Enterprise*, and several row galleys and gondolas, totaling 53 guns.[135] These ships required crews of sailors and Marines, but none existed in upstate New York.

Like Washington in Boston, General Gates turned to the army to enlist sailors and Marines. They would become known as "Arnold's Fleet" since Arnold held tactical control of the combined naval force operating on Lake Champlain.[136] Gates issued a general order on July 23, declaring "it is of the utmost consequence that a well regulated body of Seamen and Marines should be immediately draughted from the several Brigades of this Army, to the end that the Army of the United States may continue to support their Naval Superiority & Command of the Waters of Lake Champlain."[137]

Gates directed the assignment of 28 sergeants, 16 corporals, 16 drummers, and 288 privates from the army to serve as Marines in Arnold's Fleet. Gates authorized these soldier-marines an additional eight shillings per month, issuing brass blunderbusses, which looked like oversized shotguns that fired multiple projectiles in a wide pattern. Arnold was unimpressed, referring to these troops as a "wretched motley Crew; the Marines, the Refuse of every regiment, and the Seamen, few of them, ever wet with salt Water," but they would have to suffice.[138]

134 Fitzpatrick, *TWGW*, 444.

135 *Royal Savage* mounted 12 cannons, *Revenge* 8, *Liberty* 8, and *Enterprise* 12; Randall, *Benedict Arnold: Patriot and Traitor*, 280-283, 290-291.

136 Arthur Lefkowitz, *Benedict Arnold's Army: The 1775 American Invasion of Canada During the Revolutionary War* (El Dorado Hills, CA, 2008), 67; Randall, *Benedict Arnold: Patriot and Traitor*, 291.

137 Force, ed., *AA*, 5th Series, 656; Smith, *MIR*, 28.

138 Morgan, ed., *NDAR*, 6:881.

The recruitment of sailors and Marines continued for the next three months in preparation for blocking British forces moving south. The fleet eventually consisted of over 900 soldiers serving as seamen and Marines. The troops still wore army uniforms, carried army weapons and accoutrements, and fell under army regulations. Regardless, Arnold trained them to fight on the water as Washington prepared his army for battle on land. Both forces would face enormous challenges and defeat in the coming months.

Chapter Five

A Growing Crisis

"Good God! What brave fellows I must this day lose!"

— Gen. George Washington, New York[1]

By mid-August 1776, the Continental forces in New York held a precarious position. The British had assembled an army of 32,000 well-led, well-trained, and well-equipped professional soldiers, supported by a fleet of 10,000 sailors and 2,000 Royal Marines manning hundreds of vessels armed with 1,200 guns.[2] The British organized their ground forces according to each unit's unique skill. They had 27 regiments of the line (regular infantry), four battalions of light infantry (fast, mobile foot soldiers), four battalions of grenadiers (elite shock troops), two of the Guards (traditionally guarded royal residences but also acted as infantry), three artillery brigades, one regiment of light dragoons (light cavalry), and three regiments of Hessians. The fleet consisted of 10 ships of the line (60-100 guns), 20 frigates (20-56 guns), and various smaller ships and transports.[3]

George Washington assembled 19,000 men, but most of his soldiers were untrained, undisciplined, and often poorly led militiamen. Apart from the few who might have fought at Lexington and Concord, Bunker Hill, or the French and Indian War, many lacked combat experience. Unlike the British, the only uniquely skilled American troops at the time consisted of riflemen recently recruited from Virginia, Pennsylvania, and Maryland and Knox's artillerymen.

---

1 Henry Onderdonk, *Revolutionary Incidents of Suffolk and Kings Counties: With an Account of the Battle of Long Island and the British Prisons and Prison-Ships at New York* (New York, 1849), 147-148.

2 Stephenson, *Patriot Battles*, 232, hereafter cited as *PB*; Ward, *TWOR*, 211; Middlekauff, *TGC*, 347.

3 Ward, *TWOR*, 209; Leckie, *George Washington's War*, 258; Ferling, *AAM*, 125.

One of Washington's greatest shortfalls was the lack of a credible naval force that could compete with the British fleet.

As in Boston, Washington created an ad hoc local fleet using soldiers. Commodore Hopkins's depleted fleet remained in New England waters and was of little help to the Army at this time. On his own, Washington assembled several armed schooners, sloops, row galleys, and whaleboats commanded by 38-year-old Lt. Col. Benjamin Tupper of Ward's Massachusetts Regiment.[4] Tupper was a French and Indian War veteran who would achieve the rank of brigadier general by the end of the Revolution. Tupper's armada of small vessels was no match for the powerful British fleet. It cruised the New Jersey and Long Island coasts, cutting communications between Tories and the enemy fleet and providing intelligence on British movements. As this was ineffectual, Washington was often left guessing at the enemy's next move, but he would not have to wait long.

After giving the Hessian and British troops a week to acclimate and rest after arriving from England, General Howe launched an amphibious attack on Long Island. At 8:00 a.m. on August 22, the British frigates HMS *Phoenix* (44 guns), *Rose* (20 guns), *Greyhound* (20 guns) and bomb ketches HMS *Thunder* and *Carcass* (each carrying up to 12 guns and 2 mortars) entered Gravesend Bay off Long Island to provide fire support to the landing force. HMS *Rainbow* (44 guns) was anchored off Denyse Point near Staten Island, acting as a guide boat. The first British and Hessian troops, along with 40 field cannons, boarded 75 flatboats, 11 bateaux (shallow-draft flat-bottom boats), and two row galleys for the transit across the bay from Staten Island. This advance force consisted of four battalions of light infantry, four battalions of grenadiers, two infantry regiments, light dragoons, and a corps of Hessian grenadiers and jaegers (highly mobile infantry) under the command of Generals Clinton and Cornwallis.[5] According to General Howe's secretary,

> the disembarkation of about 15,000 troops, upon a fine beach, their forming upon the adjacent plain, a fleet above 300 ships and vessels with their sails spread open to dry, the sun shining clear upon them, the green hills and meadows after the rain, and the calm surface of the water upon contiguous sea and up the sound, exhibited one of the finest and most picturesque scenes that the imagination can fancy or the eye behold.[6]

4 Daughan, *If By Sea*, 86-87, 92-93.

5 McCullough, *1776*, 156-157; Stephenson, *PB*, 233; Savas & Dameron, *American Revolution Guidebook*, 55-56.

6 "Journal of Ambrose Serle, secretary to Lord Richard Howe, Thursday, 22 August 1776," quoted from Commager & Morris, *SSS*, 430-431.

Morale was strong among the waiting Americans. Colonel William Douglas of the Connecticut regiment wrote his wife, "As yet things look well on our side. . . . Our troops are really in high spirits … Let them [the British] come on as soon as they can, or dare!"[7] On August 25, the British brought in 5,000 additional men as reinforcements.

As British troops landed on Long Island, the Americans were facing challenges in getting ready for them. Washington, who had been reorganizing the army, creating new brigades and leaders, was forced to change command of the troops on Long Island for unforeseen reasons. General Nathaniel Greene became too ill to perform his duties and relinquished command to Gen. John Sullivan. Thirty-four-year-old Greene had entered the army as a private in the Rhode Island militia outside Boston the previous year but quickly became one of Washington's most gifted and dependable officers.[8] Thirty-six-year-old Sullivan was serving as a New Hampshire representative to the Continental Congress when the war began. He was among the first generals appointed in the army, and later served as governor of New Hampshire.[9] Sullivan, however, lacked knowledge of American plans, did not know the local terrain, and had little understanding of the disposition of his forces on Long Island, causing Washington to question his ability to lead his men successfully. Washington's concerns were confirmed during an inspection tour of Sullivan's defensive preparations, and he quickly replaced Sullivan with Israel Putnam.

Fifty-eight-year-old Putnam was a seasoned warfighter with knowledge of the terrain on Long Island.[10] Born near Salem, Massachusetts, and raised as a farmer, Putnam gained a reputation as a fearless soldier during the French and Indian War. He was a member of the famed Rogers' Rangers, survived Indian captivity, and was promoted to lieutenant colonel by 1759.[11] Putnam displayed exceptional leadership at Bunker Hill and was selected as one of the first major generals appointed to the Continental Army. He later commanded forces in Philadelphia during the battle of Trenton.

7 Commager & Morris, *SSS*, 431.

8 See Gerald Carbone's *Nathanael Greene: A Biography of the American Revolution* (New York, 2008) for a complete narrative of Greene's contributions during the American Revolution.

9 See Charles Whittmore's *A General of the Revolution: John Sullivan of New Hampshire* (New York, 1961) for a narrative on Sullivan's actions during the Revolution.

10 See Robert Hubbard's *Major General Israel Putnam: Hero of the American Revolution* (Jefferson, NC, 2017) for more information on Putnam.

11 Rogers' Rangers are commonly accepted as the forerunners to today's U.S. Army Rangers. The unit was originally formed as a provincial company, but later adopted as part of the British Army during the French and Indian War under Maj. Robert Rogers. Rogers trained the unit as a light infantry force to conduct independent reconnaissance and special operations against the French.

Putnam hoped to replicate Bunker Hill by forcing the British to attack his well-defended positions along key terrain. While contemplating an enemy ploy to distract them from the main attack on Manhattan, Washington sent an additional 10 battalions to reinforce Putnam. As a precaution, he kept boats to support a withdrawal, if necessary. Putnam maintained direct command of his main force, deploying it on a prominent area known as Brooklyn Heights. These troops dug in and oriented their defenses toward the east, with their backs to the East River.[12]

Generals Sullivan and William Alexander (Lord Stirling) assumed command of the remaining one-third of Putnam's force. They established forward positions along an extended ridge called the Heights of Guana, approximately two miles from Putnam's primary defensive position. The ridge ran around 10 miles in length and was heavily wooded except for five key passes that had been cleared. The Americans intended to engage the British as they funneled through these choke points, then pulverize them while falling back toward Brooklyn Heights for the decisive battle.[13] The Continentals employed 500-1000 men at each of the westernmost passes, but only sent a five-man scouting team to watch Jamaica Pass on the far eastern flank; this would prove to be a fatal mistake.[14]

The plan might have worked, but the British, having learned their lesson at Bunker Hill, had no intention of attacking head-on into well-prepared positions. Upon landing at Gravesend Bay, they aggressively sent out reconnaissance patrols to determine the Americans' dispositions, composition, and strength. They also conducted limited probing attacks to determine how the Americans might respond to their actions. The Americans' lack of cavalry prevented them from establishing an adequate counter-reconnaissance force to block British information collection efforts.

The Americans watched as the British landed unopposed. Thirty-two-year-old Col. Edward Hand led the riflemen of his 1st Pennsylvania Continental Regiment in shadowing the British at Denyse Point as they established a beachhead. Hand was a doctor who trained in Ireland, served with the British army prior to the war, and later represented Pennsylvania in the Continental Congress.[15] Unable to oppose the larger British force, Hand hid his unit in the woods, reporting on their movements. He also sent out a detachment to burn all the standing grain

12 O'Donnell, *Washington's Immortals*, 55; McCullough, *1776*, 160-163; Leckie, *George Washington's War*, 260-261.

13 Scheer & Rankin, *RR*, 162; Ward, *TWOR*, 215; Stephenson, *PB*, 233-234.

14 McCullough, *1776*, 162, Stephenson, *PB*, 234.

15 See "Edward Hand," https://www.battlefields.org/learn/biographies/edward-hand, accessed Sept. 29, 2019, for more information on Hand.

and slaughter as many cattle as possible, preventing their use by the British. Unhindered, the Redcoats continued to gather information and develop an assault plan.

With assistance from loyalists, the British identified a weakness in the American lines. They found Jamaica Pass undefended, intending to outflank the Americans by employing a three-pronged attack.[16] Fifty-six-year-old Gen. James Grant was assigned the mission to attack north up the coastal road, engaging the Americans' right wing near Gowanus Creek. At the same time, 60-year-old Hessian Gen. Leopold von Heister would attack the Americans' center lines near Flatbush.[17] These attacks were meant to serve as feints to fix the Americans' forward units in place and draw their attention toward where Putnam expected the British to attack. Generals Howe, Clinton, and Cornwallis intended to lead the main effort in a flanking attack through the Jamaica Pass toward the rear of the Americans' forward positions, cutting off their retreat to the main defensive lines on Brooklyn Heights.

This flanking movement took the Continentals by surprise. One American explained, "the main body of British, by a route we never dreamed of, had surrounded us and driven within our lines, or scattered in the woods, all our men except the Delaware and Maryland battalions who were standing at bay with double their number."[18] These brave soldiers attacked Lord Cornwallis's troops, allowing their comrades time to withdraw to the main lines while paying a heavy price in blood. The weight of the combined British and Hessian troops forced the Americans to retreat through a mill pond, causing mass confusion and casualties. One Continental private recorded, "The British, having several field pieces stationed by a brick house, were pouring the canister and grape upon the Americans like a shower of hail."[19] Washington crossed the East River and assumed overall command of the American forces in the midst of battle. He watched the heroic stand of the Delaware and Maryland battalions and was reported to say, "Good God! What brave fellows I must this day lose!"[20]

16 Stephenson, *PB*, 234-235; Chernow, *Washington: A Life*, 246-247; Ward, *TWOR*, 216.

17 Grant gained extensive experience during the French and Indian war and later served as governor of Florida before the start of the Revolution. He was with the British forces at Boston and was the first to recommend that they seize New York. See Paul Nelson's *General James Grant: Scottish Soldier and Royal Governor of East Florida* (Gainesville, FL, 1993) for more on Grant. Von Heister, the senior Hessian officer in America, also had extensive military experience from the Seven Years' War. See John Fredriksen, *Revolutionary War Almanac* (New York, 2006), 427 for more on Von Heister.

18 "A letter of an unknown Patriot Soldier, New York, 1 September 1776," Onderdonk, *Revolutionary Incidents*, 147-148, as quoted in Commager & Morris, *SSS*, 440.

19 "Narrative of a Continental private," Commager & Morris, *SSS*, 442.

20 "A letter of an unknown Patriot Soldier," 440.

The British troops were in a fury. Many could finally hold the contemptuous rebels accountable for their nefarious activities following months of inactivity. One British officer wrote to a friend,

> Rejoice, my friend, that we have given the Rebels a d--d crush. . . . The Hessians and our brave Highlanders gave no quarter; and it was a fine sight to see with what alacrity they dispatched the Rebels with their bayonets after we had surrounded them so that they could not resist. Multitudes were drowned and suffocated in the morasses—a proper punishment for all Rebels. [21]

The British had instilled hatred for the Americans in their German allies. The same British officer commented, "We took care to tell the Hessians that the Rebels had resolved to give no quarters to them in particular, which made them fight desperately and put all to death that fell into their hands."[22] The Hessians developed a deep contempt for the Americans, or *Rebellers* as they called them. They considered the Continentals cowards and traitors, viewing the American beliefs of liberty and freedom as opposite their culture of hierarchy, order, and discipline. Hessian officers demanded instant obedience and feared the thought of freedom and liberty spreading like a cancer through their ranks.

The Hessians were professional soldiers who, like the Spartans of ancient times, dedicated their lives to the profession of arms.[23] Hessian officers took a personal oath of loyalty to their prince, and soldiers began training at an early age. Both groups received extensive instruction in the military arts and in a strict code of honor and loyalty. Soldiers often received better pay than their civilian counterparts, receiving promotions based on their merits rather than their position in life. Hessians also expected to profit in the service of their prince, and captured articles were sold for prize money and shared among officers and men. One Hessian officer explained, "Never in this world was an army as well paid as this one during the civil war in America. One could call them rich."[24] The Americans learned to fear these German mercenaries, as they showed little mercy on the battlefield and aggressively pillaged homes.

---

21 "Extract of a letter from an officer in General Frazier's battalion, September 3, 1776," Force, ed., *AA*, 5th series, 1:1259-1260, quoted in Commager & Morris, *SSS*, 443.

22 Ibid.

23 David Hackett Fischer provides a comprehensive background on the Hessians in *Washington's Crossing*.

24 Johann Ewald, *Diary of the American War: A Hessian Journal*, Joseph P. Tustin, ed. (New Haven, CT, 1979), 118.

The Americans experienced a crushing defeat on the first day of battle on Long Island, losing around 300 killed and 1,100 wounded or captured, including the capture of Generals Stirling and Sullivan.[25] The British suffered 400 casualties.[26] While Howe had the rebels on the run, he did not push forward as he had done at Bunker Hill. Rather than attack the Americans' well-prepared main defensive positions, Howe paused to conduct deliberate siege operations. He was confident that the Americans faced defeat with the East River to their backs and the Royal Navy controlling the waterways. Howe saw no need to risk another costly victory, but he based his decision on a flawed assumption, which Washington would soon exploit.

As the army was fighting on Long Island, the Marines waged a different type of battle in Philadelphia. Major Nicholas faced challenges in acquiring the resources needed to man, train, and equip the Marines. Washington and the army required the same matériel, which was always in short supply. Congress was tasked with prioritizing those units to receive the much-needed equipment. Nicholas achieved a small victory on August 22, the same day the British landed on Long Island, when Congress directed the Secret Committee to deliver enough muskets to arm the Marines. This victory was short-lived, however. Sensing that Washington required assistance in New York, Congress attempted to shift these weapons to a group of German immigrants being formed into an army battalion. It ordered the Secret Committee to first arm the Germans before giving weapons to the Marines.[27] Nicholas countered by leveraging the favor of close friends in Congress, ensuring the Marines received the necessary guns.

Washington faced much larger concerns than Nicholas at this time. He was fighting for the very survival of the army and the preservation of the newly established United States. Howe's troops began systematically digging siege trenches closer to American lines, while the Royal Navy maintained control of the East River. Washington held a war council with his generals to determine the best way forward. Many argued to remain and fight, as they held a strong position. Leaning on his experiences at Bunker Hill, General Putnam said, "Give an American army a wall to fight behind and they will fight forever."[28] Washington, on the other hand, understood that defeat was inevitable, and his duty was to preserve the American army and the fight for independence. Colonel Benjamin Tallmadge, who later led

---

25 Ward, *TWOR*, 226-227; Stephenson, *PB*; 243, McCollough, *1776*, 179.

26 Ferling, *AAM*, 134.

27 *JCC*, 5:716, quoted from Smith, *MIR*, 88.

28 John Ferling, *Whirlwind: The American Revolution and the War that Won It* (New York, 2015), Kindle edition.

Washington's Culper spy ring in New York, described the Americans' situation in a letter to his father:

> To move so large a body of troops, with all their necessary appendages, across a river a full mile wide, with a rapid current, in the face of a victorious, well disciplined army nearly three times as numerous as his own, and a fleet capable of stopping the navigation so that not one boat could have passed over, seemed to present most formidable obstacles.[29]

Regardless of the challenges, the Americans had to attempt an escape, and Washington gave the order to withdraw.

The army's escape from Long Island on August 29-30 was a close-run affair, and Washington and his generals kept their intentions secret. Just as he had at Boston, Washington turned to John Glover and the fishermen and seafarers from Massachusetts for support. He employed the 14th and 27th Massachusetts regiments to man the boats he previously held at Long Island as soldiers went to the pier under the guise of shifting to another part of the battle line.

As the evacuation commenced, an uncharacteristic nor'easter rolled in, preventing the British fleet from entering the East River. This welcome situation caused some to claim divine intervention on behalf of the Americans. Additionally, Washington deceived the British by stoking campfires and having a force remain to make noises replicating that of an army girding for battle. The ploy worked, but not all the troops made it across the river by daylight, when the weather yet again helped as a heavy fog rolled in to conceal the ongoing withdrawal. Washington was among the last to board a boat to Manhattan Island. He had successfully evacuated 9,500 men, all their baggage, horses, and provisions, "even the biscuits which had not been [cooked] and the raw pork which could not be eaten."[30] British patrols cautiously advanced toward the American lines, finding three Continental soldiers who had intentionally remained behind to plunder and five cannons that were too heavy to move.[31]

Though Washington had performed a masterful stroke in saving the Army, the defeat at Long Island was the start of a four-month-long chain of losses that would test the resolve of patriotic Americans and their would-be allies. Following the withdrawal to Manhattan, General Greene reported, "the Country is struck

---

29 Henry Johnston, ed., *Memoir of Colonel Benjamin Tallmadge* (New York, 1904), 11-12.

30 Ward, *TWOR*, 235; Ferling, *AAM*, 135; Middlekauff, *TGC*, 353

31 Lengel, *General George Washington*, 148.

with a pannick, any Cappital loss at this time may ruin the cause."[32] The American ambassador to France, Silas Deane, wrote, "The Last check on Long Island has sunk our credit to nothing."[33] The defeat also caused Washington to question the competence of his troops. He told Congress, "Our situation is truly distressing. The militia . . . are dismayed, intractable and impatient to return . . . great numbers of them have gone off; in some instances, almost by whole regiments."[34] He used this opportunity to advocate for a permanent and professional army, arguing that American liberties might be lost "if their defense is left to any but a permanent standing army."[35]

Washington also began to realize the folly of confronting the British on their terms. At this point in the war, the citizen army was ill-suited to engage enemy forces on open battlefields employing European-style tactics, and the American navy was far too weak to challenge the British fleet. The Americans needed to play to their strengths while exploiting British weaknesses.

Washington decided to conduct a strategic defense by only engaging the British at the time and place of his choosing. He intended to set the conditions for victory by systematically chipping away at enemy resources and the will of the British people until they deemed the war too costly to continue. He also hoped to gain allies who could challenge Great Britain in other locations in order to drain their resources further. Washington wrote to John Hancock and Congress, "[O]n our Side the War should be defensive. It has even been called a War of Posts. That we should on all occasions avoid a general Action, or put anything to the risque, unless compelled by a necessity, into which we ought never to be drawn."[36] Washington intended to keep the British at arm's length until the time was right, when "a brilliant stroke could be made with any probability of success."

Defending New York City did not offer much hope, as British dominance of the waterways around Manhattan Island enabled them to land behind the Americans and block their escape over land. On September 7, Washington held a council of war to discuss matters with his generals. He voiced his concerns to Congress the following day, stating that the British "mean to inclose us on the Island of New York by taking post in our Rear, while the Shipping effectually secure the Front;

32 *FONA*, https://founders.archives.gov/documents/Washington/03-06-02-0180, accessed Aug. 16, 2019.

33 Ward, *TWOR*, 236.

34 *FONA*, https://founders.archives.gov/documents/Washington/03-06-02-0162, accessed Sept. 30, 2019.

35 Ibid.

36 The quotes in the next two paragraphs are cited from *FONA*, https://founders.archives.gov/documents/Washington/03-06-02-0203, accessed Oct. 1, 2019.

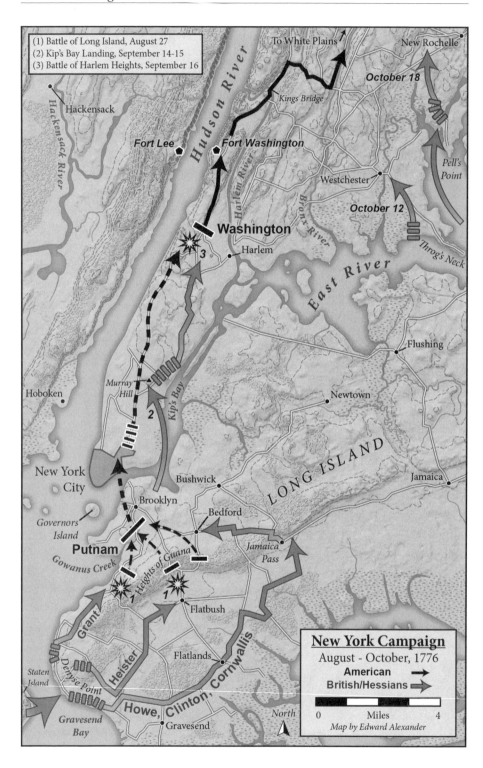

(1) Battle of Long Island, August 27
(2) Kip's Bay Landing, September 14-15
(3) Battle of Harlem Heights, September 16

To White Plains

New Rochelle

October 18

Hudson River

Kings Bridge

Hackensack River

Hackensack

Fort Lee

Fort Washington

Westchester

Pell's Point

Harlem River

Bronx River

October 12

Washington

Harlem

Throg's Neck

East River

3

Flushing

Hoboken

Murray Hill

Kip's Bay

2

Newtown

New York City

Bushwick

LONG ISLAND

Jamaica

Governors Island

Brooklyn

Bedford

Putnam

Gowanus Creek

Jamaica Pass

Grant

Heights of Guana

1

1

Flatbush

Heister

Flatlands

Cornwallis

Staten Island

Denyse Point

Howe, Clinton, Cornwallis

Gravesend Bay

Gravesend

North

New York Campaign
August - October, 1776
American
British/Hessians

0   Miles   4

Map by Edward Alexander

and thus either by cutting off our Communication with the Country oblige us to fight them on their own Terms or Surrender at discretion." He continued, "The honor of making a brave defense does not seem to be a sufficient stimulus, when the success is very doubtful, and the falling into the Enemy's hands probable. But I doubt not this will be gradually attained." Washington was preparing Congress for his inevitable evacuation of the city.

Some thought the situation called for more extreme measures. General Greene argued that the city should be abandoned and burned, preventing its use by the British. He reasoned, "Two-thirds of the property of the city of New-York and the suburbs belongs to the Tories . . . I would burn the city . . . not one benefit can arise to us from its preservation . . . ."[37] Washington posed the question to Congress. Hancock responded on September 10 that Washington's plan to abandon New York had been approved, but warned, "Congress being Apprehensive that their former Resolution of 3d Int was not rightly understood, have directed me to Send you the foregoing, by which you will perceive that their wish is to preserve N. York."[38] Against his better judgment, Washington placed his trust in the primacy of civilian leadership over the military and complied, but he continued to seek any advantage he could gain over his adversaries.

Lacking a capable fleet, Washington was desperate to take any offensive action against the British warships to disrupt their expected attack against New York City. He turned to Connecticut inventor David Bushnell, who constructed the nation's first submarine. This single-man craft, dubbed the *American Turtle* by Bushnell, used hand-cranked winches and screws to maneuver the craft below ships.[39] The pilot then used a hand-powered drill to attach an explosive primed with a simple timer that would detonate twenty to thirty minutes upon release, giving the pilot enough time to escape. Twenty-seven-year-old Sgt. Ezra Lee of Connecticut volunteered to man the *Turtle*.

On the evening of September 6, Sergeant Lee conducted his attack. Soldiers in whaleboats towed the *Turtle* toward the anchored British fleet, releasing it at a safe distance. Lee manipulated the cranks and winches to propel the craft toward the warships. It took him two hours to reach a man-of-war, believed to be HMS *Asia* (64 guns). The *Turtle* submerged and made multiple attempts to fasten the explosive charge to the bottom of the ship. Unbeknownst to the Americans, the

37 *FONA*, https://founders.archives.gov/documents/Washington/03-06-02-0180, accessed Aug. 16, 2020.

38 *FONA*, https://founders.archives.gov/documents/Washington/03-06-02-0218, accessed Aug. 16, 2020.

39 See Roy Manstan & Frederick Frese, *Turtle: David Bushnell's Revolutionary Vessel* (Yardley, PA, 2010) for the full story of the *American Turtle*.

British had lined their wooden ships with copper sheathing to protect the hulls from marine life, effectively blocking Lee's attempt to secure the explosive.

Unable to set the charge and with daylight approaching, Lee abandoned the mission and began a four-mile journey to escape. As he passed Governor's Island, hundreds of British troops on the shore spotted him and sent soldiers in a whaleboat to capture him. Lee released the explosive charge he was towing as the boat approached within 50-60 feet of the *Turtle*, hoping it would explode in their midst. The floating bomb frightened the soldiers, who rapidly rowed away. As it passed the island, the charge exploded, causing a tall water geyser, justifying the British retreat. Lee continued his journey and eventually was picked up by friendly forces.[40]

Samuel Nicholas, meanwhile, struggled to equip the Marines nearly 100 miles away in Philadelphia. He slowly progressed, and on September 5, the Marine Committee published the first formal uniform regulations for Marines. It specified that Marine officer's uniform would consist of "A Green Coat faced with white, Round Cuff, Slash'd Sleeves and Pockets; with Buttons Round the Cuff, Silver Epaulett on the right Shoulder - Skirts turn'd back, Buttons to suit the Facings. White waistcoat and Britches, edged with Green, Black Gaiters & Garters Green shirts for the Men if they can be Procured."[41] The Marines also began wearing round hats with white bindings. State marines wore their own distinct uniforms. Pennsylvania's wore brown coats faced with green, cocked hats, and the letters "I.P.B" etched on their buttons, while Maryland marines wore blue hunting shirts. Newly equipped and attired, they were probably hoping to join Washington in the pending fight in New York, but the members of Congress had other plans. They decided to maintain the Marine presence in Philadelphia rather than reinforce Washington, whom they believed would be able to confront British advances in New York.

On September 12, after debates and exchanges with Congress, Washington and his generals agreed on a plan to contain the British offensive in New York. They would leave 8,000 troops stationed at Fort Washington to coordinate with Fort Lee to block the Royal Navy's passage north. At the same time, the remaining Americans would withdraw to block British ground movements, with one group staging in Harlem and the remainder north of the fort at Kings Bridge. Washington put the plan in motion, but the British quickly disrupted it.

40 See Morgan, ed., *NDAR*, 6: Annex B, 1499-1511 for letters from George Washington, Thomas Jefferson, David Bushnell, and Ezra Lee on the topic of the *American Turtle* and Lee's mission in New York Harbor.

41 "Minutes of the Continental Marine Committee, Philadelphia, 5 September 1776," quoted from Morgan, ed., *NDAR*, 6:716.

The first Marines, like the militia, had no standard uniform. They wore civilian clothing or Army uniforms until the Naval Committee could provide the prescribed uniform, as depicted in this photo. *Author*

On the dark evening of September 13, Pvt. Joseph Plumb Martin and his comrades manned guard positions at Kip's Bay. All was quiet until an eerie exchange disrupted the still night. Martin listened as the watchword was called out down the American line: "All is well." Suddenly, a voice with a British accent responded from the water, "We will alter your tune before tomorrow night."[42] Plumb awoke the following day to see four British frigates, HMS *Phoenix* (44 guns), HMS *Roebuck* (44 guns), HMS *Orpheus* (32 guns), and HMS *Carysfort* (28 guns) move upriver and anchor right below his position.[43] An additional warship and six transports joined them the following day. Simultaneously, HMS *Renown* (50 guns), HMS *Repulse* (32 guns), HMS *Pearl* (32 guns), and three armed schooners sallied up the Hudson on the opposite side of Manhattan, drawing American attention away from the activity at Kip's Bay. Forts Washington and Lee did what they could to stop the British advance up the river, but to no avail. Though damaged, the ships easily passed the supposedly formidable forts, bringing their further usefulness into question.

By the morning of September 15, Washington was evacuating most of his artillery, troops, and provisions to the north. Private Martin and others received orders to remain in place and confront the pending British attack in order to buy time for the rest of the Army to escape. Martin recalled sitting on a stool

42 Joseph Martin, *A Narrative of Some of the Adventures, Dangers and Sufferings of A Revolutionary Soldier* (Hallowell, ME, 1830), 26.

43 Chernow, *Washington: A Life*, 253; Lengel, *General George Washington*, 153; Middlekauff, *TGC*, 355.

reading some papers, "when all of a sudden there came such a peal of thunder from the British shipping that I thought my head would go with the sound. I made a frog's leap for the ditch, and lay as still as I possibly could, and began to consider which part of my carcass was to go first."[44] Benjamin Trumbull, chaplain of the 1st Connecticut Regiment, described, "near an 100 canon [loosed] a most furious Cannonade on the Lines, which Soon levelled them almost with the Ground in some Places, and buried our men who were in the Lines almost under Sand and Sods of Earth, and made such a dust and Smoke that there was no possibility of firing on the Enemy."[45] The ships' fire protected British soldiers as they loaded boats and rowed toward the shore. According to Trumbull, this fire was so effective that the British soldiers "made good their Landing without receiving any annoyance from our Troops."[46] The naval guns served their purpose, with the remaining Americans running away, allowing the British to effect another unopposed landing.

Hearing the guns roaring in the distance, Washington mounted his horse and raced to the scene. He was enraged at what he found. He told John Hancock, "to my great surprize and Mortification I found the Troops that had been posted in the Lines retreating with the utmost precipitation and those ordered to support them . . . flying in every direction and in the greatest confusion, notwithstanding the exertions of their Generals to form them."[47] Washington tried desperately to rally his troops, yelling, "Take the walls . . . take the cornfield!"[48] Some listened, but most continued running. Private Martin thought "the demons of fear and disorder seemed to take full possession of all and everything that day."[49]

Washington's anger grew. Eyewitnesses described how the commander "dashed his hat upon the ground in a transport of rage," crying out, "Are these the men with whom I am to defend America?"[50] He reportedly lashed out with his riding cane, hitting enlisted men and officers alike. Nothing worked, and the troops continued to stream rearward. Washington blamed his undisciplined troops, calling their

44 Martin, *A Narrative*, 27.

45 *Collections of the Connecticut Historical Society, vol. 7, Orderly book and journals kept by Connecticut men while taking part in the American Revolution, 1775-1778* (Hartford, 1899), 194.

46 Ibid.

47 *FONA*, https://founders.archives.gov/documents/Washington/03-06-02-0251, accessed Oct. 5, 2019.

48 Chernow, *Washington: A Life*, 253; Ward, *TWOR*, 243; Lengel, *General George Washington*, 153

49 Martin, *A Narrative*, 27.

50 McCollough, *1776*, 212; Middlekauff, *TGC*, 355; Ferling, *AAM*, 141; Scheer & Rankin, *RR*, 182.

conduct "disgracefull and dastardly."[51] Reverend Trumbull disagreed, stating, "The men were blamed for retreating and even flying in these Circumstances, but I imagine the Fault was principally in the General Officers in not disposing of things so as to give the men a rational prospect of Defense and a Safe retreat should they engage the Enemy."[52]

Both parties were correct. Washington and his troops still had much to learn about prosecuting a war, but they first had to survive to apply these lessons on future battlefields. With that knowledge, Washington gathered what troops he could and pulled back to a consolidated position along Harlem Heights.

General Howe's cautious tendencies resulted in another missed opportunity to defeat the rebels. Although his landing force pushed quickly inland, Howe paused his troops at Murray Hill in the center of Manhattan Island to await further reinforcements before proceeding. Mrs. Murray, a local citizen, treated him to cakes and wine as General Putnam pulled the remaining Americans out of New York City. Putnam and his men slipped past the British, escaping north to join Washington and the main body.

By September 16, Washington had consolidated approximately 10,000 men on Harlem Heights.[53] He arrayed his units in a crescent along the heights between the Hudson and Harlem rivers with open terrain and clear fields of fire to his front, waiting for the British to engage on terrain of his choosing. The Redcoats advanced to within three miles of the American position before stopping. Having learned his lesson on Long Island, Washington established a special reconnaissance unit comprised of trained riflemen under the command of 36-year-old Lt. Col. Thomas Knowlton.[54] A French and Indian War veteran and father of nine, Knowlton had distinguished himself at Bunker Hill. On Washington's orders, he organized a company of 150-200 men, known as "Knowlton's Rangers," to scout ahead of friendly lines and determine enemy intentions.

As the Rangers advanced, they precipitated a meeting engagement with the advanced guard of General Leslie's 5,000-man British force, which was gathering information on the Americans. A hot firefight from Highlanders, Hessians, and British light infantry ensued, and the Rangers began to withdraw. Hearing distant firing, Washington prepared elements of his main body for battle, sending his

51 *FONA*, https://founders.archives.gov/documents/Washington/03-06-02-0251, accessed Oct. 5, 2019.

52 *Orderly book and journals*, 195.

53 Henry Johnston, *The Battle of Harlem Heights, September 16, 1776* (New York, 1897); Stephenson, *PB*, 246; Savas & Dameron, *American Revolution Guidebook*, 65-66.

54 See Ashbel Woodward, *Memoir of Colonel Thomas Knowlton of Ashford Connecticut* (Boston, 1861).

aide, Joseph Reed, forward to investigate. Reed described the situation as he arrived: "Firing began at about 50 Yards Distance; as they were 10 to 1 against our Party we immediately retreated."[55] The Americans fell back in good order, gaining Washington time to organize a defense. The British became overconfident and treated the pursuit like a sport. According to Reed, "in the most insulting manner [they] sounded their Bugle Horns as is usual after a Fox Chase . . . it seemed to crown our disgrace"[56] Yet this was far from another American defeat.

Washington ordered a counterattack. He sent a 1,000-man brigade across open ground to fix the British in position, directing the Rangers and three companies of Virginia troops to maneuver through woods on the enemy's right flank to strike his rear. Confusion ensued as the Virginians attacked too soon, exposing themselves on the British flank rather than ending up behind them. Regardless, Knowlton's force achieved the desired effect, and the British began retreating from the battlefield in disarray. The Americans drove them back over a mile before Washington ordered an end to the pursuit lest his men stumble into the main enemy defensive lines. Colonel Knowlton was killed in the engagement, depriving the Americans of a promising leader. His 16-year-old son was with him, and comforted the colonel in his final moments. Knowlton's dying words are reputed to have been, "You see my son, I am mortally wounded; you can do me no good; go fight for your Country."[57]

The battle of Harlem Heights provided Washington with his first tactical victory while commanding the American army. Numbers vary, but the Continentals likely lost approximately 30 killed and 100 wounded, with the British losing twice as many.[58] More importantly, this small victory boosted American morale. Governor George Clinton of New York noted, "It has animated our Troops, gave them new Spirits, and erased every bad Impression, the Retreat from Long Island, &c. had left on their minds, they find they are able, with inferior Numbers, to drive their Enemy, and think of nothing now but Conquest."[59] Reed shared with his wife that "[t]he men have recovered their spirits and feel a confidence which before they had

---

55 *Reed Papers*, 4:59, New York Historical Society, quoted from Johnston, *The Battle of Harlem Heights*, 137.

56 Ibid., 135.

57 Woodward, *Memoir of Colonel Thomas Knowlton*, 15; "Lt. Col. Thomas Knowlton, Connecticut's Forgotten Hero," http://connecticutsar.org/lt-col-thomas-knowlton-connecticuts-forgotten-hero/, accessed Oct. 6, 2019.

58 *FONA*, https://founders.archives.gov/documents/Washington/03-06-02-0264, accessed Oct. 5, 2019; Ward, *TWOR*, 251; Stephenson, *PB*, 247.

59 "Governor George Clinton to the New York Convention, Kings Bridge, New York, September 18, 1776," quoted from Johnston, *The Battle of Harlem Heights*, 141-142.

quite lost."[60] This was a lesson Washington would not soon forget. He was learning that victory breeds victory, but he still had a long road to traverse before he could once more put this principle into practice.

The British defeat at Harlem Heights caused William Howe to pause. He and Washington consolidated and strengthened their positions, gathering intelligence so they could plan their next moves. Washington maintained strong positions at Harlem Heights, Fort Washington, and Fort Lee, hoping that Howe would attack them. Howe had no intention of attacking into strong, prepared defenses and once again contemplated ways to leverage his strengths over the Americans.

As both sides sought to gain an advantage, New York City went up in flames. Just after midnight on September 20, fires erupted at three different locations on the city's southern end, quickly spreading due to strong winds from the south. British troops assisted local Tories in extinguishing the fires, but several structures were consumed over the next twelve hours. The tragic event outraged the British. Captain Fredrick Mackenzie claimed, "[I]t is beyond a doubt that the town was designedly set on fire, either by some of those fellows who concealed themselves in it . . . or by some villains left behind for the purpose. Some of them were caught by the soldiers in the very act of setting fire to the inside of empty houses."[61] He further claimed that "many were detected with matches and combustibles under their clothes . . . one or two of them who were found in houses with fire brands in their hands were put to death by the enraged soldiery and thrown into the flames."[62] As directed, Washington did not order the burning of the city. He informed John Hancock, "I have not been Informed how the Accident happened."[63] He was, however, elated regardless of who may have set the fires. He informed his cousin Lund, "Providence, or some good honest fellow, has done more for us than we were disposed to do for ourselves."[64]

The fire was quickly followed by the capture of an American spy who was put to death. Twenty-one-year-old Lt. Nathan Hale was a member of Knowlton's Rangers, volunteering to gather intelligence behind enemy lines.[65] Hale traveled to Long Island under the guise of a Dutch schoolmaster and was taken prisoner with

60 Ibid., 135.

61 "Diary of Captain Fredrick Mackenzie," 1:58-61, as quoted in Commager & Morris, *SSS*, 472.

62 Ibid., 472-473.

63 *FONA*, https://founders.archives.gov/documents/Washington/03-06-02-0288, accessed Oct. 6, 2019.

64 *FONA*, https://founders.archives.gov/documents/Washington/03-06-02-0379, accessed Oct. 6, 2019.

65 Barry Bishop, *Nathan Hale: The Life of a Colonial Freedom Fighter* (Pittsburgh, 2013).

sketches of enemy positions hidden in his boot. He was brought before General Howe in New York as smoke continued to rise from its ruins. Hale confessed his name, rank, and mission, and Howe ordered him hung without a trial. Hale asked for a bible and clergyman to attend him but was refused on both counts. At 11:00 a.m. on September 22, Hale reportedly said, "I only regret that I have but one life to lose for my country," before being unceremoniously hanged.[66] A similar drama played out four years later when American militiamen captured Maj. John Andre, head of British intelligence, who had conspired with Benedict Arnold to give up the plans for West Point.[67] Washington ordered Andre hung in retribution for Howe's execution of Hale.

Washington continued to face challenges more critical than dealing with spies. His army was just over a year old and still learning. He was doing everything possible to instill discipline in, train, and preserve his troops. He was further challenged by a heavy reliance on militia forces with officers selected by the states and the limited authority granted to him by Congress to select, organize, and discipline the army as he saw fit. In a letter to his brother on September 23, Henry Knox noted, "The general [Washington] is as worthy a man as breathes, but he cannot do everything nor be everywhere. . . . He wants good assistants . . . the bulk of officers of the army are a parcel of ignorant, stupid, men, who might make tolerable soldiers, but [are] bad officers."[68]

Knox also understood the challenges associated with the lack of a professional army comprised of soldiers trained to standard and held accountable to published rules and regulations. He opined, "As the army now stands, it is only a receptacle for ragamuffins." Knox quickly became a member of Washington's inner circle of trusted lieutenants. They shared a vision for "academies, in which the whole theory of the art of war shall be taught, and every other encouragement possible given to draw persons into the army that may give a luster to our arms." Washington

66 The quote was reportedly conveyed by British Capt. John Montresor, who was present at Hale's hanging, to American Capt. William Hull under a flag of truce. Hull recounted the conversation with Montresor in his memoir: "On the morning of his execution my station was near the fatal spot, and I requested the Provost Marshal [William Cunningham] to permit the prisoner to sit in my marquee, while he was making the necessary preparations. Captain Hale entered: he was calm, and bore himself with gentle dignity, in the consciousness of rectitude and high intentions. He asked for writing materials, which I furnished him: he wrote two letters, one to his mother and one to a brother officer. He was shortly after summoned to the gallows. But a few persons were around him, yet his characteristic dying words were remembered. He said, 'I only regret, that I have but one life to lose for my country.'" Samuel Clarke, *Memoir of Gen. William Hull* (Boston, 1893), 4-5.

67 D. A. B. Ronald, *The Life of John Andre: The Redcoat Who Turned Benedict Arnold* (Philadelphia, 2019).

68 The next three quotes attributed to Knox are cited from *Francis Drake, Life and Correspondence of Henry Knox* (Cambridge, MA, 1873), 31-32.

employed leaders like Knox and Greene to advocate with their home states for improvements to the army, while repeatedly engaging Congress on the topic.

On September 25, Washington shared his frustrations with Congress. "We are now, as it were, upon the eve of another dissolution of our Army," he revealed, and "unless some speedy, and effectual measures are adopted by Congress, our cause will be lost."[69] His time in command and battle experiences with the ad hoc army of a few Continental regulars augmented with local militia had strengthened his resolve in calling for a professional, national armed force. He voiced grave concerns about relying on a militia: "To place dependence upon Militia is, assuredly, resting upon a broken staff. . . . Men accustomed to unbounded freedom, and no control, cannot broke the Restraint which is indispensably necessary to the good order and Government of an Army." He explained how the militiamen "take liberties, which the Soldier is punished for, This creates jealousy; jealousy begets dissatisfaction; and these by degrees ripen into Mutiny."

Manpower shortages and the army's professionalism only comprised part of Washington's troubles. As the fall temperatures dropped, supply shortages became more prevalent. Washington shared with Hancock, "this Army is in want of almost every necessary—Tents—Camp Kettles—Blankets & Cloaths of all kinds; But what is to be done with respect to the Two last Articles I know not, as the term of Inlistment will be nearly expired by the time they can be provided."[70] The navy and Marines would do their best to assist Washington by capturing enemy materials to supply the army. Later, the Marines were placed under Washington's command, reinforcing the army in its greatest time of need.

Washington addressed these challenges with Congress, providing recommendations, such as those with respect to pay and allowances needed for the professional military men to support their families received. Many states offered their militia, state armies, state navies, and marines higher pay than national forces. Washington complained, "Men find that their Townsmen and Companions are receiving 20, 30, and more dollars, for a few Months Service."[71] He also explained how the costs of enlistments were increasing with time, writing, "I shall therefore take the freedom of giving it as my opinion, that a good Bounty be immediately offered, aided by the proffer of at least 100, or 150 Acres of Land and a suit of Cloaths and Blanket, to each non-Comd. Officer and Soldier." He stressed the

---

69 The next three quotes from Washington are cited from *FONA*, https://founders.archives.gov/documents/Washington/03-06-02-0305, accessed Oct. 6, 2019.

70 *FONA*, https://founders.archives.gov/documents/Washington/03-06-02-0306, accessed Oct. 13, 2019.

71 The next four quotes from Washington were taken from *FONA*, https://founders.archives.gov/documents/Washington/03-06-02-0305, accessed Oct. 6, 2019.

importance of "giving your Officers good pay; this will induce Gentlemen, and Men of Character to engage." Washington reinforced the fact that "something is due to the Man who puts his life in his hand, hazards his health, and forsakes the Sweets of domestick enjoyments." It should be noted that Washington himself refused a salary throughout the eight-year war.

Major Nicholas and the Marines faced many of the same challenges as the army, chief among them being a high demand for their services. On the same day as the battle of Harlem Heights, the Pennsylvania Committee of Safety resolved to apply to "the [Continental] Board of War to employ the Marines now in this City [Philadelphia], as Guards over the Frigates, Prison, and Powder belonging to the Continent."[72] The Philadelphia Associators had previously served in this role and sought relief, and Congress complied. The Marines assumed these duties only to have Congress partially reverse the order a week later so Nicholas could detach two companies to Fort Montgomery on the highlands of the Hudson River above New York City to guard Washington's northern flank. Additionally, the Marines received orders to proceed to New York to join the frigates *Congress* (28 guns) and *Montgomery* (24 guns), which were under construction.[73] Congress later rescinded all of these orders to address a perceived threat to Philadelphia. The Marines' direct support of Washington would have to wait.

As the Marines prepared for action in Philadelphia, Benedict Arnold faced another danger in upstate New York. He was busy building a fleet to block any British advance south on Lake Champlain. By October, he assembled around 500 soldiers to fill the roles of sailors and Marines manning the schooners *Royal Savage* (12 guns), *Liberty* (6 guns), *Revenge* (6 guns), and the sloop *Enterprise* (12 guns). The Americans had also built three 80-foot row galleys (8 guns each) and eight 45-foot flat-bottomed gondolas (3 guns each).[74]

Sir Guy Carleton was determined to execute the plan of cutting off New England from the rest of the colonies. He would begin by attacking south through Lakes Champlain and George and joining forces with the British fleet on the Hudson River in the vicinity of Albany. Carleton assembled 13,000 troops to man the three-masted ship *Inflexible* (18 guns), the schooners *Maria* (14 guns) and *Carleton* (12 guns), 20 gunboats (1 gun each), 30 long boats, 400 bateaux, a 30-ton gondola, *Loyal Convert* (7 guns), and a huge flat-bottomed boat with two

---

72 "Minutes of the Pennsylvania Committee of Safety, Philadelphia, 16 September 1776," quoted from Morgan, ed., *NDAR*, 6:863.

73 *JCC*, 5:811, as quoted in Smith, *MIR*, 88.

74 Journal of Lieutenant James Hadden of the Royal Artillery, quoted from Commager & Morris, *SSS*, 223; Randall, *Benedict Arnold*, 300-301.

masts called the *Thunderer* (12 guns and 2 howitzers).[75] Both hodge-podge fleets were looking for a fight.

On October 11, Arnold positioned his fleet in a narrow body of water between the western shore of Lake Champlain and Valcour Island, midway down the lake toward Fort Ticonderoga. He knew his fleet was inferior and wanted to reduce Carleton's maneuverability by positioning his vessels in this confined area. Carleton's fleet initially sailed past Arnold's hidden force but spotted it while maneuvering around the island's southern end. Carleton quickly turned his fleet into the wind for battle.

The three-day battle of Valcour Island was vicious. Both sides took a pounding on the first day of the fight. Later that evening, Arnold quietly slipped past the British in a thick fog, heading south toward the safety of Fort Ticonderoga. The British, however, discovered the movement, and a running battle ensued over the following two days. By the time it was over, Arnold had lost 11 ships and sustained roughly 200 casualties.[76] After running his damaged flagship aground, he set it on fire before leading the remaining troops over land to Ticonderoga. Three of his remaining vessels escaped. The British lost three ships and suffered 40 casualties. Carleton reported to Lord Germain, "The Rebel Fleet upon Lake Champlain has been intirely defeated."[77] While it was a tactical defeat, Arnold achieved a strategic victory. By delaying Carleton's advance and damaging the enemy fleet, he was able to convince the British to return to Canada. This bought the Americans an additional year to prepare their forces for the next British invasion.[78]

Arnold's actions at Valcour Island made possible the victory at Saratoga the following year. Naval historian and theorist Alfred Thayer Mahan later wrote, "That the Americans were strong enough to impose the capitulation of Saratoga was due to the invaluable year of delay secured to them in 1776 by their little navy on Lake Champlain, created by the indomitable energy, and handled with the indomitable courage of the traitor, Benedict Arnold."[79] More importantly, Arnold also protected Washington's northern flank. The timing could not have been better.

After weeks of inactivity, the British struck again. On October 12, Howe left three brigades under Lord Percy to pin the Americans in place on the west side

---

75 Morgan, ed., *NDAR*, 6:1234-1235, 1244; Randall, *Benedict Arnold*, 296-297.

76 Morgan, ed., *NDAR*, 6:1235; Sol Stember, *The Bicentennial Guide to the American Revolution*, vol.1 (New York, 1974), 52; Dave Palmer, *George Washington and Benedict Arnold: A Tale of Two Patriots* (Washington D.C., 2006), 178-179.

77 Morgan, ed., *NDAR*, 6:1257.

78 Tonsetic, *Special Operations*, 42.

79 Ward, *TWOR*, 397.

Defeat on Lake Champlain, 13 October 1776. Painting by Col. Charles H. Waterhouse, USMCR. General Benedict Arnold assigned soldiers to fill the role of Marines in the three-day battle of Valcour Island. Although a tactical defeat, Arnold and his soldier-Marines achieved a strategic victory, causing the British invaders to return to Canada and buying the Americans another year to prepare for the northern fighting. *Art Collection, National Museum of the Marine Corps, Triangle, Virginia*

of Manhattan, while 80 vessels carried a 4,000-man force up the East River to land at Throg's Neck in Washington's rear.[80] Howe intended to sever the American supply line to Connecticut and strike their flank. But the British failed to conduct a proper reconnaissance, and found the area to be separated from the mainland by a creek and marshy area. Colonel Hand and his Pennsylvania riflemen chose to leverage this restrictive terrain to their advantage. Hand and approximately 30 of his troops moved forward, establishing a blocking position behind a wood pile that effectively stopped the British advance long enough for reinforcements to arrive. Determining that the terrain provided no opportunity to maneuver, the British abandoned the position, re-embarked their ships, and conducted a follow-on amphibious landing three miles east on the Manhattan mainland at Pell's Point on East Chester Bay.

On October 18, British and Hessian troops moved inland from the landing beach at Pell's Point. They were met by 750 Massachusetts men organized into four regiments under the command of the indomitable Col. John Glover.[81] Glover's

80 Morgan, ed., *NDAR*, 6:1245-1246; Lengel, *General George Washington*, 160.

81 Commager & Morris, *SSS*, 486-487.

regiments were stationed at staggered intervals behind stone walls that bordered the Split Rock Road. These walls provided cover and concealment from which to ambush the British as they advanced. One regiment after another rose from behind the rocks to fire a volley, withdrawing afterward to join troops at the next interval. Glover and his troops repeated this pattern as a delaying action to buy Washington and the army's main body time to leave Manhattan Island and move north to the vicinity of the village of White Plains.

As this drama played out in New York, there were growing concerns in Pennsylvania. The Continental Congress and Pennsylvania Committee of Safety feared that General Howe would send invasion forces to Pennsylvania. They commenced joint planning for its defense and, on October 16, submitted recommendations to the Continental Board of War. The board recommended, among other measures, that two Virginia battalions, the German battalion, and Nicholas's four companies of Marines be "continued in this State, or at Trenton or Billingsport in New Jersey, as Necessary defense of this city, not only against the British Troops, but the growing party of disaffected persons, which unhappily exists at this time." These men would be used "also for the protection of the vast quantity of Stores belonging to Congress that are now in the public Magazines; and at the same time carry on such Works of defense as have been or may by thought necessary."[82]

These recommendations would keep the Marines in Pennsylvania for the time being, instead of deploying them north to assist Washington. The Marines unknowingly assisted the army in another important way. General Howe agreed to parole General Sullivan and Lord Stirling, captured at the battle of Long Island, as part of a prisoner exchange with Congress. Governor Browne, whom the Marines had captured on New Providence, became a key part of this negotiation. On October 10, Col. George Weedon of the Continental Army wrote to a friend from Harlem Heights, "Lord Stirling was yesterday Exchanged for Govr Brown of [New] providence."[83] The Marines had inadvertently assisted Washington by returning senior leaders just in time for the next major battle.

During the lull at White Plains, Washington again reorganized the army, this time into seven divisions after Sullivan's and Lord Stirling's release and General Lee's return following his victory in South Carolina. He assigned command of the divisions to Generals Greene, Lee, Heath, Sullivan, Putnam, Spencer, and

---

82 *Minutes of the Provincial Council of Pennsylvania*, vol. 10, (Harrisburg, PA, 1852), 757, found at https://babel.hathitrust.org/cgi/pt?id=mdp.39015039495919&view=1up&seq=763, accessed Oct. 13, 2019; Smith, *MIR*, 89.

83 *Weedon Papers*, quoted from Morgan, ed., *NDAR*, 6:1199.

Lincoln.[84] Washington then gave Greene 3,500 troops to defend the newly renamed Fort Lee on the New Jersey side, as Col. Robert Magaw, with 1,500 men, received orders to defend Fort Washington. He consolidated the remaining divisions with 13,000-14,000 men around White Plains under his command to face the main body of the British.[85]

Howe continued his cautious tendencies, holding his army at New Rochelle for three days following Harlem Heights. He then moved three miles to Mamaroneck, where he sat for four more days. The British had only advanced 17 miles in 10 days, diminishing the benefit gained from the maneuvering of their fleet. But Howe was getting stronger, as roughly 4,000 additional Hessians and 3,400 British troops arrived in New York on the day the British landed on Pell's Point. Howe used these forces to relieve the main body around New Rochelle, advancing toward White Plains with 14,000 soldiers.[86]

Washington was waiting for them from his defensive positions among the hills overlooking White Plains. He posted Putnam's division to the right on Purdy Hill, with Heath's division on Hatfield Hill to the left. He personally commanded the main body in the center at White Plains Village. The Americans erected two defensive lines between the Bronx River and a mill pond to protect their flanks. Early on October 28, Washington led his generals on a reconnaissance of the surrounding area after his staff informed him that the British were again on the move. They rode back to headquarters, where Colonel Reed confirmed that all guards had been pulled in and the army was ready for battle. Washington turned to his generals and stated, "Gentlemen, you will repair to your respective posts, and do the best you can."[87]

Washington deployed 1,500 Connecticut troops from Lee's division to slow the British advance. Another brigade of men from Delaware, New York, and Maryland with militia and two field pieces reinforced Chatterton Hill about a half mile beyond the Americans' right flank. The lead brigade positioned itself behind a stone wall a mile and a half in front of the main lines, holding their fire until the enemy was within 100 yards. Benjamin Tallmadge described how, "At the dawn of day, the Hessian column advanced within musket shot of our troops, when a full discharge of musketry warned them of their danger. At first they fell back,

84 Leckie, *George Washington's War*, 283; Chernow, *Washington: A Life*, 258; Lengel, *General George Washington*, 161; McCollough, 1776, 230-231; Commager & Morris, *SSS*, 484.

85 Leckie, *George Washington's War*, 284; Ward, *TWOR*, 256.

86 Stephenson, *PB*, 247-248; O'Donnell, Washington's Immortals, 89.

87 "Major General Heath's account," Heath, Memoirs, 68-71, quoted from Commager & Morris, *SSS*, 489.

but rallied again immediately, and the column of British troops having advanced upon our left, made it necessary to retire."[88] The Americans pulled back in good order, conducting a fighting withdrawal back across the Bronx River toward Chatterton Hill.

Howe arrived on the battlefield and conferred with his generals before detaching eight regiments of 4,000 men with 12 cannons across the Bronx River to attack the Continentals on Chatterton Hill. The main body then positioned itself forward of the Americans' center as the British artillery opened fire on Chatterton Hill. Colonel Haslett of Delaware wrote, "The cannonade from twelve to fifteen pieces, well served, kept up a continual peal of reiterated thunder."[89]

General Leslie and his troops were the first to attack, quickly followed by Hessians under 50-year-old Col. Johann Gottlieb Rall and 36-year-old Col. Carl Emilius von Donop. Rall was an outspoken veteran with 36 years of military service, and he did not tolerate those he perceived as fools, regardless of their rank.[90] He had a reputation for being a fighter who was liked by his men. He commanded the *Landgrenadier*, from the old Hessian *Landmiliz*, or militia. Von Donop came from the upper class and served as the personal adjutant to the Landgrave of Hesse-Cassel, gaining command of the coveted Jaeger Corps.[91] Von Donop, known for being brutal and cruel, was not liked by his men. Both officers would later play key roles in the battle of Trenton.

The combined British and Hessian pressure, reinforced by British cavalry, broke the Americans. Haslett reported, "The militia regiment behind the fence fled in confusion, without more than a random, scattering fire."[92] The American regulars attempted to hold, but they too fell back toward the main lines after the militia left their flank open to attack. The retreat from Chatterton Hill left Washington's central defensive positions untenable, forcing him to move his troops to a second defensive line along the high ground at North Castle.

The battle of White Plains was a relatively minor event. Reports vary, but most agree that both sides suffered approximately 150-200 casualties.[93] Again, Howe was slow to press his advantage, allowing Washington to preserve his army. The British occupied the abandoned American positions, and for several days "the two

---

88 Johnston, *Memoir of Colonel Benjamin Tallmadge*, 17.

89 Commager & Morris, *SSS*, 490.

90 For more about Rall, see Bruce Burgoyne, *The Trenton Commanders: Johann Gottlieb Rall and George Washington, as Noted in Hessian Diaries* (Westminster, MD, 1997).

91 For more on von Donop see Fischer, *Washington's Crossing*, 55-57.

92 Commager & Morris, *SSS*, 490.

93 Ward, *TWOR*, 266; Ferling, *AAM*, 247; Leckie, *George Washington's War*, 287.

armies lay looking at each other and within long cannon shot."[94] They engaged in short artillery duels, and the Americans prepared for the next attack, which never came. As the British withdrew on November 4, the Americans were bewildered. Washington wrote to Congress, "The design of this maneuver is a matter of much conjecture and speculation, and cannot be accounted for with any degree of certainty."[95] Later he added, "I expect the Enemy will bend their force against Fort Washington and invest It immediately. From some advices it is an Object that will attract their earliest attention."[96] Unsure of Howe's intent, Washington ensured that Greene had an adequate force to defend Fort Lee, maintained the force at Fort Washington, and deployed another 3,000 men under Gen. Lee to defend the Peekskill and the passes of the Highlands further north.

As Washington redistributed his forces, the Marines celebrated the first year of their existence in Philadelphia. Major Nicholas and his Marines began to meld into a cohesive and well-trained unit. While the frigates were still under construction, Nicholas housed the Marines in barracks on Second Street on Philadelphia's north side. He also sought medical treatment for those who had become sick during the changing seasons. On November 4, Congress directed Dr. Benjamin Rush, a signer of the Declaration of Independence, "to take them [the Marines] under his care and see them properly provided for."[97] Thirty-year-old Rush saw to the Marines' medical needs, and later provided valuable service by caring for casualties during the battle of Trenton and acting as surgeon general of the Middle Department of the Army.[98]

Nicholas needed his men to be healthy, as Congress had heard reports of a large enemy fleet heading south toward Philadelphia. The Marine Committee received orders to "make such disposition of the naval force, now in the river Delaware, or the neighborhood thereof, as will best conduce to defeat the designs of the enemy."[99] Captain Samuel Shaw and his Marines departed their barracks on Second Street, joining the frigate *Randolph* (32 guns) to prepare for action at sea. The reputed enemy fleet, however, was later identified as a group of merchant ships sailing for England. The *Randolph* was the closest of the four Philadelphia frigates

---

94 Scheer & Rankin, *RR*, 196.

95 *FONA*, https://founders.archives.gov/documents/Washington/03-07-02-0067, accessed Oct. 13, 2019.

96 Ibid.

97 Library of Congress, *JCC*, 6:921.

98 For more on Rush see Harlow Unger, *Dr. Benjamin Rush: The Founding Father Who Healed a Wounded Nation* (New York, 2018).

99 Library of Congress, *JCC*, 6:951; Smith, *MIR*, 89.

nearing completion. Preparations to sail continued as Washington shifted his flag to the New Jersey side of the Hudson River.

Washington had second thoughts about continuing to defend Fort Washington after the battle of White Plains. He wrote to Greene, "If we cannot prevent Vessells passing up [the Hudson River], and the Enemy are possessed of the surrounding Country, what valuable purpose can it answer to attempt to hold a post from which the expected Benefit cannot be had—I am therefore inclined to think it will not be prudent to hazard the Men & Stores at Mount Washington."[100] Still, Washington placed great trust in Greene and added, "but as you are on the Spot, [I] leave it to you to give such Orders as to evacuating Mount Washington as you judge best."[101] Although Greene agreed with Washington's concern about the freedom the British held on the river, he still believed Fort Washington should be defended. He informed Washington, "Upon the whole I cannot help thinking the Garrison is of advantage—and I cannot conceive the Garrison to be in any great danger."[102] He added that Colonel Magaw "thinks it will take them [the British] till December expires, before they can carry it."[103]

Unbeknownst to Washington and Greene, they had been betrayed by one of their own. Ensign William Demont of the 5th Pennsylvania had deserted and turned over plans of Fort Washington to the enemy. A British officer reported, "A man named Diamond [Demont] . . . says the Rebels remaining on this island [Manhattan] amount to about 2000 men, who, if they are obliged to abandon their advanced works, are to retire into Fort Washington and defend it to the last extremity."[104] Demont himself later admitted, "I sacrificed all I was worth in the world to the service of my King and country . . . brought in with me the plans for Fort Washington, by which plans the fort was taken."[105]

Now in possession of the fort's plans, Howe moved to reduce the last American stronghold in his rear. He consolidated his main body with that of Lord Percy, whom he had left in Manhattan, increasing his army to 20,000 men, and set out for Fort Washington. General Washington's hesitancy in abandoning the fort proved to be a fateful mistake.

100 *FONA*, https://founders.archives.gov/documents/Washington/03-07-02-0078, accessed Oct. 13, 2019.

101 Ibid.

102 *FONA*, https://founders.archives.gov/documents/Washington/03-07-02-0085, accessed Aug. 16, 2019.

103 Ibid.

104 Commager & Morris, *SSS*, 491.

105 Ibid., 492.

Fort Washington was an earthwork covering around four acres surrounded by wooden abatis. It had no casemates, shelters, barracks, or buildings besides a wooden magazine, making it ill-suited for defense against a siege. The fort had no internal water source, requiring soldiers to traverse 230 feet down a rocky height to gather water from the Hudson River. Thirty-eight-year-old Col. Robert Magaw, who had been a lawyer in Carlisle, Pennsylvania, before the war, commander the garrison. Magaw claimed he could hold Fort Washington till the end of December, and he and Greene believed they could withdraw its garrison and stores to the Jersey shore "if matters grow desperate."[106]

The situation indeed grew desperate for those defending Fort Washington. On November 15, a British officer approached under a white flag, demanding the fort's surrender. Magaw refused, determinedly responding, "[G]ive me leave to assure his excellency that actuated by the most glorious cause that mankind ever fought in, I am determined to defend this post to the very last extremity."[107] Although bold, there was little the Americans could do. Washington was aboard a boat with Greene, Putnam, and Mercer to personally assess the situation at the fort when British cannons in New York and from HMS *Pearl* (32 guns) on the Hudson opened fire. Frustrated, he and the others returned to New Jersey as the British attacked Fort Washington from three sides.

Roughly 8,000 British and Hessian troops advanced as cannons blasted the fort. Lord Percy attacked from the south. General Edward Mathew with the light infantry and Guards attacked from the east, while Hessians led the main attack from the north. Hessian troops quickly drove the Americans from their outer defenses. Hessian Colonel Rall demanded for a second time that the Americans surrender. Magaw asked for time to consider his options but was refused. He surrendered his sword, resulting in one of the worst American defeats of the Revolutionary War. The Hessian Rall and Lossberg Regiments formed two lines; the Americans marched between them, laid down their weapons, and surrendered their unit colors.

The victorious British and Hessians suffered casualties of approximately 450 killed and wounded at Fort Washington.[108] American losses were 150-275 killed and wounded, but they lost an additional 230 officers and 2,600-2,800 soldiers

---

106 *FONA*, https://founders.archives.gov/documents/Washington/03-07-02-0085, accessed Aug. 16, 2019. Abatis were sharpened stakes pointing outward at attacking troops.

107 *FONA*, https://founders.archives.gov/documents/Washington/03-07-02-0117, accessed Oct. 13, 2019.

108 Ward, *TWOR*, 274; Leckie, *George Washington's War*, 292; Commager & Morris, *SSS*, 491.

captured.[109] The Americans also lost 146 iron and brass cannons, 12,000 shot and shell, 2,800 muskets, 400,000 musket cartridges, tents, entrenching tools, and additional supplies and provisions.[110]

This devastating loss ended the New York campaign while simultaneously blemishing many senior Americans' reputations. Greene knew he had let Washington down. On November 17, he wrote to his friend Henry Knox, "I feel mad, vexed, sick, and sorry. Never did I need the consoling voice of a friend more than now."[111] Greene would maintain Washington's trust, redeeming himself later at Trenton and Princeton, as Quartermaster of the Army, and during the Southern campaign of 1780-83.

More importantly, Washington's subordinates were beginning to question his abilities. Joseph Reed doubted the general's decisiveness. He began to correspond with Charles Lee behind Washington's back, questioning the commander-in-chief's fitness for command. Lee agreed and wrote to Washington, "Oh, General, why would you be overpersuaded by men of inferior judgment to your own? It was a cursed affair."[112] All was not well in the American camp, and the pending New Jersey campaign would further exacerbate their problems.

Though the campaign fought in New York between August and November 1776 was a low point for Washington and the Continental Army, it was a formative and important period of growth for the nascent army and its commander. Although Washington experienced several defeats, what emerged was a hardened core of combat veterans with an undefeatable determination to persevere and ultimately win their freedom. Washington learned to employ the valuable lessons obtained in New York in future battles like Trenton, Princeton, and others throughout the war's remainder.

Perhaps the most important lesson Washington learned in New York was a deeper appreciation and understanding of his army. It was not like European armies, but a unique army forged in the American wilderness fighting the French and Native Americans for survival. American soldiers were raised with a strong independent streak and sense of pride that had to be shaped and molded to persevere during the toughest times. Washington admitted it was unwise "[t]o lead our young troops into open ground against their superiors, both in number and discipline."[113] He had to learn how to lead, combining the efforts of professional

---

109 Ward, *TWOR*, 274; Chernow, *Washington: A Life*, 262; Leckie, *George Washington's War*, 292.

110 Ward, *TWOR*, 274; Leckie, *George Washington's War*, 292; Commager & Morris, *SSS*, 491.

111 Drake, *Life and correspondence of Henry Knox*, 34.

112 Scheer & Rankin, *RR*, 201.

113 Fischer, *WC*, 101.

regular soldiers and Marines, serving beside masses of a local militia that joined the army for short durations.

The battles of New York also assisted Washington in identifying leaders he could rely on to succeed in battle. The New York campaign weeded out many politically appointed and popularly elected officers, allowing the most competent to rise to leadership positions. Well-led Americans could fight, and fight well. The names Haslet, Hand, Glover, Knox, and Greene would come up repeatedly throughout the remainder of the war as the true heroes who won America's freedom. Washington figured out how to leverage the unique talents of these men to gain the greatest benefit on the battlefield.

New York also helped validate earlier tactical lessons Washington had absorbed as a member of the Virginia militia, providing a broader perspective of the applications at an operational and strategical level. He learned the importance of operational security for his forces while gaining key information about his adversaries. Washington saw how deception could be employed to preserve his army. He learned the critical importance of gaining and maintaining the initiative, fighting when conditions were to his advantage. He learned how best to create the conditions for success and not allow the enemy to dictate the terms of battle. Washington employed an economy of force efforts, which allowed for the massing of troops at critical junctures to achieve a decisive victory. He learned that speed, surprise, and tempo were force multipliers on the battlefield and gained an appreciation for using the waterways while denying them to his enemies.

George Washington contemplated these lessons and others as he prepared for what was to come next. Howe did not make him wait long.

Chapter Six

The Pursuit Across New Jersey

*"As we go forward into the country the Rebels fly before us & when we come back,
they always follow us, 'tis almost impossible to catch them. They will neither fight,
nor totally run away, but Keep at such a distance that we are always above
a days march from them. We seem to be playing at Bo peep."*

— Captain William Bamford, British Officer[1]

Having driven George Washington's army from New York, the Howe brothers were contemplating their next move. In retrospect, immediately focusing on destroying the remnants of Washington's troops was the best chance to end the rebellion. The brothers believed, however, that this was a foregone conclusion, and chose not to take any undue risks. General Clinton recommended an aggressive offensive against Philadelphia to capture the rebel capital and arrest the Continental Congress, but the Howes opted to pacify the newly declared states that still bred strong bands of patriots.

The British also had to consider their logistical situation practically. After months of hard campaigning, the fleet and army needed rest and refitting. Additionally, the navy required an ice-free port to conduct repairs and sustain operations during the upcoming winter months, and New York harbor had a reputation for freezing over. General Howe needed to find housing and food for his soldiers, and the army was desperately seeking supplies. A partially destroyed city already ravaged by fire and two armies offered little to meet the general's needs.

The strategy the Howe brothers agreed upon would address their concerns.[2] Admiral Howe devised a naval campaign, consisting of 6,000 troops under General Clinton, to capture Newport, Rhode Island. Not only would he gain a

1 William Bamford, "Bamford's Diary," *Maryland History Magazine*, vol. 28 (Baltimore, 1933), 18.

2 For a comprehensive overview of the Howes' strategy for the Revolution see, David Smith, *Whispers Across the Atlantick: General William Howe and the American Revolution* (Oxford, UK, 2017) and McCollough, *1776*, 252; Ward, *TWOR*, 281; Ferling, *AAM*, 148.

port, which the navy could use for repairs, but the rich countryside would provide the necessary provisions to survive the upcoming winter. This move also had the advantage of pacifying another state.

General Howe would reduce his logistical burden by remaining in New York with a portion of his army. He wanted to keep a close watch on Washington, who he believed was still north of New York City, while sending another body of troops further north up the Hudson River. He planned for this group to combine forces with Carleton's army attacking south from Canada in a second attempt to isolate the New England states.

General Cornwallis would lead a third force into New Jersey, occupying the eastern part of that state. The Jersey countryside was untouched by the war and could provide ample supplies and provisions for the army. These actions would allow the British to expand their influence, sustain their forces, and hold a position of strength to initiate a spring offensive in 1777 to end the rebellion, or so they thought.

The Americans were far from defeated, although their position was still precarious. The Southern Department still controlled those states, but not many troops were stationed in that sector. The Northern Department had successfully blocked Carleton's invasion from Canada. But they also had very few troops, and without a substantial fleet, they expected the British to attack again in the spring. The Continental fleet and Marines were still too small to significantly contribute on the open seas. The remnants of Hopkins's force were operating around Rhode Island as others formed new crews and Marine detachments to man the 13 frigates being constructed in America's major cities. General Lee remained north of New York City with roughly 5,000 tired troops, and Brig. Gen. William Heath led four brigades around Peekskill, New York. Washington intended to transfer his main force of 4,000-5,000 across the Hudson River into New Jersey to join General Greene and his men at Fort Lee.[3]

Washington had started the New York campaign with 19,000 troops, but his force was quickly depleted by loss, desertion, and expired enlistments. He expected to lose another 2,000 soldiers on December 1 as their enlistments were ending, and the following month would bring another round.[4] The Americans also lacked adequate provisions following a hard campaign. One British officer commented, "many were without shoes or stockings and several were observed to

---

3 Ward, *TWOR*, 275.

4 Force, ed., *AA*, 5th Series, 3:822; Lengel, *General George Washington*, 169; Ward, *TWOR*, 276.

have only linen drawers on, with a rifle or hunting shirt without any proper shirt or waistcoat. They are also in great want of blankets."[5]

Washington struggled with many challenges as he attempted to determine the British's next move. He had energized his intelligence apparatus with good results. He began to receive indications and warnings that the British were planning to cross into New Jersey; they were gathering boats to cross the Hudson River while ordering their troops to prepare five days of provisions to support a rapid movement. As early as November 8, Washington wrote to General Greene, "The best Accounts obtained from the Enemy assure us of a considerable movement among their Boats last evening, and so far as can be collected from the various sources of Intelligence they must design a Penetration into Jersey, & fall down upon your Post—You will therefore immediately have all the Stores &c. removed, which you do not deem necessary for your defence."[6] Washington immediately began moving his portion of the army across the river on November 9 and established his headquarters at Hackensack, New Jersey, leaving Greene in command at Fort Lee.

Washington had hoped to maintain a strong position at Fort Lee following the fall of Fort Washington on November 16, but he began to reconsider this decision. He believed it might be necessary to withdraw deeper into New Jersey, taking steps to protect the rear of his army. On November 17, Washington moved Lord Stirling with a brigade of approximately 1,200 men 40 miles south to Brunswick, New Jersey, to guard against a possible British amphibious landing and flanking attack. On November 19, he informed John Hancock, "As Fort Lee was always considered as only necessary in conjunction with that on the East side of the River [Fort Washington], to preserve the communication across, & to prevent the Enemy from a free Navigation, It has become of no importan[ce] by the loss of the Other."[7] Washington intended to abandon the fort and consolidate his and Greene's troops, but he was one day too late in reaching this decision. Howe had already decided to invade New Jersey and take the fort. He shared with Lord Germain that the capture of Fort Lee provided the British "the entire command of the North River and a ready road to penetrate into Jersey."[8]

5 Mackenzie, *Diary of Frederick Mackenzie*, 1:97-98, quoted from Ward, *TWOR*, 275; Lee Anderson, *Forgotten Patriot: The Life and Times of Major-General Nathanael Greene* (Irvine, CA, 2002), 76.

6 *FONA*, https://founders.archives.gov/documents/Washington/03-07-02-0078, accessed Oct. 19, 2019.

7 *FONA*, https://founders.archives.gov/documents/Washington/03-07-02-0128, accessed Oct. 19, 2019.

8 Ibid.

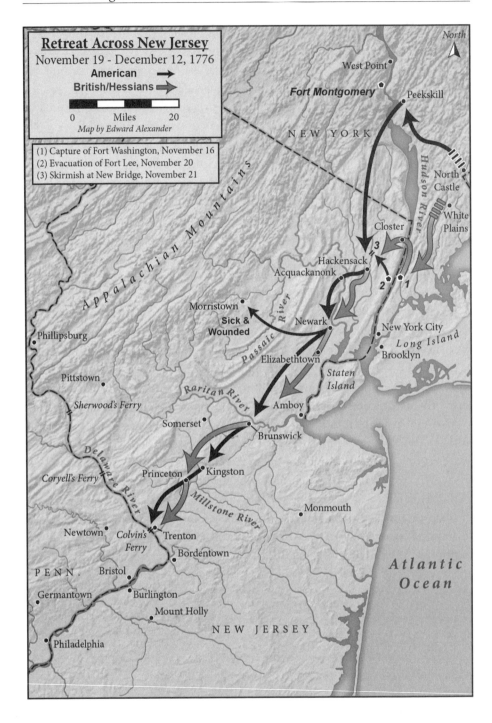

Retreat Across New Jersey
November 19 - December 12, 1776
American ➡
British/Hessians ➡

0   Miles   20
Map by Edward Alexander

(1) Capture of Fort Washington, November 16
(2) Evacuation of Fort Lee, November 20
(3) Skirmish at New Bridge, November 21

On the cold, rainy night of November 19, Cornwallis landed a force of 4,000-6,000 men at Closter, New Jersey, five miles north of Fort Lee.[9] British and Hessian soldiers scaled a 300-foot narrow slope as sailors of the Royal Navy winched heavy cannons up to the top of the cliff. Cornwallis intended to move his troops swiftly south, cutting off Greene's retreat toward Washington at Hackensack with the assistance of local loyalist guides. He further intended to trap Washington between the Passaic and Hackensack rivers to complete the destruction of Washington's army. American security patrols were fortunate to identify Cornwallis's advance and sound the alarm.

Greene jumped into action, but the evacuation of Fort Lee was a disorderly affair, as word of the British advance sent its defenders into a frenzy. Greene began removing arms and provisions per Washington's orders, but he was not fast enough. The only materials transferred out of the fort before the British attacked were gunpowder and the largest cannons. Unit leaders stirred their men from their morning routines, giving orders to withdraw toward Hackensack and join Washington rapidly. Greene led most of his force to New Bridge, a crossing site of the Hackensack River, seven miles northwest of Fort Lee. His troops continued another four miles to join Washington at Hackensack as Greene returned to the fort to gather stragglers.

Greene was unhappy with the chaotic retreat as his troops, "mostly of the Flying Camp" and who he referred to as "irregular and undisciplined," had performed poorly.[10] Congress established the "Flying Camp" in the summer of 1776 as a reserve force to the Continental regulars fighting in New York. Congress intended to raise 10,000 men from Pennsylvania, New Jersey, Delaware, and Maryland under the command of Brig. Gen. Hugh Mercer, but the force never reached more than 3,000. Mercer, a 50-year-old French and Indian War veteran, hailed from Fredericksburg, Virginia, and commanded what became the 3rd Virginia Regiment before receiving a promotion to brigadier general in the regular army.[11] He was ordered to lead the construction of Fort Lee prior to assuming command of the Flying Camp. Mercer was destined to play a vital role in the upcoming battles at Trenton and Princeton, but not before assisting Greene in driving the stragglers from his unit to Hackensack.

9 Commager & Morris, *SSS*, 495-496; Chernow, *Washington: A Life*, 262; Scheer & Rankin, *RR*, 202.

10 William Dwyer, *The Day is Ours! An inside View of the Battles of Trenton and Princeton, November 1776-January 1777* (New Brunswick, NJ, 1998), 19, hereafter cited as *TDIO*.

11 For more on General Mercer's contributions to the Revolutionary War, see Frederick English, *General Hugh Mercer: Forgotten Hero of the American Revolution* (Princeton, NJ, 1995).

Cornwallis's men arrived at Fort Lee mid-day, just as the final Americans withdrew. One British observer recalled, "On the appearance of our troops, the rebels fled like scared rabbits . . . not a rascal of them could be seen."[12] The Americans abandoned the fort so quickly that "the pots were left absolutely boiling on the fire, and the tables spread for dinner for some of their officers."[13] The British also discovered "forty or fifty pieces of cannon found loaded, with two large iron sea mortars and one brass one, with a vast quantity of ammunition, provision and stores with all their tents standing." The Americans left other provisions behind. According to one British officer, "the number of cattle taken in the Hackensack meadows, which had [been] driven from Pennsylvania and some parts of the Jerseys for the use of the grand Rebel army, is truly astonishing, and amount to many thousands."

Thirty-two-year-old Hessian Capt. Johann Ewald led his aggressive Jaegers in pursuit of the fleeing Americans.[14] He observed their rear guard withdrawing in the distance and asked Cornwallis for permission to attack. Cornwallis held him back, stating, "Let them go, my dear Ewald, and stay here. We do not want to lose any men. One Jaeger is worth more than ten rebels." Ewald, a soldier since the age of 16, had fought for the Prussians against the French in the Seven Years' War, was wounded, and was cited for bravery in battle. He was dumbfounded by Cornwallis's order but began to understand that Howe had instructed Cornwallis to maintain pressure on Washington without becoming decisively engaged. Ewald wrote, "Now I perceived what was afoot. . . . We wanted to spare the King's subjects and hoped to terminate the war amicably, in which assumption I was strengthened the next day by several English officers." This hesitancy in taking casualties helped preserve a good portion of Washington's army. On arriving at Fort Lee, Cornwallis's men "found but twelve men, who were all dead drunk."[15]

The caution exhibited by Cornwallis helped Washington more than he would know, as the Americans had lost over 4,000 soldiers in the last 12 weeks. Washington gathered 3,000-5,000 men at Hackensack, but they lacked tents, blankets, stockings, shoes, and more. Most of the local population were Tory loyalists, who would not support Washington.[16] Desertions became rampant, and

---

12 Frank Moore, *Diary of the American Revolution: From Newspapers and Original Documents*, vol. 1. (New York, 1859), 350.

13 The following three quotes are from Commager & Morris, *SSS*, 496-497.

14 The following three quotes were taken from Johann Ewald, *Diary of the American War: A Hessian Journal*, Joseph P. Tustin, ed. (New Haven, CT, 1979).

15 *Hasting Manuscripts*, 190-192, quoted from Commager & Morris, *SSS*, 496.

16 Scheer & Rankin, *RR*, 203; O'Donnell, *Washington's Immortals*, 101; Chernow, *Washington: A Life*, 264.

he saw retreat and survival as his only alternative. As he prepared to retreat south, Washington directed Generals Gates, Lee, and Heath to withdraw from New York, consolidating their forces with his in New Jersey. On November 21, he wrote to Lee, "the Enemy are evidently changing the Seat of War to this Side of the North River—that this Country therefore will expect the Continental Army to give what Support they can & failing in this will cease to depend upon or support a Force from which no Protection is given to them."[17] He added, "Unless therefore some new Event should occur, or some more cogent Reason present itself I would have you move over by the easiest & best Passage."[18] Unfortunately, a fracture was forming in the Americans' senior ranks, which contributed to a delay by some in responding to Washington's orders.

The Americans' defeats in New York and the recent loss of Fort Lee in New Jersey fueled doubt about Washington's leadership abilities. As he called for his generals to join him in New Jersey, his adjutant general, Col. Joseph Reed, wrote to praise General Lee's abilities while questioning Washington's competence. He stated, "I have some additional reasons for most earnestly wishing to have you [Lee] where the principal scene of action is laid. . . . You have decision, a quality often wanting in minds otherwise valuable . . . we are in a very awful and alarming state . . . I think yourself and some others should go to Congress and form the plan of a new army."[19] Reed's encouragement fed Lee's already overinflated sense of self-worth. Lee responded, "I received your most obliging, flattering letter— lament with you that fatal indecision of mind which in war is a much greater disqualification than stupidity or even want of personal courage . . . I really think our Chief will do better with me than without me."[20] Lee believed he was more capable than Washington and wanted to take his place as commander-in-chief. So, instead of rushing to Washington's aid as ordered, he began making plans of his own while remaining in New York.

The British did not wait for the Americans to work out their differences. On November 21, Cornwallis's light infantry and Jaegers advanced to New Bridge to attack the rebels near Hackensack. Washington reported to Hancock, "Our present situation between [the] Heckensec & Posaic Rivers being exactly similar to our late one, and our force here by no means adequate to an opposition that will promise the smallest probability of Success, we are taking measures to retire over the Waters

17 *FONA*, https://founders.archives.gov/documents/Washington/03-07-02-0137, accessed Oct. 20, 2019.

18 Ibid.

19 Commager & Morris, *SSS*, 497-498.

20 Ibid., 498-499.

of the latter, when the best disposition will be formed that circumstances will admit of."[21] Washington used three regiments to establish a rear guard, slowing the enemy advance across the bridge as he withdrew with the remainder of the army. The American rear guard conducted a stiff resistance that bought the army crucial time to escape farther west. These actions established a pattern of hold-delay-withdraw that Washington chose to employ throughout his retreat across New Jersey. Howe's cautious tendencies enabled this strategy, one the Americans would often exploit.

On Howe's orders, Cornwallis paused across the river from Hackensack to join reinforcements before continuing his pursuit. Washington halted his men at Aquackanonk Landing on the west side of the Passaic. Howe sent Cornwallis three additional brigades and the 16th Light Dragoons to bolster his troops to 10,000 soldiers while Washington's strength continued to dwindle.[22] Washington faced the additional challenge of indefensible flat terrain possessing many fordable rivers that offered few choices on which to anchor a strong defensive position. The Americans took advantage of the temporary lull to destroy the bridge spanning the 400-foot Passaic River. This did little to slow the Hessians a mile upriver, as they easily forded the frigid waist-deep waters, using their artillery for cover.

On November 23, Washington led his army 10 miles south to Newark, but Cornwallis broke off his pursuit to allow his men to forage. Although British army regulations permitted soldiers to forage for food and provisions, the Redcoats and Hessians expanded their foraging efforts to include open pillaging. An April 1777 report from Congress on the conduct of enemy troops marching across New York and New Jersey found "[t]he whole track of the British army is marked with desolation and a wanton destruction of property."[23] In a similar hearing conducted by the House of Commons in 1779, one officer admitted that "[t]he commander in chief [Howe] gave orders against it repeatedly. A number of officers who lately came into the country, and entertained a notion that Americans were enemies, perhaps did not take enough care to prevent soldiers from gratifying themselves at the expense of the people, so that plundering was very frequent."[24] When asked, "What effect had this on the minds of the people?" the officer responded, "Naturally it would lose you friends and gain you enemies."

---

21 *FONA*, https://founders.archives.gov/documents/Washington/03-07-02-0128, accessed Oct. 19, 2019.

22 McCollough, *1776*, 253; Ward, *TWOR*, 285.

23 Moore, *Diary of the American Revolution*, 419.

24 The following three quotes are from Adams, "Contemporary Opinion on the Howes," *MHS Proceedings*, 44:118-120, quoted from Commager & Morris, *SSS*, 527.

British and Hessian troops exacerbated the problem when they plundered residents regardless of political affiliation. Tory and Whig citizens lost valuables and provisions to the scavenging troops, causing many uncommitted colonists to lean toward the American cause. One old Quaker who lost property said, "Well, God made these men, though I am sure the devil governs them."[25]

Washington found a supportive population in Newark, as local citizens were sympathetic to the patriotic cause. Fearing the approaching British, hordes of townspeople packed their belongings and departed, clogging the road networks throughout the area. Washington, however, remained for five days to rest and reorganize his dwindling army. He sent his sick and wounded to Morristown, around twenty miles northwest of Newark, while deciding to continue south with his men, joining Lord Stirling's brigade holding Brunswick.

The 50-year-old Stirling had known Washington since they served together in the French and Indian War. In 1756, he traveled to England to stake a claim to a family inheritance. While the House of Lords denied him the title of earl, he was granted the lesser title of lord. When hostilities broke out between the colonists and their motherland, Lord Stirling opted to fight for the Americans.

Washington sent Lord Stirling's brigade to guard a crossing site at the Raritan River, protecting his flank against enemy forces that may land at Amboy, blocking Washington's line of retreat. Clinton had recommended a landing there, but the Howes chose to follow their plan of employing Clinton's troops to secure Newport, Rhode Island. On November 17, Lord Stirling's weary force arrived in Brunswick, quickly taking comfort in the local taverns. One lieutenant wrote, "Here our soldiers drank freely of spiritous liquors. They have chiefly got a disorder which at camp is called the 'Barrel Fever,' which differed its effects from any other fever—Its concomitants are black eyes and bloody noses."[26] Washington hoped to gather his army in Brunswick, along with the New Jersey and Pennsylvania militia and the Continental troops he had directed to join him from New York, but it was not to be.

While Washington rested his men in Newark, Thomas Paine, who had published *Common Sense*, began working on another piece. As an aide to Nathanael Greene, Paine was given unique insights into the challenges and deprivations confronting the Continental Army. He also experienced first-hand the divided loyalties of the people of New Jersey. Following the army's recent defeats, and with the cool reception it received from the citizens of Hackensack, Paine pulled up a

25 William Stryker, *The Battles of Trenton and Princeton* (Boston, 1898), 22, hereafter cited as *BTP*.

26 James McMichael, "Diary of Lieutenant James McMichael of the Pennsylvania Line, 1776-1778," *PMHB*, vol. 26, no. 2 (1892), 139.

drum to use as a desk, and under candlelight, began drafting *The American Crisis.*[27] He intended to address the American people again, challenging their patriotism and loyalty to the revolutionary cause. It would take around a month for Paine to publish his work, however. He also maintained a journal, which gave insights into the army at Newark:

> We staid four days at Newark, collected our outposts with some of the Jersey militia, and marched out twice to meet the enemy . . . both officers and men, though greatly harassed and fatigued without rest, covering or provision, the inevitable consequences of a long retreat, bore it with a manly and martial spirit. All their wishes centered in one, which was that the country would turn out and help them to drive the enemy back.[28]

As the Americans hoped for reinforcements, the British doubted any were forthcoming. Many in that army believed the final defeat of the Continental Army was inevitable. On November 25, one British officer wrote the following to a loyalist friend living in Boston, "You see my dear sir, that I have not been mistaken in my judgment of this people. The southern people [those living below New England] will no more fight than the Yankees. The fact is that their army is broken all to pieces . . . I think one may venture to pronounce that it is well-nigh over with them. All their strongholds are in the hands of his Majesty's troops." He continued,

> All their cannon and mortars, and the greatest part of their stores, ammunition, etc. are gone. The people in the country almost universally sick of it, in a starving condition, and cannot help themselves. And what is to become of them during the approaching inclement season God Only knows.[29]

While not far from the truth, British and Hessian troops continued to underestimate the Americans' resolve, determination, and commander. Eighteen-year-old James Monroe, the future president of the United States, served in the 3rd Virginia Regiment at Newark, saying about Washington, "he was always near the enemy, and his countenance and manner made an impression on me which time can never efface. . . . A deportment so firm, so dignified, so exalted, but yet so modest and composed, I have never seen in any other person."[30] Thomas Paine

---

27 For the full manuscripts of *Common Sense* and *The American Crisis* see Eric Foner, ed., *Thomas Paine: Collected Writings: Common Sense / The Crisis / Rights of Man / The Age of Reason / Pamphlets, Articles, and Letters*, 2nd edition (New York, 1995).

28 Moncure Daniel Conway, ed., *The Writings of Thomas Paine*, vol. 1 (New York, 1894), 170-173.

29 Dwyer, *TDIO*, 36.

30 James Monroe, *Autobiography*, Stuart Gerry Brown & Donald Baker, eds. (Syracuse, NY, 1959), quoted from Dwyer, *TDIO*, 37.

provided further insight into Washington, stating, "The character fits him. There is a natural firmness in some minds which cannot be unlocked by trifles, but which, when unlocked, discovers a cabinet of fortitude. . . . God hath blessed him with uninterrupted health, and given him a mind that can even flourish upon care."[31]

Although Washington appeared firm in his resolve, he continually asked for help. On November 23, he sent Colonel Reed to meet with Governor William Livingston of New Jersey to stress the need for additional militia, stating, "The critical situation of our affairs and the movements of the enemy make some further and immediate exertions absolutely necessary."[32] He also sent Philadelphia native Gen. Thomas Mifflin to ask Congress to do all in its powers to provide reinforcements without haste.

Washington attempted to strike at the British in order to slow or stop their advance into New Jersey, but he lacked the combat power to have any meaningful effect. Regardless, on November 26, he again advanced a force toward the British without gaining anything. By November 28, Washington could do nothing more than continue retreating south, splitting his force into two columns and marching on parallel roads to move faster. The pursuit continued as the British advance guard entered Newark just as the Americans exited the opposite side of the town.

On November 29, Washington's troops arrived in Brunswick, joining forces with Lord Stirling's Brigade. The joyful reunion was short-lived, however, as the army quickly faced additional hardships. The enlistments of nearly 2,000 militiamen of Maryland and New Jersey would soon expire, and despite Washington's pleas, the men refused to continue. One departing soldier wrote, "Our Brigade march'd to Philadelphia leaving our Brave Genl with a weak army."[33] General Greene recalled, "Two Brigades left us at Brunswick notwithstanding the Enemy were within two hours march and coming on. The loss of these troops at this critical time reduced his Excellency to the necessity to order retreat again"[34] Washington explained to Congress how some men deserted the army rather than wait for their enlistments to end: "I am told that some of Genl Ewing's Brigade who stand engaged to the

---

31 Conway, ed. *The Writings of Thomas Paine*, 1:170-173.

32 *FONA*, https://founders.archives.gov/documents/Washington/03-07-02-0140, accessed Oct. 20, 2019.

33 Fischer, *WC*, 129.

34 Peter Force, ed., *American Archives*, 5th series, vol.3 (Washington, D.C., 1853), 1071; Fitzpatrick, *The Writings of George Washington*, 6:318; George Washington Greene, *The Life of Nathanael Greene: Major General in the Army of the Revolution* (Princeton, NJ, 1867), 1:280. Richard Showman, Dennis Conrad, Roger Parks, Elizabeth Steven, eds. *The Papers of General Nathanael Greene* (Chapel Hill, NC, 1976), 1:360-364.

1st of January are now going away. If those go, whose service expires this day, our force will be reduced to a mere handfull."[35]

A proclamation from the Howe brothers on November 30 may have hastened desertions. They offered amnesty and full pardons to anyone, including Washington's men, if within 60 days they would take an oath of allegiance to remain obedient to the king. Although much blood had already been shed, they hoped to end the conflict and achieve reconciliation. Up to 2,700 New Jersey citizens reportedly accepted pardons. Lord Cornwallis stated, "three or four hundred came in every day for ten days to take protection."[36] These actions further complicated Washington's situation in New Jersey and fueled more hatred between Tories and Whigs across the state.

Charles Lee added to Washington's frustrations by pushing back on the calls for help and continuing to delay reinforcing the main Continental Army. On November 30, he informed Washington, "I cou'd wish you wou'd bind me as little as possible—not from any opinion, I do assure you, of my own parts—but from a perswasion that detach'd Generals cannot have too great latitude—unless They are very incompetent indeed."[37] Washington had little time for Lee's independent tendencies and responded the following day, "The force I have with me, is infinitely inferior in number and such as cannot give or promise the lest successful opposition. . . . I must entreat you to hasten your march as much as possible or your arrival may be too late to answer any valuable purpose."[38]

Although down, Washington was not beaten. In a letter he allegedly wrote to Lee on November 30, Washington explained how he thought the British originally intended to capture Newark, Elizabeth Town, and Amboy for winter quarters. He believed they were preparing for a combined sea and land attack on Philadelphia in the spring. As he explained to Lee, however, "The advantages they have gained over us in the past have made them so proud and sure of success that they are determined to go to Philadelphia this winter."[39] He added that this British hubris was fueled by their perceived weakness of Washington's army following the departure of those soldiers who terminated their enlistments. Washington stated, "Should they [the

---

35 *FONA*, https://founders.archives.gov/documents/Washington/03-07-02-0168, accessed Nov. 14, 2019.

36 Stryker, *BTP*, 23.

37 *FONA*, https://founders.archives.gov/documents/Washington/03-07-02-0169, accessed Nov. 16, 2019.

38 *FONA*, https://founders.archives.gov/documents/Washington/03-07-02-0180, accessed Nov. 16, 2019.

39 Stryker, *BTP*, 326-327. The authenticity of this letter has been questioned. See note at *FONA*, https://founders.archives.gov/documents/Washington/03-07-02-0180, accessed Nov. 24, 2019.

British] now really risk this undertaking then there is a great probability that they will pay dearly for it for I shall continue to retreat before them so as to lull them into security."[40] Washington also received the first indications that help may soon arrive from Philadelphia: "I hope to meet a considerable reinforcemt of Pensylva. Associators; it is said they seem spirited upon this occasion."[41]

On December 1, the British resumed their pursuit, advancing across the Raritan River near Brunswick. Washington employed Knox's artillery and Lord Stirling's infantry brigade to block their progress as American engineers attempted to disassemble the bridge spanning the river. Twenty-year-old Captain Alexander Hamilton commanded one of the batteries from New York. Hamilton's battery was described as "a model of discipline," while "its captain [was] a mere boy, with small, slender, and delicate frame, who with cocked hat pulled down over his eyes, and apparently lost in thought, marched beside a cannon, patting it every now and then as if it were a favorite horse or pet plaything."[42] By destroying their baggage to move quickly and evade the enemy, Hamilton and Lord Stirling bought Washington time to withdraw his forces 13 miles south to Kingston. Lieutenant Enoch Anderson of Lord Stirling's brigade recollected, "We made a double quick-step and came up with the army about eight o'clock. We encamped in the woods, with no victuals, no tents, no blankets."[43]

Before departing Brunswick, Washington ordered the collection of all boats on the Delaware River for 70 miles upriver from Philadelphia, then their staging approximately 25 miles southwest near Trenton, New Jersey.[44] He directed Israel Putnam, whom he had placed in command of the defense of Philadelphia, to begin constructing rafts for transporting the Continental Army to the south side of the river. Washington intended for the army to cross into Pennsylvania at Trenton, using the Delaware as a natural barrier to protect his troops from the advancing British and Hessian forces.

Washington realized the risks, as Cornwallis could strike the Americans with the army split between both sides of the river. To mitigate them, he set his troops in motion through Princeton and on to Trenton while directing Lord Stirling's brigade to conduct a fighting withdrawal to delay the British. Lord Stirling's men

40 Ibid.

41 *FONA*, https://founders.archives.gov/documents/Washington/03-07-02-0180, accessed Nov. 16, 2019.

42 George Morgan, *The Life of James Monroe* (Boston, 1921); Stryker, *BTP*, 15, FN2.

43 Enoch Anderson, *Personal Recollections, quoted from Historical and Biographical Papers*, vol. 16 (Willington, CT, 1896), quoted from Ward, *TWOR*, 282; Fischer, *WC*, 131.

44 *FONA*, https://founders.archives.gov/documents/Washington/03-07-02-0179, accessed Nov. 23, 2022.

welcomed the task, seeking shelter from the winter cold at Princeton College, while Cornwallis again paused his advance.

Cornwallis's lack of aggressiveness and his orders from General Howe aided Washington. On November 29, Howe replaced General Gage in the overall command of British forces in North America. He immediately ordered Cornwallis to halt at Brunswick until Howe arrived with reinforcements. Parliament later criticized Howe for these actions, as it viewed the delay as a lost opportunity to finally defeat Washington and his army. When questioned later, Cornwallis claimed that in addition to Howe's orders, he also needed reinforcements to guard the communication lines between Brunswick and Amboy. He added that he was wary of "a considerable body" of Americans under Gen. Lee that was finally moving to reinforce Washington.[45] He explained that his men and horses were fatigued and hungry after completing a 20-mile forced march to Brunswick over poor road conditions.

Howe provided additional insight into his decision to order Cornwallis to halt at Brunswick in a letter to Lord George Germain, Secretary of State for America. He shared, "My first design extend[ed] no further than to get and keep possession of East-Jersey."[46] Tragically for the British, Howe's limited objective to secure East Jersey and his hesitancy to allow Cornwallis to destroy the Continental Army gave the Americans a much-needed respite.

Unaware of the British intent to pause at Brunswick, Congress was energized by the rapid advance of the combined British and Hessian forces across New Jersey. In response, it began answering the pleas of General Mifflin, whom Washington had sent to seek its assistance. It scrambled to deploy available forces as it worked with the states to mobilize additional militia while also mobilizing 46-year-old Col. Nicholas Haussegger and his German American battalion. It further directed the national and state navies operating on the Delaware to support Washington's pending river crossing.

The Naval forces operating on the Delaware River were a conglomeration of Continental and state sailors and marines from Pennsylvania and Maryland.

---

45 William Belsham, *History of Great Britain: From the Revolution, 1688, to the Treaty of Amiens, 1802,* 12 vols. (London, 1805), 6:259.

46 "My first design extending no further than to get and keep possession of East-Jersey, Lord Cornwallis had orders not to advance beyond Brunswick, which occasioned him to discontinue his pursuit; but finding the advantages that might be gained by pushing on to the Delaware, and the possibility of getting to Philadelphia, the communication leading to Brunswick was reinforced, and on the 6th I joined his Lordship with the 4th brigade of British under the command of Major-General Grant. On the 7th Lord Cornwallis's corps, the guards excepted, who were left at Brunswick, marched to Princetown, which the enemy had quitted on the same day." Charles Cornwallis, *Correspondence of Charles, First Marquis Cornwallis* (Cambridge, UK, 2011), 24.

They were manning an eclectic collection of ships, barges, galleys, gunboats, and smaller vessels.[47] Though they paled in strength compared to the Royal Navy, they had defeated the British and now held uncontested control of the river—a luxury Washington had yet to experience. If the Continental forces had failed to secure the Delaware, the Royal Navy could block Washington's crossing, acting as an anvil as Howe's infantry hammered the remnants of the Continental Army, likely ending the war.

Pennsylvanian naval forces helped ensure that Washington's troops lived to fight another day. By December 1776, Pennsylvania had converted or built nearly 30 armed vessels operated by around 450 sailors and 250 Marines.[48] The state's flagship, *Montgomery* (14 guns), was joined by many smaller gun galleys mounting a single cannon in their bows, fire rafts, and two floating batteries (*Arnold* and *Putnam*) armed with 10-12 cannons each and manned exclusively by Pennsylvania marines.

Like their Continental brothers, the Pennsylvania marines came from varied backgrounds and would play a crucial role in upcoming battles. Twenty-nine-year-old Philadelphia native Thomas Forrest received a commission as a marine officer in the Pennsylvania Navy in March 1776. He commanded the floating battery *Arnold* on the Delaware River from May through September. On October 5, 1776, Forrest transferred to Col. Thomas Proctor's Pennsylvania artillery battalion to assume command of a 52-man battery.[49] On December 1, Proctor tasked Captain Forrest's battery, with two six-pound brass field cannons, to proceed from Philadelphia and report to Henry Knox, who was reinforcing Washington at Trenton.

Another Pennsylvania marine, Capt. William Brown, initially commanded the floating battery *Putnam* before assuming command of the marine detachment aboard the flagship *Montgomery*.[50] First Lieutenant James Morrison joined Brown in leading the 64-man detachment prior to Brown following Forrest's lead and assuming command of a battery.[51] On December 2, as Cornwallis sat in Brunswick, Washington arrived in Trenton to find Forrest and others waiting to

47 See Coggins, *SSAR*, Chapter 12, "The Navies of the States," 99-106; Howarth, *To Shining Sea: A History of the United States Navy*, 12-13; Fischer, *WC*, 134-135.

48 "The Pennsylvania State Navy," http://www.ushistory.org/march/other/pennnavy.htm, accessed Nov. 16, 2019; Edwin McClellan, *History of the United States Marine Corps*, vol.1 (Washington, D.C., 1931), 22-23.

49 Morgan, ed., *NDAR*, 6:916; "Forrest, Thomas," https://history.house.gov/People/Detail/13327?ret=True, accessed Nov. 16, 2019; *PMHB*, 4:457; Fischer, *WC*, 392.

50 Morgan, ed., *NDAR*, 6:916, 939, 1266; Stryker, *BTP*, 242, 433.

51 Stryker, *BTP*, 346.

Portrait of Thomas Forrest by Charles Willson Peale. Forrest received a commission as a Pennsylvania State Marine in March 1776. He commanded the floating battery *Arnold* from March-October 1776 before transferring to the Pennsylvania artillery battalion to serve as a battery commander. Forrest performed superbly in this role in the battles of Trenton and Princeton. *Wikimedia*

join him. Washington immediately began crossing his wounded, baggage, and stores into Pennsylvania.

Twenty-seven-year-old Capt. William Shippin ended his service as a privateer to serve as a company commander in the Pennsylvania marines. Shippin, a fish and meat merchant before the war, assumed command of the marine detachment on board the Pennsylvania Navy privateer *Hancock* in May 1776, helping disrupt British commerce and resupply efforts. The threat posed by the advancing British caused Shippin and 30 of his men to join the ground forces sent to reinforce Washington.[52]

State marines were not the only ones joining Washington's force as it crossed the Delaware. Congress initially kept Maj. Samuel Nicholas and the Continental Marines in Philadelphia to protect their ships, stores, and a prison. But the crisis had risen to such a degree that it had no choice but to direct Nicholas to form a battalion and join Washington.[53] As the army started going over the river, Nicholas assembled his men, issued them bayonets and cartouche boxes, and had them board gondolas for a trip upriver to join Washington at Trenton.[54]

Nicholas was the battalion commander. He made Capt. Isaac Craig of the *Andrew Doria* the adjutant and Capts. Robert Mullan of the *Delaware*, Benjamin Dean of the *Washington*, and Andrew Porter of the *Effingham* the company commanders. In all, the battalion numbered between 120-130 Continental Marines.[55] Nicholas ordered Capt. Samuel Shaw of the *Randolph* to remain behind

52 Ibid., 277, 327, 453-454; Dwyer, *TDIO*, 345.

53 Morgan, ed., *NDAR*, 6:863.

54 *Pennsylvania Colonial Records*, 11:26; Smith, *MIR*, 90; *JCC*, 21:1028.

55 The weekly returns from the Marine detachments on the *Washington*, *Effingham*, and *Delaware* reported 10 officers (including Nicholas and Craig) and 112 Marines fit for duty and nine sick on

with his Marines, anticipating the *Randolph* soon putting to sea. He also left small guard details and nine sick Marines to watch over the remaining three frigates still under construction.

Private John McKinley was among the Continental Marines who departed Philadelphia on December 2. McKinley enlisted in Capt. Mullan's company in August 1776 and served on the *Delaware*. Following the war, he recounted his time on the *Delaware*: "[U]ntil about the month of December in this said year [1776] . . . he, together in the other marines and sailors belonging to the said frigate Delaware, were drafted from said vessel to join the Army under the command of George Washington for the purpose of aiding and supporting said Army, which was then retreating before the British Army in the state of New Jersey."[56] Mullan later ordered a sick McKinley back to Philadelphia, where he remained until February 1777. After the battle of Princeton, he and other indisposed Marines stayed in Philadelphia until rejoining their companies in Morristown, New Jersey.

Major Nicholas and his Marines did not know what the future held other than being ordered to assist Washington and the army. Congress's records state, "In December following he [Major Nicholas] was ordered to march with three companies of Marines to the Jerseys to be under his Excellency the Commander-in-Chief, and continued in the field until the men's times of Inlistment expired."[57] So began the Continental Marines' first land campaign.

Additional Marines answered the call to support Washington on the Delaware River during this critical time. Detachments of Marines on board the brig *Andrew Doria* (14 guns), the sloops *Hornet* (10 guns) and *Independence* (10 guns), and the Pennsylvania gunboat *Champion* (8 guns) helped keep the river in American hands. Navy Capts. James Nicholson and George Cook and Continental Marine Capt. James Disney joined this group with a mix of around 70 sailors and Marines from Maryland. The British blockaded their ships—*Defense* from the Maryland navy and *Virginia* (28 guns) from the Continental Navy—in Baltimore, causing these sailors and Marines to travel over land to join the Americans in Philadelphia. Congressman Samuel Chase wrote to Captain Nicholson, "It has been reported that you are coming up to this city with a body of sailors and Marines." Chase hoped they could sail the incomplete frigates in Philadelphia to Baltimore to prevent their

---

December 20, 1776. Smith, *MIR*, 421-423; *McClellan, History of the United States Marine Corps*, 24-25.

56 *Pension Records*, Private John McKinley, cited from Edwin McClellan, *Personal Collection*, Box 30, Folder 5, "History of the USMC, Navy and Marines at the Battles of Trenton and Princeton," Archives Branch, Marine Corps History Division, Quantico, VA.

57 *JCC*, 21:1028.

capture.[58] Though this proved untenable, Congress still employed the sailors and Marines to assist Washington's defensive efforts. Chase later recalled how the group from Baltimore "arrived in high spirits and very desirous of engaging the enemy."[59]

Though a lack of accurate records makes it difficult to identify the exact number of Marines and sailors who assisted Washington at this time, their contribution is undeniable. From existing records, there are indications that between 500-600 Continental and state marines and sailors operated ashore, and as many as 700 more operated on the armed vessels controlling the Delaware River.[60] This accounts for nearly one-quarter of the total American troops who participated in the historic events that occurred between mid-December 1776 and mid-January 1777.[61]

Other forces would soon join the Marines in reinforcing Washington. Philadelphia city leaders mobilized the local militia force known as the "Associators."[62] This group was the brainchild of Benjamin Franklin, who in 1747 devised plans to create a force to protect the city against French and Spanish privateers in anticipation of the French and Indian War. The Associators were a democratically run organization in which men elected their leaders, and all ranks provided input into how the unit would operate. They had no set terms of enlistment, coming and going as they pleased. In all, Franklin recruited 10 companies of 100 men each to defend Philadelphia, with additional companies protecting the Pennsylvania countryside. The organization was disbanded at the end of the French and Indian War.[63]

In 1775, the city reestablished the Associators in response to the threat posed by the British and Hessians, eventually raising five battalions of infantry and two battalions of artillery. Although the Associators gave every man a voice, establishing a "Committee of Privates" to help run their units, they generally elected their officers from among Philadelphia's most prominent citizens. They chose 34-year-old Col. John Cadwalader to command the 3rd Battalion, and he would later assume command of the entire brigade.[64] Cadwalader, thought to be the most

58 Force, ed., *AA*, 5th Series, 3:1165.

59 John Scharf, *History of Maryland*, 1765-1812, vol. 2 (Baltimore, 1879), 290.

60 "The Pennsylvania State Navy"; McClellan, *History of the United States Marine Corps*, 1:22-23; Stryker, *BTP*, 433.

61 Edwin McClellan, & Jon Craige, "American Marines in the Battles of Trenton and Princeton," *Marine Corps Gazette*, vol. 6, issue 3 (September 1921), 279.

62 For more on the Associators see Joseph Seymour, *The Pennsylvania Associators*, 1747-1777 (Yardley, PA, 2012); Fischer, *WC*, 25-28; Ward, *TWOR*, 281, 289, 293.

63 Fischer, *WC*, 26.

64 "John Cadwalader: Senior Officer of the Philadelphia Associators," https://www.battlefields.org/learn/articles/john-cadwalader, accessed Nov. 21, 2019.

Brigadier General John Cadwalader commanded a brigade of Philadelphia militia known as the Associators. Washington assigned Major Nicholas and his battalion of Continental Marines to serve under Cadwalader during the battles of Trenton and Princeton. *Wikimedia*

affluent merchant in the city, also proved to be a competent leader on the battlefield. Author and historian David Hackett Fischer asserts that Washington was initially dubious of the Associators due to their form of democratic rule. This was counter to the strict discipline and unity of command he believed the army needed, but he quickly gained an appreciation for Cadwalader and his men.[65] Washington later described Cadwalader as "a Man of Ability, a good disciplinarian, firm in his principles, and of intrepid Bravery."[66]

On December 3, Cadwalader assembled three battalions of Associators, which agreed to remain in service for six weeks. Two days later the brigade departed Philadelphia and marched toward Trenton. Other troops joined them along the way. Captain John Barry of the frigate *Effingham* believed that stopping the British advance provided the best chance of protecting his ship, which was still under construction in Philadelphia. Barry's Marine detachment under Capt. Andrew Porter was already on route to join the Continental Marine battalion, so Barry led some sailors from his crew, "contriving to mount a light gun or two, in a manner that admitted of their being used in the field."[67] Barry joined the Associators as Cadwalader's aide-de-camp.[68] Captain William Shippin's company of Marines from the *Hancock* was assigned to join the Associators' 2nd Battalion to fight ashore. A troop of light horse under Capt. Samuel Morris and Marine Capt. William Brown's artillery provided additional firepower to the brigade.

65 Fischer, *WC*, 28.

66 *FONA*, https://founders.archives.gov/documents/Washington/03-08-02-0135, accessed Nov. 21, 2019; Stryker, *BTP*, 81.

67 James Fenimore Cooper, "Sketches of Naval Men-John Barry," in *Graham's Lady's and Gentleman's Magazine*, George Graham, ed., vol. 24 (Philadelphia, 1844), 268.

68 "John Barry," https://www.history.navy.mil/research/library/research-guides/z-files/zb-files/zb-files-b/barry-john.html, accessed Nov. 21, 2019.

By December 7, the Associators brigade had grown to 1,000-1,200 men. Cadwalader led the militiamen upriver, joining Nicholas and his Marines in Trenton, and reported to Washington. The general contemplated sending the brigade to reinforce Lord Stirling in delaying the British around Princeton but held them in Trenton due to a lack of adequate shelter for the men. Washington ordered Cadwalader to supply his troops with ammunition and "three days Provisions ready Cooked—that they may be ready to March at a Moments warning."[69] He further directed, "The Marines—Sailors &ca from Philadelphia you will take under your care till a further disposition of them can be made, if necessary, letting me know in the meanwhile if they came out resolved to act upon Land or meant to confine their Services to the Water only."[70] Washington had just assigned the Continental, Pennsylvania, and Maryland marines and sailors operating ashore to the brigade of Associators under Cadwalder's command. Although the state marines were integrated into the Associators battalions, the Continental Marines remained a separate battalion.

Washington undoubtedly remembered the challenges with the soldier-Marines and sailors he had pressed into service outside Boston, but he needed every able-bodied man he could get to assist in the continuing struggle for independence. Placing the Continental and state marines and sailors under Cadwalader's charge would streamline the chain of command ashore, reducing Washington's overall span of control and allowing him to remain focused on higher-level issues.

Commodore Thomas Seymour of the Pennsylvania Navy maintained command of the forces operating on the Delaware River. He sent nine galleys to assist the army's crossing of the Delaware and four more to patrol the river. Leaving Cadwalader in Trenton to organize and prepare his newly assembled forces, Washington departed to join General Greene in reinforcing Lord Stirling at Princeton. He also wanted to determine British intentions, but he never made it.

On December 6, General Howe arrived in Brunswick with reinforcements under Gen. James Grant and Col. Johann Rall's Hessian regiment. The latter had gained a reputation as a competent leader during the fight in New York. Cornwallis briefed Howe on the current situation, and at 4:00 a.m. the following morning, the combined force resumed the pursuit of Washington. With Princeton as their objective, Howe split his force into two columns to make good speed, with Cornwallis leading one and Grant the other. Lord Stirling was able to delay

---

69 *FONA*, https://founders.archives.gov/documents/Washington/03-07-02-0205, accessed Nov. 21, 2019.

70 Ibid.

the advance before relinquishing the town to the British and moving south to rejoin Washington.

Washington came across Lord Stirling as he withdrew toward Trenton, positioning himself with the regiment from Delaware in the rear guard. Twenty-one-year-old Capt. Enoch Anderson, who had been wounded at the battle of Long Island, recollected, "We continued on our retreat—our regiment in the rear, and I, with thirty men, in the rear of the regiment, and General Washington in my rear with pioneers—tearing up bridges and cutting down trees to impede the march of the enemy. I was to go no faster than General Washington and his pioneers. It was dusk before we got to Trenton."[71]

Wanting to ensure that his men and supplies were safely across before the British reached Trenton, Washington ordered the remainder of his Army to cross the Delaware. The operation took most of the night. Thirty-five-year-old Lt. Charles Willson Peale was a well-established artist. He had painted portraits of Washington and other prominent members of Congress before joining the Philadelphia Associators as a company commander in the brigade's 2nd Battalion. Peale observed the crossings from Trenton that evening and later explained, "All the shores were lighted up with large fires, boats continually passing and repassing, full of men, horses, artillery and camp equipage. The sick and half naked veterans of the long retreat streamed past. I thought it the most hellish scene I have ever beheld."[72] He added, "Suddenly a man staggered out of the line and came toward me. He had lost all his clothes. He was in an old dirty blanket-jacket, his beard long and his face full of sores . . . which so disfigured him that he was not known by me on first sight. Only when he spoke did I recognize my brother James."[73] Scenes like this would continue to play out as the last Americans began to cross the river, just as the British lead elements arrived in Trenton.

With bands playing, the British 4th Brigade under James Grant arrived, with two battalions of light infantry and three battalions of Hessian grenadiers. General Howe's Hessian aide and translator, Capt. Ernst von Munchausen, described how "some inhabitants came running toward us, urging us to march through the town in a hurry so we can capture many of the enemy who were just embarking." They missed their chance, however.[74] The blasts of 37 Continental cannons firing from the far side of the river greeted Howe and Cornwallis as they led the column

71 Enoch Anderson, *Personal Recollections of Captain Enoch Anderson, an Officer of the Delaware Regiments in the Revolutionary War* (Manchester, NY, 1971), 28.

72 Fischer, *WC*, 133, Dwyer, *TDIO*, 102-105.

73 Ibid.

74 Fischer, *WC*, 135.

down to the river, killing or wounding 13 of their party. Cornwallis sent other units upriver to secure boats to cross the Delaware, but Washington's earlier efforts ensured that all available craft has been secured on the Pennsylvania side of the river.

Over the years, Howe's lack of aggressiveness in defeating Washington before his escape into Pennsylvania has come under much criticism. Historian Charles Steadman asserts that Howe may have intentionally allowed Washington to escape, positing that "Howe had calculated with the greatest accuracy the exact time necessary for his enemy to make his escape."[75] Thomas Fleming takes a slightly different stance, claiming that Howe had no intention of defeating Washington but rather intended to merely drive him out of New Jersey so Howe could secure the Crown's position in that state.[76]

Regardless of where the truth lies, Howe was no longer immediately able to continue pursuing Washington, let alone defeat him. The Americans controlled the Delaware River using a combination of naval forces and shore-based artillery. As the infantry covered all the known crossings, Howe had no way to traverse it without boats. He had three options to conduct a crossing if he chose to pursue them: he could send for boats from other areas to be transported across land, and he could construct his own boats or wait for the river to freeze in the coming weeks and walk across it. Trenton possessed ample materials for such a job as well as the blacksmith shops needed to produce boats and rafts. Tory Joseph Galloway reported, "At Captain Montressor's request, I did inquire whether there were any material in or about Trenton with which pontoons, boats, or rafts might be constructed; and I found 48,000 feet of boards, a quantity of wire, and there was timber enough about Trenton for that purpose."[77] Howe decided against these options, considering the opposition he would face in crossing the river and the difficulty of a winter campaign. Instead, he chose a fourth option: he decided to put his army into winter quarters.

On December 14, Howe officially ended the New Jersey campaign. He ordered that, with "the Approach of Winter putting a Stop to any further Progress, the

75 Stryker, *BTP*, 29; Fredrick Bauer, "Notes on the Use of the Cavalry in the American Revolution," *The Cavalry Journal*, vol. 47, no.1 (1938), 136.

76 Fleming asserts, "Howe did not see total victory in military terms as the key to his policy. What he and his brother were aiming at, from the start, was peace by reconciliation. To achieve this they had to balance American extremists, who insisted on independence, against extremists of the opposite persuasion back home, who insisted on all-out repression. If they annihilated Washington and his army and captured the Congress, what would there be left to reconcile?" Thomas Fleming, "The Enigma of General Howe," https://www.americanheritage.com/content/enigma-general-howe, accessed Nov. 22, 2019.

77 Stryker, *BTP*, 37.

Troops will immediately march into Quarters and hold themselves in Readiness to assemble on the shortest Notice."[78] He further tasked all commanders with "preserving the greatest Regularity and strictest Discipline in their respective Quarters, particularly attending to the Protection of Inhabitants and their Property in their several Districts."[79] The Howe brothers saw no need to push their forces during the winter. Once spring arrived, they intended to resume their offensive, defeating Washington and his rebel forces while capturing the capital of Philadelphia.

Howe directed the establishment of 17 military cantonments across New Jersey. He wanted to secure the population and distribute his forces to forage off the land. British troops occupied towns and villages in Essex, Burlington, Middlesex, Somerset, and Hunterdon counties. Cornwallis would secure Elizabethtown, Brunswick, Princeton, Trenton, and Bordentown farther down the river toward Philadelphia. He assigned Colonel von Donop and his Hessians responsibility for Trenton, Bordentown, and Burlington. Von Donop then gave the responsibility for Trenton to Col. Johann Rall.[80]

Though the disposition of Howe's forces supported his logistical needs, protecting local citizens from the bands of rebels within New Jersey, it did little to defend against an attack by a determined enemy.[81] The dispersed positions remained relatively isolated and were too far away to provide adequate support. This did not concern Howe, as he believed Washington could not offer any credible resistance, and he explained his decision in a letter to Lord Germain.[82] Howe left General Grant in command of the forces in New Jersey and granted General Cornwallis leave to return to England to attend to his ailing wife. He then went to his headquarters in New York.

---

78 "General William Howe, General Orders, 14 December 1776, Trenton, New Jersey," quoted from Ward, *TWOR*, 291; Robert Alter, "Boots for the Battle," *Boy's Life* (December 1964), 17.

79 Dwyer, *TDIO*, 151.

80 Stryker, *BTP*, 38-39, 46-47; Fischer, *WC*, 184-188; Ferling, *AAM*, 172.

81 Leonard Lundin, *Cockpit of the Revolution: The War for Independence in New Jersey* (Princeton, NJ, 1940), 161.

82 "The passage of the Delaware being thus rendered impracticable, his Lordship took post at Pennington, in which place and Trenton the two divisions remained until the 14th, when the weather having become too severe to keep the field, and the winter cantonments being arranged, the troops marched from both places to their respective stations. The chain, I own, is rather too extensive, but I was induced to occupy Burlington to cover the county of Monmouth, in which there are many loyal inhabitants, and trusting to the almost general submission of the country to the southward of this chain, and to the strength of the corps placed in the advance posts, I conclude the troops will be in perfect security." *The Parliamentary Registry; or History of the Proceedings and Debates of the House of Commons*, Fifth Session of the Fourteenth Parliament, 16 vols. (London, 1802), 10:370.

Many within the British ranks questioned Howe's decision to end the campaign short of total victory. Some voiced their displeasure with not ending the rebellion when they had the chance.[83]

Although the rebellion was still thriving in New Jersey and Pennsylvania, the British would administer a blow to the Americans in another state. As Howe reached Trenton, his brother arrived in Rhode Island. As planned, Admiral Howe landed Clinton's expeditionary forces under Brig. Gen. Richard Prescott. They moved to seize control of Newport quickly, then blockaded the American fleet under Commodore Hopkins at Providence. The British would occupy Rhode Island for three years before being ousted. These landings only added to the anxiety felt by Americans south of the Delaware River. Unaware of General Howe's intentions, the Americans distributed their forces to guard against any possible river crossing. On December 9, Washington mobilized his troops on the Pennsylvania side of the Delaware. He established fortified positions to cover known ferry sites at Sherwood's, Coryell's, McKonkey's, Yardley's, Howell's, Kirkbride's, Beatty, and Trenton Ferry crossings.[84] He positioned the Continental brigades commanded by Generals Lord Stirling, Adam Stephen, Hugh Mercer, and Matthias Fermoy further north to cover the 11 miles of riverfront between Coryell's and Yardley's ferries. Pennsylvania and New Jersey militia under Gens. James Ewing and Philemon Dickinson occupied the center, covering nearly 14 miles of riverfront between Yardley's Ferry and a crossing site near Bordentown, New Jersey. Colonel Cadwalader and the Associators with Maj. Nicholas and the Continental Marines originally guarded the area south of Trenton Ferry in the center. While there, Washington asked Cadwalader to write to his associates on the Pennsylvania Committee of Safety to seek their assistance:

> His Excels General Washington desires me to request that you will immediately dispatch a Party of men from Philadelphia to cut down & destroy the two Bridges on the Burlington Road, one on Pensawkin & the other on Cooper's Creek [New Jersey]—as he is apprehensive the Enemy intend to pass to Philadelphia by that

---

83 One captain stated, "Thus to suffer the shattered remains of the rebel troops, a set of naked dispirited fugitives encumbered with baggage, to run a race of ninety miles and outstrip the flower of the British army, three times their number, appears to be an omission, not to give it another name. . . . We had every thing to encourage our progress: the enemy were depressed and drove from every quarter, their principal force was flying before us, the country-people eagerly assisting our advances by repairing the bridges and guiding the pursuit. Yet, for want of vigor and decisiveness, we flagged in the career of conquest and neglected to follow the blow, which would have finally crowned us with success and crushed the rebellion." Lundin, *Cockpit of the Revolution*, 151; Dwyer, *TDIO*, 113.

84 Stryker, *BTP*, 30; Fischer, *WC*, 191; Dwyer, *TDIO*, 117.

Rout. Let me beg of you in my own name that you will alarm the whole Country, South and West, nothing but their assistance can save us![85]

Washington later shifted the Associators and Marines further down river toward Bristol to cover his southern flank and guard the approximately 12 miles of riverfront between Bristol and Bordentown. Local militia and other forces made available to General Putnam in Philadelphia covered the gap between Washington's army and the city. All told, the army covered roughly 40 miles of riverfront but possessed little depth. A crossing and defeat of Americans along this thin line would place the enemy in a position to roll Washington's flank and wipe out the army. Washington established his headquarters at Colvin's Ferry, then moved to establish the village of Newtown, eight miles from the river, as the location of his commissary and quartermasters. If his front-line units were defeated, either location could be easy targets for the British, but Washington had the foresight to establish a second line of defense along the Schuylkill River, covering the high ground around Germantown approximately 30 miles southwest of Trenton and just nine miles north of Philadelphia.

Washington and his weary men were safe for now. Although forced to flee in the face of superior British and Hessian forces, they had performed admirably. Thomas Paine captured the spirit of their achievement when he stated, "With a handful of men we sustained an orderly retreat for nearly a hundred miles, brought off our ammunition, all of our fieldpieces, the greatest part of our stores, and had four rivers to pass. None can say that our retreat was precipitate, for we were three weeks in performing it, that the country might have time to come."[86] Although Paine's facts are debatable, the country had finally begun to come to Washington's aid in limited numbers. The army remained weak, but the arrival of the German battalion, the Associators, and Marines nearly doubled Washington's shrinking numbers, and Congress promised additional reinforcements. This added strength allowed Washington to seize the initiative from the British, but the question remained as to where and when to take this action.

Washington first had to address some pressing concerns. The arrival of the British on the shores of the Delaware made Philadelphia's citizens panic. Rumors rapidly spread, and many chose to flee. Packing their belongings, families departed for the countryside and other areas to stay with relatives or friends. Washington sent word to Israel Putnam in the capital city to "defend it at all hazards."

85 Stryker, *BTP*, 323.

86 Conway, ed., *The Writings of Thomas Paine*, 173.

Congress gave Putman absolute control of Philadelphia.[87] Putnam reported back to Washington, "All Things in this City remain in Confusion, for Want of Men to put them into Order."[88] He added, however, "The Citizens are generally with you." Putnam directed the construction of defensive positions across Philadelphia and shared that "[o]rders for every able Bodyed Man to be enrolled, & put to work on throwing up the Lines" had been issued.

Putnam pursued his new duties with vigor. When he heard rumors of plans to conduct nefarious activities by loyalists in Philadelphia, he immediately declared martial law and ordered that any inhabitant seen on the city streets after 10:00 p.m. would be arrested. After being informed that some "weak and wicked men" intended to burn the city, Putnam responded by stating he would consider any attempt to do so as "a crime of the blackest dye, and [would] without ceremony, punish capitally any incendiary who shall have the hardiness and cruelty to attempt it."[89]

Still unaware of British intentions, Washington took action to ensure he was informed of any potential crossing activities by his adversaries. On December 10, he informed the Pennsylvania Committee of Safety, "I immediately sent orders to Commodore Seymour to dispatch one of his gallies down to Dunk's Ferry and I shall dispose of the remainder in such a manner, and at such places, as will be most likely, not only to annoy the Enemy in their passage, but to give the earliest information of any attempt of that kind."[90] The next day, he notified Hancock that he had "received certain Information that the Enemy . . . had advanced a party of about Five hundred to Borden Town . . . it confirms me in my Opinion, that they have an Intention to land between this and Philadelphia, as well as above, if they can procure Boats for that purpose."[91] He continued, "I last Night directed Commodore Seymour, to station all his Gallies between Bordentown and Philadelphia, to give the earliest intelligence of any Appearance of the Enemy on the Jersey shore."

As he gathered information, Washington began to suspect that British efforts to cross the river would be unsuccessful. He surmised, "From their several Attempts to seize Boats, it does not look as if they had brought any with them, as

87 Stryker, *BTP*, 57.

88 The following three quotes were found at *FONA*, https://founders.archives.gov/documents/Washington/03-07-02-0250, accessed Nov. 22, 2019.

89 "Major General Putnam, General Orders, Philadelphia, 13 December 1776," in Force, ed., *AA*, 5th Series, 1200.

90 Morgan, ed., *NDAR*, 6:437.

91 This and the following three quotes are from *FONA*, https://founders.archives.gov/documents/Washington/03-07-02-0232, accessed Nov. 23, 2019.

I was at one time informed." Later he confirmed his suspicions, "I last Night sent a person over to Trenton to learn whether there was any Appearance of building any, but he could not perceive any preparations for a Work of that kind. So that I am in hopes, if proper Care is taken to keep all the Craft out of their way, they will find the crossing Delaware a Matter of considerable Difficulty." If true, and Seymour's river fleet could hold the line at the Delaware, Washington could plan for an offensive operation.

Commodore Seymour commanded all vessels, gondolas, and row-galleys above the *chevaux-de-frise* from Billingsport, approximately 20 miles southwest of Philadelphia, upriver to Trenton Falls. The sailors and Marines operating on the Delaware protected the city and Washington's eastern flank from a British attack from the sea. They would do much more, however. They collected intelligence to determine the loyalties of those towns and villages not actively occupied by British and Hessian forces. Additionally, they helped to verify the character, arrangement, and strength of the area's enemy forces and assisted in preventing them from crossing the river. The Marines also received orders to conduct raids on the Jersey side to disrupt enemy activities, capture supplies, and keep the British guessing regarding Washington's intentions. These actions kept the British and Hessian troops on constant alert, causing fatigue and conditioning them to false alarms that could play to Washington's advantage when he decided to move.

These actions did little to convince Congress of its safety. Rumors spread that the politicians intended to flee Philadelphia. On December 11, the members passed a resolution calling for a day of fasting and humiliation "to implore of Almighty God the forgiveness of the many sins prevailing among all ranks, and to beg the countenance and assistance of his providence in the prosecution of the present just and necessary war."[92] Coincidentally, the resolution also denounced the false rumors that Congress planned to leave the city. Congress asked Washington to publish the resolution, but he refused, perhaps knowing that the congressmen did intend to leave.

The very next day, on the advice of Generals Putnam and Mifflin, Congress fled Philadelphia for Baltimore, where the members could conduct business safely. Congressman Oliver Scott of Connecticut attempted to explain the departure by stating, "It was judged that the Council of America ought not to sit in a place liable to be interrupted by the rude disorder of arms."[93] Regardless of their reasons,

---

92 Abiel Holmes, *The Annals of America: From the Discovery by Columbus in the Year 1492 to the Year 1826*, 2nd ed., vol. 2 (Cambridge, MA, 1829), 255.

93 Thomas Chorlton, *The First American Republic, 1774-1789: The First Fourteen American Presidents Before Washington* (Bloomington, IN, 2011), 371; Samuel Griffin, *The War for American Independence: From 1760 to the Surrender at Yorktown in 1781* (Urbana, IL, 1976), 333; Stryker, *BTP*, 36.

the flight fueled greater panic in Philadelphia. Captain Samuel Morris of the Associators said it "struck a damp on ye spirits of many."[94] Three congressmen, Robert Morris, George Walton, and George Clymer, stayed in Philadelphia to represent Congress's interests. As they left, the members passed a resolution granting "General Washington . . . full power to order and direct all things relative to the department and to the operations of War."[95]

This was uncharacteristic of the Congress, which had made a point of directing aspects of Washington's military actions during the New York campaign. Congressmen now realized that Washington needed the flexibility to direct movements as he saw fit so as to exploit opportunities as the situation on the ground developed. They also understood that these were desperate times and while in Baltimore, they would not be in a good position to direct operations. Congress extended Washington's powers for six months to get the country through the current crisis, but not before directing other necessary actions.

Congress feared an attack from the sea and land sides of Philadelphia. It had received reports that the British Navy had posted HMS *Roebuck* near the mouth of the Delaware to block any exit to the sea.[96] As a result, the congressmen resolved on December 12 that the American frigate *Randolph*, along with the Marine detachment under Capt. Shaw that Nicholas had left back, and the sloop *Hornet* of the Continental Navy be "[p]ut under the General Commanding in Philadelphia [Putnam] to act as he shall direct for the defense of the city, and prevent the enemy from passing the Delaware."[97]

The *Randolph* was the only frigate nearing completion. Congress desperately wanted to preserve the ship and resolved that when the "General has no further occasion for the use of the frigate *Randolph*, for the defense of the city" that she be put to sea. It also enticed the ship's captain and crew with a monetary reward if they could achieve this objective, stating, "Should the *Randolph* escape to sea, this Congress will reward him [Captain Biddle] and his people with a present of 10,000 dollars."

Randolph and *Hornet* set sail on December 14 but did not get far. The *Randolph* received orders to "cruise the coast for enemy shipping destined for New York," and the *Hornet* was tasked with proceeding to the Carolinas before continuing

94 Chris Coelho, *Timothy Matlack, Scribe of the Declaration of Independence* (Jefferson, NC, 2013), 7; Elroy Avery, *A History of the United States and its People, From their Earliest Records to the Present Time*, 16 vols. (Cleveland, 1904), 6:41; Stryker, *BTP*, 61.

95 Force, ed., *AA*, 5th Series, 3:1606.

96 Samuel Hazard, *Pennsylvania Archives*, 1st series, vol. 5 (Philadelphia, 1853), 99.

97 The following three quotes are from Force, ed., *AA*, 5th series, 3:1605-1606.

to Martinique "where supplies might be obtained for the army." The unexpected arrival of HMS *Falcon* and two bomb ketches to reinforce HMS *Roebuck* caused Congress to hold the ships near Philadelphia.[98] The enemy presence, ice forming on the river, and depleted crews further delayed the ships' departure until February 3, 1777, when *Randolph* became the first of the 13 frigates authorized by Congress to put to sea.

Congress took additional actions to ensure the remaining three frigates still being built in Philadelphia did not fall into enemy hands. On December 12, it directed Putnam to appoint a person to secure combustibles "for burning such of the frigates and other continental vessels as may be in imminent danger of falling into the enemies's possession should this city come into their hands."[99]

While prudent, Congressman Morris hoped to save at least one more of these valuable ships. On December 13, he wrote Washington to seek his assistance in saving the frigate *Delaware*. Although incomplete, Morris believed its construction had progressed sufficiently to sail and complete construction at another location. The *Delaware's* captain, Charles Alexander, and the Marine detachment commanded by Capt. Robert Mullan, the owner of Tun's Tavern, had previously joined Nicholas in reinforcing Washington, and Morris requested their return. Washington forwarded this request to Cadwalader, who ordered Alexander and his crew to go back to Philadelphia. Nicholas chose to keep Mullan in his current position as a company commander in the Continental Marine battalion. He did form a 20-man detachment of personnel pulled from across the battalion's three companies under the command of Lts. Daniel Henderson and David Love. The detachment was to report to the *Delaware*.[100]

Major Nicholas and his remaining Marines settled into guard rotations to protect the Pennsylvania shore from British incursions. The Marines provided a company commander, one corporal, and eight privates on a rotating basis in support of Cadwalader's brigade guard at Bristol.[101] Nicholas and his Marines also made forays across the river. On December 15, Nicholas received orders to meet with Hessian Colonel von Donop in New Jersey to conduct a prisoner exchange

98 *PCC*, 137, quoted from Smith, *MIR*, 93.

99 Force, ed., *AA*, 5th Series, 3:1606.

100 *TWGW*, 6:375; Brigade Return, 12 & 17 December 1776, *John Cadwalader Papers*, *PHS*, quoted from Smith, *MIR*, 93, 302.

101 "Return of Robert Mullan's Company of Marines," 20 December 1776; "A Weekly Return of Captain Andrew Porter's Company of Marines to Samuel Nicholas Esqr. Major of Marines," 20 December 1776, quoted from Smith, *MIR*, 94.

under a flag of truce. Von Donop explained the engagement in a letter to General Grant the following day.[102]

These actions proved prudent, as the British and Hessians had been hard at work since arriving in Trenton. Patrols searched for boats while others reconnoitered the surrounding villages for adequate winter quarters. On December 11, von Donop led one such patrol of 100 jaegers and 400 grenadiers to the village of Burlington. They did not travel far before encountering a 100-man scouting party of Pennsylvania riflemen that crossed the Delaware to determine British intentions. A brief exchange of gunfire ensued before the Americans broke contact and withdrew. Jaeger Capt. Johann Ewald learned from a prisoner that the Americans had positioned a small fleet of five row galleys under Seymour's command just offshore from Burlington. Ewald and von Donop were concerned about this development, as they did not have artillery with which to confront the threat.

The citizens of Burlington received word of the approaching Hessians and sent a delegation to meet them. Many in the community sympathized with the British and hoped to "spare the Inhabitants from Insult and their property from pillage."[103] Von Donop assured them that the village would be spared if they remained peaceful and no one possessed "any arms, ammunition or effects belonging to persons that were in arms against the king."[104] There was still the matter of the American cannons pointing ominously at the village. Von Donop ordered its leaders to try and solicit an agreement with Commodore Seymour not to fire on Burlington. Ewald reported that Seymour requested two hours to consider the request, so von Donop and his party enjoyed a meal with the locals while awaiting his response.

Though history has lost what transpired on the American side during the two-hour delay, Seymour's response became evident when Burlington's leaders returned to the river at the designated time. The Americans answered with a shot fired from a ship's swivel gun. The locals were shocked, thinking it must be a mistake. One man waved his hat toward the ships, and a second shot erupted from an 18-inch

---

102 "Yesterday Major Nichols of the enemy brought here two English officers to exchange for those Captain Sims had taken to Bristol. The Major will be led back today to Burlington by an officer and a mounted man. He is a good looking man, and very enthusiastic for their cause. He pleased me very much in what he said about the arrival of our other Hessian troops and he appeared greatly disturbed and curious concerning our operations this winter. He seemed more desirous for permanent public good than for immediate peace." Stryker, *BTP*, 320.

103 George Hills, *History of the Church in Burlington, New Jersey; Comprising the Facts and Incidents of Nearly Two Hundred Years, From Original, Contemporaneous Sources* (Trenton, NJ, 1876), 315; Dwyer, *TDIO*, 123.

104 Margaret Morris, *Private Journal Kept During a Portion of the Revolutionary War, for the Amusement of a Sister* (Philadelphia, 1836), 8; Dwyer, *TDIO*, 123.

gun.[105] This was quickly followed by a rain of bullets and more cannon fire. Von Donop quickly withdrew from the village, vowing to return when he had adequate firepower to respond to the Americans.

Unfortunately, this was not the end of Burlington's troubles. Already known for their British sympathies, the Americans now viewed its citizens as openly sympathetic to the hated Hessians. Now, the Americans would target Burlington, preventing both the British and the Hessians from using it and driving the townspeople into their cellars to avoid injury.

On December 12, Pennsylvania Marine Capt. William Shippin, still aboard the *Hancock*, received orders to land with his company and clear Burlington of any Hessian presence. Shippin was stern with the British and Hessian sympathizers, threatening to burn the village if he found they were harboring Hessian soldiers. Having spotted the son of a local widow named Margaret Morris observing the American ships with a telescope the previous day, Shippin also sought out this British "spy" to take into custody.[106] Morris recalled how "[t]he captain, a smart little fellow . . . said he wished he could see the spy-glass." Morris provided the telescope and convinced the Marine officer of her son's innocence, but it did little to dissuade his aggressive campaign of "hunting Tories in Burlington."

Enemy activity in Burlington confirmed Washington's belief that the British intended to move toward Philadelphia. Subsequently, he redirected his militia forces, blocking any possible crossings downriver from Trenton. Washington penned orders to Colonel Cadwalader, and then issued similar instructions to Generals Ewing and Dickinson.[107] He also directed Dickinson to secure Yardley's Ferry, extending his lines two miles downriver to tie in with Ewing.[108] Dickinson, 37, was an effective leader in the New Jersey Militia and a fair politician, later serving as a congressman for Delaware and a senator for New Jersey.[109] In the winter of 1776, Dickinson watched from across the Delaware River as the Hessians occupied his home in Trenton. Washington gave Ewing the responsibility of guarding a ford near Hoop's Mill on Biles Creek and extending his lines down to Bordentown

---

105 Morris, *Private Journal*, 8-9; Hills, *History of the Church in Burlington*, 315.

106 The following three quotes are from Morris, *Private Journal*, 12.

107 See Appendix B for Washington's orders. *FONA*, https://founders.archives.gov/documents/Washington/03-07-02-0240, accessed Nov. 23, 2019.

108 *FONA*, https://founders.archives.gov/documents/Washington/03-07-02-0241, accessed Nov. 23, 2019.

109 Robert Broadwater, *American Generals of the Revolutionary War: A Biographical Dictionary* (Jefferson, NC, 2007), 33.

Ferry to tie in with Cadwalader to the south.[110] Forty-year-old Ewing began his military service in 1755, serving with James Braddock's expedition during the French and Indian War.[111] He now commanded five regiments of Pennsylvania militia across the river from Trenton.

Two days later, Washington issued orders to Lord Stirling, Mercer, Stephen, and Fermoy, emphasizing the importance of maintaining a strong defense along the Delaware. He implored the generals to "give the enemy all the opposition they possibly can. Everything in a manner depends upon the defence at the water's edge."[112] He gave his commanders the freedom to act, informing them that "one brigade is to support another, without loss of time, or waiting for orders from me." Washington also reinforced a valuable lesson from the New York campaign by asking his commanders "to find out some person who can be engaged to cross the river as a spy, that we may, if possible, obtain some knowledge of the enemy's situation, movements, and intention." He continued,

> Particular inquiry should be made by the person sent, if any preparations are making to cross the river; whether any boats are building and where; whether they are coming over land from Brunswick; whether any great collection of horses is made, and for what purpose.

At some point over the next week, Shippin and his Marines transferred from the *Hancock* to the command of Colonel Cadwalader ashore. They were assigned to the Associators' 2nd Battalion. On December 13, Cadwalader and his brigade arrived in Bristol per Washington's orders. Major Nicholas occupied Bessonet's Tavern, and his Marines were quartered at the town's Quaker Meeting House.[113]

In a letter dated December 15, Cadwalader notified Washington, "I have sent several persons over [to the New Jersey side of the Delaware River] for Intelligence, & last Night sent Capt Shippen with 20 good men."[114] Shippin continued gathering intelligence while hunting for Hessians in and around Bordentown until December 17. Nicholas and the Continental Marines also participated in intelligence gathering and security patrols on the New Jersey side.

---

110 *FONA*, https://founders.archives.gov/documents/Washington/03-07-02-0242, accessed Nov. 23, 2019.

111 Broadwater, *American Generals of the Revolutionary War*, 37.

112 These three quotes are derived from instructions issued by General Washington from Keith's, December 14, 1776, quoted from Stryker, *BTP*, 62.

113 "Quarters of the several parts of Colonel Cadwalader's Brigade," 14 December 1776, *John Cadwalader's Papers, PHS*, quoted from Smith, *MIR*, 92.

114 *FONA*, http://founders.archives.gov/documents/Washington/03-07-02-0273, accessed Nov. 23, 2019.

Cadwalader and the other militiamen appeared to be following Washington's orders, but the commanding general was still apprehensive about the militia following their poor performances up to that point in the war. He sent Colonel Reed to assess the competence of Ewing, Dickinson, and Cadwalader and their men and to assist in conveying Washington's guidance. Reed informed Washington on December 12,

> The militia are crossing over in parties—I fear they do not mean to return[.] I do not know by whose orders—but if their Colonels have Power to give Permission in a little Time there will be none left. I do not like the Situation of Things at & above Coryell's Ferry—the Officers are quite new and seem to have little sense of the necessity of vigilance.[115]

While Reed did little to increase Washington's confidence in the militia, he was in no position to refuse their service. He continued to call for the assistance of Continental regulars from New York, but they were slow in coming, and time was running out. Enlistments were close to expiring, and ice would be forming soon on the Delaware River, providing the British and Hessians access into Pennsylvania.

Washington did what he could with the few regulars remaining with the army. He bolstered Cadwalader with the attachment of the Continental Marines and sent Col. Daniel Hitchcock's brigade of Continental regulars from the New England states once they arrived with Lee's division.[116] Thirty-seven-year-old Hitchcock had fought in nearly every major battle since the siege of Boston. Sadly, he died the following month from pneumonia and battle wounds sustained in the hard campaigning. Hitchcock was a prominent and well-experienced regular officer joining the militia brigade, which caused Washington some concern in assigning him to Cadwalader.

Washington promoted Cadwalader to brigadier general, clearly establishing his authority to command Hitchcock, Nicholas, and their regular Continental forces. Washington explained, "As the Colonels of the Continental Regiments might kick up some dust about Command (unless Cadwalader is considered by them in the light of a brigadier, which I wish him to be)."[117] Washington later

---

115 *FONA*, https://founders.archives.gov/documents/Washington/03-07-02-0251, accessed Nov. 23, 2019.

116 For more on Hitchcock see Catherine Williams, *Biography of Revolutionary Heroes: Containing the Life of Brigadier General William Barton and also, of Captain Stephen Olney* (Providence, RI, 1839), 300.

117 *FONA*, http://founders.archives.gov/documents/Washington/03-07-02-0329, accessed Nov. 23, 2019.

offered Cadwalader a permanent position as a general in the Continental Army, but he politely refused, remaining with his Philadelphia Associators.

Now that there were established defensive lines on the riverfront and a fallback position toward Germantown to block the enemy crossing into Pennsylvania, Washington could pause to contemplate his options. His immediate concern was holding the line on the Delaware, giving the army enough time to consolidate with Lee and Gates. But he wanted to do more. Washington's thinking aligned with the Chinese military strategist, Sun Tzu, who theorized, "Invincibility lies in the defense; the possibility of victory in the attack. One defends when his strength is inadequate; he attacks when it is abundant."[118] Washington knew he had to build his combat power before taking decisive action against the British and Hessians. He also realized the importance of immediate action if he were to accomplish anything before the next allotment of enlistments ended, which would decimate his force further.

For now, Washington intended to make life uncomfortable for the Hessians across the river. He ordered the militia to harass, attack, and attrite the enemy, keeping them on edge and tired. This would allow time for the arrival of additional Continental regulars with which he could finally strike back with a "brilliant stroke," hopefully saving the revolution and preserving the nascent country.[119]

---

118 Sun Tzu, *The Art of War*, S. B. Griffith, trans. (New York, 1982), 85.

119 See McCollough, *1776*, 271-272, for more on the genesis of Washington's thinking on effecting a "Brilliant Stroke" against the British.

Chapter Seven

Seizing the Initiative

"If we can draw our Forces together I trust under the smiles of Providence, we may yet effect an important stroke."

— Gen. George Washington[1]

*W*ashington's army in Pennsylvania consisted of many newcomers, as the core of regular Continental soldiers who fought beside him since New York had been decimated. The Maryland regiment, described by historian and author Patrick O'Donnell as "Washington's Immortals," started the New York campaign with 1,100 men. High casualties reduced them to approximately 100 by the time they reached Pennsylvania.[2] The proud 3rd Virginia Regiment had shrunk from 600 to approximately 140 men. The capable regiment known as the "Delaware Blues" experienced the greatest attrition, having been reduced from a strength of 700 down to a mere six. The regiment succumbed to casualties, desertions, and terminated enlistments. Their commander, Col. John Haslet, explained, "Captain Holland, Ensign Wilson, Dr. Gilder and myself are all who have followed the American cause to Trenton, two privates excepted."[3]

Washington desperately sought the reinforcements he had summoned from the other Continental regulars spread across New York and New Jersey, in addition to any fresh troops he could get from New Jersey and Pennsylvania. On December 2, Horatio Gates departed Albany with a force of 600-700 New Hampshire men. Washington shared with Gates, "With a handful of men,

---

1 *FONA*, https://founders.archives.gov/documents/Washington/03-07-02-0265, accessed Nov. 24, 2019.

2 Read Patrick O'Donnell's *Washington's Immortals* for an account of the Maryland Regiment's actions throughout the American Revolution.

3 Dwyer, *TDIO*, 120.

compared to the Enemy's Force, we have been pushed through the Jerseys without being able to make the smallest opposition & to pass the Delaware. Genl Howe is now on the other side, and beyond all question, means if possible to possess himself of Philadelphia." The commander-in-chief directed Gates to hasten his seven regiments to Pittstown, consolidating his division with that of Generals Lee and Heath.[4] Washington hoped to merge his dispersed forces beyond Howe's western flank at Pittstown, around 30 miles northwest of Trenton. He sent General Stirling to the linkup point to guide the combined force of regulars 11 miles southwest, where boats were waiting at Tinicum Ferry to transport the troops across the Delaware. A frustrated Washington wrote to Lee, "I have so frequently mentioned our situation, and the necessity of your aid, that it is painful to me to add a word upon the Subject. Let me once more request and entreat you to march immediately for Pitts Town."[5]

His tone was markedly different toward Heath, to whom he stated, "I am extremely pleased by the ready attention you have paid to my Orders and have only to request that you will proceed with your Troops with all possible expedition to Pitts Town, pursuing General Lee's rout & where I expect you will join him." He added, "if we can collect our Force speedily, I should hope we may effect something of importance, or at least give our Affairs such a turn as to make 'em assume a more promising aspect than they now have."[6]

Although Lee began moving his troops south on December 2, he followed his own plan and made slow progress. Lee believed that if he could achieve a significant victory as Washington was experiencing multiple defeats, Congress would agree that he was the better choice as commander. Lee sought an opportunity to strike the British at either Princeton or Brunswick, going as far as to write the president of the Council of Massachusetts, "There are times when we must commit treason against the laws of the state, and the present crisis demands this brave virtuous kind of treason."[7] On December 13, Lee went further in trying to justify his actions in a letter to Gates:

> a certain great Man is most damnably deficient—He has thrown me into a situation where I have my choice of difficulties—if I stay in this Province I risk

4 *FONA*, https://founders.archives.gov/documents/Washington/03-07-02-0265, accessed Nov. 24, 2019.

5 *FONA*, https://founders.archives.gov/documents/Washington/03-07-02-0267, accessed Aug. 23, 2020.

6 *FONA*, https://founders.archives.gov/documents/Washington/03-07-02-0266, accessed Nov. 24, 2019.

7 Dwyer, *TDIO*, 143.

myself and Army and if I do not stay the Province is lost forever—I have neither guides Cavalry Med[i]cines Money Shoes or Stockings—I must act with the greatest circumspection—Tories are in my front rear and on my flanks—the Mass of the People is strangely contaminated—in short unless something which I do not expect turns up We are lost.[8]

Unfortunately for Lee, his hubris and vanity finally caught up with him. For reasons unknown, he chose to spend the night in a tavern, several miles away from the protection of his soldiers. He ordered General Sullivan to begin moving the army south and had just finished writing the aforementioned letter when his guards sounded an alarm.

On December 12, Lord Cornwallis sent a patrol of 30 horsemen from the 16th Light Dragoons under 33-year-old Lt. Col. William Harcourt to gather intelligence on Lee's activities.[9] Harcourt eventually served 52 years in the service of his country, retiring in 1811 as a field marshal. Among Harcourt's group was a brash 22-year-old cornet [the third and lowest grade of commissioned officer] named Banastre Tarleton.[10] Tarleton would earn the nicknames "Bloody Ban," "The Butcher," and "The Green Dragoon" due to the brutality he repeatedly demonstrated in the later years of the war. He served in Parliament after the war in America and, by 1812, achieved the rank of lieutenant general, though he would never lead troops in combat again after the Revolution. Harcourt's men captured a local rebel and an express rider who, along with British sympathizers in the area, confirmed that Lee was quartered close by.

The Dragoons quickly took advantage of this unexpected opportunity. Harcourt sent Tarleton and an advance party forward, charging the tavern where they assumed Lee was staying. An exchange of gunfire ensued as Tarleton shouted that he "knew Genl. Lee was in the house, that if he would surrender himself, he and his attendants should be safe, but if my summons was not complied with immediately, the house should be burnt and every person without exception should be put to the sword."[11]

---

8 Charles Lee, "Letter," New York Historical Society College, 5:348, quoted in Commager & Morris, *SSS*, 500.

9 T. A. Heathcote, *The British Field Marshals: 1736-1997: A Biographical Dictionary* (South Yorkshire, UK, 2012).

10 The British villain portrayed in Mel Gibson's 2000 film *The Patriot* is based on the real-life exploits of Banastre Tarleton; "Banastre Tarleton," https://www.battlefields.org/learn/biographies/banastre-tarleton, accessed Nov. 24, 2019.

11 Commager & Morris, *SSS*, 501.

Lee surrendered without incident. Tarleton described Lee's capture as "a most miraculous event—It appears like a dream."[12] Hessian Captain von Muenchhausen voiced the feelings of many upon hearing the news when he wrote, "Victoria! We have captured General Lee, the only rebel General whom we had cause to fear."[13] Washington expressed his frustration in a letter to his cousin on December 17: "Unhappy man! Taken by his own imprudence! going three or four miles from his own Camp to lodge, & within 20 of the Enemy."[14]

Neither Washington, the British, nor the Hessians realized at the time that Lee's capture provided a more valuable service to the Americans than anyone might have realized. This was proven true after his exchange when, 18 months later during the battle of Monmouth, Lee's actions almost caused the Continental Army to be defeated before Washington could save the day. Regardless, with word of Lee's capture, General Sullivan hastened the march of his army south to join Washington.

As Lee's drama played out to the northwest, the Hessians adjusted to their new winter home in Trenton. The small village served as a transportation node in 1776.[15] It was a waypoint for stagecoaches carrying passengers, cargo, and mail between New York and Philadelphia. Trenton's ferries provided the means for crossing the Delaware River. Its location, just beneath the river's falls, made it a destination for boats transporting commerce and people upriver from Philadelphia. Trenton contained roughly 100 houses, with two-thirds of them located north of Assunpink Creek; a stone bridge connected the central portion of the village with the remaining homes and mills on the south side of the creek. This bridge provided access to the River Road, which connected Trenton to Crosswicks, Bordentown, and Burlington villages on the New Jersey side of the Delaware, moving southwest toward Philadelphia over 30 miles away. The Assunpink was fordable at several locations east of the village, emptying its waters into the Delaware below Trenton Falls, where it was seven and a half feet deep, over a quarter mile wide, and fast-moving. Rising ground dominated either side of the creek.

Trenton was like most villages of the day. It possessed three taverns, a jail, three churches, a Quaker meeting house, and military barracks from the French and Indian War. Many homes were currently empty, as residents carried away or hid

12 Ibid., 502.

13 Dwyer, *TDIO*, 150.

14 *FONA*, https://founders.archives.gov/documents/Washington/03-07-02-0228, accessed Nov. 24, 2019.

15 Stryker, *BTP*, 90-93.

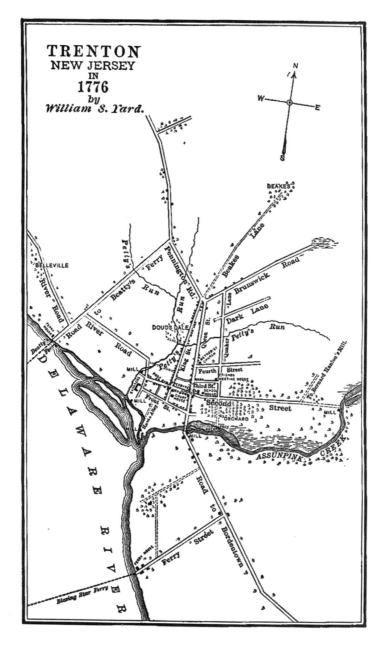

Map of Trenton. In 1776, Trenton was a small village that served as a transportation node and waypoint for stagecoaches carrying passengers, cargo, and mail between New York and Philadelphia. It would become the site of one of George Washington's greatest victories. Colonel Johann Rall led a brigade of Hessian soldiers in Trenton. Washington led a surprise attack against Trenton, defeating Rall's isolated force and helping to turn the tide of the war. *Stryker, The Battles of Trenton and Princeton, 93, https://archive.org/details/ cu31924086860784/page/n122*

their personal belongings in advance of the Hessians' arrival. Those who failed to leave before they got there would regret it.

Most homes were situated along two main streets, King and Queen, which ran north to south through the village, converging on high ground on the north side of the community. A prominent road continued north for 12 miles from this intersection that connected Trenton to Maidenhead and Princeton, while another road forked out eight miles to the northwest toward the town of Pennington. King and Queen streets terminated south at the River Road, running parallel to the Delaware, and leading to the stone bridge spanning Assunpink Creek. Toward the west was "The Hermitage," an estate owned by American militia General Philemon Dickinson, who was now with Washington. Like they did with many other houses in Trenton, Hessian mercenaries occupied The Hermitage with little regard for its treatment, which added to the public's scorn throughout the region.

American disdain for the Hessians began before their soldiers first arrived in Trenton. Congress had referred to the Hessians in drafting the Declaration of Independence months earlier when it wrote, "He [King George of England] is, at this time, transporting large armies of foreign mercenaries to complete the works of death, desolation, and tyranny, already begun, with circumstances of cruelty and perfidy scarcely paralleled in the most barbarous ages, and totally unworthy the head of a civilized nation."[16] These words were prophetic, as some citizens would experience cruelty at the hands of the Hessians during the battles of New York and New Jersey.

The Hessians' reputation was undoubtedly fed by their fierce fighting methods, acts of plunder, and differences in appearance from the familiar British. One American colorfully described the Hessian soldiers: "A towering brass-fronted cap; moustaches colored with the same material that colored his shoes, his hair plastered with tallow and flour, and tightly drawn into a long appendage reaching from the back of the head to his waist; his blue uniform almost covered by the broad belts sustaining his cartouche box, his brass-hilted sword, and his bayonet. . . . " The writer continued: "a yellow waistcoat with flaps, and yellow breeches, were met at the knee by black gaiters; and thus heavily equipped he stood an automaton, and received the command or cane of the officer who inspected him."[17]

Albeit from a different culture and raised to be professional soldiers—unlike the American citizen-soldier—the Hessians shared many similarities with Americans.

16 "The Declaration of Independence: A Transcription," https://www.archives.gov/founding-docs/declaration-transcript, accessed Nov. 25, 2019.

17 Stryker, *BTP*, 40; Margaret Moncrieffe Coghlan, *Memoirs of Mrs. Coghlan, Daughter of the Late Major Moncrieffe* (New York, 1864), 150.

Hessians were professional soldiers. The British hired several thousand Hessians to fight in America as mercenaries to help defeat the rebellious colonists. They showed little mercy toward Americans in battle and became feared opponents until Washington's army defeated the Hessian garrison at Trenton on December 26, 1776. Many Hessians settled in America following the war. *Wikimedia*

A profile of one company from the Knyphausen Regiment demonstrates that the Hessians were not the giants claimed by many reports. The tallest soldier in this company was 5'10", with the shortest being only 5'2". Many reported that the towering headgear worn by Hessians made them appear much taller. The ages of the soldiers also ranged from teenagers into their forties. Like their American counterparts, many Hessians were also men of faith, holding various skills, including weavers, tailors, shoemakers, millers, and carpenters.[18]

Howe assigned Hessian Col. Carl von Donop to guard the key terrain closest to the Americans. With his 3,000 troops, von Donop could control the area from Trenton to Burlington.[19] He believed Trenton was in an exposed position and should only be manned as a combat outpost of approximately 150 men. One of his regimental commanders, Col. Johann Rall, had grander ideas and convinced Howe to assign him the post. Rall further requested the command of an entire brigade of three regiments and reinforcements. He claimed that he had earned the right to do so based on his performance during the fighting at Chatterton's Hill during the battle of White

18 Stryker, *BTP*, 196.

19 Bardeleben Schlieffen, W. Heikennitz, Jung Kenn, Wangermann Schramm, & William Stryker, "Report of the Court-Martial for the Trial of the Hessian Officers Captured by Washington at Trenton, December 26, 1776," *PMHB* (1883), 7:45-49, found at www.jstor.org/stable/20084591, accessed Nov. 28, 2019.

Plains, and at the capture of Fort Washington. Howe granted Rall his wish and directed his posting in orders to von Donop.[20]

On December 12, Rall arrived in Trenton with his regiment and the von Knyphausen Regiment under the command of Maj. Friedrich von Dechow. The von Lossberg Regiment, under Lt. Col. Frances Scheffer, followed two days later. An artillery detachment, 50 jaegers, and 20 light dragoons joined the three regiments to round out Rall's newly formed brigade, bringing it to a strength of roughly 1400-1500 men.[21] Rall established his headquarters in the town's center, and sent his men into winter quarters. Each company from the three regiments was assigned private homes in which to quarter its troops. The dragoons established their quarters in the Friends meeting house on 3rd Street. The jaegers berthed in part of the military barracks on the village's south side and later moved to The Hermitage. The brigade established a hospital in the Presbyterian Church on 3rd Street about 100 feet east of Queen Street.

The artillery detachments were quartered in the Methodist Church on Queen Street and the English Church on King Street. Each regiment also received two brass three-pound guns. Initially, the six guns were arranged in the graveyard behind the English Church, but later they were moved next to the guardhouse by Rall's headquarters. The road's narrowness required the guns to be staged one behind the other in the middle of King Street.[22] Rall organized them for security purposes rather than employing them in defensive positions.[23] He came to regret this decision when Washington unexpectedly attacked days later.

Von Donop did not approve of Rall's "improper ambition." He directed the construction of defensive redoubts north along Pennington Road and south at Trenton Ferry to ward off any attacks that he believed would follow the occupation

---

20 "You are to command the troops to be cantoned at Trenton, Bordentown and Burlington to report and receive Orders from Major-General Grant at Brunswick and to communicate with Brigadier-General Leslie at Princetown.

The Brigade of Railee, fifty yagers and twenty Dragoons to be stationed at Trenton with six hessian three pounders. The Dragoons to be relieved once a week from Princetown.

Three Battalions of hessian Grenadiers and a Detachment of Yagers, with six hessian three pounders and if you please two British eighteen pounders, to take post at Bordentown.

A Bat. of hess. Gren and 42 d Regt. [British regulars] with two hessian three pounders and four british eighteen pounders, with two six and two three pounders, to form the Garrison of Burlington; you will fix such other posts as shall appear to be necessary to secure the communication of your cantonment." Stryker, *BTP*, 316.

21 Ward, *TWOR*, 296; Ferling, *AAM*, 173; Carbone, *Nathanael Greene*, 53; Fischer, *WC*, 396.

22 Stryker, *BTP*, 96-98.

23 Dwyer, *TDIO*, 168.

of Trenton.[24] Von Donop also assigned his engineer officer and another officer from the dragoon regiment to assist in choosing the locations of these positions. At first, Rall accepted the recommendations but ignored the order, against his better judgment. Rall's subordinates pleaded with him to erect defensive positions, to which he responded, "Let them come! We want no trenches! We'll at them with the bayonet!"[25] Von Donop later urged Rall to complete the redoubts, but Rall explained, "I have not made any redoubts or fortifications of any kind because I have enemy all around me."[26]

Rall's cavalier attitude toward the Americans and his lust for glory concerned his subordinate commanders. He underestimated the intelligence and ability of his foe. Rall referred to the Americans as "nothing but a lot of farmers," "country clowns," and a "miserable lot."[27] His desire to capture Philadelphia and destroy the Continental Army blinded Rall to some basic tenets of war. In addition to refusing to construct defensive positions, Rall failed to employ spies to gather intelligence on Washington's intentions. He also refused to move his units' baggage to a safe location to prevent its capture during unexpected attacks. This apathetic attitude was not helped by Gen. Grant's flippant response to Rall's request for additional troops: "Tell the colonel he is safe; I will undertake to keep the peace in New Jersey with a corporal's guard."[28] This overconfidence would result in additional missteps.

Rall also declined to see to the basic needs of his soldiers. He mocked his subordinate commanders' requests for winter socks, boots, and clothing by stating that he would soon run barefoot over the ice of the Delaware River to take Philadelphia.[29] When Major Dechow persisted in requesting winter clothes, Rall admonished him, stating that if Dechow did not care to share in the glory that awaited them, he could be relieved from his post. The concerns of Rall's lieutenants ran so deep that they predicted the brigade's ruin while voicing their desires to be relieved of their responsibilities to a visiting Hessian officer. The officer promised to carry their letter of concern to Lt. Gen. Philip von Heister, the senior Hessian in

24 Ibid., 151.

25 Arthur Lefkowitz, *George Washington's Indispensable Men: Alexander Hamilton, Tench Tilghman, and the Aides-de-Camp who Helped Win American Independence* (Mechanicsburg, PA, 2003), 90; Stryker, *BTP*, 107.

26 Stryker, *BTP*, 332; Dwyer, *TDIO*, 151, 153.

27 Schlieffen, Heikennitz, Kenn, Schramm, & Stryker, "Report of the Court-Martial," 296; Stryker, *BTP*, 107; Scheer & Rankin, *RR*, 211.

28 William Grimshaw, *History of the United States, from Their First Settlement as Colonies, to the Cession of Florida in Eighteen Hundred and Twenty One* (Philadelphia, 1826), 131; Stryker, *BTP*, 108; Scheer & Rankin, *RR*, 211.

29 The information in this paragraph was derived from Stryker, *BTP*, 99-100.

the United States stationed in New York. Unfortunately, the letter would not arrive in time to help the Hessians languishing at Trenton.

Even though he was not expecting a major attack, Rall did take some precautionary measures to protect against small raids at Trenton. He established six picket positions to provide early warning of rebel attacks from any direction.[30] He selected the Maidenhead, Pennington, and River roads, the Assunpink Creek bridge, the road to Trenton Ferry, and a drawbridge over Crosswicks Creek as the best locations for these outposts.

The Maidenhead Road picket was Rall's primary guard post. He assigned a commissioned officer, three under-officers, and 70 men to conduct guard duty in the town from Mrs. Joseph Bond's Fox Chase Tavern. Rall maintained a captain at this post to serve as an inspector. He assigned a corporal and 15 men to the Pennington Road picket on the village's northwest side. They operated from the home of local coopers Richard and Arthur Howell. The Hermitage became the picket site along the River Road west of Trenton. It was manned by the jaegers, who were also guarding the village to the south from potential crossings. A sergeant and 18 men comprised the picket at the Assunpink Creek bridge and were responsible for controlling the traffic there.

Rall's fifth picket was at an old tavern on the Ferry Road leading to the river. It consisted of a commissioned officer, five non-commissioned officers, and 22 men. This unit maintained guards at Dr. William Bryant's residence and the Trenton Ferry. They were ordered to remain in hiding during the day to avoid rebel cannon fire from across the river. The Hessians established a final picket at a drawbridge spanning Crosswicks Creek southwest of Trenton. They intended to keep the communication lines open with Col. Von Donop as he was stationing his garrison at Bordentown and Burlington, 13 and 18 miles from Trenton, respectively. A commissioned officer and 100 men manned the Crosswicks Creek picket, with orders to withdraw to Bordentown if Trenton came under attack.

Rall's daily routine taxed his men to their limits. Initially, each regiment served three days on duty followed by one day of rest. All guard and sentinel posts received relief at 9:00 a.m. each morning. Each day at 11:00 a.m., the regiment held a parade to inspect the troops, and at 4:00 p.m., all pickets received relief, and troops received the new password. Additionally, Rall had his men stacking their muskets in front of their commanders' quarters for quick retrieval during emergencies, and troops were to remain in their fighting gear while off duty. He

---

30 Information concerning the descriptions of the six Hessian positions found in the following paragraphs is primarily derived from Stryker, *BTP*, 101-104; a drawing of the disposition of Hessian forces during the battle of Trenton can be found in Fischer, *WC*, 406-407.

also kept the regiments' horses bridled and saddled to respond to unexpected enemy actions rapidly.

This cycle established a pattern that the Americans could exploit and would help to establish the time Washington intended to attack. The routine began wearing down Rall's men and animals. Additionally, inadequate winter clothing led to fatigue, and many succumbed to illness. Rall would change his duty rotations, having each regiment serve a full day and single night cycle before being relieved. But this did not provide much relief, as fears of a pending attack led Rall to keep his soldiers on a heightened alert and performing additional tasks while not on duty.

As Rall set about establishing his rotations, Washington struggled to increase the size of his force and awaited the arrival of the Continental regulars. The mixed loyalties of New Jersey and Pennsylvania citizens challenged his ability to determine their reliability.

They proved to be very diverse in their loyalties.[31] Pockets of Tory loyalists and patriotic Whigs were interspersed throughout the countryside. Some communities consisted of stalwart loyalists willing to support and fight for the king, while others were moderates or patriots who only claimed an oath to the king to prevent persecution and loss of property. Some changed loyalties based on what side appeared most likely to win. To them, it was a matter of survival; for others, it was a matter of morals.

Communities of Quakers and Moravians attempted to remain neutral based on their religious convictions, but this proved difficult in a country torn by conflict, and many families and communities were divided as individuals chose sides. Twenty-one-year-old Capt. John Lacey, Jr. left his family in Bucks County, Pennsylvania, in defiance of the Society of Friends to fight as a Continental soldier following Lexington and Concord. Though he was among a group of Quakers who volunteered, he was the only one to remain when the local congregation called the men in to inform them of its intent to "read them out of the meeting" if they persisted in going to war. Lacey stayed in the ranks, and the clerk of the Buckingham Meeting responded by publishing minutes that read, "Whereas John Lacey . . . hath so far deviated from the principles of Friends as to learn the art of War . . . [and] not coming to a sense of this error . . . [we] can have no further Unity with him as a Member of our Society until he comes to a sense of

---

31 For a profile of loyalists in New Jersey, see Edward Jones, *The Loyalists of New Jersey: Their Memorials, Petitions, Claims, Etc., from English Records* (reprint, Boston, 1972); for a profile of loyalists in Pennsylvania see Wilbur Siebert, *The Loyalists of Pennsylvania* (Columbus, OH, 1920), 22-31; John Lacey & John Armstrong, "Memoirs of Brigadier-General John Lacey, of Pennsylvania (continued)," *PMHB* (1902), 26:101-111, found at www.jstor.org/stable/20086016, accessed Nov. 30, 2019.

his Misconduct."[32] As a militiaman, Lacey served honorably before transitioning to the regular army, attaining the rank of brigadier general by the war's end.

Lacey was not the only patriot to sacrifice in the service of his country. Sixty-two-year-old clergyman John Rosbrugh left a wife and five children behind to join the army.[33] He was the pastor of the Allen Township Presbyterian Church in Northampton County, Pennsylvania, 50 miles northwest of Philadelphia. The Allen community had done its part in the fight for independence. The previous year, townsmen joined the "Flying Camp" under Gen. Hugh Mercer to fight in New York and were captured at Fort Washington. General Washington sought the townspeople of Allen's help again, urging the militia to come "to the assistance of the Continental army, that by our joint endeavors, we may put a stop to the progress of the enemy, who are making preparations to advance to Philadelphia as soon as they cross the Delaware, either by boats or on the ice."[34]

In an impassioned speech to his congregation, Rosbrugh encouraged those remaining men able to bear arms to join and volunteered his services as their chaplain. Many agreed, but only if Rosbrugh assumed command of their company. Rosbrugh accepted and drafted a will before departing home in which he quoted the Bible, "Jer. 49:11 'Leave the fatherless children, I will preserve them alive; and let the widows trust in me.'"[35] Sadly, Rosbrugh's prophesy came true when he was killed two weeks later in the battle of Assunpink Creek, otherwise known as the Second Battle of Trenton.[36]

The Continentals traveling south to join Washington did not experience the same patriotism and support provided by men like Lacey and Rosbrugh. On December 13, Sullivan informed Washington of Lee's capture and promised to quickly join Washington with Lee's force.[37] Sullivan now commanded approximately 2,000 men predominately from Massachusetts, Connecticut, and New York. They proceeded to Phillipsburg, New Jersey, 40 miles upriver from Trenton, and on December 16 crossed the Delaware River to Easton, Pennsylvania.

---

32 Lacey & Armstrong, "Memoirs of Brigadier-General John Lacey," *PMHB*, 1-13; Dwyer, *TDIO*, 156-160.

33 Parker Thompson, *From its European Antecedents to 1791: The United States Army Chaplaincy* (Washington, D.C., 1978), 148-153.

34 Ibid., 150; Dwyer, *TDIO*, 208.

35 Dwyer, *TDIO*, 209.

36 Thompson, *The United States Army Chaplaincy*, 148; Holger Hoock, *Scars of Independence: America's Violent Birth* (New York, 2017), 159.

37 *FONA*, https://founders.archives.gov/documents/Washington/03-07-02-0261, accessed Nov. 30, 2019.

Sullivan's men found a community already impacted by war. Most able-bodied men had departed to serve in the army, and those remaining were unwilling to help. Sullivan's men were tired and hungry but were denied homes to warm themselves, wood to burn, straw to lie on, and food to eat. The locals rejected the Continental paper currency used to pay for the requested goods. Many soldiers ignored this inhospitality by helping themselves to whatever they wanted. The soldiers' growing disdain for the locals was intensified by their refusal to serve.

Many of the remaining men in Easton openly opposed the war. Some would physically assault recruiters trying to form local militia companies. Others refused to march to Washington's aid even after they received advance payment for their service. One company of militiamen got three pounds per man but disobeyed their marching orders unless given compensation for the idle time they spent at home prior to receiving these orders.[38] Local leaders refused, and the company disbanded. Word of these payments angered the regular soldiers, many of whom had served for months in combat and under harsh conditions with no pay. Incidents like this also frustrated Washington.

On crossing into Pennsylvania, Washington began to receive reports of disaffected communities and the people's unwillingness to join the cause of freedom. On December 20, he wrote to Congress, "the Enemy are daily gathering strength from the disaffected; This strength, like a Snowball by rolling, will increase, unless some means can be devised to check effectually, the progress of the Enemy's Arms."[39] Washington voiced similar sentiments in an earlier letter to his cousin Lund: "A large part of the Jerseys have given every proof of disaffection that a people can do, & this part of Pennsylvania are equally inimical; in short your imagination can scarce extend to a situation more distressing than mine—Our only dependance now, is upon the Speedy Inlistment of a New Army; if this fails us, I think the game will be pretty well up."[40]

Although Congress was implementing steps to assist in recruiting troops, Washington had concerns about its methods, writing, "The unhappy policy of short Inlistments, and a dependance upon Militia will, I fear, prove the downfall of our cause."[41] He further voiced his concerns: "Can anything (the exigency of the case indeed may justify it) be more destructive to the recruiting service, than

---

38 Dwyer, *TDIO*, 197.

39 *FONA*, https://founders.archives.gov/documents/Washington/03-07-02-0305, accessed Dec. 1, 2019.

40 *FONA*, https://founders.archives.gov/documents/Washington/03-07-02-0228, accessed Nov. 24, 2019.

41 Ibid.

giving ten dollars bounty for six weeks' service of the militia, who come in you cannot tell how, go you cannot tell when; consume your provisions, exhaust your stores, and leave you at last at a critical moment?"[42] This problem was exacerbated by the states, who were offering bounties to locals who joined the militia for short stints. On December 12, the Philadelphia Assembly offered a bounty of 10 dollars to all volunteers who would join Washington on or before December 20, seven dollars to those who would enlist before December 25, and five dollars to those who joined before December 30.[43]

While attempting to help Washington, politicians had inadvertently made the local militia more attractive than service in the Continental Army, Navy, and Marines. Just as privateers offered a greater financial reward and lifestyle than a rough life at sea as a sailor or marine, life as a part-time militiaman was now becoming more profitable than service in the army. Furthermore, early soldiers, sailors, and marines did not receive a bounty upon enlisting. This challenged Washington's ability to maintain the morale of the regular servicemen. These troops had already given so much, and now Washington was relying on them to engage the enemy again, right before many of their enlistments were due to expire. They were ready to return home. Washington provided the Congress with a warning: "I rather think, the design of Genl Howe, is to possess himself of Philadelphia this Winter, if possible, and in truth, I do not see what is to prevent him, as ten days more will put an end to the existence of our Army."[44]

On December 15, Horatio Gates crossed the Delaware River approximately 20 miles upriver from Easton with 600 New Hampshire soldiers and found a population with mixed loyalties. Local Whigs reported Tory groups in the area that were ready to take up arms against their patriotic neighbors. Gates's men pushed forward to join Washington. They stopped in the villages of Mount Bethel, Nazareth, and Easton, where they found wounded and sick soldiers. Washington had directed the establishment of hospitals at Easton, Allentown, and Bethlehem to remove ineffective troops from the region surrounding Trenton, where he expected action against the enemy.[45]

---

42 *FONA*, https://founders.archives.gov/documents/Washington/03-07-02-0305, accessed Dec. 1, 2019.

43 Stryker, *BTP*, 19-20.

44 *FONA*, https://founders.archives.gov/documents/Washington/03-07-02-0305, accessed Dec. 1, 2019.

45 Louis Duncan, *Medical Men in the American Revolution, 1775-1783* (Carlisle, PA, 1931), 167; Richard Blanco, "American Army Hospitals in Pennsylvania During the Revolutionary War," https://journals.psu.edu/phj/article/viewFile/24277/24046, accessed Dec. 1, 2019; Dwyer, *TDIO*, 204.

On December 17, Sullivan and Gates finally converged their forces in Bethlehem, and the Continentals found a more accommodating population. Although their religious beliefs prevented them from bearing arms, the local Moravians were willing to do their part for the cause. Soldiers received food and were provided shelter from the winter weather. The Moravians were *not* willing, however, to share their women. Gates felt obligated to post a guard at each door of the "Sisters' House" until the troops withdrew. Tragically, previous wounds and sickness overcame many soldiers, taking a toll on Washington's dwindling numbers. Over the next three months, 110 soldiers were buried in Bethlehem alone, while more died at other hospitals.[46]

With the armies from the north finally arriving in Pennsylvania, an increased air of confidence permeated the American camps, although the situation remained precarious. Major Samuel Webb, one of General Washington's aides-de-camp, captured the climate well when he wrote,

> You ask me our situation. It has been the Devil, but is to appearance better. About two thousand of us have been obliged to run damned hard before ten thousand of the enemy. Never was finer lads at a retreat then we are. . . . No fun for use that I can see. However, I cannot but think we shall drub the dogs. . . . Never mind, all will come right one of these days.[47]

Webb had been wounded at Bunker Hill and White Plains, and would be again at Trenton. He was later promoted to colonel, commanded a regiment, and was captured by the British. He remained active upon his release and went on to live a happy life before dying in 1807.[48]

While Webb had reasons to remain hopeful about the Americans' ability to inflict a blow against the British, it was not a widely shared opinion. The arrival of the north's regulars was not to be as beneficial as some hoped, though it likely benefitted the Americans more mentally than it did in superior numbers. The 5,000-7,000-man force with which Lee had departed New York had dwindled to roughly 2,000 by the time it reached Pennsylvania. Gates brought an additional force of approximately 600 men. Including the Associators and Marines, Washington's force was just over 7,000 troops of combined Continental regulars and militia.

46 Mark Shaffer, "The Revolutionary War Burial Ground in Bethlehem," https://pahistoricpreservation.com/revolutionary-war-burial-ground-bethlehem/, accessed Dec. 1, 2019; Dwyer, *TDIO*, 206.

47 Webb, *Correspondence and Journals*, 1:175.

48 Phillip R. Giffin, "Samuel Blachley Webb: Wethersfield Ablest Officer," *Journal of the American Revolution*, https://allthingsliberty.com/2016/09/samuel-blachley-webb-1753-1807/, accessed Dec. 1, 2019; Dwyer, *TDIO*, 165.

He still would have to guard over 40 miles of riverfront, protect Philadelphia, and determine how best to strike the British. Though this seemed plausible on the surface, Washington only had two weeks before enlistments ending on December 31 would reduce his strength to around 1,400 men.[49] The service of the Continental Marines, their brothers in the Pennsylvania State Marines, and others who volunteered to serve into the new year bolstered Washington's diminishing army. But with such low numbers, Washington would have to act quickly if he hoped to exploit his current strength.

He once more received assistance in the form of Thomas Paine's eloquent words. Paine's newest pamphlet—*The American Crisis*— was finally finished.[50] Paine found a printer in Philadelphia to publish and disseminate thousands of copies of his latest call to service to the American people. The timing of its release could not have been better. Washington's regulars had not been paid in months, lacked many basic supplies, missed their families, and for some, the promise of returning to their normal lives was within grasp. Many could not wait to end their service. The prospects of a looming American defeat and a nation split between loyalties offered additional challenges. These issues were exacerbated by a national capital under martial law, a Congress that had fled, and economic woes, including a currency that often proved worthless. There was little confidence in a nascent government that had proven inept and a commander who experienced nothing but defeat for months. Many believed the end was near.

Paine's words had a galvanizing effect on the American psyche. He challenged them to look beyond their current troubles toward a better future, declaring,

> These are the times that try men's souls. The summer soldier and the sunshine patriot will, in this crisis, shrink from the service of their country; but he that stands it now deserves the love and thanks of man and woman. Tyranny, like hell, is not easily conquered . . . the harder the conflict, the more glorious the triumph.[51]

Paine challenged his fellow Americans to rise to the occasion and not lose this opportunity to secure their independence and freedom. He placed the onus for victory on the shoulders of those who had not yet answered the call to service, noting that "officers and men, though greatly harassed and fatigued, frequently without rest, covering or provision, the inevitable consequences of a long retreat,

---

49 Scheer & Rankin, *RR*, 210.

50 Foner, ed., *Thomas Paine: Collected Writings*.

51 The quotes in the following paragraph were derived from Conway, ed., *Complete Writings of Paine*, 1:170-173.

bore it with a manly and martial spirit." Paine concluded with a subtle reminder that it was not too late for each citizen to do their part: "All their wishes centered in one, which was that the country would turn out and help them to drive the enemy back."

Paine's words resonated with many, but Washington understood that actions are stronger than words. He energized his commanders to harass the enemy while gathering intelligence to decide what action to take before time ran out. Though Washington knew of Howe's return to New York, he still feared an attack by the British and Hessians once the Delaware River froze. He hoped to conduct what in modern terms is referred to as a "spoiling attack" by grasping the initiative from the enemy before they could execute their plans.

The local militia provided a valuable service in setting the conditions for decisive action by the commander-in-chief. As the Continental regulars recovered from their long journey and the Associators and Marines operated closer to Philadelphia, the militiamen under Generals Dickinson and Ewing went into action around Trenton. Many enlisted from the areas now occupied by the British and Hessians. Their knowledge of the terrain, along with a growing hatred for the Hessians who continued to plunder and ravage local families and property, produced a determined force employing guerrilla tactics against an increasingly fatigued enemy.

By mid-December, small groups were consistently harassing and inflicting casualties and suspicion in Rall's brigade.[52] On December 16, Ewing's men conducted a raid across the Delaware under the protective fire of shore-based artillery from Pennsylvania. The Americans attacked an isolated Hessian outpost near the river, crossing back before Rall could react. On December 17, American militia in New Jersey ambushed a patrol and severely injured a dragoon as his unit patrolled toward Pennington. The following day, they surprised another patrol on its way to Maidenhead, killing another dragoon, and Ewing's men conducted a larger raid against the same outpost it had previously attacked. On December 19, the Americans captured three Hessian soldiers who were foraging two miles north of Trenton. Hessian anxiety increased as the Americans made it increasingly dangerous to wander outside the confines of Trenton.

Rall's response to the increased attacks further degraded the willpower and readiness of his troops. He deployed larger patrols to hunt for the militiamen roaming the countryside and increased the size of his outposts. Attempting to deter militia activity, Rall sent 100 men and a cannon to deliver a single dispatch

---

52 Stryker, *BTP*, 323-324, 326, 329; Fischer, *WC*, 193-195.

to Princeton.[53] Following the raids, Rall began mustering his entire force before dawn and deploying an entire company with two guns to the river post. Although he hoped to deter future attacks, Rall only wore his troops down further. The Americans responded on December 21 by conducting another surprise raid, this time without the forewarning of artillery, burning several buildings before escaping yet again.

Frustrated, Howe and Rall issued harsh orders against any locals found opposing their troops. One stated, "His Excellency the Commander-in-Chief orders that all inhabitants that shall be found with arms, not having an officer with them shall be immediately taken and hung up."[54] Another order published on December 12 stated, "Small straggling parties not dressed like soldiers and without officers, not being admissible in war who presumes to molest or fire upon soldiers or peaceable inhabitants of the country, will be immediately hanged without trial as assassins."[55]

Rall also wrote to Colonel von Donop and Generals Leslie and Grant for assistance. He claimed that Trenton was indefensible due to the increasing American activity. Though concerned, Rall still failed to construct the redoubts von Donop had ordered. Leslie temporarily sent additional troops to Maidenhead, maintaining the line of communication between the British and Hessian outposts. Leslie's reinforcement was short-lived, as his soldiers received orders to march back to Princeton shortly after their arrival. Grant was less sympathetic. He downplayed the rebel presence operating near Trenton and refused to send Rall any additional troops.[56]

Von Donop, who was facing his own challenges, could not assist Rall. Von Donop attempted to obey Howe's orders to garrison Bordentown, but the village lacked adequate lodging for the number of troops needed. Necessity forced von Donop to distribute his men across farms and residences throughout the New Jersey

---

53 Stryker, *BTP*, 331.

54 Ralph Izard, *Correspondence of Mr. Ralph Izard, of South Carolina: From the Year 1774-1804; With a Short Memoir*, vol. 1 (New York, 1844), 269.

55 Stryker, *BTP*, 484.

56 Grant wrote to Rall, "I am sorry to hear your Brigade has been fatigued or alarmed. You may be assured that the rebel army in Pennsylvania which has been joined by Lee's Corps, Gates and Arnolds does not exceed eight thousand men who have neither shoes nor stockings, are in fact almost naked, dying of cold, without blankets and very ill supplied with Provisions. On this Side [of] the Delaware they have not three hundred men. They stroll about in small parties, under the command of subaltern officers none of them above the rank of Captain, and their principal object is to pick up some of our Light Dragoons . . . as General Howe does not approve of Maidenhead for a Post, I cannot send troops there." Ibid., 335.

side of the Delaware River. This resulted in the loss of unit cohesion, challenging the colonel's ability to reinforce Rall in Trenton.

Continued American control of the Delaware impacted von Donop's command in other ways. The Pennsylvania navy and marines operating on the river forced the Hessians out of Burlington without a fight, as the firing of the ships' cannons made it untenable. Von Donop wanted to challenge the American vessels and requested the 18-pound guns of the Hessian grenadier battalion, von Kohler, from New York, but they had not arrived.[57] Instead, Donop deployed the 42nd Highlander Regiment in Burlington to the village of Black Horse, safely outside the reach of enemy warships.

On December 22, von Donop received a report from the Highlanders' commander, 43-year-old Lt. Col. Thomas Stirling, that a large group of Americans had crossed into Pennsylvania.[58] Watching the British and Hessian movements, Israel Putnam assigned 30-year-old Col. Samuel Griffin to lead a group of 600 militiamen and volunteers against the Hessian advance in the counties across the river from Philadelphia.[59] Griffin requested that Cadwalader provide 200-300 volunteers and two pieces of artillery before moving toward Mount Holly. Griffin's activity alerted Stirling, who implored von Donop to "come here and attack them before they have time to extend themselves so as to surround us or to form a plan to drive us from hence."[60]

On December 23, von Donop personally led Stirling's Highlanders, along with the Hessian Block and Linsing Battalions, to confront the American threat. He left 80 men behind to guard Bordentown. The two forces met in front of the Mount Holly Meeting House, exchanging cannon fire before the Americans began retreating, as Cadwalader's regiment had not reinforced them. Washington had canceled Cadwalader's movement, preserving his troops for a more ambitious undertaking. Instead of pursuing the Americans, von Donop held his force at Mount Holly for two days "to let the people longing for protection take an oath of allegiance to the King," while also allowing his men to break into liquor stocks and plunder local homes.[61] Von Donop reportedly became infatuated with a local widow, whom some speculate may have been a plant to hold von Donop and his force in place. Meanwhile, Washington moved against the Hessians at

57 Ibid., 333.

58 Ibid., 335.

59 *FONA*, https://founders.archives.gov/documents/Washington/03-07-02-0324, accessed Dec. 3, 2019.

60 Stryker, *BTP*, 335.

61 Dwyer, *TDIO*, 217.

Trenton. Hessian Captain Ewald later described von Donop as "extremely devoted to the fair sex" and explained how he had "found in his quarters an exceedingly beautiful young widow."[62]

Although Griffin's force achieved little tactically, it inadvertently achieved an operational coup. They drew von Donop and his 2,000 troops away from Bordentown, and they were no longer in a position to mutually support Rall. Von Donop's regiment was now 18 miles away, a full day's march from Trenton, providing Washington an open opportunity if he chose to seize it.

Washington had a lot to consider, as according to the military records, from late December 1776, he had 679 officers and 10,804 enlisted men on hand. Nearly half of these were sick, wounded, pulling extra duty, or on furlough.[63] It is generally accepted that around 4,000-5,000 troops were available for action before the end of the year when the next group of enlistments expired.[64] While all indications showed that Howe did not intend to capture Philadelphia until spring, Washington remained concerned about the possibility of such an attack.

Although their position was still dire, there was a growing sense among the Americans that the time was right to strike their enemy. Congressman Robert Morris wrote to John Hancock, "As our enemies are still kept at bay on the other side of Delaware I cannot help flattering myself with the expectation of some favorable event that will save the city. I shall certainly remain here as long as I can with safety."[65] In a letter dated December 21, General Greene told the governor of Rhode Island, "We are now on the west side of the Delaware; our force is small when collected together; but small as it is, I hope we shall give the enemy a stroke in a few days."[66] One of Washington's staff officers noted in his diary on December 22, "From what I see I am quite certain Washington intends to make some movement soon. He keeps his own counsel, but is very much determined."[67]

Washington had been considering a counterstrike against the British since mid-December, but the time to act had arrived. He had been waiting to consolidate his forces, establish favorable conditions on the ground, and for the enemy to make a mistake he could exploit—all three aligned by the third week of December. The

---

62 Ibid.; Lengel, *General George Washington*, 191.

63 Stryker, *BTP*, 85.

64 Ibid.; Fischer, *WC*, 208-209; McCollough, 1776, 272-273; Leckie, *George Washington's War*, 319.

65 Morgan, ed., *NDAR*, 7:483.

66 Thaddeus Allen, *An Inquiry Into the Views, Services, Principles, and Influences of the Leading Men in the Origination of our Union, and the Formation and Early Administration of the Present Government* (Boston: 1847), 384; Benson Lossing, *The Pictorial Field-Book of the Revolution*, 3 vols. (1850; reprint, Gretna, LA, 2008), 2:225.

67 Stryker, *BTP*, 361.

only question remaining was where to attack. Washington relied on several sources of information to assist with this decision. He employed raiding parties, patrols, prisoners, local civilians, and spies to gather intelligence. At times, he relied on them to plant misinformation and doubt in the enemy leadership. Washington was often one of only a few individuals who knew the identity of informants.

John Honeyman of Griggstown, New Jersey, allegedly was one of Washington's most valuable spies.[68] Honeyman reportedly met Washington during the retreat through Hackensack and agreed to become a spy. To gain access to British lines, Honeyman remained in New Jersey, posing as a British sympathizer. He was a butcher, selling beef to the British and Hessian soldiers while providing access to information on the enemy's disposition, composition, and strength.

Honeyman's actions put him and his family at risk. Not only could he be hanged as a spy, but American patriots also identified him as a Tory traitor for doing business with the enemy. Washington supposedly provided Honeyman's wife with a letter that stated, "The wife and children of John Honeyman of Griggstown, the notorious Tory now within the British lines and probably acting the part of a spy," should be "protected from all harm and annoyance."[69] To preserve his cover, however, the letter offered "no protection to Honeyman himself."

Honeyman supposedly provided invaluable intelligence to Washington concerning the Hessians in Trenton that likely contributed to the commander's ultimate decision. Honeyman conducted business in and around Trenton on December 22, departing once he gathered the information sought on the Hessians. Honeyman purposely moved down the River Road to where two American scouts would be. He was quickly "apprehended" and brought to Washington's headquarters. Washington and Honeyman spent 30 minutes alone behind closed doors before Honeyman later "escaped" and made his way back to Trenton.

---

68 John Honeyman's story is depicted as true in Stryker's *BTP*, 87-89, Thomas Allen's, *George Washington, Spymaster: How the Americans Outspied the British and Won the Revolutionary War* (Washington, D.C., 2004), 48-49, and Thomas Flemings's *1776* (eBook, Boston, 2016). David Hackett Fischer, however, raises questions about the validity of the "Honeyman Legend" in *WC*, 423. Though Fischer makes a compelling argument, I present it here as plausible considering the ample evidence that Washington employed spy rings such as the Culper group in Long Island and Connecticut. Ken Daigler, an experienced intelligence officer, adds, "an experienced intelligence officer is likely to put more faith in the story, even without full documentation, than someone outside the profession. Honeyman's story is representative of Washington's capabilities and previous actions to leverage intelligence to achieve a military success. Thus, Honeyman's story deserves to be told." Quoted from Ken Daigler, "George Washington's Attacks on Trenton and Princeton, 1776-77," *The Intelligencer Journal of U.S. Intelligence Studies*, vol. 25, no. 1 (Spring-Summer 2019).

69 The following two quotes and related information are found in John Van Dyke, "An Unwritten Account of a Spy of Washington," *Our Home Magazine*, (Somerville, NJ, October 1873), as quoted in Stryker, *BTP*, 88-89.

He reportedly met with Colonel Rall to share his story while feeding him false information about the condition of the Continental Army.

Washington verified Honeyman's information through additional sources. Local militia and patriotic farmers from the counties around Trenton reported the strength and condition of the enemy, while others verified British dispositions that could impact any attack. Joseph Reed, working with Cadwalader near Bristol, informed Washington of the findings of one of his spies on December 22. Reed verified that the British appeared to be remaining in winter quarters and reported on the American militia activity drawing von Donop to Mount Holly. This intelligence reinforced the thoughts Washington had already been contemplating for weeks.[70]

Washington's generals were working with other sources. On December 23, General Fermoy shared information he received from a young boy he had hired to report back on the Hessian situation in Trenton. After hearing the boy's report, Washington remarked, "Now is our time to clip their wings while they are so spread."[71] While no accurate records of specific patrols remain, Samuel Nicholas and the Continental Marines and William Shippin's Pennsylvania marines were actively patrolling to gather intelligence on the New Jersey side of the Delaware. These combined intelligence efforts assisted Washington in deciding to attack the Hessians at Trenton. Now all he needed was a plan.

Washington gathered his senior officers at his headquarters outside of Newtown for a council of war. The division and brigade commanders present included Major Generals Sullivan and Greene and Brigadier Generals Stirling, Fermoy, Mercer, Stephen, and St. Clair. Washington also invited certain trusted regimental commanders who had proven their worth, including Colonels Sargent, Stark, Glover, and Knox. Generals Putnam, Ewing, Dickinson, and Colonel Cadwalader did not attend, presumably due to distance. General Gates, now second in command due to Lee's capture, feigned sickness and opted not to attend.

The commander-in-chief shared his ambitious vision. They would recross the Delaware and conduct near-simultaneous attacks against the British and Hessians

---

70 On Dec. 22, Reed wrote to Washington, "We are all of Opinion my dear General that something must be attempted to revive our expiring Credit, give our Cause some Degree of Reputation & prevent a total Depreciation of the Continental Money which is coming on very fast—that even a Failure cannot be more fatal than to remain in our present Situation in short some Enterprize must be undertaken in our present Circumstances or we must give up the Cause—In a little Time the Continental Army is dissolved the Militia must be taken before their Spirits & Patience are exhausted & the scattered divided State of the Enemy affords us a fair Oppy of trying what our Men will do when called to an offensive Attack—Will it not be possible my dear Genl for your Troops or such Part of them as can act with Advantage to make a Diversion or something more at or about Trenton." *FONA*, https://founders.archives.gov/documents/Washington/03-07-02-0324, accessed Dec. 3, 2019.

71 Stryker, *BTP*, 87.

at several locations. He also voiced his concern about attempting a dangerous crossing at this time of year. Colonel Glover, however, assured Washington that his Marblehead fisherman could successfully handle the boats under harsh conditions.

The council endorsed Washington's plan and began working on the details needed to assume the offensive. Forty-eight-year-old Col. John Starke of New Hampshire, frontier fighter and Battle of Bunker Hill hero, reminded his comrades that they needed to shift the mindset of their soldiers. "Your men have too long been accustomed to place their dependence for safety upon spades and pickaxes. If you ever expect to establish the independence of these States you must teach them to place dependence upon their firearms and courage."[72]

As the various commanders worked on the plans of attack, Washington wrote to his subordinates, informing them of the pending operation. He told Joseph Reed, who was still working with Cadwalader, "Christmas day at Night, one hour before day is the time fixed upon for our Attempt on Trenton. For heaven's sake keep this to yourself, as the discovery of it may prove fatal to us, our numbers, sorry I am to say, being less than I had any conception of—but necessity, dire necessity will—nay must justify any [attempt.]"[73]

Washington directed Reed to work with Cadwalader and the other militia in the area to "attack as many of their Posts as you possibly can with a prospect of success. the more we can attack, at the same Instant, the more confusion we shall spread and greater good will result from it." Washington also voiced his intention to promote Cadwalader to brigadier general, preventing concerns about the seniority of command with the colonels from the Continental regiments. Cadwalader received his promotion on Christmas Day. Washington concluded by informing Reed that if "we are successful which heaven grant & other Circumstances favour we may push on." Washington was committed to total victory and planned to attack deeper into enemy-held territory if circumstances allowed.

Rall learned of the Americans' intentions yet chose to ignore the reality of the situation. A steady stream of warnings and information about a pending attack arrived at his headquarters, but he refused to believe any of them. The Hessian commander had become numbed by the frequent raids and ambushes conducted around Trenton and continued to believe the Americans did not have the resources or will to attack in large numbers. Rall was also paranoid. He often was seen socializing with influential leaders in and around Trenton, currying their favor and

---

72 Ibid., 85.

73 The following three quotes are from *FONA*, http://founders.archives.gov/documents/Washington/03-07-02-0329, accessed Dec. 9, 2019.

issuing letters of protection for them. He was, however, beginning to suspect that many were patriot spies in disguise.

Rall's growing distrust blinded him to information about the Americans. During the week of December 22, a resident told Rall about a looming attack, but he chose to ignore this warning.[74] Two American deserters arrived at Rall's headquarters on December 23, confirming a pending attack, but he did not believe it. A respected doctor reported to the Hessian commander that he had heard similar rumblings. Rall responded, "This is all idle! it is old woman's talk."[75] A patrol sent from Princeton to Trenton by General Leslie also spoke of an assault on Trenton. Grant had a spy inside Washington's headquarters, and they warned Rall of an attack as late as Christmas Eve.[76] Some of Rall's subordinates did not share his contempt for the Americans. Major von Dechow, attempting to be prudent, requested that the brigade's baggage be moved to keep it from becoming a hindrance. Rall responded, "Fiddlesticks! These clod-hoppers will not attack us, and should they do so, we will simply fall in them and rout them!"[77]

Although Rall publicly scorned the Americans and downplayed the threat they posed, his actions show that he gave some credence to the reports. He continued to keep an entire regiment under arms each day and sent company-sized patrols reinforced with artillery to the river's edge every morning. He reinforced guard posts, continually placing the entire brigade on high alert, and sent strong security patrols into the surrounding area to detect rebel activity.

On December 24, Rall deployed two 100-man patrols west of Trenton. He sent one group from his regiment eight miles northwest to the village of Pennington. The second group, from the von Lossberg Regiment, moved west along the River Road to Johnson's Ferry. This patrol spotted a 30-man American raiding party disembarking boats on their side of the Delaware at the ferry and attacked. The Americans escaped across the river under covering artillery fire from Pennsylvania, but not before sustaining three casualties. This encounter prompted the patrol leader to recommend that a detachment be deployed daily to Pennington and make daily patrols to Johnson's Ferry. Flippantly, Rall asked the officer if he wanted to lose a detachment to the Americans and be assigned the mission himself.

---

74 Alfred Bill, *The Campaign of Princeton, 1776-1777* (Princeton, NJ, 1948), 41; Fischer, *WC*, 204.

75 Bill, *The Campaign of Princeton*, 41; Stryker, *BTP*, 111.

76 Grant wrote, "Washington has been informed that our Troops have marched into Winter quarters and have been told that we are weak at Trenton and princetown and Lord Stirling expressed a wish to make an attack upon these two places. I don't believe he will attempt it, but be assured that my information is undoubtedly true, so I need not advise you to be upon your guard against an unexpected attack at Trenton." Fischer, *WC*, 203; Dwyer, *TDIO*, 221.

77 Fischer, *WC*, 205; Dwyer, *TDIO*, 221.

Unfortunately for Rall, Washington had chosen Johnson's Ferry as the location where his army would land the following day.

Ignoring the growing level of American activity, Rall continued to believe that the rebels could do nothing more than undertake small raids. One of his soldiers agreed but also acknowledged the toll American activity was taking on the Hessians: "We have not slept one night in peace since we came to this place. The troops have lain on their arms every night, but they can endure it no longer. We have ourselves more trouble and uneasiness than is necessary." The Hessian continued,

> That men [Americans] who will not fight without some defense for them, who have neither coat, shoe nor stocking, nor scarce anything else to cover their bodies, and who for a long time past have not received one farthing of pay, should dare to attack regular troops in the open country, which they could not withstand when they were posted amongst rocks and in the strongest intrenchments, is not to be supposed.[78]

While Rall persisted in doubting an attack was imminent, Washington continued to prepare for the offensive. He ordered Commodore Seymour to move his fleet further upriver to cover the area from Burlington to Bordentown. He had the troops provided with "three days provisions ready cooked," issued additional ammunition, and ordered the men to be ready to move when called.[79] He also distributed all available shoes and uniforms to protect them from the inclement weather.

Those Continental sailors and Marines still operating on the seas continued to do what they could to support the soldiers, sailors, and marines ashore. The *Andrew Doria* captured a British sloop with some much-needed supplies off the coast of St. Eustatius, Bahamas. It managed to elude the British ships and delivered its goods to Philadelphia. On December 24, Congressman Morris provided Washington a timely Christmas gift.[80] The vital contributions of American sailors,

78 "Translation of a Hessian Diary found in Trenton," published in the *Pennsylvania Evening Post*, July 26, 1777, quoted from Stryker, *BTP*, 483; Stanley Weintraub, *Iron Tears: America's Battle for Freedom, Britain's Quagmire: 1775-1783* (New York, 2005), 85; Willard Randall, "Hamilton Takes Command: In 1775, the 20-year-old Alexander Hamilton took up arms to fight the British," https://www.smithsonianmag.com/history/hamilton-takes-command-74722445/, accessed Dec. 11, 2019; Fischer, *WC*, 204.

79 *FONA*, https://founders.archives.gov/documents/Washington/03-07-02-0332, accessed Dec. 14, 2019.

80 Morris shared with Washington a list of the goods captured by the Andrew Doria: "This Brigt. [Andrew Doria] was sent by the Secret Committee for Cloathing & Stores & has brought in the following cargo—208 Dozen pair of Woolen Stockings, 106 Dozen pair of Worsted do, 215 Sailors Jackets, 23 Great Coats, 50 ps. Dutch plains, 30 ps. 900 Yds Flannell, 45 ps. blue, brown & white Cloth, 463 Blankets, 218 ps. ⅞ Linen, 496 Muskets, 326 pair Pistols, 200 half barrells Powder,

marines, and privateers in raiding and capturing essential materials and provisions cannot be underestimated. These supplies were required to sustain Washington's land forces, which now included marines and sailors. Recognizing that the army could perish without proper logistical support, Washington requested that Morris do all he could to clothe his men and provide for them properly. Morris wrote to Hancock, "I received a letter last night from Genl. Washington by Col Moylan [Quartermaster General] requesting me to hurry Mr. Mease to have Soldiers cloths made up with all possible diligence. He says muskets are not wanted there, but that comfortable clothing is exceedingly wanted."[81] These requests speak volumes about Washington's concern for his troops; he was more worried about acquiring proper winter clothing for his men than obtaining muskets.

The American brig *Lexington* received orders to conduct the "secret business of Congress" in the West Indies to assist the war effort.[82] She also was directed to capture materials needed by the army. HMS *Pearl* lay in wait off the Delaware Capes, capturing *Lexington* with a full cargo hold of critically needed materials as she attempted to enter the Delaware River. The British removed the Continental sailors but left Marine Capt. Abraham Boyce and his detachment of Marines on board the *Lexington*, sending a prize crew of seven aboard the captured ship to bring her home. This was a mistake as Boyce and his Marines refused to remain captives. They overpowered the crew, recaptured the ship, and sailed into Baltimore, providing Washington with "336 blankets, 2,200 ells of fabric, 200,000 needles, 636,000 pins . . . 5,000 flints, 500 stands of arms, and 500 bayonets."[83]

John Paul Jones had assumed command of the *Alfred* following the amphibious assault led by Nicholas's Marines the previous year in the Bahamas. Jones led the *Alfred* and *Providence* in operations off the coast of Rhode Island, capturing the armed transport HMS *Mellish* that was carrying winter clothing for the British army. He was quoted as stating, "The news of the uniforms taken on board the Mellish raised the courage of the Army under General Washington's command, which was almost destitute of clothing. This timely and unexpected relief

---

14101 lb. Lead. I have enumerated these Articles that you may judge what part is wanted for your Army." *FONA*, http://founders.archives.gov/documents/Washington/03-07-02-0328, accessed Aug. 23, 2020.

81 *The Bulletin of the Historical Society of Pennsylvania*, vol. 1, 1845-47, (Philadelphia, 1848), 58; Martin Griffin, *Stephen Moylan, Muster-master General, Secretary and Aide-de-camp to Washington, Quartermaster-general, Colonel of Fourth Pennsylvania Light Dragoons and Brigadier-general of the War for American Independence, the First and the Last President of the Friendly Sons of St. Patrick of Philadelphia* (Philadelphia, 1909), 45.

82 Smith, *MIR*, 433.

83 Ibid.; Fischer, *WC*, 156-157.

contributed not a little to the success of the Army at Trenton."[84] Though true, evidence shows that Washington did not get all he needed. Several accounts claim that many Americans remained half naked and without shoes during the fighting at Trenton and Princeton.

Having energized his troops in meeting many of their logistical needs, Washington gathered his key leaders on Christmas Eve to convene a final war council before the attack. Sullivan, Mercer, Lord Stirling, Knox, and others joined him at Greene's headquarters to confirm the plan. The Americans intended to conduct three near-simultaneous supporting assaults against British and Hessian outposts spread across the 30 miles separating Trenton and Philadelphia. Washington would personally lead the main effort against the Hessians at Trenton.

Washington directed General Putnam and Colonel Griffin, along with 600 New Jersey and Philadelphia militiamen to conduct attacks against enemy forces in the New Jersey counties across the Delaware from Philadelphia. Washington's intended to use this force to fix the British in place while drawing attention away from Trenton. The action would also overwhelm the ability of the British and the Hessians to effectively respond to multiple concurrent threats.

General Cadwalader's brigade of 1,800 men, including Maj. Nicholas and the Continental Marines, Col. Hitchcock and his soldiers, a company of Delaware militia, and two artillery companies, would attack von Donop's forces at Mount Holly, Black Horse, and Bordentown. Like Putnam and Griffin, the Associators, Marines, and others were to fix von Donop and his troops in the Mount Holly area, 18 miles away from Trenton. These attacks would increase the enemy's inability to respond once the Americans commenced the assault.[85] Captain Shippin and his Pennsylvania marines continued to serve with the Associators' 2nd Battalion, while Capt. Brown's marines comprised one of the brigade's two artillery companies.

General Ewing's division of Pennsylvania militia would conduct the third supporting attack. General Dickinson and his New Jersey militiamen joined Ewing, forming a combined force of roughly 1,200 men. Ewing would cross the Delaware at Trenton Ferry to capture the bridge spanning Assunpink Creek and establish a blocking position. His mission was to prevent Rall's troops from escaping Trenton as Washington attacked while also blocking any attempt by von Donop to reinforce Rall.

---

84 George Clark, *A Short History of the United States Navy* (Philadelphia, 1911), 1:42; Cooper, *History of the Navy of the United States*, 1:106-107.

85 *FONA*, https://founders.archives.gov/documents/Washington/03-07-02-0329, accessed Aug. 23, 2020; Stryker, *BTP*, 113.

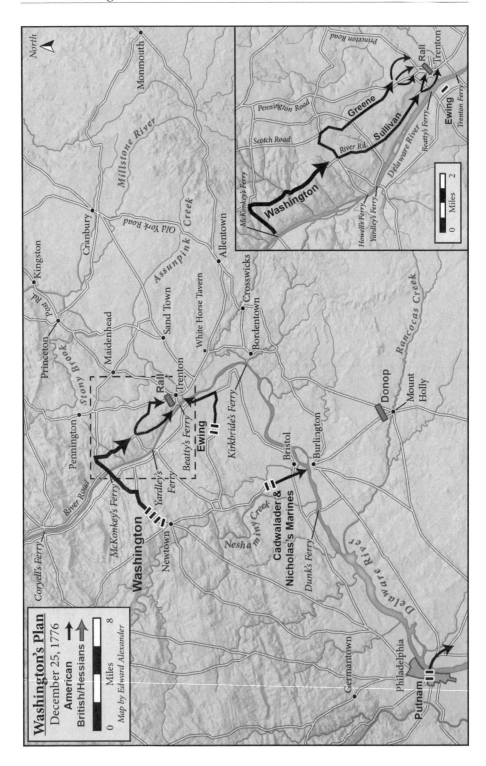

Washington's Plan
December 25, 1776
American
British/Hessians
Miles
0   8
Map by Edward Alexander

Washington himself intended to cross the Delaware with 2,400 Continentals nine miles northwest of Trenton, conducting a two-pronged attack against Rall from the north and west. This bold move required secrecy, speed, and surprise to hit and defeat the Hessians before they could respond. Former Pennsylvania marine Captain Forrest led the 2nd Company, Pennsylvania State Artillery, which added two brass six-pound guns and two five-inch mortars to Washington's force. They would play a key role in the upcoming battle.

Washington chose Christmas night to conduct the crossings along the Delaware. He hoped that due to the holiday, the enemy would lower their guard and, with luck, succumb to the effects of alcohol, slowing their responses as the Americans attacked just before dawn. If the attack on Trenton proved successful, Washington informed his officers of his intention to follow with aggressive attacks against the remaining outposts in New Jersey, focusing on Princeton and Brunswick.

Christmas Eve was a busy and demanding day for Washington. He felt the weight of the nation on his shoulders and contemplated what could be his last chance to preserve its fight for freedom. Congressman Benjamin Rush visited Washington at his headquarters on that day. Rush could see the enormous burden Washington was carrying in leading the army and described how the general "appeared much depressed and lamented the ragged and dissolving state of his army in affecting terms. I gave him assurance of the disposition of Congress to support him under his present difficulties and distress." Dr. Rush continued,

> While I was talking to him, I observed him to play with his pen and ink upon several small pieces of paper. One of them by accident fell upon the floor near my feet. I was struck with the inscription upon it. It was, "Victory or Death."[86]

The decisive moment had arrived. The following 48 hours would likely determine the fate of a nation.

---

86 Benjamin Rush, *The Autobiography of Benjamin Rush; His Travels Through Life* (London, 1948), 136.

Chapter Eight

Victory or Death

"I determined to push on at all events."

— George Washington[1]

It is unlikely that George Washington or any of his senior leaders slept well on Christmas Eve 1776. They had numerous details to work out in preparing for the pending attack against Trenton. Putnam, Cadwalader, and Ewing also conducted final coordination for their parts in the operation. Washington remained awake late into the night, publishing orders for the two-pronged attack against the Hessians to be issued to his men on Christmas morning.[2]

---

1 *FONA*, http://founders.archives.gov/documents/Washington/03-07-02-0355, accessed Dec. 18, 2019.

2 "Each brigade to be furnished with two good guides. General Stephen's brigade to form the advance party, and to have with them a detachment of the artillery without cannon, provided with spikes and hammers to spike up the enemies' cannon in case of necessity, or to bring them off if it can be affected, the party to be provided with drag-ropes for the purpose of dragging off the cannon. General Stephen is to attack and force the enemy's guards and seize such posts as may prevent them from forming in the streets, and in case they are annoyed from the houses to set them on fire. The brigades of Mercer and Lord Stirling, under the command of Major-General Greene, to support General Stephen. This is the 2d division or left wing of the army and to march by the way of the Pennington road.

St. Clair's, Glover's, and Sargent's brigades, under Major General Sullivan, to march by the River Road. This is the first division of the army, and to form the right wing. Lord Stirling's brigade to form the reserve of the left wing, and General St. Clair's brigade the reserve of the right wing. These reserves to form a second line in conjunction, or a second line to each division, as circumstances may require. Each brigadier to make the colonels acquainted with the posts of their respective regiments in the brigade, and the major-generals will inform them of the posts of the brigades in the line.

Four pieces of artillery to march at the head of each column; three pieces at the head of the second brigade of each division; and two pieces with each of the reserves. The troops to be assembled one mile back of McKonkey's Ferry, and as soon as it begins to grow dark the troops to be marched to McKonkey's Ferry, and embark on board the boats in following order under the direction of Colonel Knox." *FONA*, "General Orders, 25 December 1776," http://founders.archives.gov/documents/Washington/03-07-02-0341, accessed Dec. 18, 2019.

Henry Knox also had much critical work to do. His first priority was reorganizing his artillery regiment to fight as separate companies, directly supporting the infantry rather than keeping them consolidated as a single unit.[3] While the British had formal artillery instruction, the Americans were learning through self-study and on-the-job training. British artillery officers attended the Royal Woolwich Military Academy, where they studied algebra, trigonometry, quadratic equations, chemistry, engineering, and logistics in the course of earning artillery and engineering specialties. Henry Knox learned how to fire artillery before the war by reading books on the subject in his Boston bookstore and questioning British soldiers about what he read. The Americans had no military academies at the time. Knox recognized this shortfall and would later establish the first military schools in the newly formed United States. In December 1776, Knox would have to rely on the other self-taught and locally trained artillerymen. The Marines assisted him in this regard.

The Marines led two of Knox's artillery companies in December 1776. Captain Thomas Forrest of the Pennsylvania Marines, who previously commanded the *Arnold* on the Delaware, now headed the 2nd Company, Pennsylvania State Artillery. He was attached to Greene's Division, forming the army's left wing. Captain William Brown, the former commander of the *Putnam*, now led the newly designated 2nd Artillery Company under Capt. Jehu Eyre. His regiment was assigned to the Associator Brigade under the newly promoted General Cadwalader. In January 1777, the Continental Marines came to Knox's aid. After the battle of Princeton, Knox's ranks became depleted due to terminated enlistments. He requested, and was granted, that the Continental Marines—with their knowledge of operating naval guns—be assigned to his artillery regiment.[4]

Knox's artillery reorganization gave the Americans greater flexibility and lethality. The synchronized combined-arms effect achieved by employing artillery fire to support infantry maneuvers quickly allowed them to gain firepower superiority and overwhelm their Hessian adversaries. With the infantry being assigned direct artillery support, Knox could position his companies to respond quickly during the upcoming battle.

The artillery also maintained the advantage while fighting in inclement weather. Infantry muskets often fouled, failing to fire once moisture ruined the exposed gunpowder. American artillerymen, on the other hand, used leather covers to protect their pieces from the rain, sleet, and snow. This was the genesis of the

---

3 It was common at that time to refer to artillery units commanded by captains as companies, similar to the infantry, rather than batteries, which is the contemporary term for such units.

4 Chapter 10 covers this topic in greater detail.

still-used term, to "keep one's powder dry."[5] Washington's troops would benefit from this invaluable advantage at Trenton, as they would become soaked from their overnight march in a blizzard before the battle.

Knox's organizational skills, towering presence, and bellowing voice led to his second priority, one that would serve the Americans well on Christmas 1776. Washington chose Knox to orchestrate and lead the crossing of the Delaware, without which there would be no attack on Trenton. In speaking of Colonel Knox on the evening of the crossing, one militia officer stated, "His voice was a deep bass and resounded through the camp. . . . When on the left bank of the Delaware . . . his stentorian voice was heard above the crash of ice which filled the river with floating cakes and very much embarrassed the boats that were conveying the army."[6]

Washington was careful to first establish security on the New Jersey side before sending over his main body. Stephen's brigade was to cross and establish a secure perimeter at the landing site and detaining any persons in the area. Washington also deployed two 40-man companies to scout ahead of the two divisions to within three miles of Trenton, detaining all who attempted to exit or enter the village along those routes prior to the attack.

Washington's 24-year-old cousin, Capt. William Washington, commanded one of these units.[7] Though Captain Washington was still recovering from wounds sustained in the battle of Long Island, he and his second in command, 18-year-old Lt. James Monroe, would be valuable during the upcoming battle. William eventually achieved the rank of colonel and successfully commanded cavalry units throughout the Southern campaign later in the war. In 1798, he was promoted to brigadier general to assist in the naval war against France during President Adams's administration. James Monroe went on to become the fifth president of the United States.[8]

Captain John Flahaven and his company of New Jersey Continentals served as the advanced guard for Sullivan's division. In his late forties, Flahaven would perform well at Trenton and Princeton. He was later captured leading his men near

5 "Keep one's powder dry," https://www.dictionary.com/browse/keep-one-s-powder-dry, accessed Jan. 2, 2020.

6 Samuel Breck & Horace Scudder, *Recollections of Samuel Breck: With Passages from his Note-books, 1771-1862* (Carlisle, PA, 1877), 209; Stryker, *BTP*, 137.

7 Daniel Murphy, *William Washington, American Light Dragoon: A Continental Cavalry Leader in the War of Independence* (Yardley, PA, 2014); *FONA*, "General Orders, 25 December 1776," accessed Dec. 18, 2019.

8 Gary Hart, *James Monroe: The 5th President, 1817-1825* (New York, 2005).

Amboy, New Jersey, in what became known as "The Forage War."[9] Surgeon's Mate Ebenezer Elmer of Flahaven's regiment, who later served in Congress, described him as follows: "I believe his bravery was indisputable, but his enterprising disposition and thirst for honor led him beyond the bounds of true bravery or conduct."[10] Flahaven was later released and returned to action as a privateer.

Washington's orders directed the sequence for units crossing the Delaware, offered guidance on security measures to be taken on the far side of the river, and provided final instructions for organizing units prior to the attack.[11] If the assault on the Hessians in Trenton were to happen at 5:00 a.m. as Washington wanted, he would need to get his troops moving early. He projected that it would take around five hours to transport the army across the Delaware from McConkey's Ferry in Pennsylvania. After that, it would take an additional five hours to march the nine miles to Trenton from the Garret Johnson Ferry landing in New Jersey. Washington intended to conduct these movements in the dark in order to conceal them from the enemy. The sun was projected to set at 4:43 p.m. on December 25, 1776. The Americans would remain in a concealed assembly area along the Pennsylvania side of the river until boarding the boats at dark.

Officers issued additional orders for ammunition and rations on Christmas Day to prepare their men for battle.[12] A sergeant and six men from each brigade remained behind to guard their units' baggage, while the remaining troops received word to parade at precisely 4:00 p.m. with their weapons, rolled blankets, and packed provisions. They assembled in a concealed valley behind McConkey's Ferry. The officers affixed white pieces of paper on their headgear to be easily recognizable

9 "Washington's Revolutionary War Battles," https://www.mountvernon.org/george-washington/the-revolutionary-war/washingtons-revolutionary-war-battles/, accessed Dec. 18, 2019; Fischer, *WC*, 346-362, 373.

10 Tim Abbott, *"Another Pair Not Fellows": Adventures in Research and Reinterpreting the American Revolution*, http://notfellows.blogspot.com/2015/11/his-enterprising-disposition-and-thirst.html, accessed Dec. 18, 2019; *FONA*, "General Orders, 25 December 1776," accessed Dec. 18, 2019.

11 "General Stephen's brigade, with the detachment of artillerymen, to embark first; General Mercer's next; Lord Stirling's next; General Fermoy's next, who will march into the rear of the second division and file off from the Pennington to the Princeton road in such direction that he can with the greatest ease and safety secure the passes between Princeton and Trenton. The guides will be the best judges of this. He is to take two pieces of artillery with him.

St. Clair's, Glover's, and Sargent's brigades to embark in order Immediately upon their debarkation, the whole to form and march in subdivisions from the right.

The commanding officers of regiments to observe that the divisions be equal and that proper officers be appointed to each. A profound silence to be enjoined, and no man to quit his ranks on the pain of death. Each brigadier to appoint flanking parties; the reserve brigades to appoint the rear-guards of the columns; the heads of the columns to be appointed to arrive at Trenton at five o'clock." *FONA*, "General Orders, 25 December 1776," accessed Dec. 18, 2019.

12 Stryker, *BTP*, 359-360.

General Washington used this house as a temporary headquarters as his army assembled and conducted its famous crossing of the Delaware River on December 25, 1776. Washington crossed with the first troops into New Jersey, leaving Henry Knox to control the crossing from Pennsylvania. Although still the original house, it was expanded in later years to its current configuration. The white line down the center of the house distinguishes the original structure from the expansion. *Author*

and passed the word for the men to observe strict silence while awaiting further instructions. The men could sense that they were part of something big, but very few knew the details of what was about to transpire. Washington had purposely kept them secret to maintain operational security.

Washington took other clandestine measures to facilitate his army's crossing of the river. Over the prior week, members of the New Jersey militia and Pennsylvania regulars familiar with the area were busy collecting all the boats on the Delaware and Lehigh rivers. They consolidated these vessels with those previously collected when Washington crossed into Pennsylvania. The boats were staged out of view behind the thick woods of Malta Island two miles upriver from McConkey's Ferry. The small fleet was comprised of scows, ferries, and Durham boats. The Durham boats were the best-suited vessels to transport personnel, while the ferries proved ideal for transporting horses and artillery pieces. Originally designed to haul heavy iron ore to Philadelphia, the flat bottom Durhams were 40-60 feet in length with eight-foot beams and shallow drafts. Each one could carry approximately 40 men.[13]

13 David Bonk, *Trenton and Princeton, 1776–77: Washington Crosses the Delaware* (Oxford, UK, 2009), 50; Edwin Tunis, *The Tavern at the Ferry* (Baltimore, 1973), 29.

Picture of reenactors replicating Washington's crossing of the Delaware River using a replica of the "Durham boat" used by the Americans in their Christmas Night 1776 attack. Originally designed to carry iron ore, the Durham boats were perfect for moving Washington's force across the river in groups of 40 men. *Wikimedia*

Pole men on either side of the boats would propel them forward as steer sweeps on the bow and stern guided the craft away from the shore. Oar men would row them once in open waters.

Colonel John Glover's sea-wise soldiers from Marblehead were primarily responsible for shuttling Washington's troops across the river. These sailors had helped the Americans escape during the battle of Long Island and were referred to as "Glover's Marine Regiment."[14] Lieutenant Anthony Cuthbert, along with Capt. John Moulder's artillery company, would also work with Glover during the river crossing. Twenty-five-year-old Cuthbert was a shipbuilder from East Philadelphia. He had helped enlist former seamen, riggers, longshoremen, shipwrights, and other seafaring men to establish a company of volunteer artillerymen under Moulder.

It is plausible that former Pennsylvania marines, like those of Captains Forrest's and Brown's artillery companies, might have joined the ranks of Moulder's company, assisting Glover in the crossing.[15] A third group consisting of civilian ferry and boatmen from New Jersey and Pennsylvania were also present to help transport troops across the Delaware. Some would act as guides and scouts for the Americans once the army safely landed in New Jersey. After completing the crossing, Glover's

14 Edwin McClellan, *History of the United States Marine Corps*, vol. 1 (Washington, D.C., 1931), 65, 118; Smith, *MIR*, 466.

15 McClellan, *History of the United States Marine Corps*, 1:65; Fischer, *WC*, 217.

Replica of the flat bottom ferries used by Washington's army to haul horses and artillery pieces across the Delaware River. *Washington Crossing Historic Park, New Jersey. Author.*

and Moulder's men would pick up their muskets, joining Sullivan's 1st division in the attack along the River Road.

Generals Putnam, Ewing, and Cadwalader made similar preparations for their crossing. Putnam already had 300-400 men under Colonel Griffin in New Jersey south of Mount Holly and was trying to get more. Joseph Reed wrote Cadwalader at 11:00 a.m. on Christmas day from Philadelphia, "General Putnam has determined to cross the river with as many men as he can collect, which he says will be about 500; he is now mustering them and endeavouring to get [Thomas] Proctor's company of artillery to go with them. I wait to know what success he meets with, and the progress he makes; but at all events I shall be with you this afternoon."[16] Ewing's men did not have far to travel to their launch site. They were to land at Trenton Ferry, an area they had become familiar with during their raids against Rall.

16 William, Reed, *Life and Correspondence of Joseph Reed: Military Secretary of Washington at Cambridge; Adjutant General of the Continental Army; Member of the Congress of the United States; and President of the Executive Council of the State of Pennsylvania*, vol. 1 (Philadelphia, 1847), 275; *FONA*, http://founders.archives.gov/documents/Washington/03-07-02-0347, accessed Dec. 18, 2019.

Cadwalader and the Continental Marines were to launch from Neshaminy Ferry, across the river from Burlington. The 2nd Artillery Company, comprising Pennsylvania Marine Capt. William Brown and his men, would be ferrying Cadwalader's Associators, Hitchcock's Continentals, and other units attached to Cadwalader's brigade across the river. There is no record of whether Major Nicholas and the Continental Marines assisted in operating the boats or crossed as passengers.

The stage was set for Washington's masterpiece. The general had devised a plan that, in today's jargon, would be referred to as employing maneuver warfare. Modern-day United States Marines describe maneuver warfare as "a warfighting philosophy that seeks to shatter the enemy's cohesion through a variety of rapid, focused, and unexpected actions which create a turbulent and rapidly deteriorating situation with which the enemy cannot cope."[17] It calls for focusing on the enemy, bypassing his strengths, and striking his weaknesses with a faster tempo, against which he cannot effectively respond. The goal is to present one's adversaries with dilemmas from which there is no escape. Washington hoped his forces would confront Rall with a dilemma for which there was no alternative but to surrender.

Independently minded subordinates with boldness of thought and action are necessary to implement the concept of maneuver warfare successfully. It is a strategy that requires the commander to employ a philosophy that enables decentralized action based on a leader's intent for operation and mission tactics that encourage initiative and freedom of action.

Washington had voiced his overarching intent for the pending operation and, as was his custom, provided commanders with mission-type orders. He tasked them with assignments that articulated "what" he needed them to accomplish without dictating "how" they went about achieving success. For instance, Washington wrote to Cadwalader shortly after being informed that the latter's force may have difficulty in crossing the river, "Notwithstanding the discouraging Accounts I have received from Col. Reed of what might be expected from the Operations below, I am determined, as the night is favourable, to cross the River, & make the attack upon Trenton in the Morning. If you can do nothing real, at least create as great a diversion as possible."[18]

The time and conditions were finally right for the Americans to turn the tide of the war. Washington synchronized his officers' watches with his own and sent for the doctors caring for the sick and wounded at the hospital in Bethlehem,

17 Marine Corps Doctrinal Publication 1, *Warfighting*, Headquarters, United States Marine Corps, (Washington, D.C., 1997), 73.

18 *FONA*, http://founders.archives.gov/documents/Washington/03-07-02-0343, accessed Dec. 18, 2019.

Pennsylvania, in anticipation of casualties. The Continental brigades began departing their camps at approximately 2:00 p.m. and, by 4:00 p.m., were mustered for the parade as directed. There was an energy in the air as the soldiers realized they would not be returning to their quarters. Following the parade, unit leaders marched their troops directly toward the Delaware River and assembled for boarding the boats. Although energized, some still suffered that evening. Major Wilkinson described how the soldiers' "route was easily traced, as there was a little snow on the ground, which was tinged here and there with blood from the feet of the men who wore broken shoes."[19]

Although he hoped to remain focused on the mission, Washington was continually confronted with other matters requiring his attention. His ally in the Continental Congress, Robert Morris, was still attempting to get the frigates *Randolph* and *Delaware* out to sea. Morris now wanted to add the smaller vessels *Andrew Doria, Independence, Hornet, Fly, Mosquito,* and several merchant ships to the list.[20] Many of the men needed to crew these ships, however, were ashore, ready to join Washington in the attack he had already put into motion. Washington wrote Morris, "The security of the Continental ships of war in Delaware is a capital object, and yet to draft, the many hands necessary to fit them out, from the militia, might be dangerous just now, perhaps in a little while hence, their places may be supplied with Country militia, and then of the exigency of affairs requires it, they certainly ought to be spared."[21] Washington's letter also proposed an alternative, as he thought of the troops he had used to establish a navy in Boston. He knew the enlistments for many of his New England troops were ending on January 1, 1777, and that these "men would be willing to go on board the frigates and navigate them round to any of the ports in New England, if it was thought they would be safer there than in [the] Delaware."[22]

With the letter to Morris and other administrative work complete, Washington departed his headquarters. As he was about to mount his horse, he was stopped by General Gates's aide, 19-year-old Maj. James Wilkinson. To Washington's surprise, Wilkinson delivered a note from Gates with information that the general was on his way to meet with the Continental Congress. Washington was flabbergasted, as he had requested that Gates lead the attack against Trenton. When Gates refused

---

19 James Wilkinson, *Memoirs of my Own Times*, vol. 1 (Philadelphia, 1816), 127.

20 *FONA,* https://founders.archives.gov/documents/Washington/03-07-02-0328, accessed Dec. 19, 2019.

21 Morgan,   ed.,   NDAR,   7:596;   *FONA,*   https://founders.archives.gov/documents/Washington/03-07-02-0344, accessed Dec. 19, 2019.

22 Ibid.

due to an illness, Washington asked if he could at least join Cadwalader in Bristol for a few days, but Gates declined again, stating that his ailment prevented him from doing so. Wilkinson shared that Gates, like Lee, held the commander-in-chief in low regard, and claimed to have heard Gates state that "instead of vainly attempting to stop Sir William Howe at the Delaware, General Washington ought to retire to the South of the Susquehanna, and there form an army; he said it was his intention to propose the measure to Congress at Baltimore."[23]

Once again, one of Washington's senior leaders was conspiring against him while following his ambition. But just as Lee's capture was a blessing in disguise, Gates's departure was likely for the best. Although Gates would be credited with the victory at Saratoga the following year, many understood that Gen. Benedict Arnold's bold actions were the real reason for the American victory. Just as Lee's true colors and downfall occurred at the battle of Monmouth Courthouse in 1778, Gates showed his true colors and inept leadership at the battle of Camden in 1780.[24] Both officers' reputations were severely tarnished following their dismal performances in these later battles.

Nine miles downriver, Rall and his men were experiencing some excitement. General Grant had warned Rall again that morning that General Stirling was nearby and was concerned that Trenton might come under attack that day.[25] Rall had toured his outposts on the outskirts of the village to inspect his troops' readiness and determine if his men were experiencing any indications of an imminent attack. Satisfied that no such attack was forthcoming, Rall returned to his headquarters as a late afternoon rain began to fall. He sat down for a game of checkers with Mr. Stacy Potts, the owner of the home Rall used as his headquarters. As the Hessians took shelter from the worsening weather, the Americans implemented their plan.

Washington's army moved to the river as darkness crept in and began crossing the Delaware around 6:00 p.m. A steady rain fell as the temperatures hovered around freezing, resulting in a rain/snow mix that worsened throughout the night. The rains swelled the river and added to its already swift currents. Warmer temperatures during the previous two days had caused cakes of ice on the river's edge to break free, causing floating hazards on the river as Glover's and Moulder's men maneuvered the boats to take on their first passengers.

---

23 Wilkinson, *Memoirs*, 127.

24 For more on the battle of Monmouth see Brendan Morrissey, *Monmouth Courthouse, 1778: The Last Great Battle in the North* (Oxford, UK, 2004). For more on Camden see Jim Piecuch, *The Battle of Camden: A Documentary History* (Charleston, SC, 2006).

25 Stryker, *BTP*, 117.

Emanuel Leutze's famous 1851 painting, *Washington Crossing the Delaware*. Although dramatic and representative of the participants, the painting is not a true representation of the crossing. Regardless, it gives one a sense of the danger, determination, and significance surrounding this historic event. *Wikimedia*

Stephen's brigade, with the advance guards, crossed first, establishing a secure perimeter around the landing site. The guards moved to their designated routes. Washington crossed with Stephen's men to ensure that he was in position to provide orders from the Jersey shore, and Knox controlled the movement from Pennsylvania. The remainder of Greene's division, with former Pennsylvania marine Thomas Forrest's artillery company, was the next to cross. Lord Stirling and his men followed Mercer's brigade. Sullivan's division followed with Roche de Fermoy's brigade in the lead and St. Clair's and Sargent's brigades in trace. Glover's brigade and Moulder's artillerymen would join them once the crossing was complete.

As the Americans continued their crossing upriver, Rall's checkers game was interrupted by gunfire from the direction of the Hessian post on the Pennington Road. Sometime between 7:00-8:00 p.m., a group of 40-50 Americans attacked the advance picket, injuring six of the 15 Hessian soldiers stationed there. The Americans withdrew toward Johnson's Ferry, unaware that Washington was in the process of landing his army at that site. The gunfire alerted the entire Hessian brigade, as the company commander from the von Lossberg Regiment, responsible for the picket, rushed his company forward from its headquarters. Six jaegers ran to their assistance from their picket on the River Road. The commander ordered a squad to sweep the vicinity beyond their position to make sure the Americans were

A modern-day view of the stretch of the Delaware River Washington's army crossed on the night of December 25, 1776. This view is from McKonkey's Ferry landing in Pennsylvania. The Johnson Ferry house, where the army landed on the New Jersey shore, can be seen on the right-hand side of the photo. The river was fast-moving and full of floating cakes of ice that evening. *Author*

gone. A larger group from the main guard position at the Fox Chase Tavern joined in the search. The combined group patrolled two miles toward Johnson Ferry but did not discover the crossing site.

Back in Trenton, Rall mobilized the remainder of the brigade. He led the Rall Regiment to the intersections of Princeton and Pennington roads as the von Knyphausen and the remainder of the von Lossberg regiments formed outside their quarters to await orders. On determining the Americans had fled and there was no pending attack, the Hessians reinforced the Pennington Road picket with an officer and 20 men and dismissed the remaining troops. Rall and his officers gathered to discuss the incident, which he believed to be another harassing attack that validated Grant's earlier warning. Major von Dechow requested that Rall immediately send out a heavy patrol to each ferry site in the area, but Rall responded that there was plenty of time for that in the morning. Unsatisfied, Dechow placed guards in front of the houses his troops occupied and ordered his men to remain on alert throughout the night. Rather than return to his checker game, Rall stopped at Abraham Hunt's home to enjoy a Christmas party.

Historians still debate the source of the American attack on the Pennington Road post. Some believe the patrol was the advance guard led by Capt. William Washington.[26] Others believe it was an unsanctioned scouting party headed by Capt. Richard Anderson of the 5th Virginia.[27] Author David Hackett Fischer identified evidence that points to a Captain Wallis of the 4th Virginia, who led a patrol to seek revenge for the loss of one of that unit's soldiers.[28] Regardless, the Americans avoided discovery during their crossing thanks to Rall's complacency and failure to answer von Dechow's request to send patrols to observe the major ferry sites. Luck and an overconfident adversary had once again aided Washington.

Putnam, Ewing, and Cadwalader were not as fortunate as Washington. All three faced challenges in accomplishing their assigned missions. Putnam struggled to muster the reinforcements needed to join Griffin in New Jersey, while Ewing and Cadwalader encountered difficulties getting across the river. Ewing's crossing site, just below Trenton Falls, was teeming with large, floating cakes of ice, which formed into a jagged mess that extended far downriver. Ewing's boats were worthless in this environment, and the ice proved too unpredictable for his men to attempt to cross by foot.

Cadwalader and the Continental Marines faced similar problems farther south. The strong currents, floating ice, and high winds created conditions that convinced Cadwalader to abandon the crossing at Neshaminy Ferry. At 8:00 p.m., he ordered his force a mile downriver to Dunk's Ferry. Thirty-two-year-old Capt. Thomas Rodney of the Delaware militia recalled, "the wind blew very hard and there was much rain and sleet, and there was so much floating ice in the River that we had the greatest difficulty."[29]

Cadwalader's troops started crossing around 11:00 p.m., just as the effects of a nor'easter rolled in, bringing freezing rain, sleet, and snow. Rodney and three companies of 46-year-old Col. Timothy Matlack's Philadelphia militia rifle battalion were the first to cross, and they established a secure perimeter to protect the others during their crossing. Rodney was eventually promoted to colonel and later served in the Continental Congress. Matlack, a beer brewer, also became a member of Congress. Rodney remembered, "when we reached the Jersey shore we were obliged to land on the ice, 150 yards from shore."[30] Upon landing, the

---

26 Ibid., 121.

27 Ibid., 373-374; Dwyer, *TDIO*, 249-250.

28 Fischer, *WC*, 231-233, 423.

29 Thomas Rodney, *Diary of Captain Thomas Rodney, 1776-1777, Papers of the Historical Society of Delaware* (Wilmington, 1888), 8:23.

30 Ibid., 22.

militiamen pushed inland for 200 yards, posting security to await the others. The Associators' 1st Battalion went over next. Cadwalader accompanied the 1st Battalion with two field guns to test the feasibility of landing artillery under these conditions. He later told Washington that "upon examination I found it was impossible the ice being very thick."[31]

Cadwalader's second attempt to cross the Delaware quickly became untenable, as swift currents and forming ice made it impossible for him to land his artillery to support the infantry. According to Rodney, "the boats with the artillery were carried away in the ice and could not be got over."[32] The Associators' 3rd Battalion successfully followed the 1st Battalion. The 2nd Battalion, accompanied by Nicholas and his Marines, was preparing to board the boats when Cadwalader canceled the movement. He noted, "Upon reporting this [failure to get the artillery across] to the field-officers, they were all of opinion, that it would not be proper to proceed without cannon."[33]

Approximately 1,000 men who had successfully crossed the river were ordered to return to the Pennsylvania side. Rodney explained, "This greatly irritated the troops that had crossed the River, and they proposed making the attack without both the Generals and the artillery."[34] Wiser heads prevailed as the men agreed that it was more important to keep the force together. Joseph Reed agreed with Cadwalader's decision. He reported to Washington, "the ice began to drive with such force and in such quantities as threatened many boats with absolute destruction. To add to the difficulty, about daybreak there came the most violent storm of rain, hail, and snow."[35]

The weather had a similar effect on Washington's force 22 miles upriver. The commander's frustration and anxiety grew as the expected five-hour crossing at McConkey's Ferry dragged out to over nine hours. He was afraid of risking the Americans' advantage of achieving the element of surprise. Washington later told John Hancock, "This made me despair of surprising the Town, as I well knew we could not reach it before the day was fairly broke, but as I was certain there was no

31 *FONA*, http://founders.archives.gov/documents/Washington/03-07-02-0347, accessed Dec. 20, 2019.

32 Rodney, *Diary of Captain Thomas Rodney*, 23.

33 *FONA*, http://founders.archives.gov/documents/Washington/03-07-02-0347, accessed Dec. 20, 2019.

34 Rodney, *Diary of Captain Thomas Rodney*, 23.

35 Fischer, *WC*, 215; Dwyer, *TDIO*, 244.

making a Retreat without being discovered, and harassed on repassing the River, I determined to push on at all Events."[36]

Stephen's men pushed inland, gaining the top of a high plateau overlooking the landing site to provide room for the arriving units while remaining alert for any Hessian patrols or prying loyalists. Other soldiers did what they could to dry off and keep warm by fires stoked by burning fence rails as they awaited the rest of the army. Wrapped in a long cloak, Washington remained by the river's edge as a physical presence, bolstering his men's morale as they arrived in New Jersey by showing that their commander was willing to share in their hardships. The blistering winter weather continued, adding misery to an already challenging night, but it did not dampen the Americans' determination.

Although delayed, Henry Knox, with the assistance of Glover, Moulder, and others, had once again accomplished an extraordinary feat. After the battle, Knox wrote to his wife Lucy how the army "pass'd the River on Christmas night with almost infinite difficulty, with eighteen field pieces. floating Ice in the River made the labour almost incredible however perseverance accomplished what at first Seem'd imposible."[37] Knox successfully crossed 2,400 personnel, approximately 150 horses, and 18 cannons without a loss.[38]

Although the Americans had completed one difficult task, they now faced another. Washington's force was four hours behind schedule. The men now had a nine-mile hike to complete during a blizzard without being detected by the enemy. Luckily, the inclement weather helped to dissuade the Hessians from any unnecessary outdoor activity.

Rall enjoyed the Christmas party as many of his troops remained on alert. Abraham Hunt was one of Trenton's wealthiest men. To accommodate his guests, he had tobacco, food, and spirits. Rall partook of Hunt's offerings, settling down to play cards with the other guests in the parlor.[39] Unbeknownst to Rall, a loyalist farmer had arrived at the residence with some critical information. But his entrance was blocked by a house servant, who had been ordered not to disturb the holiday guests. Earlier, the farmer had observed Washington's men forming to cross the river and attempted to notify Rall of the movement. With his entrance blocked, the farmer quickly scratched a note on a piece of paper and asked the servant to deliver

---

36 *FONA*, http://founders.archives.gov/documents/Washington/03-07-02-0355, accessed Dec. 19, 2019.

37 Commager & Morris, *SSS*, 513; Drake, *Life and Correspondence of Henry Knox*, 36.

38 Phillip Tucker, *George Washington's Surprise Attack: A New Look at the Battle that Decided the Fate of America* (New York, 2016); Puls, *Henry Knox*, 73-75; McCollough, *1776*, 277.

39 Stryker, *BTP*, 125; Ward, *TWOR*, 297; Fischer, *WC*, 205; Dwyer, *TDIO*, 265.

it. On being handed the note, Rall unfolded it but could not read the English wording. With no one around who could translate it into German, he refolded it and placed it in his pocket for later. This was perhaps the gravest mistake of what remained of Rall's life. The party continued into the night, and Rall did not return to his headquarters until well after midnight, as Washington was about to get his men moving toward Trenton.

At their designated positions, American officers were forming their units and preparing for the long march. Torches affixed to field guns provided weak lighting as the lead units stepped off at around 4:00 a.m. The column stretched nearly a mile through a winding forest trail over rolling hills. Although the freezing temperatures helped to harden the ground, the thousands of feet, wagon wheels, and horses' hooves churned it into a morass of slush and mud, retarding progress. The rolling terrain also caused the slow-moving column to stop and start like a giant accordion continually. The troops continued for a mile and a half before reaching the Bear Tavern and turning toward Trenton. A few farmers, learning of the Continentals' presence, grabbed their weapons and joined the column to share knowledge of the area and help oust the Hessian occupiers. Washington was encouraged by this support but was undoubtedly concerned about his men's ability to arrive in fighting order. He lamented, "Many of our poor soldiers are quite barefoot and ill-clad."[40]

The weather, terrain, and lack of sleep were starting to take a toll on the men. As they trudged on, the weather shifted between snow, sleet, and rain. Steep ravines required them to unharness the horses hauling munitions wagons and field guns, as men used ropes and shear strength to lower the heavy loads down one side and hoist them up the other. The guns alone weighed nearly 2,000 pounds each. Knox documented how "the troops marched with the most profound silence and good order."[41] Marching under such conditions caused many men to focus inward as they continued to mindlessly go through the motions of their tasks until someone, or something, broke them out of their stupor. Sixteen-year-old John Greenwood, a fifer in Sullivan's division, wrote, "At one time when we halted on the road, I sat down on the stump of a tree and was so benumbed with cold that I wanted to go to sleep, Had I been passed unnoticed I should have frozen to death without knowing it. But as good luck always attended me, Sergeant Madden came and, rousing me

40 Bruce Chadwick, *George Washington's War: The Forging of a Revolutionary Leader and the American Presidency* (Naperville, IL, 2004), 71; Stryker, *BTP*, 129; O'Donnell, *Washington's Immortals*, 115.

41 Commager & Morris, *SSS*, 513; Drake, *Life and Correspondence of Henry Knox*, 36; Stryker, *BTP*, 129.

up, made me walk about."[42] Two other soldiers were not as fortunate and froze to death when they fell out of the formation.[43]

The column continued for another three miles before Washington ordered a short respite in the small village of Birmingham. This was the predesignated location for Greene's and Sullivan's divisions to split and follow separate routes toward Trenton. Washington allowed the men to eat their prepared rations as the column reorganized. Some men quickly fell asleep on the side of the road and had to be awakened. Twenty-seven-year-old Lt. Elisha Bostwick recalled seeing General Washington ride by and encourage his soldiers, stating, "Soldiers, keep by your officers. For God's sake, keep by your officers."[44]

Washington gathered his senior officers and provided final guidance as he ate quickly while sitting on horseback. Afterward, in a letter to John Hancock, he explained, "As the Divisions had nearly the same distance to march, I ordered each of them, immediately upon forcing the out Guards, to push directly into the Town, that they might charge the Enemy before they had time to form."[45] Washington hoped to have both columns attack Trenton simultaneously but thought it was more important to achieve surprise. As the commanders discussed the plan, word arrived that many weapons were inoperable due to the weather and that "snow and sleet melted into the cartridge boxes." Washington cleared any doubt about his intent when he stated, "Advance and charge."[46] If necessary, Washington intended to attack with artillery and bayonets alone.

With that clear direction, the Americans commenced the final leg of their journey. Washington directed the left wing of the army under Greene to depart first since they had a more challenging route. Greene's column headed uphill to the northeast on a stretch of Scotch Road before connecting to Pennington Road, then turning southeast for the final stretch toward Trenton. Stephen's men led the column, followed by Mercer's, Lord Stirling's, and Fermoy's brigades. Washington, accompanied by Knox, followed the lead elements of this division with a troop of

42 Joseph R. Greenwood, ed., *The Revolutionary Service of John Greenwood of Boston and New York, 1775-1783* (New York, 1922), 39.

43 Fischer, *WC*, 228; Dwyer, *TDIO*, 227; Chadwick, *George Washington's War*, 16.

44 Bentton Rain Paterson, *Washington and Cornwallis: The Battle of America, 1775-1783* (Lanham, MD, 2004), 87; Chernow, *Washington: A Life*, 274; James Rees & Stephen Spignesi, *George Washington's Leadership Lessons: What the Father of Our Country Can Teach Us About Effective Leadership and Character* (Hoboken, NJ, 2007), 49.

45 *FONA*, http://founders.archives.gov/documents/Washington/03-07-02-0355, accessed Dec. 22, 2019.

46 Steven Siry, *Greene: Revolutionary General* (Washington, D.C., 2006), 27; James McNabney, *Born In Brotherhood: Revelations About America's Revolutionary Leaders* (Bloomington, IN, 2006), 494; Fischer, *WC*, 230.

light horse to provide security. Captain Forrest's artillery company accompanied Stephen's men in the vanguard so as to be placed into action quickly. Bauman's artillery traveled with Mercer's troops, while Hamilton and his artillerymen traveled with the reserve brigade. There had been no word from the advance guards, or indications that the Hessians were aware of their presence outside Trenton. The Americans apparently still held the element of surprise.

Sullivan received instructions to pause temporarily to allow Greene's men to get a head start, as his downhill route was more direct and was expected to take less time. After a few moments, Sullivan gave Captain Flahaven's company and Col. John Stark's New Hampshire regiment the order to move. They led the army's right wing toward the River Road, followed by the remainder of St. Clair's brigade, Glover's hardy soldiers, and Sargent's brigade. Capts. Neil, Moulder, Sargent, and Hugg provided artillery support for this division.

As the duty regiment on Christmas morning, Rall's grenadiers remained in uniform with weapons stacked and cartouche boxes, bayonets, and other gear within arm's reach. Unlike their commander, the troops did not party into the night, as has been falsely reported. The loosening of the men's leggings was the only relief afforded them overnight. Most remained sheltered in their barracks to protect against the blizzard. The often-cautious Major von Dechow of the von Knyphausen Regiment uncharacteristically provided some relief for his men when he canceled the morning's daily company-sized patrol to Trenton Ferry following the American raids. This could have proven a fatal flaw if Ewing's force had made it across the river. Nevertheless, this company was not ready to respond when the Continentals attacked.

Washington and his men could sense that they were close to their objective. Their anxiety likely increased as the first hints of daylight appeared. Sunrise came at 7:18 a.m. on that stormy December morning, but the Americans still had some distance to go. One of Washington's officers reported, "It was daybreak when we were two miles from Trenton. But happily the enemy were not apprized of our design, and our advanced parties were on their guard."[47] Washington pushed his men, encouraging them to "Press on Boys, press on!"[48] At 7:30 a.m., Greene's division joined Captain Washington and his advance guard on the Pennington Road. Washington likely pondered Sullivan's progress on the River Road and whether Cadwalader, the Marines, and Ewing had been successful in their missions.

---

47 John Barber & Henry Howe, *Historical Collections of the State of New Jersey* (New York, 1846), 294.

48 "Washington's Triumph at Trenton," https://www.mountvernon.org/george-washington/the-man-the-myth/washington-stories/the-triumph-at-trenton/; Chadwick, *George Washington's War*, 16; Stryker, *BTP*, 143.

The Americans possibly picked up the pace with renewed energy knowing they were nearing the end of their march. This was their opportunity to grasp victory after the many defeats in New York and the humiliating retreat across New Jersey.

A warning sounded from the front of the column: A body of troops was approaching the lead units. A surge of excitement coursed through the ranks as men prepared to engage the enemy. To Washington's surprise, it was a company of his soldiers, the group that attacked the Hessian picket the previous night. Washington became enraged as he listened to the story of how Stephen ordered the company to conduct the raid to avenge the death of one of their men. The company departed before the order to attack Trenton was given, unaware of the developing operation. Washington summoned Stephen to validate the information. When he did so, Washington erupted, "You Sir, may have ruined all my plans by having them on their guard."[49] Many had never seen Washington so angry, but it was too late to turn back. Washington directed the troops to join the column and gave the order to push forward into the attack.

Despite several opportunities, the Hessians failed to discover Washington's men. The jaegers on the River Road and the fusiliers on Pennington Road sent out pre-dawn security patrols, knowing the enemy traditionally attacked just before dawn. While it had been Washington's plan, the delays in getting to Trenton worked to the Americans' advantage. The column was still miles away when the Hessian patrols returned to their units to report no enemy activity. At approximately 8:00 a.m., Lt. Andreas Wiederholdt, who commanded the Pennington Road picket, exited the home his troops occupied and spotted a group of men emerging from the woods about 200 yards away. The falling snow made it difficult to identify them, and Wiederholdt thought they might be a returning Hessian patrol. After one of the individuals raised his musket and fired at the officer, however, his doubts were erased. Wiederholdt shouted, "Der Feind! Der Feind! Heraus! Heraus!" ("The enemy! The enemy! Turn out! Turn out!")[50]

Aware of the guard post on Pennington Road, Washington placed Greene's division into assault formation before advancing. He positioned Mercer's brigade on the right with orders to attack the western side of Trenton. Washington put Stephen's brigade in the middle to attack down Pennington Road, assaulting Trenton from the north; the general would accompany Stephen's column. Fermoy, on the left, had orders to swing past Stephen's men to isolate Trenton to the north and prevent any enemy attempts at escape or reinforcement. Lord Stirling was the reserve and formed the second line of the assault.

---

49 Fischer, *WC*, 232; Dwyer, *TDIO*, 250; Chernow, *Washington: A Life*, 275.

50 Stryker, *BTP*, 147; Fischer, *WC*, 240; Dwyer, *TDIO*, 265.

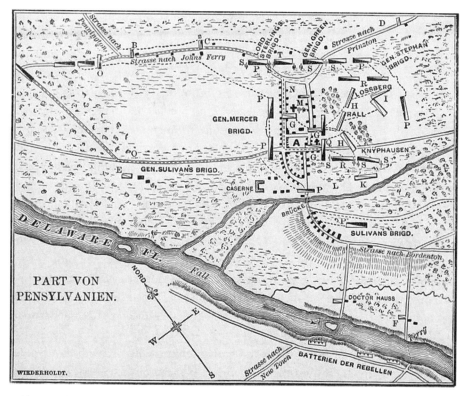

This reproduced sketch depicting the battle of Trenton was drawn by a captured Hessian officer the day after the battle. It depicts Washington's forces maneuvering from the west of the village and attacking Trenton from the north, west, and south. The Hessians vainly attempted to regroup east of the village. American artillery cleared fields of fire down the long axes of King and Queen streets, with Mercer's infantrymen firing into the Hessian flank. *Wikimedia*

Captain Washington and his trusty second, Lt. James Monroe, were the vanguard of Greene's attack. A surge of adrenaline rushed through the Americans as they broke out of the woods and formed on the open ground in front of the Hessian post. They fired three volleys at Wiederholdt's men and pushed forward. The Hessians responded with a single volley but pulled back when they saw General Washington leading an entire brigade toward them in a steady trot across the field. Approximately three minutes after the initial contact along Pennington Road, Washington heard a cannon roar from the direction of River Road, verifying that Sullivan's division had commenced its attack.

Lieutenant Friedrich Wilhelm von Grothausen commanded the jaegers posted at The Hermitage on the River Road west of Trenton. When the gunfire erupted from the direction of Pennington Road, von Grothausen assembled a squad and started running across a field to assist the Pennington post. They did not get far. From his position west of The Hermitage, Von Grothausen heard shots and looked back to see an onslaught of Americans charging toward his men. Things worsened as cannon fire roared from across the Delaware, exploding around von Grothausen's troops. While they could not cross the river, Ewing's and Dickinson's men supported Sullivan's attack with artillery from the Pennsylvania shore.

Captain Flahaven and his New Jersey Continentals led the attack down the River Road, with John Stark's New Hampshire regiment closely behind. Sullivan followed in trace. Glover's and Sargent's men came next, and St. Clair's brigade brought up the rear. Stark had his men fix bayonets, not wanting to slow their tempo by pausing the assault for the nearly 20 seconds it took to reload their muskets.[51] Seconds could mean the difference between life and death, and Stark aggressively led his men with a purpose. Major Wilkinson, who had joined Sullivan's division after delivering Gates' note to Washington, had praise for the "dauntless Stark. Who dealt death wherever he found resistance, and broke down all opposition before him."[52] Many of the American troops, however, were without bayonets. John Greenwood of St. Clair's brigade described how "although there was not more than one bayonet to five men, orders were given to 'Charge Bayonets and Rush In!' and rush on we did."[53]

Seeing the danger to his men, von Grothausen turned those with him around and ran back, angling toward the village to keep ahead of the American advance. The remainder of his troops near The Hermitage broke contact with the Americans and retreated toward Trenton. Both Hessian groups consolidated near the old military barracks at Front Street on the village's south side. Reinforcements joined them as they fired a volley toward the wave of Americans bearing down on their position. Greenwood explained, "Within pistol-shot, they again fired point-blank at us; we dodged and they did not hit a man, while before they had time to reload we were within three feet of them, when they broke in an instant and ran like so many frightened devils into the town."[54]

Greene's division pressed the Hessians hard on the northern side, denying them the time to organize a cohesive resistance. Wiederholdt attempted to lead his men across a field directly toward Rall's headquarters, but his path was blocked by another brigade advancing from the west. Hugh Mercer and his troops prevented

51 Harry Schenawolf, "Loading and Firing a Brown Bess Musket in the Eighteenth Century," http://www.revolutionarywarjournal.com/brown-bess/, accessed Dec. 22, 2019; "How Long Does It Take to Reload a Musket?" https://www.reference.com/world-view/long-reload-musket-f38b9c2f3e79ce7a, accessed Dec. 20, 2019.

52 James Wilkinson, *Memoirs*, 130.

53 Joseph R. Greenwood, *The Revolutionary Service of John Greenwood*, 41.

54 Ibid.

Wiederholdt's escape as they conducted a flanking attack on the village's west side. Fermoy's brigade, with Col. Edward Hand's Pennsylvania riflemen and a battalion of German Americans, drove the pickets guarding the Princeton Road toward Trenton. Captain Bauman joined them and employed his three-pound cannons to seal the north from escape. The Americans had successfully enveloped Trenton from the north, west, and south and continued to close in, with hopes that General Ewing had blocked the Hessian escape route across the Assunpink bridge to the east.

The Hessians unsuccessfully attempted to establish a forward defense north of Trenton. The advance companies behind the pickets sounded the alarm and began to form as soon as they heard the first shots fired. Wiederholdt withdrew to his company's position as Mercer blocked his route toward the village's center. Other pickets north of Trenton also fell back, gathering near Captain von Altenbockum's quarters where he had formed his company on the road. The combined group fired a single hasty volley before being forced to withdraw or risk being surrounded. Captain Washington took a knee and with a well-aimed shot killed 18-year-old Lt. Georg Christian Kimm of the von Lossberg Regiment as that unit retreated. Other Hessians became casualties as they conducted a fighting withdrawal to join the main body in the village. Altenbockum led one group down Queen Street, while Wiederholdt led another down King Street. Henry Knox described how "we forc'd [the guards] & enter'd the Town with them pell-mell, & here succeeded a scene of war of Which I had often Conceived but never saw before. The hurry fright & confusion of the enemy was [not] unlike that which Will be when the last Trump shall sound."[55]

Rall was asleep when Washington began his attack. Hearing gunfire, his adjutant, Lt. Jacob Piel, raced to the nearby guard house and sent the officer in charge to the aid of the Pennington Road picket. Piel believed the attack to be another American raid, like the one conducted the previous evening. With the duty guard on the move, Piel rushed to Rall's quarters and banged on the door. Rall appeared in an upper floor window still in his nightgown and asked, "Was ist Los?" (What is the matter?)[56] Piel asked if Rall had not heard the shooting, and Rall said he would be right down. When Rall stepped out of his quarters, American cannon fire was already ripping down Trenton's main streets.

---

55 Francis Drake, *Life and Correspondence of Henry Knox* (Boston, 1873), 36-37; Commager & Morris, *SSS*, 513.

56 Schlieffen, Heikennitz, Kenn, Schramm, and Stryker, "Report of the Court-Martial," 47; Scheer & Rankin, *RR*, 213.

Former Pennsylvania Marine Thomas Forrest led his artillery company in firing down the length of Queen Street, while Alexander Hamilton's New York artillery company fired down King Street during the battle of Trenton. Both units had a devastating effect on Hessian troops attempting to organize to repulse Washington's attack. *Wikimedia*

Upon reaching the high ground where King and Queen streets intersected north of town, Washington directed Knox to put his artillery into action. Knox immediately positioned Captain Forrest's company to fire two six-pound cannons and two five-and-a-half-inch howitzers down Queen Street. Hamilton was ordered forward from the reserve brigade to fire his two six-pound guns down the length of King Street. Their effect was devastating. Both companies were able to achieve plunging and enfilading fire down Trenton's two main throughways.[57] The deadly combination of controlling the high ground and having clear fields of fire resulted in dire consequences for the Hessians. The Americans' shots from the high ground could "plunge" down into the lower part of the village while also wreaking havoc along the long axis of any Hessian formations on the roads. This could kill or injure multiple soldiers with a single shot. The effect was like a bowling ball driving down a lane to smash into pins, except these were human beings. Nevertheless, this was only part of the Hessian's problems.

57 Dictionary.com defines "plunging fire" as "artillery or other fire that strikes the ground at a steep angle, as from high ground overlooking the target or from a weapon fired at a high angle of elevation," https://www.dictionary.com/browse/plunging-fire, accessed Dec. 23, 2019. Merriam-Webster defines "enfilading fire" as "gunfire directed from a flanking position along the length of an enemy battle line," https://www.merriam-webster.com/dictionary/enfilade, accessed Dec. 23, 2019.

Mercer's attack along the western flank also denied Rall's men shelter from the American artillery. As the Hessians sought cover behind Trenton's buildings from the cannon fire slamming into them from the north, Mercer's infantrymen poured musket volleys into them from the west, placing the Hessians in a dilemma. Attempting to seek cover from the fire from one direction merely exposed them to fire from another. The Americans achieved what in modern terms is described as a "combined arms" effect, where one maximizes the complimentary effects of two or more weapons systems to place an adversary in a no-win situation.[58] Knox explained this phenomenon to his wife: "They [Hessians] endevord to form in streets the heads of which we had previous[l]y the possession of with Cannon & Howitzers, these in the twinkling of an eye cleard the streets, the backs of the houses were resorted to for shelter, these prov'd ineffectual the musketry soon dislog'd them[.]"[59]

Amid the chaos, Rall attempted to organize a defense. He directed Lt. Col. Franz Scheffer, commanding the von Lossberg Regiment, to gather his men behind the English church to await the Rall regiment forming farther down King Street. Rall rode to his regiment and ordered Lt. Col. Balthasar Brethauer to clear the enemy north up King Street in concert with Scheffer, who would go parallel up Queen Street. Rall also directed one battalion from the von Lossberg Regiment to take position to the south, protecting the Hessians' rear from Sullivan's attack moving across the southern side of Trenton. Brethauer's horse was shot, causing him to place Major Matthaus in command, as he left to find another mount. The von Knyphausen Regiment formed beside the Friends meetinghouse to await Rall's orders. Washington watched as the Hessians attempted to organize, later reporting, "We presently saw their main Body formed, but from their Motions, they seem'd undetermined how to act."[60]

The Hessians' two lead regiments began moving north, sustaining several casualties along the way. The fusillade from Forrest's and Hamilton's guns continued to rip into their ranks as Mercer's men fired into their flank. Mercer's troops entered Trenton's dry buildings on the west side and used the opportunity to clear their fouled muskets and put them back into firing order. Several Americans climbed to second and third-story rooms and began firing down on the Hessians. The weather

58 The United States Marine Corps defines combined arms as the "full integration of combat arms is such a way that to counteract one, the enemy must become more vulnerable to the other." *Marine Corps Doctrinal Publication 1-0: Marine Corps Operations* (Washington, D.C., 2011), Glossary-8.

59 Drake, *Life and Correspondence of Henry Knox*, 36-37.

60 *FONA*, http://founders.archives.gov/documents/Washington/03-07-02-0355, accessed Dec. 23, 2019.

that had earlier corrupted the Continentals' muskets now began to have the same effect on Hessian weapons as they scrambled about in the open.

The Hessians continued trying to establish order out of the mayhem as Rall ordered his artillery into action. The two cannons that had been pre-staged at the guardhouse were the only ones ready for use, as the others were sitting in front of Rall's headquarters. Without infantry support, two artillery officers and 17 men moved forward with the pieces but were forced to stop after 150 feet by enemy fire. Though the Hessians unlimbered the guns and commenced an artillery duel with the Americans, they quickly found themselves outgunned. The Hessians fired six rounds of solid shot without effect before Continental artillery and musketry rendered their position untenable. Five horses and eight Hessians quickly fell as casualties. The Hessians called for reinforcements, but none were forthcoming. After firing one final round of grapeshot, those able to retreat abandoned their guns and rushed toward the town center.

As the artillery duel played out on the north side of Trenton, Sullivan's division moved swiftly across the south. Unaware of whether Ewing had succeeded in capturing the bridge across the Assunpink, Sullivan rightly directed Glover to attack east to secure it. Unfortunately, 20 British dragoons, elements of Rall's and the von Lossberg regiments, and several noncombatants had already retreated across the bridge. Following the battle, von Donop reported to General Knyphausen, "Lieutenant von Grothhausen with fifty yaegers who had his command in Trenton, with a detachment of light infantry and dragoons, except one yaeger who was killed and one sick soldier, escaped from the fight."[61] Over 400 Hessians avoided capture to fight another day.

The remaining Hessians were not as lucky. The Rall and von Lossberg regiments, still moving north, were only able to get off two volleys before being forced back by the Americans' superior firepower. Rall led both regiments east, moving out of the line of fire to the rear of an apple orchard outside the village. Washington observed this movement and described how "they then filed off to their Right and I suspected were attempting to gain a Road leading to Princetown, upon which I ordered Colo. Hands and the German Battalion to throw themselves before them, this they did with Spirit and Rapidity and immediately checked them."[62] Realizing their escape route was blocked and loath to return to the devastating artillery in Trenton, some Hessians attempted to cross Assunpink Creek. The Americans quickly began shooting at them, preventing further attempts to cross the creek.

61 Ibid., Stryker, *BTP*, 400.

62 *FONA*, http://founders.archives.gov/documents/Washington/03-07-02-0355, accessed Dec. 23, 2019.

With his way north blocked, and the two cannons abandoned on King Street, Rall turned his unit and attacked back into Trenton. He yelled, "Alle was meine Grenadir seyn, vor werds!" (All who are my grenadiers forward!)[63] Rall led his men into the fray, ordering the von Knyphausen Regiment to keep a path open to the Assunpink Creek bridge. Rall's grenadiers aggressively fought through a hailstorm of fire and reclaimed their guns, but their victory was short-lived.

Captain Washington and Lt. Monroe led Lord Stirling's brigade in commencing an assault south into the village. Sergeant John White and his gun crew joined the mêlée after their cannon's axle broke, rendering it inoperable. Knox rode up and directed them to capture the Hessian guns, stating, "My brave lads, take your swords and go up there and take those two pieces their holding! There is a party going; and you must join them."[64] The combined force charged the Hessian artillery. Monroe recalled, "Captain Washington rushed forward, attacked and put the troops around the cannon to flight and took possession of them. Moving on afterwards, he received a severe wound and was taken from the field."[65] Washington was injured in both hands, leaving Monroe in command. He continued the assault before he was wounded in the shoulder and carried from the battlefield. The sword-wielding Sergeant White and his men assisted in capturing some of the guns, which they turned, loaded with canister, and fired at the fleeing Hessians. The Hessians managed to drag off their four remaining cannons, keeping them safe for the time being.

A fire was burning inside the bellies of the onrushing Americans. Trenton was their retribution for the months of defeat, loss, and humiliation. It was their turn to strike a blow against those who had invaded their homeland. While mercenaries fought for money, the Americans were fighting for a cause.

The fight was raging in Trenton's center as they began tightening the noose around the Rall and von Lossberg regiments. While the Hessian counterattack was valiant, it was a futile attempt, as the Americans' speed, tempo, and coordinated fires overwhelmed them. Continental riflemen also began to target Hessian officers, and many lieutenants and captains would meet their fate on that cold morning. Rall attempted to aid a lieutenant who had been shot as he ordered his men to

---

63 Iain Martin, ed., *The Greatest U.S. Army Stories Ever Told: Unforgettable Stories Of Courage, Honor, and Sacrifice* (Guilford, CT, 2006), 14; Fischer, *WC*, 246.

64 Joseph White, *An [sic] Narrative of Events, As They Occurred from Time to Time, in the Revolutionary War, with an Account of the Battle of Trenton, Trenton-Bridge, and Princeton*, (Charlestown, MA, 1833), as quoted in Dwyer, *TDIO*, 256.

65 James Monroe, *Autobiography*, Stuart Gerry Brown & Donald Baker, eds. (Syracuse, NY, 1959), 30; Brad Lookingbill, *American Military History: A Documentary Reader*, 2nd ed. (Hoboken, NJ, 2019), 25.

Captain William Washington (the general's cousin), Lt. James Monroe (the future president of the United States), and Sgt. John White attacked, capturing two Hessian cannons as they advanced into Trenton. White and his artillerymen turned a gun around and fired canister shot into the retreating Hessians. *Wikimedia*

retreat toward the orchard but was himself shot twice in the side, knocking him from his horse. With the assistance of two soldiers, Rall walked to the nearby Methodist church and lay down on a pew. Meanwhile, his men sought shelter in the orchard in order to evade the Americans' relentless pursuit.

As the battle raged in the village center, Sullivan's division systematically secured the south side of Trenton. Sullivan led Glover's and Sargent's brigades, supported by artillery, in an attack east along Front Street. Twenty-two-year-old Pvt. Jacob Francis of Sargent's brigade, an African-American freedman, recollected, "General Washington was at the head of that street [King] coming down toward us and some Hessians between us and them. We had the fight."[66] Sullivan's men captured the old military barracks, quickly beating back the Hessian sergeant and 18 men who were attempting to keep open the bridge over Assunpink Creek, thus closing the only remaining escape route. After crossing the creek, Glover and

<hr />

66 John Dann, ed., *The Revolution Remembered: Eyewitness Accounts of the War for Independence* (Chicago, 1980), 395; Dwyer, *TDIO*, 257. Francis survived the war, married an enslaved woman, and purchased her freedom. They settled in New Jersey and had four sons before Francis died in Trenton in 1836.

Sargent turned their units north, occupying the high ground and establishing blocking positions overlooking Trenton.

With Moulder's artillery supporting, Stark continued leading St. Clair's brigade east down 2nd Street, paralleling Sullivan's advance. St. Clair had his men expand their lines to the north in order to connect with Greene's division. Together they pushed the Hessians out of the village, taking many prisoners. Captain Moulder positioned his cannons on the corner of 2nd and Queen streets and fired on the Hessians as they retreated toward the orchard. Fifer John Greenwood recalled how Hessians hid in cellars and churches to avoid the ongoing fight as others fled in confusion and stated that General Washington rode up to his unit and declared, "March on, my brave fellows, after me!" before riding off to apply the *coup de grâce* to the Rall and von Lossberg Regiments. [67] Sergeant White shared his recollection of the horrific scene as the battle continued: "My blood chill'd to see such horror and distress, blood mingling together, the dying groans, and 'Garments rolled in blood.' The sight was too much to bear."[68] But bear it he did, as he and his comrades continued to push the Hessians back.

Washington maneuvered his forces, placing a stranglehold on the Hessians in the orchard. Forrest pushed his guns forward, ensuring their continued support of the infantry and their ability to deal a death blow against their enemy, if needed. The von Lossberg and Rall Regiment soldiers were in disarray as they gathered in the orchard. Some probably questioned how these half-naked and undisciplined rebels could administer such a severe blow to their professional force. As the sergeants and remaining junior officers tried to organize the intermingled units, their commanders, Scheffer of the von Lossberg Regiment and now-Major Matthaus of the Rall Regiment, discussed their options. Lieutenant Piel had reported that the Americans held the Assunpink Creek bridge. Their only viable options were to attempt a breakthrough to the north through the American lines or force a crossing of Assunpink Creek northeast of Trenton. As they started moving north, their options dwindled as they began taking heavy fire from Stephen's and Fermoy's men. Continentals from the German American battalion of Fermoy's brigade supposedly called out to their fellow Germans to surrender.

As Hessian commanders continued discussing their next actions, Washington prepared his artillery to deliver the fatal blow. Washington ordered Captain Forrest to load his guns with canister, knowing that these anti-personnel rounds would

---

67 Greenwood, *The Revolutionary Service of John Greenwood*, 42; James R. Arnold, ed., *Americans at War: Eyewitness Accounts from the American Revolution to the 21st Century* (Santa Barbara, CA, 2018), 21; Chadwick, *The First American Army*, 146.

68 White, *An Narrative of Events*, 77, quoted from Fischer, *WC*, 248.

rip the Hessians to shreds. Forrest was beginning to carry out the order when he observed the Hessians lower their regimental colors to the ground, signifying their surrender. The former Marine turned to Washington and said, "Sir, they have struck." Washington responded, "Struck!" "Yes, their colours are down," replied Forrest. Washington looked over at the Hessians and admitted, "So they are."[69] The Americans, who had endured many hardships over the last year, watched as enemy soldiers lowered their muskets to the ground and their officers raised their hats on the tips of their swords as a sign of submission.

Although the battle had taken a turn in the Continentals' favor, the Hessians still had another hand to play. The von Knyphausen Regiment was still in the fight, but it too was feeling the pressure. Major von Dechow attempted to reinforce Rall with two of the Hessian's six cannons but was beaten back. While fighting Sullivan's men along 2nd Street, Dechow was shot in the hip. He relinquished command to Capt. Bernard von Biesenrodt, who hoped to escape with the regiment across Assunpink Creek. Von Biesenrodt, however, was unaware of the size of the American force holding the bridge.

Biesenrodt started moving the regiment toward the bridge and quickly realized his folly. Fire from Sargent's and Glover's brigades forced the men to turn, following a path parallel to the creek. The ground was marshy, causing the cannons to become stuck in the mud; the Hessians ultimately abandoned them. Seeing no way out, von Dechow sent a message to Biesenrodt to surrender. Biesenrodt ignored the command and searched for a place to cross the creek. Growing weaker due to his injury, von Dechow left Biesenrodt to his own devices and surrendered himself to the Americans, infuriating some of the von Knyphausen Regiment. Von Dechow's action and the cheering of the Americans stiffened some of the men's resolve to escape.

St. Clair, supported by Moulder's artillery, advanced with his brigade, which fired a volley into the rear of the von Knyphausen Regiment as it desperately attempted to flee. Several Hessians successfully traversed the creek in spite of its neck-high waters. Roughly 50 men made it across, but not before the creek's swift current carried three soldiers away. Those who got away reached Princeton 10 hours later to join the British garrison there. Back in Trenton, St. Clair ordered the Hessians to surrender, but Biesenrodt refused. After further negotiations, Biesenrodt realized the futility of his situation and agreed to submit. The battle was over. St. Clair ordered Wilkinson to notify Sullivan of the surrender. Sullivan then sent Wilkinson to tell Washington, who was riding down King Street toward their

69 Ibid., 251.

The Capture of the Hessians at Trenton, December 26, 1776. Painting by John Trumbull. It celebrates the American victory at the battle of Trenton, but like many paintings of the time, it creates a scene that did not occur as depicted. It was meant to place as many key figures in the painting as possible. It depicts General Washington seeing to the needs of the mortally wounded Hessian Col. Johann Rall. Rall, however, was receiving medical treatment in a building at the time of the surrender. The painting also depicts a severely wounded Lt. James Monroe being helped by Dr. John Riker on the left and Gen. Nathanael Greene on horseback with Henry Knox standing beside him. *Wikimedia*

position. On hearing the good news, Washington extended his hand to Wilkinson, stating, "Major Wilkinson, this is a glorious day for our country."[70]

From the first shot at the Pennington picket to the surrender of the von Knyphausen Regiment, the battle of Trenton only lasted around an hour and a half, but it likely changed the nation's fate. While it was a great American victory, it was not as complete as Washington had wanted. He later confided in John Hancock, "I am fully confident, that could the Troops, under Generals Ewing and Cadwallader, have passed the River, I should have been able, with their Assistance, to have driven the Enemy from all their posts below Trenton."[71] Though true, Washington's victory was still significant. He told Hancock, "In justice to the Officers and Men, I must add, that their Behaviour upon this Occasion, reflects the highest honor upon them."[72] And so it was, but the greatest credit for the victory belongs to Washington.

70 Wilkinson, *Memoirs*, 131.

71 *FONA*, http://founders.archives.gov/documents/Washington/03-07-02-0355, accessed Dec. 23, 2019.

72 Ibid.

While Washington received input from various sources, he was solely responsible for deciding when and where to strike the enemy, and he personally led the attack. His sheer determination and grit throughout the trying months leading to the battle of Trenton ensured the survival of his army. Washington made the attack possible by preserving what he could of his force while demanding reinforcements like that of Major Nicholas and the Continental Marines.

In the weeks before the battle, Washington's ability to effectively employ his limited resources was instrumental in rebuilding and restoring his army. He used this time to gather critical intelligence about the enemy so as to determine their strengths and weaknesses. Washington skillfully employed the local militia and others familiar with the area to constantly harass the British and Hessian forces, systematically wearing them down and conditioning them to expect more attacks by smaller forces. Washington arguably used deception and misinformation to validate his enemy's perceptions of the Continental Army's weakness and inability to stage any large-scale attacks.

Having established the conditions, Washington devised a scheme that embraced the tenets of maneuver warfare. He planned to avoid the enemy's strength, hitting their isolated and weakest positions. By using the element of surprise, speed, tempo, and simultaneous attacks at multiple locations to overwhelm the enemy's ability to react effectively, Washington could also break their will to resist. He provided clear and concise directions that informed his commanders of what he wanted while allowing them to determine how they accomplished their specific tasks. These mission-type orders gave his lieutenants the flexibility to adjust on the run when the original plan did not play out as expected.

Washington also placed himself at the most significant point of potential friction to exert his leadership when needed. He was among the first to cross the Delaware, ensuring he could pull his force across as Knox pushed from the opposite shore. He placed himself toward the front of the column in the march to Trenton and took a position with his designated main effort for the attack. Washington went where he could best control his units, observe enemy reactions, and make timely decisions for his forces. The reports of his soldiers indicate that he was actively moving about the battlefield throughout the fight, exposing himself to the same dangers and providing a personal example to all. Washington instilled positive energy and confidence in his men, evident in much of the correspondence leading up to the battle. His belief in himself, his men, and their cause was a force multiplier on the battlefield that the Hessians lacked.

As is often the case when an organization faces defeat, people look for someone to blame. Many pointed to Rall's poor decisions, lack of adequate preparations, and hubris as the primary drivers of defeat. Although true, several additional factors contributed to the Hessian loss. Their culture valued discipline and instant obedience to orders, which did not leave room for the free-thinking that spurs initiative like that of the Americans. The loss of Rall and other officers during the battle further degraded the Hessians' cohesion. The high tempo established by the Continentals left their adversaries with no time to work through this friction, and the surprise they achieved left little time for the Hessians to organize a defense. The weather worsened Hessian troubles, as the fouling of their muskets weakened their defense. While the Americans effectively employed overwhelming artillery support, the Hessians barely got their guns into action. Part of the blame for this defeat must also fall on the senior leadership of the British and Hessian forces. They implemented a cantonment plan, which spread their forces across widely dispersed and unsupported positions.

Trenton was a devastating defeat for the Hessians and their British allies. They lost 22 killed and 83 seriously wounded. Rall and von Dechow died of their wounds the day after the battle. More importantly, the Americans captured 896 Hessian soldiers, six brass cannons, three munitions wagons, 40 horses, 1,000 muskets with bayonets, 15 regimental and company battle colors, 40 hogsheads of rum, and a band's worth of instruments.[73] Fifer John Greenwood recalled that in the midst of battle, "I passed two of their cannon . . . and a brass drum. This latter article was, a great curiosity to me and I stopped to look at it, but it was quickly taken possession of by one of the drummers, who threw away his own instrument."[74] In a letter to Colonel Procter, commander of the Pennsylvania artillery, Thomas Forrest wrote, "we have taken, exclusive of what were not able to march off, with a Compleat band of Musick."[75] Forrest, however, kept his joy over the victory in perspective when he added, "The men are not able to move for want of Shoes and Watch coats which I expect you'll forward . . . immediately."[76]

Forrest captured the essence of the Americans' situation following this historic victory. Not a single American died, aside from the two men who had frozen to death on the march, and only four were wounded.[77] Washington attributed this to the Hessians' lack of a cohesive defense. He wrote to Hancock, "they [Hessians] never made any regular Stand. Our Loss is very trifling indeed."[78] The Americans'

73 Bonk, *Trenton and Princeton*, 61; Ferling, *AAM*, 178; Fischer, *WC*, 254, 256; Ward, *TWOR*, 302.

74 Greenwood, *The Revolutionary Service of John Greenwood*, 42.

75 Stryker, *BTP*, 373.

76 Ibid.

77 Bonk, *Trenton and Princeton*, 61; Ferling, *AAM*, 178; Fischer, *WC*, 254, 256; Ward, *TWOR*, 302.

78 *FONA*, http://founders.archives.gov/documents/Washington/03-07-02-0355, accessed Dec. 23, 2019.

Washington Inspecting the Captured Colors After the Battle of Trenton. Painting by Percy Moran. The American victory at Trenton was complete. The Hessians sustained 22 killed and 83 wounded. The Americans captured 896 Hessian soldiers, six brass cannons, three munition wagons, 40 horses, 1,000 muskets with bayonets, 15 regimental and company battle colors, 40 hogsheads of rum, and a band's worth of instruments. *Wikimedia*

victory and its rewards were substantial, but Washington knew that while this win would bolster the spirit of his army and the nation, ultimate victory was still far away. Many challenges lay ahead, but so too did opportunities. Washington's trustworthy subordinate, Henry Knox, put into words what Washington must have been thinking as he reflected on what they had just achieved on the shores of the Delaware: "Providence seemed to have smiled upon every part of this enterprise. Great advantages may be gained from it if we take proper steps."[79] With no time to waste, Washington gathered his commanders to determine the next "proper steps."

79 Commager & Morris, *SSS*, 513.

Chapter Nine

Going for Broke

"The bridge looked red as blood, with their killed and wounded, and their red coats."

— Sgt. Joseph White[1]

*B*efore the smoke had cleared from the Trenton battlefield, Washington and his senior leaders gathered for an impromptu council of war. They assessed their situation, discussing how best to proceed in what had been a successful operation up to that point. Washington originally envisioned continuing the offensive, defeating the British at Princeton, and capturing their main supply depot at Brunswick, if possible. But with the situation rapidly changing, he was still unsure of the overall status of his other forces operating downriver and of additional enemy units in the area.

Washington determined that he had four courses of action from which to choose. His army could continue the offensive and attack another British or Hessian post in New Jersey. It could advance south along the Delaware River to join forces with Cadwalader's and Putnam's men to continue operations in New Jersey. The army could remain in place, fortify its position, and let the enemy come to him, or it could recross the Delaware and seek sanctuary in Pennsylvania.

Throughout deliberations, Washington first considered the condition of his men. Although they renewed their self-confidence and morale was soaring following the defeat of the feared Hessians, Washington realized his troops were exhausted. Most soldiers had been awake for over 24 hours, remained ill-clad, and were shoeless. Additionally, they were soaked from exposure to the ongoing

---

1 Nathaniel Philbrick, *Valiant Ambition: George Washington, Benedict Arnold, and the Fate of the American Revolution* (New York, 2016), 342; Chadwick, *The First American Army*, 154; Fischer, *WC*, 307.

blizzard. The army had endured a river crossing, a nine-mile forced march over rough terrain, fought a battle, and had not enjoyed a hot meal in over 24 hours. To make matters worse, Washington's men now had roughly 1,000 angry Hessian prisoners with which to contend.

Washington understood that his army was quickly approaching its culmination point. In military terms, the culminating point is the one at which a unit starts to experience diminishing returns if it continues in its current form of operation. History has demonstrated that armies pushing beyond this point can quickly turn a victory into a defeat.

Washington was also considering the enemy's situation. Though they had defeated the Hessians at Trenton, somewhere, in the rear of Washington's army, lurked von Donop and his 1,500 men. He hoped that Putnam, Cadwalader, and the Marines had achieved similar success against von Donop, but he had received no information concerning their statuses. He did know that Ewing had failed in his endeavor. General Leslie still commanded a brigade of four regular infantry and two light infantry battalions, with a company of light dragoons in Princeton, 12 miles north of Trenton. If pushed, the British infantry could easily make it to Trenton within three to four hours, and the mounted dragoons could start harassing his forces much sooner. Grant commanded an additional brigade of two guards and two grenadier battalions, with a company of light dragoons in reserve 16 miles farther north at Brunswick. He could join Leslie and confront Washington within a few hours.

With the Delaware River to their backs, Washington understood that the Americans in Trenton were vulnerable. They could face attacks to their front and rear by an overwhelming number of enemy troops. Washington's boats remained staged at the Johnson Ferry landing, nine miles upriver. Before his troops had become fatigued by battle, it had taken them roughly four hours to cover that distance. Now, they also had 1,000 prisoners in tow. Washington also recalled how it took his men 10 hours to conduct that unopposed crossing. Plus, the river was still clogged with ice and the inclement weather persisted. A crossing on this day promised to be challenging enough without fighting off a pursuing enemy.

Washington and his commanders argued the merits of each course of action. Greene, Knox, Haslet, and others called for pressing the attack. They reasoned that "[s]uccesses & brilliant strokes ought to be pursued—that History shewed how much depended upon improving such Advantages—& that a Pannick being once given no one could ascertain the beneficial Consequences which might be derived from it if it was push'd to all its Consequences."[2] Others contended that the Americans should not push their luck and risk the great advantage they had gained. Joseph Reed later recalled yet another factor that needed to be considered: "There were great Quantities of Spirituous Liquors at Trenton of which the Soldiers drank too freely to admit of Discipline or Defence in Case of Attack."

Prudence prevailed, and Washington decided to move the army back to the safety of Pennsylvania. As one officer explained, "The weather was so amazingly severe, our arms so wet, and the men so fatigued, it was judged prudent to come off immediately with our prisoners and plunder."[3] Haslet later agreed, noting, "We should have gone on and, panick struck, they would have fled before us, but the inclemency of the weather rendered it impossible."[4]

Their defeat at Trenton profoundly impacted the Hessians and British. The shock and surprise Washington created by this unexpected move placed doubt, and perhaps a bit of fear, in their minds. Von Donop immediately withdrew from Mount Holly and ordered his remaining forces at Bordentown to join him in Allentown, eight miles inland from the Delaware River and 12 miles southeast of Trenton. Those in Burlington also evacuated. Some joined the British in Princeton, while the remainder went north to Brunswick. Although Ewing and Cadwalader were unsuccessful, Washington's actions caused the Hessians to abandon every post along the Delaware. Lord Stirling wrote, "we are now in possession of all those places, and the spirit of that part of the country is roused."[5]

Von Donop explained the decision to abandon his posts to Lieutenant General von Knyphausen in New York by citing exaggerated numbers threatening his brigade. Von Donop claimed that he was told the Americans attacked Trenton with 10,000-12,000 men, which we know to be five times the amount Washington actually employed. With both this large number and the uncertainty of what might happen in mind, von Donop reported,

I did not think it advisable for me to remain any longer in so dangerous a situation, surrounded on all sides by the enemy and cut off from all communication with Princeton. I was also assured that a large part of the rebels had turned to Princeton and I had not the slightest word from General Leslie. My ammunition had run

2 Both quotes in this paragraph were derived from Joseph Reed, *General Joseph Reed's Narrative of the Movements of the American Army in the Neighborhood of Trenton in the Winter of 1776-77*, 391, https://ia801906.us.archive.org/35/items/jstor-20084674/20084674.pdf, accessed Dec. 24, 2019.

3 "Extract of a letter from an officer in the American Army, Newton, Pennsylvania, December 27, 1776," quoted from Force & St. Clair Clarke, eds., *AA*, 3:1443.

4 Rodney, *Diary of Captain Thomas Rodney*, 51; Fischer, *WC*, 255.

5 Force & St. Clair Clarke, eds., *AA*, 3:1462; Stryker, *BTP*, 394.

low, only about nine cartridges to a cannon and very little indeed for the fire-locks. Even if I had thought proper to face all attacks from the enemy in my dangerous position, to remain in Bordentown and wait for a doubtful success I would not dare to do it on account of the shortage of ammunition.[6]

Von Donop also explained how his withdrawal forced him to "leave about twenty sick and wounded at Bordentown, with a stock of provisions and forage. Some of the men were not able to be carried and the wagons were too scarce to carry the rations." He failed to explain how wagons were unavailable, as the Hessians used several to haul off the plunder they had stolen from local citizens. Von Donop described how he "organized all the escaped men from the Rail [Rall] brigade and made up a force of two hundred and ninety-two men."

Fearing Washington was on his way to attack, on December 28 General Leslie sent frantic notes to von Donop. He was requesting that von Donop and his troops reinforce the British in Princeton. He later rescinded the request after hearing that Washington had recrossed the Delaware.[7] Now that the immediate threat was gone, the British assessed the Hessians' defeat by the Americans.

The British were unhappy with their allies, or, more accurately, the mercenaries they hired to squash the rebellion. Howe found it hard to believe "[t]hat three old established regiments of a people, who made war a profession, should lay down their arms to a ragged and undisciplined militia."[8] On hearing of the battle, he immediately canceled Lord Cornwallis's departure for England, directing that he replace Grant in overall command in New Jersey. Grant maintained an indignant tone when he wrote von Donop the day following the battle, "I did not think that all the Rebels in America would have taken that Brigade Prisoners."[9] Still unwilling to believe the Americans posed a serious threat, he added, "if I was with you, your Grenadiers and Yagers I should not be afraid of an attack from Washington's Army, which is almost naked and does not exceed 8000 men," using the same language he had with Rall right before his defeat and subsequent death. Perhaps Lord Germain back in England captured the true impact of the defeat when he shared how he envisioned "a fair prospect of a successful campaign, and the happy termination of the war. . . . But all our hopes were blasted by that unhappy affair at Trenton."[10]

6 The following three quotes are from Stryker, *BTP*, 399-400.

7 Ibid., 424-425.

8 *Washington Irving, Life of George Washington* (New York, 1859), 2:500; Ward, *TWOR*, 305.

9 The following two quotes were taken from Stryker, *BTP*, 400-401.

10 *The Parliamentary Register; Or, History of the Proceedings and Debates of the House of Commons . . . during the Fifth Session of the Fourteenth Parliament of Great Britain* (London, 1802), 11:392; Dwyer, *TDIO*, 279.

Determined to end the rebellion for good, Howe began gathering reinforcements for Cornwallis. Washington, however, would soon have his reinforcements of his own.

Cadwalader and his force remained frustrated by having missed their chance for action. In fact, Cadwalader doubted any of the American units had made it across the river. On the morning of December 26, he wrote to Washington, "I imagine the badness of the night must have prevented you from passing as you intended."[11] He went on to explain why his force failed in its mission. Cadwalader and his commanders, including Major Nicholas, assessed their situations with hopes of joining what they believed to be an ongoing operation. Cadwalader recommended to Washington that his force attempt another crossing farther down river to consolidate with Putnam's men:

> Would it not be proper to attempt to cross below & join General Putnam, who was to go over from Philada today with 500 men, which number added to the 400 Jersey Militia which Col. Griffin left there would make a formidable Body— This would cause a Diversion that would favour any Attempt you may design in future, & would expose their Baggage & Stores, if they attempt to cross.

Further analyzing his force, Cadwalader understood that the "Militia will be easier kept together by being in motion & we shall have some Service from Col. Hitchcock's Brigade, whose time of Enlistment will be up in a few Days."

Cadwalader grasped what was perhaps the greatest challenge confronting Washington's army at the time. He had to gainfully employ the militia or risk losing them, which would be devastating enough without the added challenge of possibly losing most of his regulars to enlistments terminating within a week. Before completing his letter to Washington, Cadwalader received reports of the sound of battle coming from upriver.

Word of Washington's attack moved swiftly downriver. At 11:00 a.m., Ewing notified Cadwalader of Washington's success. Reports soon followed of enemy activity on the New Jersey side: "The Light Horse & Hessians were seen flying in great confusion towards Bordentown, but without Cannon or Waggons, so that the Enemy must have lost the whole, a party of our men intercepted about a Dozen Hessians in sight of our people on this side &: brought them to the Ferry & huzza'd."

The battle noise and the sight of a fleeing enemy energized Cadwalader's men and the Marines at Bristol. They did not want to miss the opportunity to strike

---

11 The following four quotes are from *FONA*, http://founders.archives.gov/documents/ Washington/03-07-02-0347, accessed Dec. 24, 2019.

back and oust the enemy from their posts in New Jersey. Cadwalader acted without waiting for Washington's response. He intended to carry out the last orders from Washington. While some of Cadwalader's men completed recrossing the river as late as 4:00 a.m., he informed them to prepare to cross back into New Jersey once again the following morning. Cadwalader wrote to the Pennsylvania Committee of Safety, "I have ordered the boats from Dunk's and shall pass as soon as possible— we can muster here about eighteen hundred men, if the Expedition last night in the storm does not thin our Ranks."[12]

Back in Trenton, Washington permitted his men some rest before putting them back on the move at noon. He and General Greene visited the dying Colonel Rall, who had been carried back to his quarters in Mr. Pott's home. Rall requested, and Washington agreed, to allow his men to keep their possessions. Washington then paroled Rall and the other wounded Hessian soldiers he intended to leave at Trenton and went on his way. Rall died later that day.

Lord Stirling and his brigade were ordered to escort the remaining Hessian prisoners across the river. The ice had cleared sufficiently to allow one group to cross from Trenton Ferry. Another contingent would cross at Beatty's Ferry five miles upriver, while the main body hiked nine miles to go over with the remainder of the army at Johnson's Ferry, where several more boats waited.

This crossing proved to be more difficult than the previous one. Jacob Francis, the freedman, described how "about noon it began to rain and rained very hard. We were engaged all the afternoon in ferrying them [prisoners] across till it was quite dark."[13] Fifer John Greenwood described how the boat he rode in with some prisoners "was half a leg deep with rain and snow and some of the poor fellows were so cold that their underjaws quivered like an aspen leaf."[14] Americans and Hessians worked together to keep ice from forming on their boats by jumping up and down to break the forming ice free so they could maneuver their craft. Some failed in doing so. Hessian Lieutenant Wiederholdt of the Pennington Road post recalled "[t]he wind blowing against us and the ice jams prevented the boat I was in from landing on the bank. As a result it drifted almost two miles down the Delaware."[15] They decided to jump in the river and wade ashore rather than

12 Force & St. Clair, eds., *AA*, 3:1441.

13 Jack Crowder, *African Americans and American Indians in the Revolutionary War* (Jefferson, NC, 2019), 57; John Dann, ed., *The Revolution Remembered: Eyewitness Accounts of the War for Independence* (Chicago, 1999), 395; Dwyer, *TDIO*, 272.

14 Greenwood, *The Revolutionary Service of John Greenwood*, 43.

15 Dwyer, *TDIO*, 269; Fischer, *WC*, 259.

continue drifting. Wiederholdt described how they "had to walk seventy feet in water up to our chest and break through the ice in some places."[16]

Other Hessians were more concerned about their treatment in captivity by the Americans than they were about the weather. The British had attempted to instill fear of the Americans in their Hessian partners to get them to fight more fiercely. The Germans were told that the American rebels were "a race of cannibals who would not only tomahawk a poor Hessian and haul off his hide for a drum's head, but would just as [soon] leave barbecue and eat him as he would a pig."[17] The opposite was true, as the Hessians would discover.

Washington demanded that all prisoners be treated with dignity and respect. Besides being right, Washington also thought it would entice more Hessians, who he believed involuntarily served in America, to surrender. Lord Stirling reinforced this thought in a letter to Governor Livingston: "I had the honour to make two regiments of them surrender prisoners of war and to treat them in such a style as will make the rest of them more willing to surrender than to fight."[18] The Pennsylvania Committee of Safety understood Washington's intent when it published a proclamation after the prisoners reached Philadelphia. It stated, "There arrived yesterday in this City near one thousand Hessian prisoners taken by his Excellency Gen'l Washington. . . . The General has recommended . . . to provide suitable quarters for them and it is his earnest wish that they may be well treated and have such principles instilled in them . . . that when they return . . . they may fully open the Eyes of their Countrymen."[19]

Washington also realized the necessity of obtaining and keeping the support of the American public. He and his army had already experienced first-hand the privations associated with operating in an area with a disaffected population. Washington intended to keep the backing of those supportive of liberty, while hoping to win over, or at least keep neutral, those whose loyalties were divided. He observed the negative impacts of the plundering and other atrocities by the British and Hessians on the population, understanding that his troops could succumb to similar temptations. As such, he later published a proclamation addressing the issue:

16 Fischer, *WC*, 259.

17 Dwyer, *TDIO*, 273.

18 Theodore Sedgwick, *A Memoir of the Life of William Livingston: Member of Congress in 1774, 1775, and 1776; Delegate to the Federal Convention 1787; and Governor of the State of New Jersey from 1776 to 1790* (New York, 1833), 221; Stryker, *BTP*, 394.

19 Samuel Hazard, *Pennsylvania Archives* (Philadelphia, 1853), 5:146; "Proclamation of the Pennsylvania Committee of Safety, December 31, 1776," quoted from Stryker, *BTP*, 395.

His Excellency General Washington strictly forbids all the officers and soldiers of the Continental army, of the militia and all recruiting parties, plundering any person whatsoever, whether Tories or others. The effects of such persons will be applied to public uses in a regular manner, and it is expected that humanity and tenderness to women and children will distinguish brave Americans, contending for liberty, from infamous mercenary ravagers, whether British or Hessians.[20]

This guidance was shared with the American army and displayed in public areas throughout New Jersey.

Washington, his army, and their prisoners began arriving back at his headquarters in Newtown, Pennsylvania, on December 26. The movement continued into the following day. The troops did what they could to warm up and get a hot meal while officers returned to ever-present piles of paperwork. On December 27, Washington thanked the men for their actions in his General Orders: "THE GENERAL, with the utmost sincerity and affection, thanks the Officers and soldiers for their spirited and gallant behavior at Trenton yesterday."[21] He continued, "The Commissary is strictly ordered to provide Rum for the Troops that it may be served as Occasion shall require." Many soldiers collapsed and slept for several hours, grateful for the warmth in their bellies. The men were so worn by sickness, disease, and fatigue that nearly 1,000 were unfit for duty. They received a short reprieve as Washington corresponded with his commanders and Congress to plan the army's next move. Little did he know that other parts of his army were already in motion.

As Washington crossed into Pennsylvania, Cadwalader, who believed the commander-in-chief to still be in New Jersey, attempted to coordinate his actions with the army he thought was still at Trenton. He wrote Washington, "if a part of your Army was to take possession of the other side of Crosswix Bridge, which is a pass easily defended, and the main Body march round by Crosswix we might perfectly surround the Troops at Bordenton so as to prevent one man from escaping."[22] Unfortunately, Washington did not receive Cadwalader's letter before recrossing the river. Cadwalader decided to continue the offensive and push on even though he had not received a response from Washington.

---

20 *FONA*, https://founders.archives.gov/documents/Washington/03-07-02-0393, accessed Dec. 24, 2019; "Proclamation of General George Washington, Trenton, New Jersey, January 1, 1777," quoted from *The Scots Magazine*, vol. 39 (Edinburgh, 1777), 141.

21 The following two quotes are from "General Orders December 27, 1776," https://www.mountvernon.org/education/primary-sources-2/article/general-orders-december-27-1776/, accessed Dec. 24, 2019.

22 *FONA*, https://founders.archives.gov/documents/Washington/03-07-02-0348, accessed Dec. 25, 2019.

Early on December 27, Cadwalader commenced his second crossing of the Delaware. Commodore Seymour's river fleet of sailors and Marines maneuvered to support the crossing as the ice began to clear. Thomas Rodney of the Delaware militia recalled, "We got down to Bristol about Daylight, and the whole army under General Cadwalader began crossing about 10 o'clock, about one mile above Bristol. The light Infantry covered the landing as before and about 3 o'clock the whole army got in motion towards Burlington."[23] Nicholas, Shippin, Brown, and their Marines moved with the brigade of Associators. Shortly after landing in New Jersey, Cadwalader received word of von Donop's retreat from Black Horse and Mt. Holly. Later that day, after the preponderance of his force had already landed, he discovered that Washington had crossed back into Pennsylvania.

On receiving news of Washington's return to Pennsylvania, and believing his mission no longer valid, Cadwalader contemplated returning. The free-willed Associators and gregarious Marines were not pleased, and with some coaxing and help from Colonel Reed, convinced Cadwalader to remain in New Jersey. Cadwalader sent a dispatch to Washington explaining, "This [Washington's movement back to Pennsylvania] defeated the Scheme of joining your Army— We were much embarrassed which way to proceed—I thought it most prudent to retreat; but Col. Reed was of [the] opinion that we might safely proceed to Burlington—and recommended it warmly least it should have a bad Effect on the militia who were twice disappointed."[24]

Reed had correctly read the mood of Cadwalader's men. They wanted action. Accepting his situation, Cadwalader shared with Washington that "A pursuit would keep up the Panic—They [British and Hessians] went off with great precipitation, & press'd all the Waggons in their reach—I am told many of them are gone to South Amboy [nearly 40 miles north of Trenton]—If we can drive them from West Jersey, the Success will raise an Army by next Spring, & establish the Credit of the Continental Money, to support it."

For better or worse, Cadwalader's Associators, Hitchcock's regulars, Nicholas's Continental Marines, and other units were in Pennsylvania looking for a fight. Captain Benjamin Dean, who had previously commanded the marines on the frigate *Washington* and now headed a company of Continental Marines in Nicholas's battalion, welcomed the arrival of his ship's commanding officer, Capt. Thomas Read. Read brought with him "a detachment of sailors used to firing

---

23 Rodney, *Diary of Captain Thomas Rodney*, 24; Hezekiah Niles, *Principles and Acts of the Revolution*, 248-249, quoted in Commager & Morris, *SSS*, 515.

24 The following two quotes are from *FONA*, http://founders.archives.gov/documents/ Washington/03-07-02-0353, accessed Dec. 25, 2019.

guns."[25] Cadwalader's force was taking on an increased naval presence. In addition to Major Nicholas and the Continental Marines, and Capts. Shippin's and Brown's Pennsylvania state marines, sailors now joined the ranks. Others would do so in the coming days.

In Baltimore on December 27, Congress, still unaware of the American victory, signed a resolution granting Washington extraordinary powers to address the nation's crisis. It resolved,

> That general Washington shall be and he is hereby vested with full, ample and complete powers to raise and collect together, in the most speedy and effectual manner, from any or all of these United States, sixteen battalions of infantry in addition to those voted by Congress.[26]

The resolution gave Washington powers "to appoint officers for the said battalions of infantry; to raise, officer and equip 3000 light horse; three regiments of artillery and a corps of engineers and to establish their pay; to apply to any of the states for such aid of the militia as he shall judge necessary." Congress added an extraordinary measure empowering Washington "to take, wherever he may be, whatever he may want for the use of the army, if the inhabitants will not sell it, allowing a reasonable price for the same; to arrest and confine persons who refuse to take the Continental Currency or are otherwise disaffected to the American cause."

Washington received more than he asked for. His newly vested powers enabled him to establish the professional army he sought. It also allowed him to appoint and displace officers rather than accept officers selected by the states or units. Now he could legally commandeer the supplies needed to sustain the army, arrest those unsympathetic to the American cause, and work directly with states to gain assistance in mobilizing militias.

Washington was granted these powers for six months, "unless sooner determined by Congress." One can only speculate whether Congress would have given him such powers if it had received word of his victory before passing the resolution. The fact that it did not rescind this authority upon learning of the victory three days later indicates that it would not have done so. Further evidence of the confidence Congress held in Washington can be found in a letter forwarded to him by Robert Morris, announcing the details of the resolution: "Happy it is for this country, that the General of their forces can safely be entrusted with the most

25 Stryker, *BTP*, 433.

26 The following quotes are from Jared Sparks, *The Writings of George Washington* (Boston, 1834), 4:550-552.

unlimited power, and neither personal security, liberty nor property be in the least degree endangered thereby."

Washington affirmed the trust bestowed upon him, responding to the Executive Committee of the Continental Congress on January 1, 1777:

> I find they have done me the honour to intrust me with powers, in my military capacity of the highest nature and almost unlimited in extent. Instead of thinking myself freed from all civil obligations, by this mark of confidence, I shall constantly bear in mind, that as the sword was the last resort for the preservation of our liberties, so it ought to be the first thing laid aside, when those liberties are firmly established.[27]

While he now had greater authority, Washington still lacked sufficient troops. He relied on Generals Putnam and Mifflin to continue recruiting in and around Philadelphia as he addressed more immediate needs with the army in the field.

Washington attempted to gain control of the fast-moving events on hearing of Cadwalader's crossing. He immediately dispatched a letter, voicing his intent and asking for Cadwalader's patience before taking further action:

> . . . it is my earnest wish to pursue every means that shall seem probable to distress the enemy and to promise success on our part. If we could happily beat up the rest of their Quarters, bordering on and near the River, it would be attended with the most valuable consequences. I have called a meeting of the General Officers to consult of what measures shall be next pursued & would recommend that you & Gen. Putnam should defer your intended operations till you hear from me.[28]

Washington described possible scenarios, including his army again crossing the Delaware near Trenton, or possibly shifting farther south, joining Cadwalader near Bristol.

Washington assembled his local commanders in Newton after dispatching a rider with the letter for Cadwalader. He informed his lieutenants of Cadwalader's presence in New Jersey and spoke of the opportunity this now provided the army. He received a tepid response. Washington guided the discussion, careful not to be directive in the approach. He wanted his commanders to make the right decision, ensuring their "buy-in" for the plan, as it would be difficult. Eventually, each one came to the same conclusion. While they would not have advised Cadwalader's

---

27 *FONA*, https://founders.archives.gov/documents/Washington/03-07-02-0395, accessed Dec. 25, 2019.

28 *FONA*, http://founders.archives.gov/documents/Washington/03-07-02-0353, accessed Dec. 25, 2019.

crossing, the opportunity was open to clear the enemy from a larger portion of New Jersey and demonstrate that the American victory at Trenton was not a fluke. It was settled. Once more, Washington ordered his army to cross the Delaware River.

Having settled on regaining the initiative, Washington ordered his commanders to apply pressure on the enemy on all fronts. On December 27, he wrote to General Heath in Peekskill, New York, who was keeping the British at bay, "I some time ago mentioned to you the importance of attacking the enemy's detached posts, when it can be done with a quick prospect of success. The best of consequences must result from their being on every occasion on that quarter."[29] The next day, he implored Gen. Alexander McDougal and other leaders of local troops operating from Morristown, New Jersey, 30 miles north of Brunswick, urging them to "exert themselves in encouraging the Militia and assuring them that nothing is wanting, but for them to lend a hand, and driving the Enemy from the whole province of Jersey. Pray watch the Motions of the Enemy, and if they incline to retreat or advance, harass their Rear and Flanks."[30] On December 30, he followed up by adding, "I beg you will collect all the men you possibly can about Chatham, and, after gaining the proper intelligence, endeavor to strike a blow at Elizabethtown [45 miles north of Trenton] or that neighborhood."[31]

After opting to recross the river, Washington dispatched a second letter informing Cadwalader of the decision and that Generals Ewing and Mifflin were en route to join him with more troops. Washington also explained that he intended to delay his crossing for two days so his weary troops could rest. The letter stated that he "therefore desires that you would keep your ground, and not attempt anything, (without you see a certainty of success,) till he [Washington] passes the river, because a miscarriage would defeat all the good effects of our late victory."[32] Unfortunately, Cadwalader was already on the move.

Once ashore in New Jersey, Cadwalader wasted no time, attacking the areas surrounding Burlington under the protection of the guns from Commodore Seymour's ships. He deployed scouts forward and on the flanks for security and employed rifle and light infantry battalions as an advance guard. The artillery followed in trace. The Continental Marines and the remainder of the main body advanced by platoons behind the artillery. Their approach was slow and deliberate due to the uncertainty of enemy activity in the area. The brigade arrived

29 Force & St. Clair, eds., *AA*, 3:1446.

30 *FONA*, http://founders.archives.gov/documents/Washington/03-07-02-0366, accessed Dec. 25, 2019.

31 Sparks, *The Writings of George Washington*, 253.

32 Force & St. Clair, eds., *AA*, 3:1447-1448.

in Burlington at approximately 9:00 p.m. only to discover that the enemy had already fled. Cadwalader assigned a small scouting party, led by Colonel Reed, to push ahead on horseback and determine the location and strength of the retreating enemy. Meanwhile, his commanders placed the remainder of the brigade in quarters for the evening.

Reed and his companions also found Bordentown abandoned by von Donop's men. Reed sent a rider to inform Cadwalader, urging him forward as he and the others continued toward Trenton. Cadwalader issued orders to continue heading for Bordentown, commencing at 4:00 a.m. in hopes of catching the enemy rear guard. Captain Rodney, moving with the advance guard, lamented how the Hessian occupiers had ravished the land: "The whole country as we passed appeared one scene of devastation and ruin. Neither hay, straw, grain or any livestock or poultry to be seen."[33] Around 9:00 a.m., the main body and Marines departed Burlington, causing resident Margaret Morris to reflect, "My heart sinks when I think of the numbers unprepared for death, who will probably be sent in a few days to appear before the Judge of Heaven."[34] Her words proved to be prophetic.

Cadwalader's column stretched out for miles. His advance guard reached Bordentown just as the main body departed Burlington. Upon entering the village, the troops found the wounded Hessians and much-needed military stores abandoned by von Donop. The hungry Americans appreciated the several hundred barrels of salted pork and captured beef. When Reed arrived in Trenton that morning, he found the village as Washington had left it two days earlier. He sent a dispatch to Washington, urging him to return to New Jersey as Cadwalader's force continued its trek toward Trenton.[35]

Cadwalader's main body got to Bordentown at approximately 2:00 p.m. and learned that von Donop's rear guard was only a few miles away. The general immediately deployed a force of 100 riflemen, 100 light infantry, and 100 militiamen to the village of Crosswicks four miles east along the Old York Road with orders to harass the rear of von Donop's column. Cadwalader kept Washington apprised of his progress: "We shall pursue with my Troops to-morrow before day—about 500 go this Evg to Cross-wix—The Enemy are much encumbered with Baggage & Cattle—I hope to fall on their Rear."[36] The advance guard arrived at Crosswicks around 8:00 p.m., finding that the enemy had retreated ahead of their arrival.

33 Rodney, *Diary of Captain Thomas Rodney*, 25.

34 Margaret Morris, "Revolutionary Journal of Margaret Morris," *Bulletin of Friends' Historical Society of Philadelphia*, vol. 9, no. 2 (Nov. 1919), 71; Dwyer, *TDIO*, 282.

35 Reed, *Life and Correspondence of Joseph Reed*, 281.

36 *FONA*, http://founders.archives.gov/documents/Washington/03-07-02-0361, accessed Dec. 25, 2019.

As Cadwalader's brigade pressed its advantage, British and Hessian forces consolidated around Princeton and Brunswick. Von Donop was ordered to Princeton, relieving Leslie with his grenadiers, jaegers, and what remained of Rall's brigade. This would allow Leslie to reposition his forces elsewhere. On December 28, von Donop departed Allentown. When he reached Princeton later that day, he immediately began construction of two small redoubts south of the village. Leslie was ordered to send a light infantry unit and the Highlanders to Maidenhead village and establish a forward outpost five miles south of Princeton and seven miles north of Trenton along the Princeton Road. Leslie also deployed detachments to Rocky Hill four miles north, Kingston four miles northeast, and Stonybrook eight miles west of Princeton. He established a final post at Six Mile Run just south of Brunswick. Grant continued gathering additional forces for Cornwallis to renew the offensive, and the Americans consolidated their troops in New Jersey.

Israel Putnam and Thomas Mifflin had been busy recruiting a new army. The victory at Trenton had a galvanizing effect on unifying the Americans sympathetic to the cause of freedom, resulting in new-found patriots rushing to join the Continental regulars and militias. The timing could not have been better, as many soldiers were preparing to depart for home. There is no record of any Marines terminating their enlistments at the time.

On December 28, Mifflin notified Washington, "Pennsylvania is at length rousd & coming in great Numbers to your Excellency's Aid."[37] Putnam, Mifflin, and others found willing participants rushing to join the rapidly forming units. They filled the ranks of the newly formed 2nd, 10th, 11th, and 12th Pennsylvania regiments and a Philadelphia rifle regiment for the Continental Army. Thirteen newly recruited regiments of Pennsylvania Associators and four additional companies of Philadelphia militia joined them. Mifflin merged these new troops and hurried to join Cadwalader in New Jersey while Putnam maintained the defense of Philadelphia. Mifflin wrote to Washington,

> I came here [Bristol] at 4 OClock this Afternoon. 500 Men sent from Philad. Yesterday crossd to Burlington this Morning. this Evening I sent over near 300 more—To Morrow 7 or 800 shall follow—I will cross in the Morning and will endeavour to form them into Regiments & a Brigade—they consist of many different Corps & want much Regulation. If your Excellency has any Orders for me, other than to join General Cadwalader as soon as possible, please to favor me with such as are necessary and I will punctually obey them.

37 The following two quotes are from *FONA*, http://founders.archives.gov/documents/Washington/03-07-02-0368, accessed Dec. 25, 2019.

Washington awoke to Mifflin's letter the following morning and dictated a response to one of his staff. Demonstrating a high degree of confidence in Mifflin, who had fought with him since New York, Washington stated he "will not undertake to give you any particular Orders, but leaves it to your Judgment, either to join General Cadwallader or proceed up towards Trenton, as, from Circumstances, you may think most proper."[38] Washington referenced the army's need for provisions and directed Mifflin to collect what goods he could find. He concluded by requesting Mifflin to provide advice to Cadwalader, who had yet to see action and may have been prone to being duped by the enemy: "Caution Cadwallader not to suffer the Enemy to turn too quick upon his young Troops, he may play the devil by waiting properly upon Flank and Rear." Washington closed by assuring Mifflin of his trust in his judgment: "You see you have full Powers and I am sure you will use them to the best Effect."

By December 29, Cadwalader's and Mifflin's combined efforts resulted in approximately 3,300 fresh American troops assembling in New Jersey. While he had pleaded for assistance for months, the momentum created by Washington's victory at Trenton created a situation that was moving fast out of his control. It would take some time before Washington fully understood the scope of the force he now had at his disposal and determined how best to employ it while he still had the services of those whose enlistments would soon expire.

Acting on Washington's intent, Cadwalader continued pursuing von Donop, who he thought was still within grasp. On December 29, he reinforced his unit at Crosswicks with several militiamen, who advanced on Allentown eight miles northeast of Bordentown only to find it also recently abandoned. This unit pressed on in one last attempt to engage von Donop and his men, who had arrived safely in Princeton just ahead of their pursuers.

Although they captured approximately 20 stragglers during this pursuit, Cadwalader's force had yet to engage the enemy in battle. Thomas Rodney, whose Delaware volunteers had been in the vanguard of Cadwalader's movements, recalled, "We had then been on duty four nights and days, making forced marches, without six hours sleep in the whole time."[39] Cadwalader ordered his men back to Allentown, from which he commenced a period of aggressive patrolling from Bordentown and Crosswicks, gathering intelligence, harassing the enemy, protecting his forces, and awaiting Washington's return to New Jersey.

---

38 The following three quotes from R. Biddle, "Selections from the Military Papers of General John Cadwalader," *PMHB*, vol. 32 (January 1, 1908), https://archive.org/stream/jstor-20085424/20085424_djvu.txt, accessed Dec. 25, 2019.

39 Rodney, *Diary of Captain Thomas Rodney*, 25; Commager & Morris, *SSS*, 514.

On December 28, Washington put the main body of his army back in motion. After sending the Hessian prisoners with guard escorts toward Philadelphia, he directed his commanders to commence crossing back into New Jersey. Sergeant Joseph White of Knox's artillery regiment recalled, "Our whole army crossed over to Trenton again with about one half the number less than we had when we retreated over the river Delaware."[40] Washington was racing the clock, hurrying to deliver another bold stroke against the enemy before losing hundreds of his regular Continental soldiers to terminated enlistments in three days.

It took the Americans four days to cross the river. On December 28, General Greene went over at Trenton Ferry with 300 soldiers, quickly reoccupying Trenton. The remainder of his division crossed the following day during a heavy snowstorm using a combination of Yardley's, Beatty's, and Howell's Ferries five miles upriver. Washington, traveling with Sullivan's division, was not as lucky. He described to Congress how the ice on the river at McKonkey's Ferry "will neither allow us to cross on foot or give us an easy passage for the boats."[41] Washington and Sullivan successfully crossed on December 30. Knox joined Washington with his artillery on December 31. Knox was busy repairing and acquiring additional cannons, and he had reportedly crossed the river with between 30-40 cannons, including the six Hessian guns captured in Trenton. Lord Stirling became ill and remained at Newton, Pennsylvania, with a rear party to guard the army's baggage.

Washington had finally maneuvered the separate elements of his army in the region into a position of advantage. His nearly 6,000 combined troops occupied the villages of Trenton, Bordentown, and Crosswicks, all within 10 miles or less of the other and all on the north side of the Delaware River, and were arrayed in a fashion that would allow them to offer one another mutual support. Washington's actions proved fortuitous, as the British were gathering in strength for an expected attack. But he first had to address a more pressing issue.

The day fast approached when many soldiers' enlistments were due to expire. Washington faced an enormous challenge in convincing his men to extend their service, as many were ready to go. They had served for months without pay and missed their families, and many had inadequate clothing. They were cold, hungry, and fatigued. Many were simply exhausted after months of hard campaigning. Washington had little to offer to entice them to stay. He had worked with Robert Morris in Philadelphia to secure a promise of 10 dollars hard currency for any

---

40 "The Good Soldier White," *American Heritage*, vol. 7, issue 4 (1956), https://www.americanheritage.com/good-soldier-white#3, accessed Dec. 25, 2019; Dwyer, *TDIO*, 292.

41 Sparks, ed., *The Writings of George Washington*, 250.

man who agreed to serve six additional weeks. But even this was insufficient to convince many.

Washington and his commanders appealed to the men's honor, commitment to the cause, and to each other. Shared hardship builds cohesion within military units, a lesson still employed today. For example, Marine Corps drill instructors instill high-stress levels, while physically and mentally exerting their recruits, breaking them down as individuals only to build them back up as a team. The recruits learn that they can accomplish anything when they work together. They also learn to embrace misery, work through the toughest challenges, and thrive in chaotic and uncertain situations. Experiencing, surviving, and succeeding under these circumstances creates a bond that is hard to break. Shared experiences in combat create even stronger bonds.

Colonel John Stark exemplified the leadership that bound patriotic Americans together during those trying times. One of his officers described how Stark "appealed to the patriotism of the men of the Granite hills who composed the New Hampshire regiments."[42] Stark explained to his men "that if they left the army all was lost, [and] reminded them of their deeds at Bunker's Hill and other occasions." Stark further demonstrated his commitment to his men when he "assured them that if Congress did not pay them their arrears, his own property should make it up to them. He proposed a re-enlistment for six weeks, and such was his influence and popularity that not a man refused."

General Mifflin addressed another group of Continental regulars, convincing them to extend their service. After establishing temporary headquarters in Bordentown on December 29, he rode to Crosswicks the following day to speak with Colonel Hitchcock's brigade of New Englanders. Sergeant John Smith described how "the General who was present with all the field officers and after making many fair promises to them he begged them to tarry one month longer in service and almost every man consented to stay longer who received 10 dollars bounty."[43] Mifflin's efforts were likely helped by Hitchcock's men having just been supplied with new breeches, shirts, and socks that the Continental Navy and Marines had captured and delivered to Philadelphia. Many locals watched as the patriots extended their enlistments, applauding the men when they valiantly stepped forward. Sergeant Smith shared how "the General ordered us to have a gill of rum per man and set out to Trenton to acquaint General Washington with his good success."

---

42 The following three quotes are from Caleb Stark, *Memoir and Official Correspondence of Gen. John Stark, With Notices of Several Other Offices of the Revolution* (Boston, 1972), 38.

43 The following two quotes from were found in Dwyer, *TDIO*, 289.

The men addressed personally by General Washington required a little more coaxing. A sergeant from the ranks described how Washington paraded the troops, appealing to their patriotism to remain in the service. "He alluded to our recent victory at Trenton; told us that our service was greatly needed . . . and in the most affectionate manner entreated us to stay."[44] The sergeant described the scene, stating that "[t]he drums beat for volunteers, but not a man turned out. The soldiers, worn down with fatigue and privations, had their hearts fixed on home."[45] He further explained how Washington wheeled his horse about and rode in front of the regiment to continue his plea, "My brave fellows, you have done all I asked you to do, and more than could be reasonably expected; but your country is at stake, your wives, your houses and all that you hold dear. You have worn yourselves out with fatigues and hardships, but we know not how to spare you." Washington made his final appeal: "If you will consent to stay only one month longer, you will render that service to the cause of liberty and to your country which you probably never can do under any other circumstances. The present is emphatically the crisis which is to decide our destiny." In response, a few men stepped forward, and then a few more. By the time it was done, nearly the entire regiment had agreed to give their commander-in-chief six more weeks.

Not everyone decided to stay. Freedman Jacob Francis served for months without pay and had had enough. He recalled, "At the time I had seven and a half months' pay due to me, and I believe others had the same. I received three months' pay, and all the rest of the regiment received the same."[46] Fifer John Greenwood was also done. He described how his lieutenant tried to convince him to stay: "You are not going to, I hope, leave us, for you are the life and soul of us and are to be promoted to an ensign."[47] Greenwood responded, "I told him I would not stay to be a colonel. I had the itch then so bad that my breeches stuck to my thighs, all the skin being off, and there were hundreds of vermin upon me."

Perhaps the greatest loss was felt with the departure of many of John Glover's Marblehead fishermen, who had rendered such valuable service in the escape from Long Island and the crossings of the Delaware. The temptation to return home and continue service as privateers was too strong for most to resist. Glover led

---

44 "An Account of Sergeant R--, March 24, 1832," quoted from Commager & Morris, *SSS*, 519-520; *FONA*, https://founders.archives.gov/documents/Washington/03-07-02-0385, accessed Dec. 25, 2019.

45 The following three quotes from *FONA*, https://founders.archives.gov/documents/Washington/03-07-02-0385, accessed Dec. 25, 2019.

46 Dwyer, *TDIO*, 291.

47 The following two quotes were found in Greenwood, *The Revolutionary Service of John Greenwood*, 44.

his men home to see his ailing wife but would return to serve again later in the war. Approximately 1,500 of the 2,400 Continental regulars, just over 60 percent, agreed to continue their service.

Still unaware of Washington's intentions, the British and Hessians sought to thwart any rebel actions. On December 30, rumors of increased American activity at Pennington, Maidenhead, and Cranberry led von Donop to deploy strong patrols to confirm a rebel presence, but they found nothing. Further reports of American activity and a planned attack arrived the following day, causing the Hessians to remain at arms starting in the early morning, employing additional security patrols. They also erected defensive works along the main roads leading to their positions. Captain Ewald, who was stationed with his jaegers at Kingston at the time, stated, "Four weeks ago we expected to end the war with the capture of Philadelphia, and now we had to render Washington the honor of thinking about our defense."[48] He described how "such a fright came over the army that if Washington had used the opportunity, we would have flown to our ships and let him have all of America." Ewald also admitted, "we had thus far underestimated our enemy, from this happy day onward we saw everything through a magnifying glass." Although surprised by Washington's bold move at Trenton, the British intended to regain the initiative by attacking the Americans as quickly as possible.

The Americans were also unaware of British intentions, aggressively pursuing any information they could gather on their adversaries. Again, Washington and his commanders employed a combination of patrols, prisoners, deserters, local sympathizers, captured documents, and spies to move about the enemy lines, reporting back with the information. Washington requested Robert Morris' assistance in acquiring "hard Money, to pay a certain set of people who are particular use to us."[49] On December 30, the ever-resourceful Morris scrapped together "two canvas bundles" filled with "410 Spanish milled dollars . . . 2 English crowns. 7 French Crowns. 1072 English shillings" to pay Washington's spies.[50] He also delivered $50,000 of paper currency for use in paying out the bounties for Continental soldiers. Morris collected both sums using his connections and personal credit. He added a quarter-cask of wine for Washington's personal use.

48 The following three quotes are from Joseph Tustin, ed., *Diary of the American War: A Hessian Journal* (New Haven, CT, 1979), 44.

49 *FONA*, https://founders.archives.gov/documents/Washington/03-07-02-0382, accessed Dec. 25, 2019.

50 Force & St. Clair, eds., *AA*, 3:1486.

American efforts to gather information began drawing a clear picture of the enemy's situation. Washington dispatched Colonel Reed and seven men of the Philadelphia Light Horse, his personal bodyguard, to collect intelligence on the British in and around Princeton. Reed was the perfect choice for this mission. He was intimately familiar with the area, having graduated from Princeton in 1757 and practiced law in Trenton. Reed and his group captured several prisoners and interrogated them. He described how "a very perfect Account was obtained that Ld Cornwallis with a Body of pickd Troops & well appointed had the Day before reinforced Grant at Princeton & that this Party was pressing Waggons to begin their March the next Morning in order to dislodge us from Trenton. That their whole Force could not be less than 7 or 8000."[51]

After pondering this information, Washington convened a council of war in Trenton to determine the army's best course of action. The Americans had yet to consolidate their forces but expected to muster 5,000-6,000 troops. This was insufficient to attack the British, who they believed had access to additional reinforcements. The logical choice was to go on the defensive and let the enemy come to them. Washington hoped to leverage the strength of the defensive to achieve results similar to those obtained at Bunker Hill. No evidence suggests that he had read the works of Chinese military strategist Sun Tzu, who proclaimed, "Invincibility lies in the defense; the possibility of victory in the attack. One defends when his strength is inadequate; he attacks when it is abundant." He was, however, certainly operating under the same principles.[52] Experience had demonstrated the challenges faced in attempting to defend Trenton, but the high ground south of Assunpink Creek provided excellent defensible terrain.

Assunpink Creek was a natural barrier that provided great advantages to the Americans. The steep terrain on either side would break any British formations attempting to advance. It would also cause the enemy to funnel into predesignated "kill zones" established at the bridge crossing and several fording sites.[53] Recalling how the British had outflanked the Americans at the battle of Long Island; they protected their flanks at Trenton by placing the Delaware River on their left and woods and marshland on their right. On the south side of the creek, the dominating terrain provided clear fields of fire against any enemy troops advancing from the

51 Reed, *General Joseph Reed's Narrative*, 400.

52 Sun Tzu, *The Art of War*, 85.

53 The United States Marines Corps defines a "kill zone" as a "site where fire is concentrated to isolate, fix, and destroy the enemy." *Marine Corps Doctrinal Publication 1-0: Marine Corps Operations*, Glossary-18.

village. Knox stated this ground "may be said to command Trenton completely."[54] It also allowed the Americans to establish tiered lines of artillery and infantry, maximizing the firepower they could bring to bear on the enemy as they attempted to cross the creek. Knox further described the situation:

> . . . the creek was in our front, our left on the Delaware, our right in a wood, parallel to the creek. The situation was strong, to be sure, but hazardous on this account, that had our right wing been defeated, the defeat on the left would almost have been an inevitable consequence, and the whole thrown into confusion or pushed into the Delaware, as it was impassable by boats.

Regardless, Washington and his commanders believed the benefits of the terrain outweighed the risks and began having their troops erect defensive positions.

As Washington's staff finalized defensive plans, one of Cadwalader's hired spies provided critical information that supplemented the Americans' understanding of British dispositions. On December 31, Cadwalader wrote Washington from Crosswicks, "A very intelligent young gentleman is returned just now from Princetown."[55] Cadwalader's informant was detained by the British but escaped, sharing that approximately 5,000 enemy troops occupied Princeton with more reinforcements expected in the coming days. He added that he fed the British officers with false information concerning American forces in the area. The informant told his captors that Washington had 16,000 men at his disposal, which was three times the army's actual size. He stated, "No sentries on the back or east end of the town. They parade every morning an hour before day and some nights lie on their arms. An attack has been expected for several nights past—the men are much fatigued. All the baggage is sent to Brunswick, where there are but few men."

Washington contemplated having Cadwalader capture Brunswick. In addition to being the British's main supply depot, the village reportedly housed a war chest of 70,000 English pounds. Washington also received word that Brunswick was where General Lee was being held prisoner. Initial reports from the village stated that 250 troops were left as guards when General Grant departed, making it an irresistible target. But Washington canceled the plan to capture Brunswick when additional reports indicated it had been reinforced with 1,500 troops.

Perhaps more important than the information provided to Washington, Cadwalader produced a sketch of the enemy positions at Princeton. Cadwalader wrote, "I have made a rough draft of the road from this place, the situation of

54 The following two quotes are from Brooks, *Henry Knox*, 83.

55 The following four quotes were found at *FONA*, https://founders.archives.gov/documents/Washington/03-07-02-0386, accessed Dec. 25, 2019.

A modern-day photo of Assunpink Creek, Trenton. Washington established a strong defensive position on dominating high ground on the south side of the creek to await Lord Cornwallis and a combined British/Hessian force to attack in what became known as the Second Battle of Trenton, or the battle of Assunpink Creek. Samuel Nicholas and the Continental Marines joined those called to reinforce and hold the line as the British attempted to breach the American position. *Author*

the cannon and works begun and those intended this morning." This sketch and corresponding information later proved essential to Washington as he developed a plan for the attack on Princeton.

First, however, he needed to address the threat of the British approaching Trenton. Washington knew he needed to consolidate his dispersed army if he hoped to defeat the growing enemy force. Keeping his troops spread between Trenton, Bordentown, and Crosswicks risked their isolation and defeat. He also needed to pull in the many patrols and raiding parties he had deployed. Major John Mifflin, the brother of General Mifflin, had recently departed with a force of 200 men to harass the British. Samuel Nicholas, his Continental Marines, and other groups were actively patrolling and gathering intelligence to attack the enemy. Cadwalader informed Washington, "Major Nicholas of the Marines informs me that Elisha Laurence, late sheriff of Monmouth, is now collecting men at Monmouth Court House: he has got together about seventy men. He has put twenty men into prison for refusing to bear arms. . . . Major Nicholas is

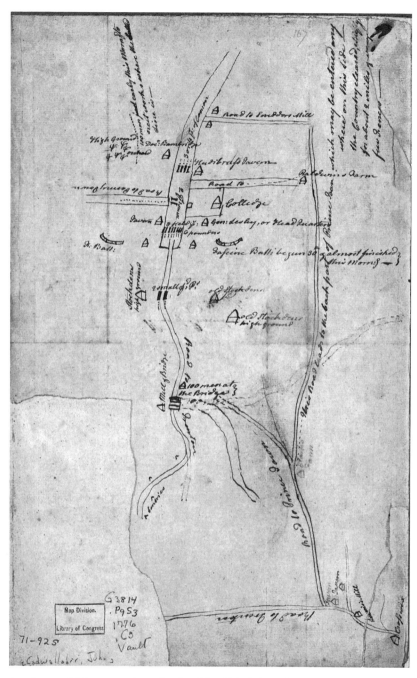

A spy's map of Princeton, as drawn by Gen. John Cadwalader and sent express to Gen. George Washington on New Year's Eve, 1776. Washington used this sketch to help develop his plan of attack for Princeton following the Second Battle of Trenton. *Wikimedia*

desirous of going after Laurence's party." Anticipating a pending move against the British, Cadwalader denied Nicholas's request and instead awaited orders from Washington. He did not have to wait long.

On the evening of December 31, Washington established a defense to slow and attrite a British advance. He instructed General Fermoy to establish a forward defensive position along Five Mile Run, just over a mile south of Maidenhead and halfway to Princeton. Fermoy's task was to slow the British, buying time for the American forces to consolidate. Fermoy was given Cols. Charles Scott's 5th Virginia Regiment, Edward Hand's regiment of Pennsylvania and Maryland riflemen, Nicholas Haussegger's German battalion, and former Marine Captain Forrest's artillery company to perform this mission. Fermoy sent a detachment to Maidenhead to serve as an advance picket and to provide early warning of enemy movements. The Americans quietly got into position under cover of darkness, occupying the high ground overlooking the stream below their position. The forward British outpost lay just a mile north of Maidenhead at Eight Mile Run.

After remaining on high alert for several nights, General Grant and his troops departed Brunswick for Princeton on January 1, 1777. He left 600 men behind to guard military stores. At 10:00 a.m., Grant entered Princeton with 1,000 men to reinforce Leslie and von Donop. Grant found Leslie's men "drawn up with their Arms expecting [the] Enemy as a small Skirmish had happened Close to our out Piquets when the Rebels lost 4 men Killed."[56] Cornwallis, who had traveled 50 miles from New York to take command of the forces in New Jersey, arrived later that day with additional reinforcements. He planned to attack the Americans the following day.

Meanwhile, Washington gathered Greene, Sullivan, Knox, St. Clair, Reed, and others for a final council of war in Trenton before the pending battle. Doctor Benjamin Rush, who had been physician to the Continental Marines in 1775, had signed the Declaration of Independence in 1776, and was currently a member of the Continental Congress, sat in an outer room. He was providing medical services to Cadwalader's men and the Marines at Crosswicks but had decided to visit his friend, General St. Clair, while in Trenton.

Since Cadwalader was not going to be attacking Brunswick, the council discussed having his and Mifflin's units join them at Trenton or having Washington's force combine with the others at Crosswicks. As Rush had just come from Cadwalader's position, Washington asked him to join the council and offer his views. He responded that he was not a judge of the council's business, but "I

---

56 *FONA*, https://founders.archives.gov/documents/Washington/03-07-02-0386, accessed Dec. 25, 2019.

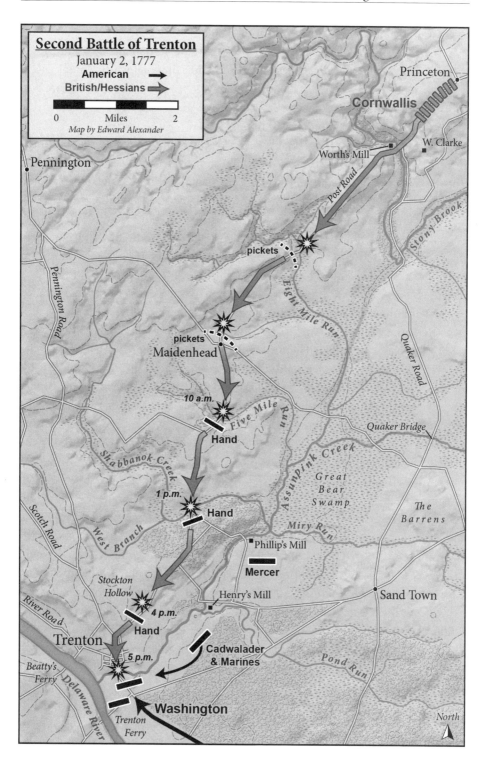

Second Battle of Trenton
January 2, 1777
American
British/Hessians
0   Miles   2
Map by Edward Alexander

Princeton

Cornwallis

W. Clarke

Worth's Mill

Pennington

Post Road

Stony Brook

pickets

Eight Mile Run

Quaker Road

pickets
Maidenhead

10 a.m.

Five Mile Run

Hand

Quaker Bridge

Shabbanok Creek

Assunpink Creek

Great Bear Swamp

1 p.m.

Hand

Miry Run

The Barrens

West Branch

Phillip's Mill

Mercer

Scotch Road

Sand Town

Stockton Hollow

Henry's Mill

River Road

4 p.m.

Hand

Trenton

Cadwalader & Marines

Pond Run

Beatty's Ferry

5 p.m.

Washington

Delaware River

Trenton Ferry

North

knew well, that all the Philadelphia militia would be very happy in being under his [Washington's] immediate command."[57] Washington responded by asking Rush to deliver a message to Cadwalader. The commander-in-chief wrote, "Some pieces of Intelligence render it necessary for you to March your Troops immediately to this place [Trenton]—I expect your Brigade will be here by five O'clock in the Morning without fail. at any rate do not exceed 6."[58]

Rush and a sergeant from the Philadelphia Light Horse for an escort mounted their horses and departed Trenton at 10:00 p.m. to deliver Washington's orders. The darkness, muddy roads caused by recent rain and mild temperatures, and an alert sentry slowed their progress. Rush reached Cadwalader's headquarters at 1:00 a.m. on January 2, rousing the general from his sleep. On reading Washington's orders, Cadwalader immediately woke his brigade and Marines and got them marching toward Trenton. Mifflin received similar orders. Cadwalader moved his force west along the White Horse Road, joining Mifflin's group at the White Horse Tavern. It was now a race to see who would arrive at Trenton first: Cadwalader, Mifflin, and the Marines, or the British and Hessians under Cornwallis.

The Americans relied on Fermoy's advance force to delay the British, but Cornwallis had other plans. He put his army in motion shortly after Cadwalader received Washington's orders and determined to lead a predawn attack with British light infantry, Hessian grenadiers and jaegers, and light dragoons under von Donop in the vanguard. Von Donop and the other Hessians relished the assignment as an opportunity to seek revenge for the loss at Trenton. According to Ewald, "It was planned . . . to give the enemy a beating and thereby repair the damage done at Trenton."[59]

Cornwallis's intention was clear. He meant to attack with an overwhelming force along a single axis of advance, destroying what remained of the understrength American army. Von Donop, who was well-acquainted with the surrounding countryside, advised against this approach. He recommended Cornwallis employ two columns. One would fix the Americans to their front, while a second would maneuver around their flank. This movement through Cranbury, Allentown, and Crosswicks would assault the rebels' right flank and rear, just as the Americans feared.

Cornwallis rejected von Donop's advice. He led a formidable force of nearly 9,000 of England's finest troops supported by a strong Hessian contingent and 28 cannons ranging up to 12-pounders. Cornwallis opted for a direct approach

---

57 Rush, *Autobiography*, 126.

58 *FONA*, https://founders.archives.gov/documents/Washington/03-07-02-0404, accessed Dec. 25, 2019.

59 Ewald, *Diary*, 146.

south down the Post Road toward Trenton via Maidenhead. Behind von Donop's vanguard came two battalions of British light infantry, artillery, four Hessian and two British grenadier battalions, the remnants of Rall's brigade, the British Guards, Highlanders, the four infantry regiments of Leslie's brigade, and more artillery. Cornwallis left the British 4th Brigade, 1,200 troops and two cannons under 48-year-old Lt. Col. Charles Mawhood, as a reserve in Princeton. The British were moving slowly due to the thousands of troops, horses, and heavy cannon through the road's deep mud. After sustaining their first casualty by American pickets posted near Maidenhead, their pace slowed even more.

Though Fermoy positioned his men well, using the terrain to their advantage, he abandoned his unit on the battlefield for some unknown reason and returned to Trenton alone.[60] Colonel Edward Hand assumed command of the remaining Americans, commencing a masterful delaying action and buying the time needed to prepare for the coming assault. Hand and his Pennsylvania and Maryland riflemen were ideal for this mission. These marksmen fired spiral-grooved long rifles that were effective up to 150-250 yards. The smoothbore muskets carried by most soldiers were only effective to about a third of that distance. Conversely, the rifle took twice as long to load; riflemen could only get off one to two shots off a minute, while those carrying muskets could fire four to five rounds per minute.[61] Riflemen fought as dispersed sharpshooters who relied on well-aimed fire, while infantry fought in massed formations and relied on volley fire. Riflemen employed accuracy, speed, and stealth to survive on the battlefield, as their rifles could not mount a bayonet. The predecessors of today's modern snipers, they liked to target enemy officers in order to confuse and misdirect their foes.

Hand and his force contested every foot of terrain gained by the British. In addition to the precise, deadly fire from his riflemen, Hand combined the devastating effects of Forrest's artillery and massed fire of Scott's and Haussegger's infantrymen. They systematically engaged the advancing enemy from behind covered positions, reminiscent of Lexington and Concord, as they conducted a fighting withdrawal along the road to Trenton. Though this small American force was outnumbered six-to-one, it stopped the British advance at Five Mile Run at 10:00 a.m. before falling back to alternate positions. Expertly using the terrain

60 Fermoy was determined to have an alcohol problem which contributed to his poor performance. In July 1777, he failed to give the order for his unit to withdraw at a critical point in a battle around Fort Ticonderoga due to being in a drunken stupor. Later that night he set his quarters on fire, silhouetting and exposing his soldiers to enemy fire. He resigned his commission in 1778 after the Congress refused to promote him.

61 David Johnson, "Revolutionary War Weapons: The American Long Rifle," https://warfarehistorynetwork.com/2015/11/11/revolutionary-war-weapons-the-american-long-rifle/, accessed Dec. 25, 2019.

again, the Americans halted the enemy at 1:00 p.m. at Shabbanok Creek, three miles from Trenton. Hand hid his troops in the woods, from which they ambushed the advancing light infantry and jaegers. The enemy fell back, and the Americans pursued. The British then deployed their main body of troops thinking this would be the decisive battle. Ewald reported, "140 [were] lost on both sides."[62]

At approximately 4:00 p.m., Hand withdrew to a final position of earthworks, reinforced with four cannons, at Stockton Hollow, one-half mile north of Trenton. He placed his riflemen on the left of the road, with Forrest's cannons on the high ground overlooking the enemy's avenue of approach. Hand placed Scott on the right to cover the ground between the road and upper fords of Assunpink Creek. The British advance guard of 1,500 men expended another hour in clearing them from those positions. Hand and his stalwart soldiers had done their duty, buying the main force even more time.

Cadwalader, Mifflin, Hitchcock, and Nicholas drove their men hard in order to reach Trenton before the British. Their movement began in the early morning during a rainstorm that created a morass of mud on the roads. Captain Willson Peale of the Associators' 2nd Battalion described the tiresome hike:

> The roads are very muddy, almost over our shoe tops. The number of troops, the badness of the roads, so many runs [creeks] to cross, and fences to remove, make it a tedious march. The sun had risen more than an hour before we reached the town, and afterwards, the difficulty of getting quarters kept us a long time under arms. At last we were provided and had made a fire. I took a short nap on a plank with my feet to the fire; but was suddenly awakened by a call to arms—the enemy approaching.[63]

Twenty-one-year-old Lt. Stephen Olney of Hitchcock's regiment recalled, "having been all night travelling . . . we took quarters in the houses [at Trenton] and began to prepare for breakfast. But before it was ready, the drums beat to arms."[64] Doctor Rush, back in Trenton after making the night movement with Cadwalader, was attempting to get some sleep at St. Clair's headquarters. He had just dozed off when an alarm gun woke him. St. Clair entered the room, and Rush asked, "What was the matter?" St. Clair said that the enemy was advancing. Rush

62 Fischer, *WC*, 281.

63 Peale, "Journal by Charles Wilson Peale," 278.

64 Williams, *Biography of Revolutionary Heroes*, 193; Fischer, *WC*, 285.

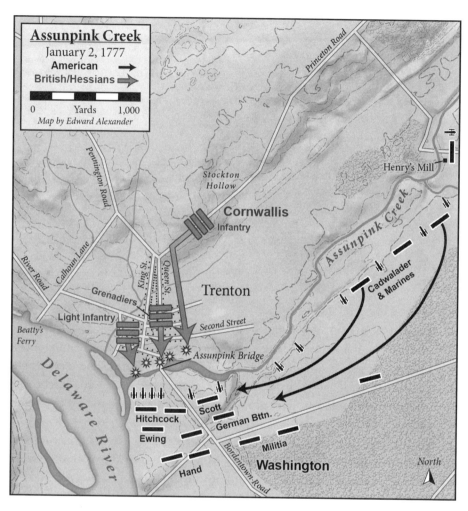

Assunpink Creek
January 2, 1777
American →
British/Hessians →

0   Yards   1,000
Map by Edward Alexander

Princeton Road

Henry's Mill

Stockton Hollow

Pennington Road

Cornwallis
Infantry

Assunpink Creek

Cadwalader & Marines

River Road

Calhoun Lane

King St.

Queen St.

Grenadiers

Trenton

Light Infantry

Beatty's Ferry

Second Street

Assunpink Bridge

Delaware River

Scott

Hitchcock

German Bttn.

Ewing

Militia

Bordentown Road

Hand

Washington

North

queried, "What do you intend to do?" to which the general responded, "Why, fight them," as he strapped his sword to his side.[65]

Washington energized his commanders when he received word of the approaching enemy. He established a three-mile-long defensive line along the high ground on the south side of Assunpink Creek oriented toward Trenton. The defense centered on four principle crossing sites, including the stone bridge spanning the Assunpink south of Trenton, two upper fords at Phillip's and Henry's Mills two to three miles up the creek, and a lower ford between the bridge and the Delaware River. The stone bridge was deemed the most likely crossing point for the enemy and was therefore the primary focus.

65 Rush, *Autobiography*, 127.

Colonel Henry Knox, who was promoted to brigadier general on the day of the Second Battle of Trenton, expertly emplaced nearly 40 cannons along a three-mile-long defensive line that repulsed repeated British attacks. He later requested the service of Major Nicholas and the Continental Marines to serve in the army artillery following the termination of many of his soldiers' enlistments. *Wikimedia*

Washington anchored his defense with artillery, weighting each likely crossing site by placing his most experienced troops to cover them. Knox had received word of his promotion to brigadier general that day and had masterfully gathered 40 guns for this battle. He employed nearly half of them in covering the bridge. Washington assigned Scott's Virginia regiment this important post, backing him with Hand's riflemen and the remnants of the German battalion. Knox placed 12 cannons to cover the upper fords, supporting St. Clair's Continentals and the army's right wing. He then positioned his remaining guns to cover the lower ford. Hitchcock's regiment was detached from Cadwalader's brigade and assigned the lower ford on the left wing.

Washington directed two additional lines to form in reserve on the high ground behind the main line of defense, with 250 yards of separation between units. He employed Ewing's New Jersey militia on the left and Cadwalader and the Marines on the right, with the bridge being the central position. The Associators and Marines were initially positioned opposite Samuel Henry's Mill "in a field on the right about a mile from the town, on the main road, to prevent the enemy from flanking."[66] But later they were moved to directly support the defense as the British attempted to force the bridge. General Mercer and his brigade deployed at Phillips Ford, two miles above the bridge at Trenton and on the extreme right of the army. Washington also deployed pickets covering the other roads leading to Trenton, sending mounted security patrols to screen in all directions. The Americans hastily constructed defensive works as the British advance drew closer.

As Hand defended his final position north of the village, Washington, Greene, and Knox rode out to assess the situation. Greene assumed local command as the British put their artillery into action. One soldier recalled Greene running up

66 Rodney, *Diary of Captain Thomas Rodney*, 31.

to his company, which was tasked with reinforcing Hand's position, and yelling, "Push on, boys! Push on!"[67] The Americans slowly withdrew, fighting house to house down King and Queen streets, buying precious time for the army to get into position. The Hessians pressed hard to regain some of the credibility they lost at Trenton. As they progressed through the village, Von Donop's men found many of Rall's wounded soldiers. They saw that the injured had been treated well by the Americans, but this did not sway their determination. This was no American rout like the one in New York. It was an organized and coordinated fighting withdrawal conducted by men seasoned in battle.

The British and Hessians maintained pressure on the Americans as the sun set. Knox's cannons on the far side of the creek spotted the enemy, opening fire on them as they passed 2nd Street. Hitchcock's Continentals received orders to move forward and support Hand's withdrawal. The New England men opened ranks, allowing the Pennsylvania and Maryland riflemen, Virginia and German infantrymen, and Forrest's artillerymen into the safety of their lines. The tired troops crossed the bridge; the commander-in-chief was mounted on horseback to greet them. With no time to waste, he directed them to their positions, turning his attention back to the running battle on the far side of the creek.

It was now Hitchcock's turn to withdraw across the Assunpink Bridge. Knox's guns covered the infantry's movement, with the enemy in close pursuit. Thirty-two-year-old Pvt. John Howland recalled, "the British made a quick advance in an oblique direction to cut us off from the bridge. In this they did not succeed, as we had a shorter distance . . . our artillery . . . played into the front and flank of their column, which induced them to fall back."[68] Knox described the scene to his wife Lucy: "Their retreat over the bridge was thoroughly secured by the artillery. After they had retired over the bridge, the enemy advanced within reach of our cannon, who saluted them with great vociferation and some execution."[69] Washington positioned Hitchcock back on the left wing just as British artillery commenced firing on the American positions.

In the confusion of combat, not all the Americans made it over the creek. Seeing the bridge was congested, elements of the German battalion under Colonel Haussegger attempted to cross the lower ford of the Assunpink. They were captured along with their commander by the British light infantry. Sixty-two-year-old Chaplain John Rosbrugh was enjoying a meal in a local tavern when he heard

67 Greene, *The Life of Nathanael Greene*, 1:302; Carbone, *Nathanael Greene: A Biography*, 59.

68 Andrew Sherburne, *Memoirs of Andrew Sherburne: A Pensioner of the Navy of the Revolution* (Providence, RI, 1831), 299; Fischer, *WC*, 299.

69 Drake, *Life and Correspondence of Henry Knox*, 38; Arnold, ed., *Americans at War*, 1:24.

the quickly approaching sounds of battle. He exited the tavern to find his horse stolen, leaving him stranded in the village. Rosbrugh attempted to flee on foot but was captured by a group of Hessian soldiers looking for revenge. They took the chaplain's weapon, stole his watch and money, and stripped him naked. Rosbrugh dropped to his knees, began to pray, and was bayonetted to death. His body was later discovered in a field with several bayonet wounds and saber slashes to his head.

It was now past 5:00 p.m., and the sky was growing increasingly dark. Many Americans described how they observed the British army in all its glory, with bands playing as they formed above Trenton, as the winter sun was setting. Major Wilkinson recorded, "Lord Cornwallis displayed his columns, and extended his lines . . . to the westward, on the heights above the town … If there ever was a crisis in the affairs of the Revolution, this was the moment."[70] The flashing of muskets and cannons from the sporadic fire of both sides punctuated the growing dark. Many were overcome with simultaneous sensations of excitement and anxiety over the approaching clash of arms. Perhaps 17-year-old Ens. Robert Beale captured best what most of the Americans were thinking at that moment:

This was a most awful crisis. No possible chance of crossing the [Delaware] river; ice as large as houses floating down, and no retreat to the mountains, the British between us and them. Our brigade . . . was ordered to form in column at the bridge and General Washington can and, in the presence of us all, told Colonel Scott to defend the bridge to the last extremity. Colonel Scott answered with an oath, "Yes, General, as long as there is a man alive."[71]

This was the moment of truth. What some refer to as "The Second Battle of Trenton," others call "The Battle of the Assunpink," or "The Cannonade at Trenton" was about to come to a head.[72]

The British and Hessians were determined to drive the Americans from their positions, defeat Washington's army, and finally end the wretched war. Accustomed to seeing the Americans flee, the British now believed they had Washington in a position from which there was no escape. British light infantry and Hessian jaegers advanced to probe the enemy line for weak spots at which to create a breach to send their army pouring through. A group of light infantry and jaegers discovered the lower ford. They attacked across the creek but were met by a hail of gunfire

70 Wilkinson, *Memoirs*, 138.

71 Dennis Ryan, ed., *A Salute to Courage*, 57.

72 Stryker, *BTP*, 266.

from Hitchcock's men and Knox's artillery. The Americans had correctly read the terrain, positioning their forces to provide interlocking fields of fire that maximized the devastating effects of their weapons. The assault was quickly defeated, and the enemy was sent reeling back toward Trenton.

The Hessian grenadiers took a more deliberate approach. They brought four cannons forward, posted marksmen in the buildings closest to the bridge, and engaged the defending Americans before attempting to cross. Hessian gunners opened fire, providing roughly 12 minutes of preparatory volleys before the assault. It was not enough. Captains Moulder's and Forrest's artillerymen, sailors from the *Washington* under Captain Read, and others responded with a thunderous volume of fire. Colonel Scott's men added to the fray. He had forewarned his infantrymen to pick their targets carefully, for "nothing must be wasted, every crack must count. For that reason, boys, whenever you see those fellows begin to put their feet upon this bridge do you shin 'em."[73] Scott understood that injuring a man required two more to carry him off, while dead men required no assistance.

The Hessians assaulted with a ferocity that may have caused the Americans to run in the past, but not this evening. Their overwhelming firepower and determination to hold their position stopped the enemy in their tracks. The grenadiers made it halfway across the bridge but lost 31 men in doing so. Twenty-nine more surrendered on the spot.[74]

The British infantry tried next. Sergeant White, who had performed admirably during the first battle of Trenton, was again in the thick of the fight. He was among the artillerymen Knox positioned to cover the stone bridge and provided a vivid account of the action. "We had all our cannon placed before it, consisting of 18 or 19 pieces. The enemy came on in solid columns; we let them come on some ways, then by a signal given, we all fired together. The enemy retreated off the bridge and formed again, and we were ready for them." White continued,

> Our whole artillery was again discharged at them. They retreated again and formed; they came on the third time. We loaded with cannister shot, and let them come nearer. We fired altogether again, and such destruction it made, you cannot conceive. The bridge looked red as blood, with their killed and wounded, and their red coats. The enemy beat a retreat.[75]

---

73 Harry Ward, *Charles Scott and the Spirit of '76* (Charlottesville, VA, 1988), 27; *The Army and Navy Chronicle*, vol. 3 (1 July-31 December 1836), 258.

74 Fischer, *WC*, 305.

75 "The Good Soldier White."

The infantrymen near the bridge added to the destruction of the British columns, but the enemy's persistence concerned Washington. He called for reinforcements in order to ensure an American victory. Captain Rodney of Cadwalader's brigade reminisced, "the enemy came down in a very heavy column to force the bridge. The fire was very heavy, and the Light troops were ordered to fly to the support of that important post."[76] Captain Peale of the Associators' 2nd Battalion wrote, "We were now ordered to take arms. . . . We then marched in platoons back towards the town. . . . Platoon firing was now pretty frequent . . . a very heavy firing kept up on the bridge. . . . We were now in the field below the town, and one of our cannon and a howitzer played on the town. . . . Some unlucky shot from a cannon killed 1 or 2 of the 3d Battalion of Philadelphia troops."[77]

Though no complete account of Maj. Nicholas's and the Continental Marines' participation in this battle survive, circumstantial evidence leads one to believe that they joined the fight. The Marines had been operating with Cadwalader's brigade since their first Delaware River crossing on December 8, 1776. Nicholas was still receiving orders from Cadwalader as late as December 31, when the general informed Washington that he had denied Nicholas's request to conduct an operation against the former sheriff of Monmouth. Clear evidence also exists that Nicholas and the Marines remained under Cadwalader's command at the upcoming battle of Princeton. Additionally, a story on Captain Andrew Porter, a Marine company commander, in an 1880 issue of *Pennsylvania Magazine of History and Biography* stated that Porter "engaged in the cannonade at Trenton."[78] One can surmise that the Continental Marines were active participants in this second battle of Trenton. It is likely that the Pennsylvania marines under Captain Shippin, who served in the 2nd Battalion with Peale, and Captain Brown, who likely commanded the artillery that fired into the town Peale mentioned in his diary, also actively participated in this battle.

The Americans' victory that day was complete. Washington was pleased with his men's performance and the few casualties he had sustained. He described the success to John Hancock, boasting that the troops had "receiv[ed] the fire of their Field pieces which did us but little damage."[79] Rodney reported, "We lost but few men; the enemy considerably more."[80] The patriots cheered as each successive

76 Rodney, *Diary of Captain Thomas Rodney*, 31.

77 Peale, "Journal by Charles Wilson Peale," *PMHB*, 279.

78 Porter, "A Sketch of the Life of General Andrew Porter," *PMHB*, 264.

79 *FONA*, https://founders.archives.gov/documents/Washington/03-07-02-0411, accessed Dec. 25, 2019.

80 Rodney, *Diary of Captain Thomas Rodney*, 31.

enemy wave was repulsed. Knox's artillery continued firing into the British ranks as they faded into the darkness. Knox wrote to his wife, "a few shells we now and then chucked into town to prevent their enjoying their new quarters securely."[81] The guns sustained a harassing fire until approximately 7:00 p.m., convincing the British to pull back to the high ground outside Trenton, beyond the range of the American cannons, to camp for the night.

Once Cornwallis arrived with the main body, he gathered his senior leaders to assess the situation. Actually, he had already made up his mind. Although his army had sustained between 150 and 500 casualties, he was still confident that Washington could not escape his trap. Cornwallis understood that his men had been under arms all day following a 10-hour fighting advance into battle, but it was dark, and he was unfamiliar with the terrain. In his mind, there was no reason to push the attack. He directed his officers to allow their troops to "make fires, refresh themselves, and take repose."[82] He sent word to Leslie and Mawhood to bring their forces forward to reinforce him because he intended to "dispose of" Washington's army and "bag the fox" in the morning.

Not all Cornwallis's officers agreed. While General Grant concurred with his superior's assessment, von Donop called for caution. He recommended that the British send a force across the upper fords to provide early warnings of any pending attacks. Von Donop was unwilling to be surprised again by his foe. Forty-eight-year-old Sir William Erksine, Cornwallis's quartermaster, advised, "My Lord, if you trust these people to-night, you will see nothing of them in the morning." Erksine would be correct in his assessment.

81 Drake, *Life and Correspondence of Henry Knox*, 38

82 The following three quotes are from Wilkinson, *Memoirs*, 139.

Chapter Ten

An Unexpected Battle

". . . though it was once the fashion of this army to treat them [Americans] in the most contemptible light, they are now become a formidable enemy."

— Lt. Col. William Harcourt, British officer[1]

Cornwallis and Washington had much to consider following the battle along Assunpink Creek. Although Cornwallis chose not to attack that evening, he did not remain idle. After ordering Leslie forward from Princeton, he ensured proper security to prevent a surprise attack from the Continentals. Cornwallis employed two battalions of British light infantry as forward pickets in the open fields within 150 yards of the enemy lines just over the creek. To avoid detection, Cornwallis forbade the troops from starting fires to warm themselves even though temperatures dropped to around 20 degrees. With security in place, Cornwallis shifted his remaining forces, staging for a morning attack on Washington's right flank.

Cornwallis developed a plan of attack that was reminiscent of his actions during the battle of Long Island, and one that he would use again in future battles. He deployed approximately 2,000 of his trusted British regulars in the woods across from the northern fords of the Assunpink while pulling von Donop's Hessians back from the front lines. He likely intended to have the Hessians attack Washington's front along the creek at first light, fixing the rebels in place while the British attacked across the ford at Phillip's Mill to crush the Americans' right flank. Leslie's force would be held in reserve and used to exploit any achieved success. The plan was straightforward and had a high chance of success considering the British's greater numbers and more disciplined and experienced soldiers.

---

1 Harcourt, ed., *Harcourt Papers*, 2:207-209, quoted from Commager & Morris, *SSS*, 524.

On January 2, 1777, General Washington held a council of war with his commanders at the Douglas House to determine the army's next actions. Nearly 10,000 British and Hessian soldiers were preparing to attack from across Assunpink Creek. Rather than attempt to retreat, Washington boldly decided to attack deeper into the enemy's rear at Princeton. The Douglas House has been moved from its original position but still stands in Trenton. *Author*

Washington was aware of Cornwallis' intentions. His security patrols reported the British activity, and earlier reconnaissance had identified the possible fording sites. The Americans were busy constructing defensive positions at each one. With his own security in place, Washington called his commanders together shortly after nightfall. They met at St. Clair's headquarters at the Douglas house. He also had Colonel Reed send word to General Putnam to bring additional reinforcements forward in anticipation of further action: "His Excellency begs you will march immediately forward with all the force you can collect at Crosswicks where you will find a very advantageous post: your advanced party at Allentown."[2]

While the senior leaders met to discuss the army's fate, their soldiers attended to other duties. Doctor Rush's timely arrival to offer his services proved invaluable. He led a group of young surgeons in rendering aid to several injured men. He recollected, "The first wounded man who came off the field was a New England

2 Reed, *Life and Correspondence of Joseph Reed*, 287.

soldier. His right hand hung a little above his wrist by nothing but a piece of skin. It had been broken by a cannon ball."[3] Rush and his colleagues treated around 20 men that evening before lying in some dirty straw beside the wounded to rest. For Rush, "It was now for the first time war appeared to me in its awful plenitude of horrors."

Twenty-one-year-old Capt. Stephen Olney of Hitchcock's regiment had been on the move for nearly 24 hours. He had started his day marching from Crosswicks with Cadwalader's brigade and the Continental Marines. It was not until after the fight at the Assunpink Bridge and darkness fell that he and his comrades "were dismissed to get our breakfast, dinner, and supper."[4] Olney, who had participated in the siege of Boston, the battles in New York, the retreat across New Jersey, and the battle of Trenton, paused to contemplate the army's position. He recalled,

> It appeared to me then that our army was in the most desperate situation I had ever known it. We had no boats to carry us across the Delaware, and if we had, so powerful an enemy would certainly destroy the better half before we could embark. To cross the enemy's line of march between this and Princeton seemed impracticable; and when we thought of retreating in the south part of New Jersey, where there was no support for an army, that was discouraging. Notwithstanding all this, the men and officers seemed cheerful and in good spirits.

The morale of Olney and his fellow soldiers remained high because they had developed trust in and devotion to their commander-in-chief, who shared in their hardships, defeats, and victories. While Washington experienced strained relationships with some senior leaders in the army and Congress, his men developed strong loyalties to their general. Many remained cheerful, confident that Washington and their commanders would once again lead them to victory.

Except for Putnam, who still defended Philadelphia, the war council conducted on January 2, 1777, was the first time Washington could assemble all his operational senior commanders around the Delaware River. In attendance were his two division commanders, Nathanael Greene and James Sullivan, and his brigade commanders, Hugh Mercer, Arthur St. Clair, Adam Stephen, Daniel Hitchcock, Thomas Mifflin, John Cadwalader, and James Ewing. Also attending were the ever-present Henry Knox and Joseph Reed. Some of his previous commanders had left for home after their enlistments ended, causing Washington to consolidate what remained of his Continental troops under the remaining leaders. As usual, Washington opened the discussion by reviewing the situation, challenges, and

---

3 The following two quotes are from Rush, *The Autobiography of Benjamin Rush*, 128.

4 The next two quotes were found in Williams, *Biography of Revolutionary Heroes*, 193-194.

opportunities faced by the army and then stepped aside to allow an open and frank discussion among his lieutenants.

The Americans had five choices in front of them. They could attempt to retreat across the Delaware or withdraw downriver toward Bordentown. The army could conduct a spoiling attack, seizing the initiative by assaulting across the Assunpink ahead of the expected British attack. It could remain in its strong defensive positions and again force the enemy to assault its prepared earthworks, or Washington could take a page out of the British playbook and strike a weakened flank or rear. Each choice offered certain risks and opportunities.

The discussion was lively and explored each option. Washington injected the belief that "the loss of the corps he commanded might be fatal to the country" as a consideration to be weighed in the debate.[5] Knox undoubtedly voiced his concern about remaining in place, as articulated in a letter to his wife written the following week: "[T]he situation was strong to be sure but hazardous on this account that had our right wing been defeated the defeat of the left would almost [have] been an inevitable consequence, & the whole thrown into confusion or push'd into the Delaware as it was impassable by Boats."[6] Cadwalader and Mifflin may have argued that there was little to no subsistence remaining to sustain the army at the villages downriver. All understood that the British likely outnumbered them and possessed a core of professional soldiers, while their force was now predominantly comprised of newly joined militiamen. Reports differ on who made the initial recommendation, but someone offered a flanking attack against the enemy rear at Princeton.[7]

Several officers endorsed this course of action. Reed was from the area and familiar with its backroads. He had also recently led a patrol of light horse as far as Princeton, reporting no enemy activity along these routes. St. Clair conveyed how his men, who had been patrolling beyond the army's right flank, reported a hidden route through woodlands that provided a concealed way to reach the Quaker Lane and bridge outside Princeton. Mercer also "immediately fell in with it, and very forcibly pointed out its practicability and the advantages that would necessarily

---

5 Wilkinson, *Memoirs*, 140; Chernow, *Washington: A Life*, 280; Fischer, *WC*, 258.

6 Drake, *Life and Correspondence of Henry Knox*, 38.

7 Wilkinson asserted that St. Clair, whose men had patrolled the trails leading toward Princeton while they were in their defensive position along Assunpink Creek, had made the recommendation to attack Princeton. This was refuted in 1824 by John Lardner, who said that he was one of four light horsemen who patrolled the Quaker Bridge Road on the night of Jan. 1 as per Washington's orders. Lardner claimed the attack on Princeton was an earlier idea of Washington's and that his mission was to conduct the reconnaissance for the route to be taken for that assault. See *FONA*, https://founders.archives.gov/documents/Washington/03-07-02-0411, accessed Dec. 26, 2019, and Stryker, *BTP*, 442-443.

result from it."[8] An attack against Princeton leveraged Washington's consolidated strength against the British's weakest and most vulnerable point.

Washington had again expertly guided his commanders into agreeing on a plan he had contemplated weeks before. While he was still open to being persuaded otherwise, allowing them to come to a consensus, rather than being ordered, endeared the officers to their commander, resulting in each of them assuming personal ownership for the operation's success. In addition to capturing Princeton, they agreed to continue the attack to take Brunswick if the conditions were right.

Washington was pleased with the result of the meeting. He told John Hancock, "One thing I was certain of, that it would avoid the appearance of a retreat, (which was of course of consequence or to run the hazard of the whole Army being cut off) whilst we might by a fortunate stroke withdraw Genl Howe from Trenton and give some reputation to our Arms."[9] Washington hoped to maintain the positive momentum the country experienced following the success at Trenton. He envisioned another victory to achieve that end.

The American forces began readying for movement, preparing to attack deeper into enemy-held territory. They were also implementing an elaborate deception plan. For security reasons, Washington directed his generals to maintain strict secrecy as to the true intent of the evening's activities. Sergeant White recalled how "orders came by whispering, (not a loud word must be spoken)."[10] Washington ordered the heaviest cannons and the army's baggage to be "removed silently to Burlington soon after dark" under the command of General Stephen.[11] Soldiers were to tie rags to wagon wheels and gun carriages to muffle any noise during the movement.

The men remained uncertain as to the pending action. Captain Rodney recalled, "no one knew what the Gen. meant to do. Some thought that we were going to attack the enemy in the rear; some that we were going to Princeton."[12] Others believed they were going to retreat.

One unit of 400-500 New Jersey militiamen did not have to guess. They were on a special mission, tricking the enemy as part of the deception plan by replicating the actions of the entire American army. Just as Washington had done when he escaped from Long Island, he kept campfires burning, moving this small

---

8 Philbrick, *Valiant Ambition*, 84; Fischer, *WC*, 315.

9 *FONA*, https://founders.archives.gov/documents/Washington/03-07-02-0411, accessed Dec. 26, 2019.

10 "The Good Soldier White."

11 *FONA*, https://founders.archives.gov/documents/Washington/03-07-02-0411, accessed Dec. 26, 2019.

12 Rodney, *Diary of Captain Thomas Rodney*, 32.

force up and down the American lines as if the army were still occupying them. He also had the troops continue improving the earthworks guarding the fording sites, making as much noise as possible while doing so. The militiamen, who knew nothing of the army's plans, were ordered to maintain the charade for a minimum of three hours following the army's departure, after which they could either follow the main force or withdraw to a safe position.

As final preparations continued, the weather seemed to favor the Americans. Captain Olney remembered, "As the night advanced, it became extremely cold."[13] This worked to their advantage, as the "roads, which the day before had been mud, snow, and water, were congealed now, and had become hard as pavement and solid." Major Wilkinson added, "The night, although cloudless, was exceedingly dark, and though calm most severely cold."[14] The Continentals' movement thus was concealed without the challenges of moving through the quagmires of mud experienced on the roads earlier that day.

Units began receiving orders around midnight, abandoning their positions on the line, and moving into a marching formation in the dark. All the while, enemy pickets were posted just across the creek. Rodney recalled how "secret orders were issued to each department and the whole army was at once put in motion."[15] The 26th Regiment of Massachusetts Continentals, once part of Glover's brigade, formed the advance guard, with assistance from local guides who volunteered their services.

Captain Rodney's company of Delaware militia led the main body. Rodney recalled, "I, with the Dover Company and the Red Feather Company of Philadelphia Light Infantry led the van of the army and Capt. Henry with the other three companies of Philadelphia Light Infantry brought up the rear."

General St. Clair and his brigade, accompanied by General Washington and his staff, followed closely behind Rodney. They departed between 1:00-2:00 a.m., with the remainder of General Sullivan's division, including Mifflin's new brigade of Pennsylvania Continentals, trailing behind. General Greene's division followed with Mercer's brigade, Cadwalader's Associators, and Nicholas's Continental Marines.

Washington devised a two-pronged attack on Princeton. He intended to march the army along a single route until it crossed Stony Brook outside the town. Once across the creek, Sullivan's division, as the main effort, would turn right, following a new route and conducting a flanking attack against Princeton. Greene

---

13 The following two quotes were taken from Williams, *Biography of Revolutionary Heroes*, 196.

14 Wilkinson, *Memoirs*, 140.

15 The following two quotes are from Rodney, *Diary of Captain Thomas Rodney*, 32.

would continue moving forward with a portion of his division, securing a bridge at Worth's Mill along the Post Road. This would block attempts by Cornwallis to advance from Trenton to the southwest while preventing any British from escaping from Princeton. Greene's remaining troops would move to attack east down the Post Road toward Princeton, drawing the enemy's attention from Sullivan's main attack on the flank. To get into position for this assault, the Americans first had to complete another tiring hike through a cold winter night without being detected by the enemy.

British sentries began to suspect the rebels were up to something as the Americans prepared for their march. They observed unusual movements about the enemy camps, including glimpses of Continental soldiers forming. Captain Hall reported, "The sentries who were advanced, heard the rattling of carriages, and patrols, in going their rounds, made their reports of an uncommon hurry in the enemy's camp that indicated they were in motion."[16] One British officer, observing excessive movement behind the American lines, speculated that Washington "meditated a blow on Prince Town, which was but weak."[17] Cornwallis received these reports and believed that the rebels might be staging to attack. He ordered the British and Hessian grenadier battalions that he was going to use to spearhead the attack against the American right flank the following morning to establish defensive positions.

Washington's plan worked, and his long column began its trek down Sand Town Road, a small, unimproved path cut through a forest. Henry Knox told his wife, "[O]ur Troops march'd with great silence & order."[18] Many Americans facing the night-long march had not had any sleep. Sergeant White of Knox's artillery detailed his challenges in remaining awake: "I being exceeding sleepy, I pitched forward several times, and recovered myself. Said he, you are the first person I ever see, sleep while marching."[19] The weariness felt by the soldiers was exacerbated by the many tree stumps and ruts found on the road. John Howland of Hitchcock's brigade recalled that "these trees stopped the movement of some of the guns, and caused many a fall and severe bruise to some of the over-weary, sleepy soldiers."[20]

Though the army was on its way, not all went according to plan. The Americans inadvertently left some men behind in Trenton in their efforts to keep the British

16 Dwyer, *TDIO*, 327; Fischer, *WC*, 317.

17 *FONA*, https://founders.archives.gov/documents/Washington/03-07-02-0411, accessed Dec. 26, 2019; Dwyer, *TDIO*, 327.

18 Drake, *Life and Correspondence of Henry Knox*, 39.

19 "The Good Soldier White."

20 Stryker, *BTP*, 276-277.

from discovering their scheme. After working on some of the wounded, Dr. Rush recalled, "I slept two or three hours. About 4 o'clock Dr. Cochran went up to Trenton to inquire for our Army. He returned in haste, and said they were not to be found. We now procured waggons, and after putting our patients in them directed that they should follow us to Bordentown, to which place we supposed our Army had retreated."[21] Upon arriving at that place, Rush's group heard firing in the distance and determined that Washington had attacked Princeton. They hastily changed course, moving to join the army.

Others started the march but did not arrive at their destination. Shortly after departing Trenton, several recently recruited and inexperienced militiamen became spooked when they spotted a group of soldiers they mistook for Hessians. According to Rodney, "on the march great confusion happened in the rear. There was a cry that they were surrounded by the Hessians and several corps of Militia broke and fled towards Bordentown but the rest of the column remained firm and pursued the march without disorder."[22] Those who fled were so frightened they did not stop running until they reached Burlington.

In Burlington, Margaret Morris encountered a group of wayward soldiers seeking shelter in a neighbor's home. She wrote, "heart was melted to see such a number of my fellow-creatures, lying like swine on the floor fast asleep. . . . Upon my questioning them pretty close, I brought several to confess that they had run away, being scared."[23] Realizing their error, most prepared to return to the army, leaving Morris to ponder, "There were several pretty innocent-looking lads among them, and I sympathized with their mothers when I saw them preparing to return to the army."

This incident was another example of why Washington called for a professional standing army the country could rely on for its defense. The militia that fled to Burlington was comprised of farmers, artisans, and merchants who volunteered bravely but lacked training, cohesion, and proper leadership. The order Mifflin issued to his brigade the day before this event provides insight into the rudimentary training and understanding his men possessed as they marched into battle at Assunpink Creek. He shared how his troops had ignored a previous order to parade the brigade, admonishing them, "Had the enemy advanced towards this Town at that time, the Army here might have been, to their eternal Disgrace and the Ruin of their Country, made Prisoners of War." He then proceeded to provide the most simplistic direction so there would be no further misunderstandings:

21 Rush, *The Autobiography of Benjamin Rush*, 140.

22 Rodney, *Diary of Captain Thomas Rodney*, 32.

23 The following two quotes are from Morris, "Revolutionary Journal of Margaret Morris," 73.

In future when the Brigade is ordered to be assembled by Night or by Day, the long roll will be beat: upon which signal every Officer and Soldier must turn out with the greatest alacrity and form on their proper Ground in the Street. They are not to wait for the Drums beating to Arms. The long roll is the proper signal for turning out, and must be attended to, as much as beating to Arms.[24]

The fact that Mifflin had to explain the basic signals used by the army in the face of a far superior enemy force is telling. The hot exchange of fire and the image of thousands of British and Hessian troops formed on the heights above Trenton undoubtedly spooked many of Mifflin's rookie troops, resulting in their flight the next morning. Cadwalader's Associators had been together for a longer period, but they too were neophytes, as we will soon see. Many of the Continental Marines attached to Cadwalader's brigade were seasoned fighters who had been blooded at sea. Their numbers, however, were too few to positively affect the militiamen in the short time they had served together. Unfortunately, no records exist of the interactions between the Marines and Associators during their movement to Princeton.

Conditions improved slightly for the foot-sore and weary soldiers and Marines as they emerged from the forest north of Sand Town. They crossed a small creek called Miry Run, continuing north. The army traversed an area called "The Barrens" due to the stunted oaks in the area, with Bear Swamp to their left providing protection from a British attack. They continued along Quaker Road, so named because the Quaker "Friends" would use it for travel from Crosswicks to a Quaker meeting house near Stony Brook, close to Princeton. Unfortunately, the Quaker Bridge could not support the weight of the heavy artillery and ammunition wagons, stopping the army in its tracks. Washington called the engineers forward and began working on a second bridge that could handle them.

Washington used the time to prepare for the final leg of the army's journey. He pulled Rodney's men to the side of the road and moved Sullivan's division forward to take the lead, as those troops would be turning right after passing Stony Brook to conduct their flanking attack. The army also gathered stragglers and returned them to their units. Sergeant White recalled how his company commander prepared his men in the final moments before the battle: "The captain sent me a sergeant with a bucket full of powder and rum, every man must drink a half gill."[25] This concoction was likely not meant to provide liquid courage but to remove the morning chill.

---

24 "General Mifflin, Bordentown Brigade Orders, January 1, 1777," quoted from *Proceedings of the New Jersey Historical Society*, 2nd series, vol. 1, 1:867-69 (Newark, 1869), 39; Stryker, *BTP*, 431.

25 "The Good Soldier White."

The Quaker meeting house outside of Princeton was the waypoint where Washington's army split into two elements. Sullivan's division, the main effort, turned east to conduct a flanking attack on Princeton while Greene's division continued north along Stony Brook to draw the enemy's attention, blocking British reinforcements coming from Trenton. The original meeting house still stands in the same location. *Author*

Meanwhile, Lt. Col. Charles Mawhood prepared to reinforce Cornwallis. With Leslie's earlier departure, Mawhood was temporarily placed in command of the 4th Brigade, consisting of his 17th and the 40th and 55th regiments and three troops of dragoons, to guard Princeton. Captain Johann Ewald, who had been in Princeton earlier that week, described it as consisting of "about three hundred and twenty houses besides the college building [Nassau Hall], in which an entire regiment was quartered. Six redoubts were constructed and mounted with 12- and 6-pounders on the heights toward Trenton."[26] Captain Rodney of the Delaware militia considered Princeton "a very pretty little town . . . the houses are built of brick and very elegant especially the college [Nassau Hall] which had 52 rooms in it."[27] As Cornwallis was sure he had Washington trapped, he ordered Mawhood forward with two regiments, artillery, and supplies to help deliver a *coup de grâce* to the rebel army.

26 Ewald, *Diary*, 44.

27 Rodney, *Diary of Captain Thomas Rodney*, 36.

Mawhood was a professional with 24 years of faithful service to the crown. Though committed to doing his duty, like others he questioned the wisdom of making war on the colonies. He shared his feelings with a physician who roomed with him just before Washington attacked Trenton. The physician shared how Mawhood "often expressed himself very freely, lamenting the American contest very much, and pronouncing Lord North a villain for being the cause of it."[28] He further described how on Christmas night, Mawhood proclaimed that "if he were in Gen. Washingtons place he would make an attack on several of the principal posts at the same time;—that they were all so weak that he could certainly cut them off, and be in possession of all Jersey in a few days."[29] One wonders whether Mawhood saw Princeton as another weak "principal post" as he prepared to engage Washington following his prophetic words.

Mawhood formed his unit for an early departure. He selected the 17th and 55th regiments and reinforced them with 10 artillery pieces, 30 mounted dragoons, supply wagons, and several stragglers from units who hoped to join their parent organizations in Trenton. Approximately 700 troops gathered before sunrise as Mawhood mounted a brown pony, calling for his two small spaniels. The 40th Regiment, with a few hundred more men, was left to defend Princeton as the column began its march. The 17th Regiment was making good progress with Mawhood in the lead and the 55th and others following in trace down the Post Road toward Trenton. The 17th and part of the 55th crossed Stony Brook at Worth's Mill, Greene's designated objective, and made its way up Millett Hill on the west side when Mawhood saw a small body of troops moving north along the east side of Stony Brook. He immediately sent two officers on horseback to investigate.

The Continentals traversed the northern branch of Assunpink Creek at the beginning of morning nautical twilight and quickly made their way north to Stony Brook, crossing the bridge over it around sunrise. Major Wilkinson recalled, "The morning was bright, serene, and extremely cold, with an hoar frost which bespangled every object."[30] As planned, Sullivan's division turned northeast to follow Saw Mill Road. They passed the Quakers meeting house and continued toward Princeton. Mercer's brigade was leading Greene's division north along a sunken road parallel to Stony Brook, working its way across the rolling hills toward its objective, when Mawhood saw it.

28 Ibid., 46, Fischer, *WC*, 326.

29 Rodney, *Diary of Captain Thomas Rodney*, 47; Fischer, *WC*, 326; Philbrick, *Valiant Ambition*, 69; Dwyer, *TDIO*, 336.

30 Wilkinson, *Memoirs*, 141.

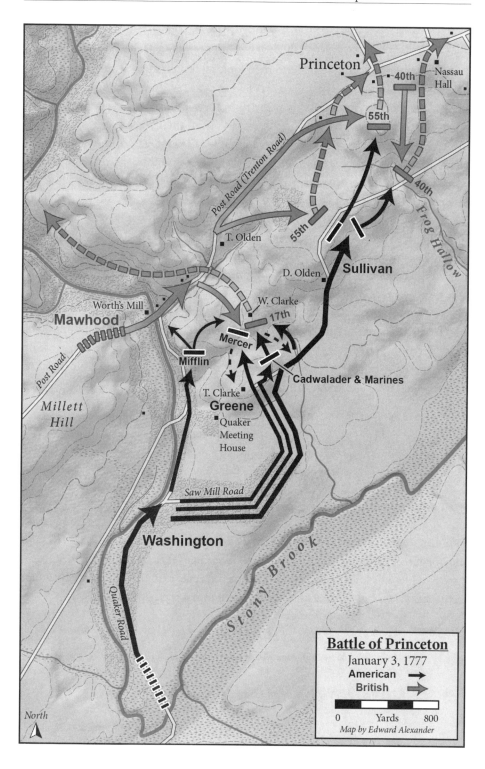

Battle of Princeton

January 3, 1777

American →

British →

0   Yards   800

Map by Edward Alexander

The Americans became alerted to the British presence at nearly the same time. A sergeant in Mercer's unit recalled that, on "reaching the summit of a hill near Princeton, we observed a light-horseman looking towards us, as we view an object when the sun shines directly in our faces. Gen. Mercer, observing him gave orders to the riflemen who were posted on the right to pick him off. Several made ready, but at that instant he wheeled about and was out of their reach."[31]

The British were unsure whether the body of troops before them was friend or foe. Believing Washington was still at Trenton, some thought they might be a group of Hessians or other friendly stragglers from the previous day's fight. All doubt was dismissed when the two officers found Sullivan's division a couple of miles east, just as Wilkinson glimpsed the British body moving west down Post Road. He recalled, "when casting my eyes towards the Trenton Road, I discerned the enemy, by the reflection of their arms against the rising sun."[32] The British unit disappeared behind a rise in the ground as Wilkinson reported his sighting, but they were quickly replaced as "two horsemen leaped a fence, advanced to . . . reconnoitre us for a minute or two, and returned to the road, soon after which we observed the line come to the right about and descend the hill in quick time." According to Knox, "we did not suprize them at Trenton; for they were on their march down to Trenton, on a road about a quarter of a mile distant from the one in which we were." He continued,

> You may judge of their suprize when they discoverd such large Columns marching up, they could not possibly suppose it was our army, for that they took for granted was coop'd up near Trenton. They could not possibly suppose it was their own army returning by a back road; in short I believe they were as much astonished as if our Army had dropped perpendicularly upon them.[33]

The Americans and British stumbled into a classic "meeting engagement." In modern terms, a meeting engagement is a "combat action that occurs when a moving force, incompletely deployed for battle, engages an enemy at an unexpected time and place."[34] In this situation, the force that more quickly gains an advantage in maneuver, terrain, or fire superiority usually wins the battle.

31 Sergeant R___, "Account of Princeton," March 24, 1832, *PMHB*, vol. 20, 515-519, quoted from Commager & Morris, *SSS*, 520.

32 The following two quotes are from Wilkinson, *Memoirs*, 141-142.

33 Drake, *Life and Correspondence of Henry Knox*, 39.

34 *Joint Publication 1-0, Department of Defense Dictionary of Military and Associated Terms* (Washington, D.C., 2001), 337.

Mawhood had three choices at this point. He could push on to Maidenhead, join Leslie, and continue supporting Cornwallis, as ordered. He could retreat to Princeton, defending from prepared positions; or he could attack. Though ignorant of the size of the force he faced, he decided to attack. Mawhood ordered the wagon trains back to Princeton, directing eight pieces of artillery and the 55th Regiment to a prominent position on what became known as Mercer Hill, supporting the 17th Regiment's attack.

The Americans and British raced to see who could occupy the area's key terrain first. Mawhood turned the 17th Regiment, reinforced by two cannons, dragoons, and the stragglers accompanying him—about 450 in total—and quickly moved back across Stony Brook to an area that offered some protection.[35] He maneuvered his force up a hill to an orchard near William Clark's house that offered a hedge fence behind which his troops could achieve some cover. Rodney recalled, "they turned off from the main road and posted themselves behind a long string of buildings and an orchard, on the straight road to Princeton."[36] Mawhood sent his dismounted dragoons forward to hide behind the fence as he formed the regiment and two cannons in a line approximately 400 yards to their rear.

Mercer rushed his men to the same area, attempting to gain the high ground. He too was unsure of the size of the force he confronted and initially sent forward a battalion of approximately 100 Pennsylvania riflemen along with a company of 20 Virginia infantrymen. Mercer followed with the remainder of his brigade of approximately 350, supported by Captain Neil's two cannons.[37] Cadwalader, with Moulder's seafaring artillerymen, Rodney's militiamen, Nicholas, and the Continental Marines, and Shippin and Brown with the Pennsylvania marines—a force over 1,200-1,500 strong—remained in the ravine near Stony Brook, allowing the situation to develop and awaiting orders.

A hot engagement ensued in the orchard. The first Americans arriving on the scene broke through a fence, found the British forming in line on the next hill over, and fired a volley in their direction before continuing to advance. The British dragoons responded by rising from their hiding place and firing at the Continentals when they were no further than 40 yards away. An American sergeant described the action: when "we were descending a hill through an orchard, a party of the enemy who were entrenched behind a bank and fence rose and fired upon us.

35 Fischer, *WC*, 330; Ward, *TWOR*, 312; Stryker, *BTP*, 280.

36 Rodney, *Diary of Captain Thomas Rodney*, 33-34.

37 Fischer, *WC*, 330; Wilkinson, *Memoirs*, 141; Stryker, *BTP*, 280.

Their first shot passed over our heads, cutting the limbs of the trees under which we were marching."[38]

The Americans responded with another volley as Mercer, mounted on a grey steed, brought the rest of his brigade into play. A British captain explained how this fire "brought down seven of my platoon at once, the rest being recruits, gave way."[39] While Neil rushed his cannon forward, Colonel Haslet, Mercer's second in command, advanced with Capt. John Fleming's 1st Virginia Regiment and other infantry on foot. The artillery continued chipping away against the enemy formations as the riflemen targeted individual British officers. One soldier described, "We formed, advanced, and fired upon the enemy. They retreated about eight rods (44 yards) to their packs, which were laid in a line."[40] A grenadier captain and another from the 17th Regiment quickly fell. An American soldier recalled, "Our fire was most destructive; their ranks grew thin and the victory seemed nearly complete when the British were reinforced . . . we were unable to withstand much superior numbers of fresh troops."[41]

The British refused to yield ground. Although their dragoons fell back after the initial fire, Mawhood's artillery commenced firing as they attempted to reform while his infantry advanced against the rebels. The British loosed another volley at the Continentals, but it too went high, so they reverted to the weapon that served them well in previous engagements—the bayonet. The Americans dreaded the 12-inch cold steel blades mounted on the muzzles of British muskets. Nothing instilled more fear in new or undisciplined troops than a mass formation of bayonet-wielding enemy soldiers bearing down before they could reload their weapons. Mawhood's men charged with ferocity. Unfortunately for the Americans, their long rifles and many old muskets could not mount bayonets.

The result was predictable, and the American line began breaking. Mercer rushed forward to lead his men in holding the line, but his horse was shot out from under him. Knocked to the ground, Mercer jumped to his feet to continue fighting, but the onrushing British were quickly on top of him. One of Mercer's soldiers reported, "I soon heard Gen. Mercer command in a tone of distress, 'Retreat' . . . I discharged my musket at a part of the enemy, and ran for a piece of woods."[42]

38 "Account of Princeton," 520.

39 John Nagy, *George Washington's Secret Spy War: The Making of America's First Spymaster* (New York, 2016), 84; Fischer, *WC*, 331.

40 Ebenezer Thomas, *Reminiscences of the Last Sixty-five Years, Commencing with the Battle of Lexington*, 2 vols. (Hartford, 1840), 1:286.

41 Ibid.; "Account of Princeton," 520; Henry Melchior Muhlenberg Richards, *The Pennsylvania-German in the Revolutionary War, 1775-1783* (Lancaster, PA, 1908), 122.

42 Commager & Morris, *SSS*, 520; Richards, *The Pennsylvania-German in the Revolutionary War*, 122.

General Hugh Mercer gallantly led his Continental soldiers forward against British regulars in the battle of Princeton before they fell back in the face of bayonet-wielding Redcoats. Mercer's horse was shot from under him as he attempted to rally his men. British soldiers quickly surrounded and bayonetted him several times as he tried to defend himself. Mercer lived for nine more days before succumbing to his wounds. *Wikimedia*

British soldiers surrounded Mercer, shouting, "Call for quarter, you damned rebel!"[43] In response, Mercer drew his sword to defend himself, but was quickly overpowered. A soldier knocked him to the ground with the butt of his musket, while others bayonetted and slashed him repeatedly. Mercer feigned death and claimed he heard a soldier say, "Damn him, he is dead. Let us leave him."[44] Some believed they had killed General Washington since Mercer was wearing a general's uniform. Mercer lived for nine more days, receiving care from Dr. Rush before finally succumbing to his wounds.

Others from Mercer's command were not as fortunate. Several key leaders met their fate while bravely leading their men in this brief, fierce engagement. The British killed Captain Neil and captured one of his guns as he continued aggressively firing into the onrushing enemy. Seeing that Mercer was down and the American line was collapsing, Colonel Haslet rushed forward to rally the men. He was shot in the head and fell dead on the spot, costing the Americans another competent

43 McNabney, *Born in Brotherhood*, 520; Chernow, *Washington: A Life*, 281; Fischer, *WC*, 332.

44 Wilkinson, *Memoirs*, 147; Fischer, *WC*, 333.

The Thomas Clarke house on the Princeton battlefield still stands. General Cadwalader deployed Captain Moulder's battery of two cannons on high ground near the monument at the base of the flagpole seen in this photo as the Associator Brigade and Samuel Nicholas's Continental Marines marched into battle to Moulder's right. The mortally wounded General Mercer was carried off the battlefield and into the Clarke home, where he died nine days later. *Author*

commander with a promising future. The loss of two senior commanders and the British advancing while "screaming as if so many devils had got hold of them" was too much for Mercer's men.[45] They broke and began running toward the rear.

Hearing the firing increasing in intensity, Cadwalader advanced his brigade and the Marines toward the fighting. General Greene ordered him to form on a hilltop opposite the British line 200-300 yards away. Cadwalader found a chaotic and deteriorating situation as he approached. He deployed Captain Moulder's battery of two cannons on high ground near Thomas Clarke's house and ordered a company of light infantry to maneuver around to strike the enemy's right flank. But they became pinned in by the artillery firing from that flank and moved back toward the center.

The Associators advanced in a column, accompanied by the Marines. According to Cadwalader, "Our column was formed from the right by divisions. . . . I immediately rode in front of the column, and ordered the second divisions to double up, to the right, the third to the left and so on alternately. This was done in the face of the enemy and under a shower of grapeshot."[46] Nicholas

45 Stryker, *BTP*, 285; Fischer, *WC*, 331; Dwyer, *TDIO*, 342.

46 Styker, *BTP*, 447. The evidence in this letter clearly identifies the officer as General Cadwalader.

A modern-day view of the Princeton battlefield from the vicinity of Captain Moulder's artillery position. The British advanced from the tree line in the distance and pushed Mercer's men back. Mercer was reportedly bayonetted near the site of the oak tree surrounded by the split rail fence in the left-center of the photo. Cadwalader and the Continental Marines advanced toward the British from the right side of the photo. *Author*

and the Continental Marines maneuvered into position on the Associators' right as Pennsylvania marine Capt. William Brown brought his company of artillery forward.

Confusion reigned as Mercer's men ran headlong into Cadwalader's Associators and the Marines as they attempted to close and organize their lines before attacking the British. The unexpected appearance of this larger body of Americans caused Mawhood to pause, buying the Americans valuable time. Rodney described how "Gen. Cadwalader's Philadelphia Brigade came up and the enemy checked by their appearance took post behind a fence and a ditch in front of the buildings before mentioned and so extended themselves that every man could load and fire incessantly."[47]

Caught up in the moment's excitement, Cadwalader rushed his brigade and Marines forward. For many Associators, this was their first experience attacking a

47 Rodney, *Diary of Captain Thomas Rodney*, 34.

determined enemy under fire. Adrenaline pumped through the Americans' veins as they closed with the long line of Redcoats. Fear of their enemy and seeing Mercer's Continentals retreating caused some of the inexperienced Philadelphia militia to break formation and begin to move toward the rear. Captain Peale of the Associators' 2nd Battalion recalled, "We marched on quickly, and met some troops retreating in confusion. We continued our march towards the hill where the firing was, though now rather irregularly. I carried my platoon to the top of the hill, and fired, though unwillingly, for I thought the enemy too far off."[48] Rodney shared how Cadwalader led his troops "with the greatest bravery to within 50 yards of the enemy, but this was rashly done, for he was obliged to recoil."[49] Cadwalader noted, "About half the first battalion was formed when they broke, fell back upon the column, [and] threw the whole into confusion."[50]

Cadwalader pulled his men back approximately 40 yards to reform them, but enemy fire was starting to take a toll. The Redcoats fired from behind the cover of the fence while "on the hill behind the British line they had eight pieces of artillery which played incessantly with round and grape shot on our Brigade, and the fire was extremely hot."[51] The Americans reloaded and loosed another volley at their enemy, but the number of men turning away from the firing line increased.

Mercer's and Cadwalader's men became entangled, making it difficult to control large units in the smoke, noise, and combat stress. Out of necessity, command and control reverted to the company level. Rodney said, "some companies did form and gave a few vollies." Captain Shippin was shot in the head, dying while leading his company forward. Captain Fleming of Mercer's brigade remained on the field, trying unsuccessfully to rally his regiment of Virginia Continentals. He, too, was shot and killed while leading his men. Continental Marine Capt. Andrew Porter performed admirably that day. It was later reported that Porter "received on the field in person the commendation of General George Washington."[52] According to Rodney, "the fire of the enemy was so hot, that, at the sight of the regular troops running to the rear, the militia gave way and the whole brigade [the Associators] broke and most of them retired to the woods about 150 yards in the rear."[53] Captain Brown led his artillery company in the thick of the battle and may have abandoned one of his guns toward the center of the action as the brigade pulled back.

48 Peale, "Journal by Charles Wilson Peale," *PMHB*, 279.

49 Rodney, *Diary of Captain Thomas Rodney*, 34-35.

50 Stryker, *BTP*, 447.

51 The following two quotes are from Rodney, *Diary of Captain Thomas Rodney*, 34.

52 Porter, "A Sketch of the Life of General Andrew Porter," *PMHB*, 264.

53 Rodney, *Diary of Captain Thomas Rodney*, 35.

Unfortunately, scant records exist of Major Nicholas's and his Continental Marines' actions at this point in the battle. Nicholas's battalion fielded around 100 or fewer Marines, equating to five to ten percent of Cadwalader's total force. Understanding that Marines were moving with Cadwalader's brigade, it is possible that they were in the wave of men falling back to the woods until they rallied for a renewed attack.

As the firing began near the Clarke farms Washington was moving with the army's main body to outflank the village. Wilkinson accompanied this column and remembered catching glimpses of the battle raging to their rear between the trees and rolling terrain. He wrote, "I well recollect that the smoke from the discharge of the two lines mingled as it rose, and went up in one beautiful cloud."[54] Not waiting to admire these sights, Washington turned his horse and raced toward the sound of the guns with the Philadelphia Light Horse in tow.

Arriving in the woods, Washington began assessing the situation as Cadwalader attempted to reform the men. The Americans had fallen back, but they were not beaten. The brave Captain Moulder and his two four-pound cannons, manned by gunners recruited from the Philadelphia docks, temporarily checked the British advance with effective fire. Washington and Cadwalader conferred and developed a plan. Rodney and others would protect Moulder's men while Washington called for additional infantry and artillery. Rodney stated that an officer "was sent to order me to take post on the left of the artillery until the brigade should form again, and with the Philadelphia Infantry keep up a fire . . . to assist the artillery in preventing the enemy from advancing."[55]

Sergeant White and the New England artillerymen joined Moulder on the battlefield. He recalled observing the British as he prepared his gun for action: "They were to the north of us, the sun shone upon them, and their arms glistened very bright, it seemed to strike an awe upon us."[56] White led one of the two cannon crews in his company. They fired solid rounds into the enemy until the formation got closer. He stated, "We then loaded with cannister shot, they made a terrible squeaking noise." White described how "[o]ur company being on the extreme left, had to face the enemy's right; consisting of granadiers, highlanders, &c. their best troops." This caused White to withdraw with his crew, leaving Moulder's company to hold the line.

Washington attempted to reorganize the Americans in the face of the enemy but found it challenging to gather the dispersed troops. Cadwalader recalled, "Gen.

---

54 Wilkinson, *Memoirs*, 143.

55 Rodney, *Diary of Captain Thomas Rodney*, 35.

56 The following three quotes were taken from "The Good Soldier White."

Marines with Washington at Princeton, 3 January 1777. Painting by Col. Charles H. Waterhouse, USMCR. Mercer's brigade fell back into the advancing Associator brigade and a battalion of Continental Marines, causing confusion until Cadwalader and Washington gained control of the group and resumed the attack. The British broke, causing Washington to yell, "It is a fine fox chase, my boys!" *Art Collection, National Museum of the Marine Corps, Triangle, Virginia*

Washington came down and exposed himself very much but expostulated to no purpose."[57] The troops had already withdrawn to the woods. Mawhood intended to exploit the confusion, sending his light horse around the Americans' right flank, but Moulder's men checked their progress with accurate fire. Cadwalader asked Washington "if it would not be proper to form about a hundred yards in the rear. He desired me to try, which succeeded beyond my expectation."

Hitchcock's New England Continentals detached from Sullivan's division, arriving on Cadwalader's and the Marines' right flank as they prepared to reattack the British. Thirty-seven-year-old Maj. Israel Angell commanded the regiment due to Hitchcock's illness. The volume of fire increased as the British observed the Americans preparing to advance. Rodney experienced several close calls as he continued to defend Moulder's guns: "[T]he enemies fire was dreadful and three balls, for they were very thick, had grazed me; one passed within my elbow nicking my great coat and carried away the breech of Sergeant McNatt's gun, he being close

---

57 The next two quotes are from Stryker, *BTP*, 447.

behind me, another carried away the inside edge of one of my shoe soles, another had niched my hat and indeed they seemed as thick as hail."[58]

The Continentals refused to be denied. One soldier remembered, "Washington appeared in front of the American army, riding towards those of us who were retreating, and exclaimed, 'Parade with us, my brave fellows! There is but a handful of the enemy, and we will have them directly.' I immediately joined the main body and marched over the ground again."[59] Others recalled how Washington rode between the two armies as they continued firing at one another. Major Apollos Morris, a volunteer from England, noted that Washington "was exposed to both firings for some time."[60] Washington's aides tried to hold him back, but he was having none of it. Colonel John Fitzgerald recalled losing sight of Washington in the thick, white smoke from the heaving firing. Fitzgerald thought there was no way that Washington could survive, only to see him riding out of the cloud shouting, "Away my dear Colonel, and bring up the troops!"[61]

Cadwalader assembled his brigade, the Marines, and the New England Continentals and advanced. His force "advanced obliquely to the right, passed a fence, and marched up to the left of the enemy."[62] The British countered and "[l]eft their station and inclined to the left, and gave us several heavy fires, in which two were killed and several wounded." General Mifflin and Colonel Hand soon joined Cadwalader, deploying their units on his right. The British offered stiff resistance, but the superior number of Americans arriving on the battlefield overwhelmed Mawhood's smaller force. The new arrivals bounded forward by platoons, with one platoon firing to cover the movement of another as they closed on the enemy. Sergeant White remembered how "[t]he British lines were broken, and our troops followed them so close, that they could not form again."[63] As the Redcoats turned and ran, Cadwalader "pressed my party forward, huzzaed, and cried out 'They Fly, the day is our own.'"[64] He recalled, "They all dropped their packs and flew with the utmost precipitation, and we pursued with great eagerness." Captain

58 Rodney, *Diary of Captain Thomas Rodney*, 35.

59 "Account of Princeton," 520.

60 Major Apollos Morris was a British officer who disagreed with the war against America and resigned his commission to serve on the American side. He used a false name to protect his property holdings in Ireland. This quote is from Dwyer, *TDIO*, 348.

61 "Col. John Fitzgerald to General Washington: On the Conway Cabal Against Washington (Alexandria 17 March 1778)," *The American Catholic Historical Researches*, vol. 17, no. 3 (July 1900), 107; Irving, *Life of George Washington*, 232; Dwyer, *TDIO*, 348.

62 The following two quotes are from Stryker, *BTP*, 447.

63 "The Good Soldier White."

64 The following two quotes are from Stryker, *BTP*, 447.

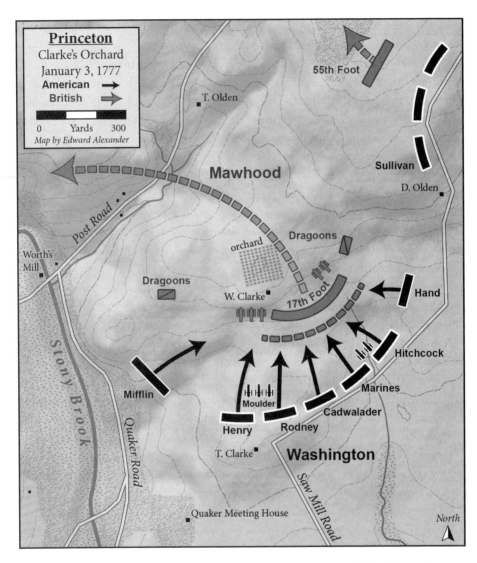

Stephen Olney stated, "The enemy perceiving we were not all dead and that we continued to advance in order with a reserved charge for them, turned their back and fled in disorder."[65]

Mawhood failed to maintain order. He turned his regiment, which now had Americans closing in on it from three directions, and ordered a bayonet charge to break out of the trap. Approximately 100 British soldiers lay dead. The remaining 17th Regiment troops abandoned their cannons, rushing across the Post Road to move west along the bank of Stony Brook away from the slaughter. Washington,

65 Williams, *Biography of Revolutionary Heroes*, 199.

his Light Horse, and several infantrymen continued in hot pursuit. Feeling the moment's excitement, Washington called out, "It is a fine fox chase, my boys."[66] Washington's aides reined him in before he was drawn too far from the main battle, but others kept after the enemy for three or four miles; 50 British soldiers were captured before the chase was abandoned. One British officer described how far some troops marched to avoid capture: "[W]e went twenty miles round that day to join our troops and marched all the following night to Brunswick, in all upwards of forty miles without halting two hours."[67] Mawhood and another small contingent crossed Stony Brook further north, eventually joining General Leslie and the remainder of their brigade to the south.

Others were not as fortunate. As Washington joined Cadwalader in the attack against Mawhood, General Sullivan turned his division and began moving against the element of the 55th Regiment and artillery positioned on Mercer Hill. Before retreating, Mawhood had ordered the portion of the 55th who had originally crossed Stony Brook with him to rejoin their regiment on the 17th's left near Mercer Hill. As the regiment attempted to reform, Sullivan's attack caused them to fall back toward Princeton where they established a defensive position along a ravine called Frog Hallow to block the Americans advance toward the town.

Sullivan relentlessly pursued the fleeing men of the 55th Regiment. On reaching Frog Hallow, he maneuvered his men into a battle line to stage for an assault. The British responded by ordering a platoon to attack the American flank. Undeterred, Sullivan extended his line, sending soldiers across the ravine. The Americans' superiority became evident as their flanks stretched well beyond those of the British. At imminent risk of being encircled by the stronger American force, the 55th hastily pulled back to another prepared position on the edge of town.

Momentum was on the Americans' side. After defeating the 17th Regiment, Cadwalader's force shifted, joining Sullivan in time to capture Princeton. According to Rodney, "We then pushed forward toward the town spreading over the fields and through the woods to enclose the enemy and take prisoners."[68] The British fled in disorder, shedding weapons and gear along their retreat. Rodney said "[t]he fields were covered with baggage which the Gen. ordered to be taken care of."

Sullivan maintained pressure on the 55th Regiment. Seeing the Redcoats taking cover behind a fortified position, the Americans called their artillery forward and

---

66 Wilkinson, *Memoirs*, 145; Ron Chernow, *Alexander Hamilton* (New York, 2004), 84; William Betts, *The Nine Lives of George Washington* (Bloomington, IN, 2013), 104.

67 Fischer, *WC*, 336.

68 The following two quotes were found in Rodney, *Diary of Captain Thomas Rodney*, 36.

commenced firing on their earthworks. Realizing the futility of their defense, the 55th broke and fled into Princeton, where the 40th Regiment remained. Seeing the American masses charging into the village, elements of the 55th and 40th regiments, about 200 men in total, raced out of Princeton, eventually escaping to Brunswick 16 miles to the north. The remaining British barricaded themselves in Nassau Hall at Princeton College.

The Continentals continued swarming through the village as Sullivan's men surrounded the college. British soldiers broke the windows of Nassau Hall and started shooting at them. Sullivan responded by summoning Capt. Alexander Hamilton's battery. Legend says Hamilton's first round entered the building, decapitating a picture of King George hanging on the wall. Major Wilkinson reported that a subsequent shot almost killed him as it ricocheted off the stone wall of the Hall: "the ball recoiled, and very nearly killed my horse as I was passing near the building."[69] Hamilton may have fired one last round before a group of local militiamen entered the building, forcing the British to surrender. The Americans took 194 prisoners in Nassau Hall and also liberated a group of American captives. One witness recalled how the British "discharged their Continental prisoners that they had confined in the College . . . among whom . . . was about 30 of our Country people that were accused either of being Rebels of aiding . . . them."[70] The capture of Nassau Hall ended enemy resistance in Princeton.

Washington was ecstatic, but he had little time to bask in the victory. He still faced a major threat to his rear, and Cornwallis was undoubtedly angry at finding that Washington had again slipped from his grasp. To slow Cornwallis's advance from the south, Washington ordered a detachment of New Jersey militia to disassemble the Stony Brook bridge. He sent another group north to destroy the bridges between Princeton and Brunswick, slowing any counterattack that might develop from that direction.

Cornwallis was skillfully duped again. As dawn broke and his pickets recognized that the Americans had withdrawn, Cornwallis was unsure of their destination. Royal engineer Archibald Robertson, recalled, "At Day Break reported that the Rebels were all gone which it was generally thought was towards Borden's Town. Until about 8 o'clock [when] a very Brisk fire of Small Arms and Smart Cannonading was heard in our Rear towards Prince Town."[71] Realizing his folly in

---

69 Wilkinson, *Memoirs*, 145.

70 "An account of the Battle of Princeton completed on April 18, 1777, by an 85-year-old resident, name unknown, Anonymous," *Brief Narrative of the British and Hessians at Princeton*, 32-39, quoted from Commager & Morris, *SSS*, 521; Patterson, *Washington and Cornwallis*, 100.

71 Harry Lydenberg, *Archibald Robertson, Lieutenant General Royal Engineers. His Diaries and Sketches in America, 1762-1780* (New York, 1930), 120.

Nassau Hall of Princeton College [University] had 52 rooms and housed an entire regiment of British soldiers. During the battle of Princeton, the British fell back to establish a final defensive position at Nassau Hall before Capt. Alexander Hamilton had his New York artillerymen fire into the building, causing the British to surrender. Scars from the cannon fire can be seen on Nassau Hall today. *Wikimedia*

not pressing the attack the previous evening, Cornwallis quickly began moving his army toward Princeton.

In Princeton, the Americans scavenged supplies, reformed their dispersed units, and cared for the wounded. One resident recounted that "almost as soon as the firing was over our house was filled and surrounded with Genl Washington's men, and himself on horseback at the door."[72] The Americans carried in two wounded British soldiers to render aid, countering the lack of compassion often displayed by the British and Hessians toward the Continentals. The witness from Nassau Hall also observed the joy of the Americans who survived: "Though they were bo[th] hungry and thirsty some of them [were] laughing out right, others smiling, and not a man among them but showed joy in his countenance."[73] One soldier's recollection captured the ferocity of the battle, providing insights into the joy of surviving the fight. He wrote, "The ground was frozen and all the blood which was shed remained on the surface, which added to the horror of this scene of carnage."[74]

72 Commager & Morris, *SSS*, 521; Patterson, *Washington and Cornwallis*, 100.

73 Commager & Morris, *SSS*, 522; Patterson, *Washington and Cornwallis*, 100.

74 "Account of Princeton," 515-519.

In a report to John Hancock and Congress, Washington praised to Mawhood and his men for their staunch defense while citing British losses,

> These three Regiments, especially the Two first, made a gallant resistance and in killed wounded and Prisoners must have lost 500 Men, upwards of One hundred of them were left dead in the Feild, and with what I have with me & what were taken in the pursuit & carried across the Delaware, there are near 300 prisoners 14 of which are Officers—all British.[75]

General Howe was extremely conservative in his report to Lord Germain. He cited only "seventeen killed and nearly two hundred wounded and missing."[76] Author David Hackett Fischer conducted an in-depth analysis of the evidence, concluding that the British lost "450 killed, wounded, captured, and missing."[77] The Americans lost fewer men, but those killed included several key leaders, with Mercer, Haslet, Fleming, Neil, Shippin, among them. Concerning these officers, Washington reported, "who with about twenty five or thirty privates were slain in the feild—Our whole loss cannot be ascertained, as many who were in pursuit of the Enemy, who were chaced three or four Miles, are not yet come in."[78] Wilkinson wrote, "In this affair our numerical loss was inconsiderable—It did not exceed thirty; fourteen only were buried in the field."[79] On January 7, Dr. Rush wrote to Richard Henry Lee, "Our loss at Princeton amounted to about twenty-five killed and about forty wounded."[80]

Arriving on the battlefield, Rush found Mercer severally wounded, but, unbeknownst to Washington, still alive. Mercer was carried into Thomas Clarke's home with other wounded soldiers. Rush described Mercer as being "wounded in seven places with a bayonet. One of these wounds is in his forehead, but the most alarming of them are in his belly." He later wrote, "General Mercer had been wounded by a bayonet in his belly in several places, but he received a stroke with

75 *FONA*, https://founders.archives.gov/documents/Washington/03-07-02-0411, accessed Dec. 28, 2019.

76 C. C. Haven, *Thirty Days in New Jersey Ninety Years Ago: An Essay Revealing New Facts in Connection with Washington and His Army in 1776 and 1777* (Trenton, NJ, 1867), 61.

77 Fischer, *WC*, 340.

78 *FONA*, https://founders.archives.gov/documents/Washington/03-07-02-0411, accessed Dec. 28, 2019.

79 Wilkinson, *Memoirs*, 146.

80 The following two quotes are from L. H. Butterfield, ed., *Letters of Benjamin Rush* (Princeton, NJ, 1951), 1:125-126.

a butt of a musquet on the side of his head, which put an end to his life a week after the battle."[81]

Knowing Cornwallis was on his way, Washington and his troops rushed to gather supplies before departing. He reported, "We took Two Brass Feild pieces but for want of Horses could not bring them away. We also took some Blankets—Shoes—and a few other trifling Articles—burnt the Hay & destroyed such other things as the shortness of the time would admit of."[82] Knox wrote his wife, "We took all their Cannon which consisted of two brass six pounders a Considerable quantity of military stores blankets guns &c."[83] Unable to transport all the cannons, the American artillerymen exchanged one of their iron pieces for a better British brass gun, threw another into a well, and positioned a large 32-pounder that could not be moved to fire at the British once they advanced from Trenton. Sergeant White and Major Wilkinson sat down at separate locations to enjoy breakfasts that had been prepared for the British but were abandoned when the Americans unexpectantly attacked. White also recalled,

> Orders came for all the men to throw away their dirty old blankets, and take new ones—The barrels of flour were great indeed, after filling all the waggons, they knocked the heads out of the remainder and strewed it about the ground. The women came and looked at it, but seemed afraid to meddle with it. I being nigh, told them to scoupe it up by aprons full, before the enemy come.[84]

The Americans continued scrounging for supplies for about an hour before being alerted by the sound of gunfire in the vicinity of Worth's Mill on Stony Brook. Rodney recounted how they had "not been an hour in possession of the town before the enemy's light horse and advanced parties attacked our party at the bridge but our people by a very heavy fire kept the pass until our whole army left town."[85] New Jersey militiamen and Captain Forrest's artillery company tried to delay the quickly approaching British and Hessians for as long as possible. The militiamen skirmished with the light horse for around an hour before the van of the enemy army arrived. Knox wrote his wife, "After we had been about two hours at Princeton, word was brought that the enemy were advanci[n]g from Trenton—

---

81 Rush, *Autobiography*, 141.

82 *FONA*, https://founders.archives.gov/documents/Washington/03-07-02-0411, accessed Dec. 28, 2019.

83 Drake, *Life and Correspondence of Henry Knox*, 39.

84 "The Good Soldier White."

85 Rodney, *Diary of Captain Thomas Rodney*, 37.

this they did as we have since been inform'd in a most infernal Sweat, running puffing & blowing & swearing at being so outwitted."[86]

Sergeant Thomas Sullivan was with General Leslie's force in Maidenhead. He recalled his unit quickly advancing toward Princeton upon hearing the firing that morning and described how the British paused on the high ground overlooking the bridge spanning Stony Brook: "A party of rebels were formed on one side on the bridge and another party cutting it down. . . . The Fifth Battalion, which marched in front of the brigade with two six-pounders, engaged them from the opposite side and in a few minutes drove them from the bridge, which they had cut down."[87]

Washington wasted no time in moving his army. He quickly paroled 56 wounded British soldiers and put his troops back on the road. He later reported to Congress, "The rear of the Enemy's Army laying at Maidenhead (not more than five or Six miles from Princeton) was up with us before our pursuit was over, but as I had the precaution to destroy the Bridge over Stoney Brooke (about half a mile from the field [sic] of action) they were so long retarded there as to give us time to move off in good order for this place."[88]

The Associators and Marines had yet to enter Princeton. Captain Peale remembered, "we were resting, on our arms, waiting for leave to enter the town to refresh ourselves, when we heard the sound of cannon in our rear. We thought it was at Trenton, but finding it approached nearer, we perceived the enemy close upon our heels."[89] Cadwalader received orders to move his people out, with Nicholas to follow. Peale continued, "We now began to march on through the town. I expected we should be collected in order when we got into the back of the town, but we were still continued on. I then expected we would halt when we should have crossed the bridge . . . Here, again, I found my mistake. We were continued on about three or four miles."

The Americans moved north up the Post Road on the heels of the escaping British toward Brunswick, Washington's next intended target. He gave up the pursuit after reaching the village of Kingston, four miles away and across Millstone Creek. Washington destroyed the bridge over the creek and posted Captain Moulder and his hearty artillerymen to cover the army's rear from Cornwallis's advance scouts. He then called for an impromptu council of war on the roadside.

---

86 Drake, *Life and Correspondence of Henry Knox*, 40.

87 The following two quotes are from Thomas Sullivan, "The Battle of Princeton (excerpts from the journal of Sergeant Thomas Sullivan of Her Majesty's Forty-Ninth Regiment of Foot)," *PMHB*, vol. 32, no. 1 (1908), 56.

88 *FONA*, https://founders.archives.gov/documents/Washington/03-07-02-0411, accessed Dec. 28, 2019.

89 The following two quotes are from Peale, *Journal*, 280.

Washington's blood was up. He wanted to make his victory complete by capturing Brunswick, but he realized that his army was again approaching its breaking point. Many men had marched near continuously for the last 48 hours. Some had been under arms for nearly 40 hours without a decent meal. The American commanders quickly deemed it unwise to continue toward Brunswick. Some argued for heading back to the Delaware to cross into the safety of Pennsylvania, which was rejected. Washington decided to move the army to Morristown, joining the portion of it already positioned there. He directed Israel Putnam to remain in the south and pose a threat to the British in that sector. He informed Putnam, "It is thought advisable for you to march the Troops under your command to Cross[w]ix and keep a strict watch upon the enemy in that quarter."[90] He followed this by dispatching a report to Congress:

> My Original plan when I set out from Trenton was to have pushed on to Brunswic, but the harrassed State of our own Troops (many of them having had no rest for two nights & a day) and the danger of loosing the advantage we had gained by aiming at too much induced me by the advice of my Officers to relinquish the attempt, but in my Judgement Six or Eight hundred fresh Troops upon a forced march would have destroyed all their Stores and Magazines—taken as we have since learnt their Military Chest containing 70,000£ and put an end to the War.[91]

Henry Knox agreed with Washington's decision, sharing with his wife, "[W]e at first intended to have made a forc'd march'd to Brunswick at which place was the baggage of their whole army & Genl Lee—but our men having been without either rest rum or provision for two nights & days were unequal to the task of marching 17 miles further."[92] He also wished for fresh troops to complete the victory that day: "[I]f we Could have procur'd 1000 fresh men at Prince[ton] to have push'd for Brunswick we should have struck one of the most Brillant strokes in All history."

It was not meant to be. Concerned that Washington intended to seize Brunswick and the British war chest, Cornwallis raced forward. Washington, however, managed to stay one step ahead of his enemy. The American rear guard effectively delayed the British, keeping them under fire and destroying the bridge, which "obliged [the British] to cross the brook at the ford with their artillery

90 *FONA*, https://founders.archives.gov/documents/Washington/03-07-02-0416, accessed Dec. 28, 2019.

91 *FONA*, https://founders.archives.gov/documents/Washington/03-07-02-0411, accessed Dec. 28, 2019.

92 The following two quotes were found in Drake, *Life and Correspondence of Henry Knox*, 40.

almost middle deep in water."[93] Rodney recollected, "Just as our army began its march through Princeton with all their prisoners and spoils the van of the British army we had left at Trenton came in sight, and entered the town about an hour after we left it, but made no stay and pushed on towards Brunswick for fear we should get there before him."[94]

The British advance guard made initial contact with the rear guard of the Americans at Princeton. Unfortunately for the Redcoats, their column stretched so far back that their rear guard did not reach Princeton until about 4:00 p.m. on January 3. Captain Ewald detailed the frantic situation on their arrival: "the enemy now had wings, and it was believed that he had flown toward Brunswick to destroy the main depot, which was protected by only one English regiment. Hurriedly, the army was issued three days' rations of biscuit and brandy, left behind the stores, all the sick, the wounded and the greater part of the baggage."[95] The British stay in Princeton was short, as Cornwallis drove the entire force to Brunswick to thwart Washington's plan. The tired British and Hessian troops arrived around 6:00 a.m. the following morning, only to find that Washington had marched his army in the opposite direction.[96] One officer recalled, "We arrived at daybreak on the 4th at the heights above Brunswick and remained there several hours, should the enemy have showed any disposition to attack us, we were prepared for them, but finding every thing quiet, the troops . . . marched into cantonments."[97] Cornwallis sent the dragoons to locate Washington, but he was more concerned with protecting his resources in Brunswick then chasing the rebels.

January 3, 1777 was a trying day for the residents of Princeton. One recalled "that the poor and almost wholly desolate town of all its late inhabitants had changed of masters two if not three times on that day, for they had the Regulars in the morning, the Continentals at noon, the Regulars again at night."[98] Of his arrival in Princeton, Doctor Rush wrote, "The college and church are heaps of ruin; all the inhabitants have been plundered; the whole of Mr. Stockton's [Congressman Richard Stockton] furniture, apparel, and even valuable writings, have been burnt; all his cattle, horses, and hogs, sheep, grain and forage have been carried away."[99]

---

93 Commager and Morris, *SSS*, 521.

94 Rodney, *Diary of Captain Thomas Rodney*, 37.

95 Ewald, *Diary*, 50.

96 Lydenberg, *Archibald Robertson*, 120-121.

97 Dwyer, *TDIO*, 364.

98 Commager and Morris, *SSS*, 521.

99 Butterfield, ed., *Letters of Benjamin Rush*, vol.1, 126.

One witness reflected, "So unconstant is the state of war and so certain and sure are the mischiefs and miserys attending it that it is a wonder that wise men should ever depend on it."[100]

Unfortunately, Washington's men experienced more "miserys" after leaving Princeton. They were still cold, tired, hungry, and ill-clad, but Washington marched them for another 13 miles by way of Rocky Hill before stopping at Somerset Court House to the northeast for the evening. The first troops arrived at dusk, with the last units not arriving until 11:00 p.m. They were exhausted. Captain Peale recalled, "The roads had now become very sloppy, and the troops so fatigued that many stopped by the way—some of my men declared they could go no further. I told them of the danger of them falling into the hands of the enemy, yet this could not induce all to keep up."[101] Rodney noted in his journal, "Our army is now extremely fatigued not having had any refreshment since yesterday morning, and our baggage had all been sent away the morning of the action at Trenton, yet they are in good health and high spirits."[102]

Commanders posted guards as the troops prepared to rest for the night, but very few got any decent sleep. In their haste to secretly depart from Assunpink Creek, Cadwalader's men had placed their blankets in the wagons that departed for Bordentown, thinking they would meet their baggage at a forward location. Unfortunately, many of them had nothing other than the clothes on their backs to protect them from the night's elements and winter temperatures. The blankets captured in Princeton had been disseminated to other units before the Associators and Marines entered the village.

Washington woke the men before sunrise on January 4 and continued their movement toward Morristown. They made it to Pluckemin, 12 miles away, "but the troops were so much exhausted, that they required a short respite from fatigue."[103] They made their way into the New Jersey highlands, protected from British attacks but exposed to harsher weather conditions than in the low country. Rodney explained why Washington had to pause in Pluckemin for two days: "Here he was obliged to encamp and await the coming up of nearly 1000 men who were not able through fatigue and hunger to keep up with the main body . . . the army in this situation was obliged to encamp on the bleak mountains whose tops were covered with snow, without even blankets to cover them."[104] Making matters

---

100 Commager and Morris, *SSS*, 521.

101 Peale, *Journal*, 281.

102 Rodney, *Diary of Captain Thomas Rodney*, 38.

103 Wilkinson, *Memoirs*, 149.

104 Rodney, *Diary of Captain Thomas Rodney*, 38.

worse, many still lacked proper shoes. According to Peale, "Many of the men, in their hard march on an icy road, were entirely barefooted. I got a raw hide to make them moccasins; but made a bad hand of it, for want of a proper needle or awl."[105]

As Washington rested his army in Pluckemin, he reflected on what his brave men had achieved over what has become known as the "Ten Crucial Days" between December 25, 1776, and January 3, 1777.[106] Subtly, Washington drafted a report to Congress describing the tenuous situation the Americans faced and how they again had turned looming defeat into a brilliant victory. His goal was to force the British and Hessians out of much of New Jersey, and as he described to John Hancock, "happily we succeeded."[107]

Washington's lieutenants agreed with the significance of their achievements. Henry Knox, who often shared the same views as his commander, explained, "[The British] have Collected the Whole Force and drawn themselves to one point to wit Brunswick. The enemy were within 19 miles of Philadelphia, they are now 60 miles we have driven [them] from almost the Whole of West Jersey—the Panic is still Kept up . . . in short my Lucy America has a prospect of seeing this part of it entirely rid of her Foes."[108] General Greene described, "The two last actions at Trenton and Princeton have put a very different face upon affairs."[109] He later wrote to the Governor of Rhode Island, "Ever since the Trenton affair we have had a continual train of success. The Lord seems to have smote the enemy with a panic. They are near three thousand weaker than they were a month ago." Alexander Hamilton recorded,

> After escaping the grasp of a disciplined and victorious enemy, this little band of patriots were seen skillfully avoiding an engagement until they could contend with advantage and then by the masterly enterprises of Trenton and Princeton, cutting them up in detachments, rallying the scattered energies of the country, infusing terror into the breasts of their invaders and changing the whole tide and fortune of the war.[110]

---

105 Peale, *Journal*, 283.

106 "Ten Crucial Days Campaign: 25 December 1776—3 January 1777," https://www.battlefields. org/learn/topics/ten-crucial-days-campaign, accessed Dec. 29, 2019.

107 *FONA*, https://founders.archives.gov/documents/Washington/03-07-02-0411, accessed Dec. 28, 2019.

108 Drake, *Life and Correspondence of Henry Knox*, 40.

109 The following two quotes are from Stryker, *BTP*, 463.

110 Hamilton, *The Life of Alexander Hamilton*, 1:60-61.

Although true, the war was far from over, and Washington's most immediate task was to find shelter for his army.

On January 6, after sending his report to Congress, Washington called on his men to take to the road to complete a final 12-mile leg on their journey to Morristown. Morristown was the perfect location to rebuild the tired American army during winter. Wilkinson described it as "a most safe one for the winter quarters of an army of observation . . . the approach to it from the sea-board is rendered difficult and dangerous by a chain of sharp hills."[111]

Washington established his headquarters at Morristown's Freeman Tavern on January 7, remaining there until May. The town was easily defendable and ideally located to monitor, harass, and attack the remaining British outposts in New Jersey. It was situated on a high plateau, with a mountain to its back and terrain that dropped into narrow draws to its sides, channeling those approaching. The nearby Whippany River provided ample water to sustain the army, and the town was within striking distance of the main post road, which connected New York to Philadelphia. Morristown was 20 to 30 miles from the main enemy posts in New York, Amboy, and Brunswick. Washington would leverage this position to his advantage in the coming weeks.

Howe and Cornwallis had learned the folly of widely dispersing their forces. By January 10, they consolidated the remaining 10,000-14,000 British and Hessian troops in New Jersey in Amboy and Brunswick. Placing this many troops in centralized locations provided greater security, but it also stretched their ability to sustain such a force adequately. Housing was inadequate and overcrowded, and fuel, food, and forage were sparse.

The Americans added to British challenges by consistently attacking foraging parties attempting to gather supplies. One British officer admitted that "Amboy and Brunswick were, in a manner besieged."[112] He shared how the Americans were "incessantly insulting, surprising, and cutting off their [British and Hessian] pickets and advanced guards; firm and undaunting amidst want, inclemency of weather, and difficulty and danger of any kind."[113]

Washington's persistence and victories galvanized the public behind the American cause, resulting in ample intelligence on British movements. The Americans used this knowledge to exploit every opportunity. Emboldened bands of

111 Wilkinson, *Memoirs*, 149.

112 Charles, Stedman, *The History of the Origin, Progress, and Termination of the American War,* 2 vols. (London, 1794), 240; Ward, *TWOR*, 322.

113 Tobias Smollett, ed., *The Critical Review: Or, Annals of Literature*, "Steadman's History of the American War," (London, 1795), 13:313-314; John Frost, *The Book of the Army: Comprising a General Military History of the United States* (New York, 1845), 77.

New Jersey militia spread across the countryside seeking to attack detached groups of British and Hessian soldiers venturing outside their armed camps. In some instances, Washington sent large armed groups to attack enemy concentrations. For example, 400 militiamen and 50 Pennsylvania riflemen led by General Dickinson defeated enemy troops and captured 40 wagonloads of plunder, 100 horses, and many cattle and sheep.[114] The Marines actively participated in these operations.

Casualties began mounting as the British and Hessians struggled through the winter, while Howe, secure in New York, planned a spring campaign to capture Philadelphia. Howe had 27,000 troops at his disposal, yet he chose to remain idle as Washington, with approximately 4,000 men, continued his harassing attacks. Author and soldier Charles Stedman asserted, "In this unfavourable and indecisive warfare it is supposed that more of the British were sacrificed than would have been lost in an attack on General Washington's whole force."[115] Blaming them for their losses, many British in New Jersey became displeased with their leaders. Just as some were quick to blame Rall following the defeat at Trenton, some began questioning Howe's leadership. One officer wrote,

> Indeed, I find our mistakes in the campaign were many and some very capital ones. . . . [Howe] makes a very good executive officer under another's command, but he is not by any means equal to a C. in C. [commander-in-chief] . . . He has, moreover, got none but silly fellows about him—a great parcel of old women—most of them improper for American service. . . . Gen. Howe is by no means equal to his present command.[116]

Another growing trend in letters sent home by British troops was a growing respect for the American fighting man. In March 1777, Lt. Col. William Harcourt, who had led the unit that captured General Lee, wrote his father,

> . . . whenever we attempt to return to our quarters we may be assured of their harassing us upon our retreat; that detached corps should never march without artillery, of which the rebels are extremely apprehensive . . . they possess some of the requisites for making good troops, such as extreme cunning, great industry in moving ground and felling of wood, activity and a spirit of enterprise upon any advantage . . . though it was once the fashion of this army to treat them in the most contemptible light, they are now become a formidable enemy.[117]

114 Ward, *TWOR*, 322.

115 Stedman, *History of the American War*, 240.

116 Commager & Morris, *SSS*, 524.

117 Edward Harcourt, ed., *The Harcourt Papers*, 13 vols. (Oxford, 1880-1905), 2:207-209.

Although becoming more formidable, the Continental Army and Marines still faced challenges. They, too, had to find shelter and subsistence for their men and animals. Morristown was a small village of around 50 buildings and was thus insufficient to house Washington's troops. Some slept in tents until they could build permanent cabins in the Lowantica Valley along the road leading to Morristown. Samuel Nicholas led his Marines to the village of "Sweet Town," two miles outside Morristown, to find billeting. Sergeant William Young of the Associators' 3rd Battalion recalled visiting the Marines in their quarters. "This afternoon went about 2 miles to see Major Nicholas at Sweet town to get a wagon . . . saw at Sweet town Captain Mullen and Peter Bedford, both well."[118]

The Marines and their army brothers also faced difficulties in acquiring food. Shortages due to the war and enterprising merchants resulted in increased costs at local markets. Major Nicholas was responsible for his Marines and had to submit a request to General Cadwalader for additional funds to feed his men. On January 11, Cadwalader responded by providing 10 additional pounds of currency for the Marines' use.[119]

In addition to food, the men also needed new clothing. It is well-documented how many Continental soldiers remained ill-clad throughout the winter campaign. The Marines were fortunate, having arrived from Philadelphia with serviceable uniforms. But after a month of hard campaigning under harsh weather conditions, they needed replacement uniforms and winter clothing. On January 16, Cadwalader provided the Marines with 21 pairs of shoes and 18 pairs of mittens, and an additional 28 pairs of shoes and mittens arrived on January 19. Though appreciated, these provisions were insufficient to meet the Marines' needs.

The shortage of personnel continued to be one of Washington's biggest challenges at Morristown. Washington had approximately 4,000 troops in the winter camp, but disease, desertions, casualties, and terminating enlistments continued to dwindle his numbers. The Marine battalion's muster report from January 8 provides insight into how these factors affected troop levels. The Continental Marines, who began the campaign with 120-130 men, had been reduced to only 78 men a month later. Nicholas reported one major, three captains, three first lieutenants, one second lieutenant, 10 sergeants, seven corporals, one fifer, one drummer, and 55 rank and file with 36 rounds per man on the rolls. The Marines did what they could to increase their numbers. Private John McKinley,

---

118 William Young, *Journal of Sergeant William Young, 3rd BN, Pennsylvania Militia*, PMHB, vol. 8 (1884), 272.

119 The information found in the following three paragraphs was derived from Smith, *MIR*, 102-104.

who in December was ordered by Captain Mullan to return to Philadelphia due to illness, was ordered by his company commander "to bring on certain Marines and Sailors who had been left sick in the Hospital, and to join the Army then in Morristown."[120] Though this helped, the battalion had limited days as a cohesive unit remaining.

The army was disintegrating before its commander-in-chief's eyes. Beginning on January 10, Rodney and his company of Delaware volunteers started leaving for home. On January 12, Captain Peale described how Cadwalader pleaded with the Associators to extend their service: "General Cadwalader harangued our Philadelphia militia, to induce them to stay over their limited time, but I think to little effect."[121] Cadwalader's 2nd Battalion remained one week longer, departing on January 19. Washington desperately wrote to Hancock and Congress that same day. "The fluctuating State of an Army composed chiefly of Militia, bids fair to reduce us to the Situation in which we were some little time ago, that is, of scarce having any Army at all, except [if] Reinforcements speedily arrive. One of the Battalions from the City of Philadelphia goes home to day, and the other two remain only a few days longer upon Courtesy." Washington's plea continues,

> The time for which, a country Brigade under Genl Mifflin, came out, is expired, and they stay from day to day by dint of Sollicitation. . . . We have about Eight hundred of the Eastern Continental Troops remaining. . . . The five Virginia Regiments are reduced to a handful of Men, as are Colo. Hands, Smallwoods and the German Battn.[122]

Even though Washington and other Continental regular officers had questioned the militiamen's ability following their experiences in New York, they now had nothing but praise for Cadwalader and his troops from Philadelphia, hoping they would remain. Washington wrote, "I fear those from Philadelphia will scarcely submit to the hardships of a winter Campaign much longer. . . . I must do them justice however to add, that they have undergone more fatigue and hardship than I expected Militia (especially Citizens) would have done at this inclement Season."[123] Greene agreed: "Great credit is due to the Philadelphia militia, their

120 Pension Records, Pvt. John McKinley, cited from Edwin McClellan, Personal Collection, Box 30, Folder 5, "History of the USMC, Navy and Marines at the Battles of Trenton and Princeton," Archives Branch, Marine Corps History Division, Quantico, VA.

121 Peale, *Journal*, 284.

122 *FONA*, https://founders.archives.gov/documents/Washington/03-08-02-0110, accessed Dec. 29, 2019.

123 *FONA*, https://founders.archives.gov/documents/Washington/03-07-02-0411, accessed Dec. 28, 2019.

behaviour at Trenton in the cannonade, and at Princeton was brave, firm and manly; they were broken at first in the action at Princeton, and soon formed in the face of grapeshot, and pushed on with a spirit that would do honor to veterans."[124]

On January 23, William Brown and the Pennsylvania State Marines departed with Cadwalader.[125] Brown later received a promotion to major, but no other records remain of his service. Thomas Forrest was promoted to major in March 1777 and lieutenant colonel in December 1778 before leaving the service. He later was a member of Congress.

The loss of William Shippin, "a Capt of Marines," was widely felt.[126] After he died in the early stages of the fighting at Princeton, soldiers buried Shippin at the Friends cemetery near Stony Brook. The army later disinterred his remains and transported them with that of General Mercer across the Delaware River, which finally froze over on January 17. The following day, the *Pennsylvania Evening Post* chronicled,

> Yesterday the remains of Captain William Shippin who was killed at Princeton the third instant, gloriously fighting for the liberty of his country were interred at St. Peters church-yard. His funeral was attended by the Council of Safety, the members of Assembly, officers of the Army, a troop of Virginia Light Horse, and a great number of inhabitants. This brave and unfortunate man was in his twenty-seventh year and has left a widow and three young children to lament the death of an affectionate husband and tender parent.[127]

Washington could not afford any more personnel losses. On January 19, he informed Congress,

> Thus you have a Sketch of our present Army, with which we are obliged to keep up Appearances, before an Enemy already double to us in Numbers, and who from every account are withdrawing their Troops from Rhode Island to form a junction of their whole Army, and make another Attempt either to break up ours, or penetrate towards Philada a thing by no means difficult now.[128]

---

124 Stryker, *BTP*, 472.

125 William Egle & John Linn, eds., *PAH*, 2nd series (Harrisburg, PA, 1874), 1:234.

126 Biddle, *Selections from the Military Papers of General John Cadwalader*, 158.

127 Extract from *Pennsylvania Evening Post*, 18 January 1777, quoted from McClellan, *History of the United States Marine Corps*, 1:68.

128 *FONA*, https://founders.archives.gov/documents/Washington/03-08-02-0110, accessed Dec. 29, 2019.

Terminating enlistments also impacted Henry Knox's indomitable artillerymen. According to Sergeant White, "The term of my enlistment being out, General Knox addressed the artillery in a pathetic manner to stay two months longer."[129] White chose to reenlist, but many more did not. Entire companies of artillerymen turned in their cannons and ammunition and headed home, resulting in "an excess of fieldpieces and a deficiency of men to work them by the end of the month."[130] These were desperate times. Searching for a way to mitigate the losses, Washington and Knox found a ready solution in the Continental Marines. These seafaring men who had previously operated ships' cannons would now man cannons in the field.

The Marine battalion was transferred to the artillery, moving from "Sweet Town" to Morristown to work directly under General Knox. Captain Isaac Craig, who previously commanded the Marines on the *Andrew Doria* and was later Nicholas' battalion adjutant, recalled, "In February we were ordered to join the Artillery and learn that Duty which Orders I gladly received As I had already acquired a considerable Knowledge both in the Theory and Practice of Gunnery and Projectives—Arts."[131] Nicholas's three companies, under the commands of Captains Mullan, Porter, and Dean, transitioned from infantry units to artillery companies over the coming months.

Captain Mullan's company was the first to receive a new assignment. On February 20, Mullan was ordered to escort 25 British prisoners to Philadelphia, where he was to await additional instructions from the Pennsylvania Committee of Safety. Mullan's Marines completed their assignment and established barracks on the east side of 2nd Street between Mulberry (now Arch) and Sassafras (now Rice) streets.[132] The Marines did not comport themselves well in their new home, later receiving charges for property damage. In April, Mullan and his men reestablished the Marine detachment on board the newly completed frigate *Delaware* and set sail to harass British ships.

Captains Craig and Porter continued to lead their Marines for approximately six weeks longer. Both resigned their commissions as the Marines prepared to return to sea duty, deciding to remain with the army as artillerymen. Porter received a commission in the 2nd Continental Artillery under Henry Knox, serving honorably throughout the remainder of the war. He later obtained the

129 "The Good Soldier White."

130 "Memorandum Book of Henry Knox, 16 January-21 March 1777," *Knox Papers*, MHS, quoted from Smith, *MIR*, 104.

131 *FONA*, https://founders.archives.gov/documents/Washington/03-19-02-0517, accessed Dec. 29, 2019.

132 Smith, *MIR*, 104.

rank of major general in the Pennsylvania militia. Before Porter's death at age 70 in 1813, President James Madison offered to name him secretary of war at the start of the War of 1812.[133] Craig received a commission in Col. Thomas Proctor's Pennsylvania artillery regiment, which later became the 4th Continental Artillery. He also served honorably throughout the war, obtaining the rank of major. Craig settled in Pittsburgh and was described as "one of the few remaining patriarchs of our land" on his passing in 1826.[134] The *Pittsburgh Gazette* described how Craig "sunk to his grave in a ripe old age, leaving to his family that best of all inheritances, an honorable name; not to be traced on monumental marble, or depending on a parchment record, but inscribed by the pen of valor, on the fields of American glory, and us immortal as the freedom of his country."

Captain Dean and his company continued to serve in the army artillery until April 1. They returned to Philadelphia to reestablish the Marine detachment on the frigate *Washington*, only to find her still unprepared for sea. The detachment remained in the shipyard while construction continued until their enlistments expired in June. Dean resigned his commission the following month; no accurate records exist covering the remainder of his life.

Serving in the artillery provided the Marines with an added benefit in the form of extra pay. Artillerymen received compensation for the special skills required to operate their cannons. Major Nicholas petitioned Congress to ensure that he and his men received their additional pay. On August 8, 1777, Congress agreed, proclaiming, "That there is due, to Major Samuel Nicholas, for himself and a detachment of three companies of Marines which he commanded on artillery duty, for which they were to receive additional pay, viz. Captain Porter's company, from 1st February to 1st July; Captain Mullen's company, from 1st February to the 1st April; and Captain Deane's company, from 1st February to the 1st April, the sum of 895 15/90."[135]

Following the various transfers to artillery units, the Marine battalion all but ceased to exist. It was an inglorious ending to a fast but historic run in support of Washington and the Continental Army. Once his companies had been dispersed, Maj. Samuel Nicholas returned to Philadelphia. He arrived in March, continuing to serve as the new nation's senior Marine. He performed several special projects for the government, including setting up new barracks in Philadelphia and leading

133 Ibid., 465.

134 The following two quotes are from Samuel Hazard, ed., *The Register of Pennsylvania: Devoted to the Preservation of Facts and Documents, And Every Kind of Useful Information Respecting the State of Pennsylvania* (Philadelphia, 1828), 304.

135 Library of Congress, *JCC*, 8:624.

the recruiting effort of new Marines to serve with the fleet. Nicholas continued his active service until 1781, when he requested assignment to the new frigate *America*. That ship, however, did not launch for another year and was given to France once complete. Congress determined that Nicholas's services were no longer needed. It resolved that his accounts be settled to August 25, 1781, at which point he was considered on the retired list. Nicholas returned to the job of tavernkeeper at the Conestoga Wagon on Market Street in Philadelphia. He remained active in community affairs until his death at the age of 46 in August 1790.[136]

While the formal designation of "Commandant of the Marine Corps" was not created until years later, Nicholas is commonly referred to as the first Commandant of the United States Marines. Through their efforts at Trenton and Princeton, Nicholas and his Marines provided an invaluable service to their country.

Reflecting upon the sentiments of the American people following the hard-won victories of Trenton and Princeton, author William Stryker noted,

> They [Americans] believed a final victory was near at hand, and that these successes were the dawn of a bright morning for the young republic. They were persuaded the great generals whose military genius and experience had been highly lauded could be outgeneraled by their Washington and could be beaten in detail by the division of the young New Hampshire attorney [Sullivan], the battalions of the New England blacksmith [Greene], or the guns directed by the bookseller of Boston [Knox].[137]

Perhaps a battalion of Marines, led by a Philadelphia tavernkeeper, should be added to this list. While they may have been few, Washington's Marines, comprised of Samuel Nicholas's Continental Marines and the state Marines under Thomas Shippin, William Brown, and others, served a critical role in the American Revolution. Rushing to the aid of George Washington and the Continental Army in their most desperate hour, their actions helped turn the tide of the war through the stunning victories at Trenton and Princeton. One can only speculate whether the army would have survived without the reinforcements provided by the Marines and others who answered the call. Few can argue that the fledgling nation could have endured without an army to defend her. Washington's Marines helped preserve the freedoms and liberties they and their fellow patriots held dear. In doing so, they established a legacy that generations of Marines strive to emulate to defend their great nation.

---

136 Smith, *MIR*, 460.

137 Stryker, *BTP*, 305-306.

Epilogue

The War of American Independence continued for six more years, but Princeton was the last time Marines received an assignment to conduct a land campaign directly under General Washington or the Continental Army. Though Marines operated shore batteries in defense of Charleston, South Carolina, in 1780, they primarily reverted to their principal duties of guarding naval installations ashore, providing ships' detachments at sea, and leading landing parties. They served particularly well in these roles under bold Continental Navy captains such as John Paul Jones. In 1778, Jones effectively employed Marines from the *Ranger* (18 guns) to invade the British homeland by harassing ports along the English coast. In 1779, defeating HMS *Serapis* (50 guns) while captain of the *Bon Homme Richard* (42 guns), Jones uttered those famous words, "I have not yet begun to fight."[1]

That same year, Marines participated in their next significant battle ashore as part of a naval campaign. The British established an advanced base at Penobscot Bay, guarded by an armed bastion dubbed Fort George, in what is now the state of Maine. The Americans devised a plan to clear the enemy from the area using an armada of 21 warships operating 200 cannons along with several support ships and a ground force commanded by Brig. Gen. Solomon Lovell of the Massachusetts Militia. Lovell's force consisted of nearly 1,000 militiamen, six field pieces, and 227 Continental and Massachusetts State Marines under the command of Continental

1 Morison, *John Paul Jones*, 231.

Marine Capt. John Welsh.[2] The Marines led the assault, resulting in the deaths of Welsh and 13 others, with 20 more wounded. Ultimately, the expedition failed after Lovell refused to attack the main British position after the navy failed to clear the area of enemy ships.

Marines participated in several other smaller landings and engagements at sea until the war's end. The absence of a credible threat and significant debt following the war resulted in the disbanding of the Continental Marines. In 1798 a new crisis involving France resulted in the permanent establishment of the United States Marine Corps.[3] That year, Congress sent President John Adams "An Act for Establishing and Organizing a Marine Corps," which created the United States Marine Corps as a separate, independent, and permanent branch of military service.[4] The act stated,

> Be it enacted by the Senate and House of Representatives of the United States of America, in Congress assembled, that in addition to the present military establishment, there shall be raised and organized a corps of marines, which shall consist of one major, four captains, sixteen first lieutenants, twelve second lieutenants, forty eight serjeants [sic], forty eight corporals, thirty two drums and fifes, and seven hundred and twenty privates, including the marines who have been enlisted, or are authorized to be raised for the naval armament; and the said corps may be formed into as many companies or detachments as the President of the United States shall direct, with a proper distribution of the commissioned and noncommissioned officers and musicians to each company or detachment.[5]

This act preserved the close tie between Marines and the Navy and authorized the president to deploy Marines ashore and at sea. But it confused matters when it stipulated that Marines would follow the Articles of War (Army regulations) when ashore but Navy regulations at sea. This created a situation in which policymakers and senior leaders of the U.S. Army and Navy believed the Marine Corps fell under their respective services, when in fact, this proved untrue.[6]

---

2 Welsh led the Marine detachment on the *Cabot* and participated in the raid on New Providence under Nicholas. He later commanded the detachment on the *Alfred* before being captured and imprisoned in England. Welsh escaped, returned to America, and was assigned to the *Warren*, at which time he led the Marine assault at Penobscot Bay. Smith, *MIR*, 477.

3 This conflict was referred to as the "Quasi-War." It was an undeclared war that was almost exclusively fought at sea between the United States and France from 1798 to 1800.

4 Richard Peters, ed., *The Public Statutes at Large of the United States of America; From the Organization in the Government in 1789, to March 3, 1845* (Boston, 1846), 1:594.

5 Ibid.

6 Millet, *Semper Fidelis*, 29.

This confusion led Congress to ratify another statute in 1834 to clarify the organization, entitlements, and regulations regarding Marines. The Act of June 30, 1834, "For the Better Organization of the Marine Corps," updated the size and organization of the Corps and solidified the Navy's control over certain aspects of the Marines, but was consistent with the act of 1798 in the provision that Marines "shall perform such other duties as the President may direct."[7] This provision opened the possibility of Marines operating ashore in extended land campaigns if that was what the president deemed necessary in achieving the country's national security interests.

Several presidents have enacted this provision throughout the Corps' history. In 1805, Lt. Presley O'Bannon led his Marines hundreds of miles across the Libyan desert to attack Derna on "the shores of Tripoli."[8] Marines fought ashore on numerous occasions in the War of 1812, including the defense of Washington, D.C., and under Andrew Jackson at the battle of New Orleans. In the 1830s, they supported the U.S. Army in the fight against the Seminoles in Georgia and Florida, and again in 1846 to secure California as a future state. Marines stormed the "Halls of Montezuma" in Mexico City in 1847 during the Mexican-American War, once again fighting beside their army brothers.[9] While under the command of Army Lt. Col. Robert E. Lee in October 1859, Marines recaptured the U.S. Arsenal at Harpers Ferry, Virginia, from abolitionist John Brown. During the American Civil War, Marines participated in the battles of Bull Run in 1861 and Fort Fisher in 1865 as part of larger army forces. In 1899, Marines fought an extended land campaign in the Philippines following the Spanish-American War and responded to a Chinese uprising in Peking during the Boxer Rebellion at the start of the 20th century.

The new century brought dramatic changes in the size and missions of Marines, but they continued to serve with the fleet while also conducting missions ashore. In 1914, Marines once again fought beside the Army in Mexico and conducted

---

7 Estes, *The Marine Officer's Guide*, 51.

8 The "Marines' Hymn" references "the shores of Tripoli" in recognition of O'Bannon's achievement. The first verse of the "Hymn" reads:

> From the Halls of Montezuma
> To the shores of Tripoli;
> We fight our country's battles
> In the air, on land, and sea;
> First to fight for right and freedom
> And to keep our honor clean;
> We are proud to claim the title
> Of United States Marine.

For more information, see https://www.loc.gov/item/ihas.200000011/, accessed Dec. 31, 2019.

9 Ibid.

several extended land campaigns in the Caribbean nations of Haiti, Nicaragua, Panama, and Santo Domingo during the "Banana Wars." The modern-day Marine Corps emerged between 1917-18 during the First World War. Assigned to the army's 2nd Infantry Division, the Marines gained fame and lore for their fighting ability at such battles as Belleau Wood, Soissons, and Blanc Mont, France. In 1941, Marines defended Wake Island, Iceland, and fought beside the Army in defense of the Philippines at the start of World War II. Yet they did not venture far from the fleet throughout the island-hopping campaigns in the Pacific until the end of the war. Following the Japanese surrender in 1945, Marines were charged with occupying China for the next two years to keep Chinese Nationalists and Communists separated from one another.

The 1950s found the Marines fighting ashore again during the Korean War. Marines came to the aid of the 8th Army in the Pusan Perimeter and recaptured the capital of Seoul following an amphibious assault at Inchon. They concluded the year 1950 by fighting in the mountains of North Korea in an area known as the Chosin Reservoir and began 1951 by fighting in central Korea at the start of a two-year struggle known as the "Outpost War."

The National Security Act of 1947 unified the armed forces of the United States following the Second World War. In 1951, as the Marines were decisively engaged against the Chinese in Korea, the 82nd Congress of the United States ratified the Douglas-Mansfield Bill (Public Law 416) which made amendments to the National Security Act that proved most important to the Marines. The Bill made the following provisions for the Marine Corps:

1. It reaffirms the Corps' status as a service within the Department of the Navy.

2. It provides for Fleet Marine Forces, ground, and aviation.

3. It requires that the combatant forces of the Corps be organized on the basis of three Marine divisions and three air wings and sets a 400,000-man peacetime ceiling for the regular Corps (the Marine Corps consisted of approximately 186,000 personnel in 2020).

4. It assigns the Corps the missions of seizures and defense of advanced naval bases, as well as land operations incident to naval campaigns.

5. It gives the Marine Corps a primary responsibility for development of amphibious warfare doctrines, tactics, techniques, and equipment employed by landing forces.

6. It seats the Commandant of the Marine Corps on the Joint Chiefs of Staff.

7. It affords the Marine Corps appropriate representation on various joint Defense Department agencies, notably the Joint Staff.

8. It assigns the Marine Corps collateral missions of providing security forces for naval shore stations; providing ships detachments; and performing such other duties as the president may direct.[10]

In passing this Bill, Congress had codified the roles and missions of Marines in public law. It recognized the Marines' expanded role to serve in air, land, and at sea. It established a permanent structure to prevent political leaders from attempting to diminish or disband the Corps. Congress's actions proved justified throughout the remainder of the 1950s and 1960s. In 1965, Marines deployed as the first U.S. combat troops to land in Vietnam and remained there for the next 10 years. Marines conducted several missions other than war throughout the 1970s and 1980s and faced further changes in its operations with the ratification of the Goldwater-Nichols Department of Defense Reorganization Act of 1986.[11] The Goldwater-Nichols Act represented the first significant shift in the U.S. National Defense apparatus since the creation of the Department of Defense in 1947. Congress enacted it partly to mitigate inefficiencies by forcing the armed services to organize and operate more effectively as a joint force.

Marines adapted well to this new approach since they habitually operated in all warfighting domains, and the Corps augmented its implementation in 1989 by introducing a new warfighting philosophy for Marines—"maneuver warfare."[12] The Marines operationalized this new concept the following year during Operation Desert Storm.

During the 1990s, the Marine Corps reaffirmed its role as the nation's premier crisis response force, demonstrating its versatility in responding to crises and contingencies across a vast spectrum. In the new millennium, the direction of the Marine Corps took a dramatic shift following the tragic events of September 11, 2001. Following the invasions of Afghanistan and Iraq, Marines once again conducted protracted land campaigns, causing some to see them as a second land army.

---

10 Estes, *The Marine Officer's Guide*, 53.

11 "H.R.3622 - Goldwater-Nichols Department of Defense Reorganization Act of 1986," https://www.congress.gov/bill/99th-congress/house-bill/3622, accessed Dec. 31, 2019.

12 *Marine Corps Doctrinal Publication 1, Warfighting*, 72-76.

As of 2020, Marines have maintained a presence in Afghanistan and Iraq (with a four-year hiatus in Iraq) approaching twenty years in length. Some voiced concern that employing Marines in this way degraded their ability to perform their primary role of supporting naval campaigns. Dakota Wood, senior research fellow for the Heritage Foundation, writes,

> The Corps is currently very good at land-based crisis response missions, contributing to America's special operations community, conducting sustained land operations in support of U.S. partners, and supporting regional combatant command requirements to work with partner nations to improve mutual capabilities. However, it lacks meaningful experience in and relevant organizations and capabilities for its primary role: contributing to the prosecution of a naval campaign.[13]

While there is truth in Wood's assertion, the distinction between land and naval campaigns is becoming blurred. The 21st century has ushered in a new era of warfare. The traditional domains of air, land, and sea are now joined by cyber and space. Information operations and controlling the narrative have also risen in prominence. Globalization, the "Internet of Things," and the proliferation of advanced and emerging technologies have created a situation in which the levels of war now overlap, and tactical actions can have strategic implications. Marines today must be proficient in achieving kinetic and non-kinetic effects to accomplish their assigned missions. They must not only be proficient in operating on air, land, and sea but also in the virtual and cognitive worlds and within the electromagnetic spectrum.

The increased capacity, reach, and lethality of today's weapons platforms allow Marines to shape and influence operations far from the sea. Improved sensors, intelligence, surveillance, reconnaissance systems, long-range precision weapons, and transport capabilities enable Marines to effectively operate hundreds of miles from sea-based platforms as part of naval campaigns. For example, the MV-22 Osprey tilt-rotor aircraft employed by Marines can lift 24 Marines over 400 nautical miles, with the ability to conduct aerial refueling and travel farther if required.[14] This new capability and many others increase the versatility of Marines in achieving national security objectives, whether at sea or ashore.

Recognizing the need to remain a step ahead of would-be adversaries and to adapt to an evolving operating environment, the Marine Corps embarked on

13 Dakota Wood, *Rebuilding America's Military: The United States Marine Corps,* The Heritage Foundation's Rebuilding America's Military Project, Special Report, No. 211 (Mar. 21, 2019), 1.

14 "Boeing MV-22 Osprey," https://www.boeing.com/defense/v-22-osprey/, accessed July 14, 2019.

a journey to reaffirm its close ties to the fleet while modernizing to address new and emerging threats. In 2016, the Commandant of the Marine Corps published the *Marine Operating Concept* (MOC). The MOC acknowledged the Marine Corps' shortfalls in meeting the demands of the future operating environment and "describes the steps we [Marines] will take to design, develop, and field a future force for the 21st century."[15]

The Marines followed the MOC by devising three operating concepts that describe the way Marines may operate in the future. The *Littoral Operations in a Contested Environment* (LOCE) reaffirms the Marine Corps' role in support of naval campaigns. It acknowledges that Marines' power projection capabilities extend their operations hundreds of miles inland.[16] The *Expeditionary Advanced Base Operations* (EABO) concept describes how Marines will employ land-based systems to complement and extend the reach of sea-based systems in influencing and controlling the seas.[17] Finally, Marines devised *A Concept for Stand-in Forces* to describe how Marines will disrupt an adversary's plans at every point on the competition continuum while operating from inside contested areas.[18] These concepts assist Marines in coordination with the Navy to prepare for the most-dangerous scenarios at the high end of the spectrum of conflict. Additionally, it provides the flexibility to address the most-likely scenarios that have frequently resulted in the president invoking the clause of "all other missions as may be directed."[19]

In 2019, Gen. David Berger, Commandant of the Marine Corps, published his guidance to drive the United States Marines' preparations for future conflicts.[20] He clearly stated his vision for the Marines:

15 Robert Neller, *The Marine Operating Concept: How an Expeditionary Force Operates in the 21st Century*, Washington, D.C., Headquarters, United States Marine Corps, Sept. 2016, i.

16 Robert Neller and John Richardson, *Littoral Operations in a Contested Environment*, Washington, D.C., Headquarters, United States Marine Corps, 2017.

17 Art Corbett, *Expeditionary Advanced Base Operations (EABO) Handbook*, Marine Corps Warfighting Lab, Concepts & Plans Division, 2018, found at https://mca-marines.org/wp-content/uploads/Expeditionary-Advanced-Base-Operations-EABO-handbook-1.1.pdf, accessed Dec. 31, 2019.

18 David Berger, *A Concept for Stand-in Forces*, Washington, D.C., Headquarters, United States Marine Corps, Dec. 2021.

19 Estes, *The Marine Officer's Guide*, 53.

20 David Berger, "Commandant's Planning Guidance: 38th Commandant of the Marine Corps," https://www.hqmc.marines.mil/Portals/142/Docs/%2038th%20Commandant%27s%20Planning%20Guidance_2019.pdf?ver=2019-07-16-200152-700, accessed Sept. 5, 2020.

The Marine Corps will be trained and equipped as a naval expeditionary force-in-readiness and prepared to operate inside actively contested maritime spaces in support of fleet operations. In crisis prevention and crisis response, the Fleet Marine Force—acting as an extension of the Fleet—will be first on the scene, first to help, first to contain a brewing crisis, and first to fight if required to do so.[21]

Regardless of the crisis or contingency, Marines will continue to answer the nation's call, whether on sea or ashore, virtually, or cognitively. Today's Marines will follow the legacy established under Samuel Nicholas, who adapted their seafaring abilities to support General Washington and the Continental Army in their greatest time of need. They will forever remain *Semper Fidelis*.

21 Ibid.

Marine Corps Birthday Message

John A. Lejeune, 13th Commandant of the United States Marine Corps

On November 10, 1775, a Corps of Marines was created by a resolution of the Continental Congress. Since that date many thousand men have borne the name Marine. In memory of them it is fitting that we who are Marines should commemorate the birthday of our Corps by calling to mind the glories of its long and illustrious history.

The record of our Corps is one which will bear comparison with that of the most famous military organizations in the world's history. During 90 of the 167 years of its existence the Marine Corps has been in action against the Nation's foes. From the battle of Trenton to the Argonne, Marines have won foremost honors in war, and in the long eras of tranquility at home generation after generation of Marines have grown gray in war in both hemispheres, and in every corner of the seven seas, that our country and its citizens might enjoy peace and security.

In every battle and skirmish since the birth of our Corps Marines have acquitted themselves with the greatest distinction, winning new honors on each occasion until the term "Marine" has come to signify all that is highest in military efficiency and soldierly virtue.

This high name of distinction and soldierly repute we who are Marines today have received from those who preceded us in the Corps. With it we also received from them the eternal spirit which has animated our Corps from generation to generation and has been the distinguishing mark of Marines in every age. So long as that spirit continues to flourish Marines will be found equal to every emergency in the future as they have been in the past, and the men of our Nation will regard us as worthy successors to the long line of illustrious men who have served as "Soldiers of the Sea" since the founding of the Corps.

Appendix B

Gen. Washington's Orders to Col. John Cadwalader, 12 December 1776

Head Quarters—Trenton Falls

*Y*ou are to post your Brigade at and near Bristol. Colonel Nixon's Regiment to continue where it is at Dunk's Ferry—but if you find from reconnoitering the ground, or from any movements of the enemy, that any other disposition is necessary, you'll make it accordingly without waiting to hear from me, but to acquaint me with the alterations and the reasons for it as soon as possible. You'll establish the necessary guards and throw up some little Redoubts at Dunk's Ferry and the different passes in the Neshamine.

Pay particular attention to Dunk's Ferry, as its not improbable something may be attempted there. Spare no pains or expense to get intelligence of the enemy's motions and intentions. Any promises made, or sums advanced, shall be fully complied with and discharged. Keep proper Patrols going from guard to guard. Every piece of intelligence you obtain worthy notice, send it forward by express.

If the enemy attempt a landing on this side, you'll give them all the opposition in your power. Should they land between Trenton Falls and Bordentown Ferry or any where above Bristol, and you find your force quite unequal to their force give them what opposition you can at Neshamine ferry and fords. In a word you are to give them all the opposition you can without hazzarding the loss of your Brigade.

Keep a good guard over such boats as are not scuttled or rendered unfit for use. Keep a good lookout for spies, and endeavor to magnify your number as much as possible. Let the troops always have three days' provisions cookt beforehand. Indeavor to keep your Troops as much together as possible, night and day, that they may be ever in readiness to march upon the shortest notice.

You'll consult with the Commodore of the Gallies, and indeavor to form such an arrangement as will most effectually guard the river. To your discretion and prudence I submit any further regulations and recommend the greatest degree of vigilence.

If you should find yourself unable to defend the passes of the Neshamine or the enemy should rout you from your post, you are to repair to the strong ground, near Germantown unless you have orders from me or some other general officer to the contrary. Be particularly attentive to the roads and vessels and suffer no person to pass over to the Jerseys without a permit.[1]

1 *FONA*, https://founders.archives.gov/documents/Washington/03-07-02-0240, accessed Nov. 23, 2019.

Bibliography

Primary Sources

Manuscript Collections

Congressional Library, Washington, D.C.

Nicholas, Samuel, "Report to the President of the Congress, August 10, 1789," Congressional Library; MS Division, Papers of the Continental Congress, 78-17-301

Connecticut Historical Society, Hartford, CT

Collections of the Connecticut Historical Society, Vol. 7, "Orderly book and journals kept by Connecticut men while taking part in the American Revolution." 1775-78, 1899

Historical Manuscripts Commission, London, England

Hastings Manuscripts

Historical Society of Pennsylvania, Philadelphia, PA

Cadwalader Papers

Historical Society of Pennsylvania, Trenton, PA

Clyde, John, Rosbrugh, "A Tale of the Revolution," Paper read before the Historical Society of Pennsylvania, 15 January 1880

Marine Corps History Division, Archives Branch, Quantico, VA

McClellan, Edwin, Personal Collection

Massachusetts Historical Society, Boston, MA

Newell, Timothy, Personal Journal of Timothy Newell, Massachusetts Historical Society Collection, 4th Series, Vol. 1

Proceedings of the Massachusetts Historical Society, 3rd Series, Vol. 59 (Oct. 1925-Jun. 1926)

Navy History Division, Washington, D.C.

Clark, William, ed., *Naval Documents of The American Revolution*, Vols. 1-3, Washington, D.C.: U.S. Naval History Division, 1964-68.

Morgan, William, ed. *Naval Documents of the American Revolution*, Vols. 4-7, Washington, D.C.: U.S. Naval History Division, 1972-76.

Parliament of the United Kingdom, London, England

The Parliamentary Register; or, History of the Proceedings and Debates of the House of Commons containing an account of the most interesting speeches and motions; accurate copies of the most remarkable letters and papers; of the most material evidence, petitions, &c. laid before and offered to the House, during the Fifth Session of the Fourteenth Parliament of Great Britain, 16 Vols. (Vols. 10 & 11). London: Wilson and Co. Wild Court, 1802.

Pennsylvania State Archives, Harrisburg, PA

Egle, William and Linn, John, eds. 2nd Series, Vol. 1., Harrisburg, PA: State Printer, 1874

Pennsylvania State Archives, Philadelphia, PA

Hazard, Samuel, 1st Series, Vol. 5. Philadelphia: Josh Severns and Co., 1853

Revolutionary War Pension Records, National Archives, Washington, D.C.

Case of Private John McKinley

Online Collections

"Founders Online" Articles and Documents

Author's Note: The following sources were consulted at "Founders Online," an online database of the National Archives consisting of historical documents produced by the Founders of the United States.

"Address from the Massachusetts Provincial Congress, July 3, 1775," https://founders.archives.gov/documents/ Washington/03-01-02-0026 [Original source: *The Papers of George Washington*, Revolutionary War Series, Vol. 1, June 16-September 15, 1775, Philander D. Chase, ed. Charlottesville: University Press of Virginia, 1985, 52-53], accessed Aug. 11, 2019.

"Editorial Note: Declaration of the Causes and Necessity for Taking Up Arms," https://founders.archives.gov/ documents/Jefferson/01-01-02-0113-0001 [Original source: *The Papers of Thomas Jefferson*, Vol. 1, 1760-76, Julian P. Boyd, ed. Princeton, NJ: Princeton University Press, 1950, 187-192], accessed Aug. 11, 2019.

"Enclosure: Inventory of Artillery, 17 December 1775," https://founders.archives.gov/documents/ Washington/03-02-02-0521-0002 [Original source: *The Papers of George Washington*, Revolutionary War Series, Vol. 2, September 16-December 31, 1775, Philander D. Chase, ed. Charlottesville, VA: University Press of Virginia, 1987, 565-566], accessed Aug. 25, 2019.

"From George Washington to Brigadier General Alexander McDougall, December 28, 1776," last modified June 13, 2018, http://founders.archives.gov/documents/Washington/03-07-02-0366 [Original source: *The Papers of George Washington*, Revolutionary War Series, Vol. 7, October 21, 1776-January 5, 1777, Philander D. Chase, ed. Charlottesville, VA: University Press of Virginia, 1997, 471-472], accessed Aug. 11, 2019.

"From George Washington to Brigadier General Alexander McDougall, December 28, 1776," last modified June 13, 2018, http://founders.archives.gov/documents/Washington/03-07-02-0366 [Original source: *The Papers of George Washington*, Vol. 7, 471-472], accessed Dec. 25, 2019.

"From George Washington to Colonel John Cadwalader, December 7, 1776," https://founders.archives.gov/ documents/Washington/03-07-02-0205 [Original source: *The Papers of George Washington*, Vol. 7, 268-269], accessed Nov. 21, 2019.

"From George Washington to Colonel John Cadwalader, December 24, 1776," https://founders.archives.gov/ documents/Washington/03-07-02-0332 [Original source: *The Papers of George Washington*, Vol. 7, 425-426], accessed Dec. 14, 2019.

"From George Washington to Colonel John Cadwalader, December 25, 1776," last modified June 13, 2018, http://founders.archives.gov/documents/Washington/03-07-02-0343 [Original source: *The Papers of George Washington*, Vol. 7, 439], accessed Aug. 11, 2019.

"From George Washington to Colonel John Cadwalader or Brigadier General Thomas Mifflin, January 1, 1777," https://founders.archives.gov/documents/Washington/03-07-02-0404 [Original source: *The Papers of George Washington*, Vol. 7, 510-511], accessed Aug. 11, 2019.

"From George Washington to Colonel Joseph Reed, December 23, 1776," http://founders.archives.gov/documents/Washington/03-07-02-0329 [Original source: *The Papers of George Washington*, Vol. 7, 423-424], accessed Nov. 23, 2019.

"From George Washington to Colonel Richard Humpton, 1 December 1776," https://founders.archives.gov/documents/Washington/03-07-02-0179 [Original source: *The Papers of George Washington*, Vol. 7, 248-249], accessed Nov. 23, 2022.

"From George Washington to John Augustine Washington, July 27, 1775," https://founders.archives.gov/documents/Washington/03-01-02-0115 [Original source: *The Papers of George Washington*, Vol. 1, 183-185], accessed Aug. 11, 2019.

"From George Washington to John Hancock, August 4-5, 1775," https://founders.archives.gov/documents/Washington/03-01-02-0150 [Original source: *The Papers of George Washington*, Vol. 1, 223-239], accessed Aug. 11, 2019.

"From George Washington to John Hancock, September 21, 1775," https://founders.archives.gov/documents/Washington/03-02-02-0025 [Original source: *The Papers of George Washington*, Vol. 2, 24-30], accessed Aug. 15, 2019.

"From George Washington to John Hancock, November 19, 1775," https://founders.archives.gov/documents/Washington/03-02-02-0367 [Original source: *The Papers of George Washington*, Vol. 2, 398-400], accessed Aug. 12, 2019.

"From George Washington to John Hancock, November 28, 1775," https://founders.archives.gov/documents/Washington/03-02-02-0404 [Original source: *The Papers of George Washington*, Vol. 2, 444-448], accessed Dec. 31, 2019.

"From George Washington to John Hancock, December 4, 1775," https://founders.archives.gov/documents/Washington/03-02-02-0437 [Original source: *The Papers of George Washington*, Vol. 2, 483-487], accessed Aug, 11, 2019.

"From George Washington to John Hancock, March 7-9, 1776," https://founders.archives.gov/documents/Washington/03-03-02-0309 [Original source: *The Papers of George Washington*, Revolutionary War Series, Vol. 3, January 1-31 March 1776, Philander D. Chase, ed. Charlottesville, VA: University Press of Virginia, 1988, 420-428], accessed Aug. 25, 2019.

"From George Washington to John Hancock, September 2, 1776," https://founders.archives.gov/documents/Washington/03-06-02-0162 [Original source: *The Papers of George Washington*, Revolutionary War Series, Vol. 6, August 13-20 October 1776, Philander D. Chase and Frank E. Grizzard, Jr., eds. Charlottesville, VA: University Press of Virginia, 1994, 199-201], accessed Sept. 30, 2019.

"From George Washington to John Hancock, September 8, 1776," https://founders.archives.gov/documents/Washington/03-06-02-0203 [Original source: *The Papers of George Washington*, Vol. 6, 248-254], accessed Oct. 1, 2019.

"From George Washington to John Hancock, September 16, 1776," https://founders.archives.gov/documents/Washington/03-06-02-0251 [Original source: *The Papers of George Washington*, Vol. 6, 313-317], accessed Oct. 5, 2019.

"From George Washington to John Hancock, September 18, 1776," https://founders.archives.gov/documents/Washington/03-06-02-0264 [Original source: *The Papers of George Washington*, Vol. 6, 331-337], accessed Oct. 5, 2019.

"From George Washington to John Hancock, September 22, 1776," https://founders.archives.gov/documents/Washington/03-06-02-0288 [Original source: *The Papers of George Washington*, Vol. 6, 369-370], accessed Oct. 6, 2019.

"From George Washington to John Hancock, September 25, 1776," https://founders.archives.gov/documents/ Washington/03-06-02-0305 [Original source: *The Papers of George Washington*, Vol. 6, 393-401], accessed Oct. 6, 2019.

"From George Washington to John Hancock, September 25, 1776," https://founders.archives.gov/documents/ Washington/03-06-02-0306 [Original source: *The Papers of George Washington*, Vol. 6, 401-402], accessed Oct. 13, 2019.

"From George Washington to John Hancock, November 6, 1776," https://founders.archives.gov/documents/ Washington/03-07-02-0067 [Original source: *The Papers of George Washington*, Vol. 7, 96-100], accessed Oct. 13, 2019.

"From George Washington to John Hancock, November 19-21, 1776," https://founders.archives.gov/documents/ Washington/03-07-02-0128 [Original source: *The Papers of George Washington*, Vol. 7, 180-186], accessed Oct. 19, 2019.

"From George Washington to John Hancock, November 30, 1776," https://founders.archives.gov/documents/ Washington/03-07-02-0168 [Original source: *The Papers of George Washington*, Vol. 7, 232-234], accessed Nov. 14, 2019.

"From George Washington to John Hancock, December 11, 1776," https://founders.archives.gov/documents/ Washington/03-07-02-0232 [Original source: *The Papers of George Washington*, Vol. 7, 296-298], accessed Nov. 23, 2019.

"From George Washington to John Hancock, December 20, 1776," https://founders.archives.gov/documents/ Washington/03-07-02-0305 [Original source: *The Papers of George Washington*, Vol. 7, 381-389], accessed Dec. 1, 2019.

"From George Washington to John Hancock, December 27, 1776," http://founders.archives.gov/documents/ Washington/03-07-02-0355 [Original source: *The Papers of George Washington*, Vol. 7, 454-461], accessed Aug. 11, 2019.

"From George Washington to John Hancock, January 5, 1777," https://founders.archives.gov/documents/ Washington/03-07-02-0411 [Original source: *The Papers of George Washington*, Vol. 7, 519-530], accessed Aug. 11, 2019.

"From George Washington to John Hancock, January 19, 1777," https://founders.archives.gov/documents/ Washington/03-08-02-0110 [Original source: *The Papers of George Washington*, Revolutionary War Series, Vol. 8, 6 January-27 March 1777, Frank E. Grizzard, Jr., ed. Charlottesville, VA: University Press of Virginia, 1998, 102-104], accessed Dec. 29, 2019.

"From George Washington to John Hancock, January 22, 1777," https://founders.archives.gov/documents/ Washington/03-08-02-0135 [Original source: *The Papers of George Washington*, Vol. 8, 125-129], accessed Nov. 21, 2019.

"From George Washington to Lund Washington, October 6, 1776," https://founders.archives.gov/documents/ Washington/03-06-02-0379 [Original source: *The Papers of George Washington*, Vol. 6, 493-495], accessed Oct. 6, 2019.

"From George Washington to Lund Washington, December 10-17, 1776," https://founders.archives.gov/ documents/Washington/03-07-02-0228 [Original source: *The Papers of George Washington*, Vol. 7, 289-292], accessed Nov. 24, 2019.

"From George Washington to Major General Charles Lee, November 21, 1776," https://founders.archives.gov/ documents/Washington/03-07-02-0137 [Original source: *The Papers of George Washington*, Vol. 7, 193-195], accessed Oct. 20, 2019.

"From George Washington to Major General Charles Lee, December 1, 1776," https://founders.archives.gov/ documents/Washington/03-07-02-0180 [Original source: *The Papers of George Washington*, Vol. 7, 249-250], accessed Nov. 16, 2019.

"From George Washington to Major General Charles Lee, December 14, 1776," https://founders.archives.gov/ documents/Washington/03-07-02-0267 [Original source: *The Papers of George Washington*, Vol. 7, 335-336], accessed Nov. 24, 2019.

"From George Washington to Major General Horatio Gates, December 14, 1776," https://founders.archives. gov/documents/Washington/03-07-02-0265 [Original source: *The Papers of George Washington*, Vol. 7, 333-334], accessed Nov. 24, 2019.

"From George Washington to Major General Israel Putnam, January 5, 1777," https://founders.archives.gov/documents/Washington/03-07-02-0416 [Original source: *The Papers of George Washington*, Vol. 7, 535-536], accessed Dec. 28, 2019.

"From George Washington to Major General Nathanael Greene, November 8, 1776," https://founders.archives.gov/documents/Washington/03-07-02-0078 [Original source: *The Papers of George Washington*, Vol. 7, 115-117], accessed Oct. 13, 2019.

"From George Washington to Major General Philip Schuyler, July 28, 1775," https://founders.archives.gov/documents/Washington/03-01-02-0118 [Original source: *The Papers of George Washington*, Vol. 1, 188-190], accessed Aug. 11, 2019.

"From George Washington to Robert Morris, December 25, 1776," https://founders.archives.gov/documents/Washington/03-07-02-0344 [Original source: *The Papers of George Washington*, Vol. 7, 439-441], accessed July 12, 2020.

"From George Washington to Robert Morris, December 30, 1776," https://founders.archives.gov/documents/Washington/03-07-02-0382 [Original source: *The Papers of George Washington*, Vol. 7, 489], accessed Dec. 25, 2019.

"From George Washington to the Commanding Officer at Morristown, December 30, 1776," https://founders.archives.gov/documents/Washington/03-07-02-0385 [Original source: *The Papers of George Washington*, Vol. 7, 490-491], accessed Dec. 25, 2019.

"From George Washington to the Executive Committee of the Continental Congress, January 1, 1777," https://founders.archives.gov/documents/Washington/03-07-02-0395 [Original source: *The Papers of George Washington*, Vol. 7, 499-501], accessed Dec. 25, 2019.

"From George Washington to William Livingston, November 23, 1776," https://founders.archives.gov/documents/Washington/03-07-02-0140 [Original source: *The Papers of George Washington*, Vol. 7, 198], accessed Oct. 20, 2019.

"General Orders, January 1, 1777," https://founders.archives.gov/documents/Washington/03-07-02-0393 [Original source: *The Papers of George Washington*, Vol. 7, 499], accessed Dec. 24, 2019.

"Instructions to Colonel Henry Knox, November 16, 1775," https://founders.archives.gov/documents/Washington/03-02-02-0351 [Original source: *The Papers of George Washington*, Vol. 2, 384-385], accessed Aug. 12, 2019.

"Orders to Brigadier General James Ewing, December 12, 1776," https://founders.archives.gov/documents/Washington/03-07-02-0242 [Original source: *The Papers of George Washington*, Vol. 7, 306-307], accessed Nov. 23, 2019.

"Orders to Brigadier General Philemon Dickinson, December 12, 1776," https://founders.archives.gov/documents/Washington/03-07-02-0241 [Original source: *The Papers of George Washington*, Vol. 7, 305], accessed Nov. 23, 2019.

"Orders to Colonel John Cadwalader, December 12, 1776," https://founders.archives.gov/documents/Washington/03-07-02-0240 [Original source: *The Papers of George Washington*, Vol. 7, 304-305], accessed Nov. 23, 2019.

"General Orders, July 9, 1776," https://founders.archives.gov/documents/Washington/03-05-02-0176 [Original source: *The Papers of George Washington*, Revolutionary War Series, Vol. 5, 16 June-12 August 1776, Philander D. Chase, ed. Charlottesville, VA: University Press of Virginia, 1993, 245-247], accessed Sept. 1, 2019.

"To George Washington from Colonel John Cadwalader, December 15, 1776," http://founders.archives.gov/documents/Washington/03-07-02-0273 [Original source: *The Papers of George Washington*, Vol. 7, 341-344], accessed Nov. 23, 2019.

"To George Washington from Colonel John Cadwalader, December 26, 1776," https://founders.archives.gov/documents/Washington/03-07-02-0347 [Original source: *The Papers of George Washington*, Vol. 7, 442-444], accessed Dec. 15, 2019.

"To George Washington from Colonel John Cadwalader, December 31, 1776," https://founders.archives.gov/documents/Washington/03-07-02-0386 [Original source: *The Papers of George Washington*, Vol. 7, 491-495], accessed Dec. 25, 2019.

"To George Washington from Colonel Joseph Reed, December 12, 1776," https://founders.archives.gov/documents/Washington/03-07-02-0251 [Original source: *The Papers of George Washington*, Vol. 7, 317-318], accessed Nov. 23, 2019.

"To George Washington from Colonel Joseph Reed, December 22, 1776," https://founders.archives.gov/documents/Washington/03-07-02-0324 [Original source: *The Papers of George Washington*, Vol. 7, 414-417], accessed Dec. 3, 2019.

"To George Washington from John Adams, January 6, 1776," https://founders.archives.gov/documents/Washington/03-03-02-0023 [Original source: *The Papers of George Washington*, Vol. 3, 36-38], accessed Aug. 30, 2019.

"To George Washington from John Hancock, October 5, 1775," https://founders.archives.gov/documents/Washington/03-02-02-0099 [Original source: *The Papers of George Washington*, Vol. 2, 106-107], accessed Aug. 11, 2019.

"To George Washington from John Hancock, December 8, 1775," https://founders.archives.gov/documents/Washington/03-02-02-0465 [Original source: *The Papers of George Washington*, Vol. 2, 513-515], accessed Dec. 31, 2019.

"To George Washington from John Hancock, September 10, 1776," https://founders.archives.gov/documents/Washington/03-06-02-0218 [Original source: *The Papers of George Washington*, Vol. 6, 273], accessed Oct. 1, 2019.

"To George Washington from Brigadier General Thomas Mifflin, December 28, 1776," http://founders.archives.gov/documents/Washington/03-07-02-0368 [Original source: *The Papers of George Washington*, Vol. 7, 473-475], accessed Aug. 11, 2019.

"To George Washington from Captain Isaac Craig, March 18, 1779," https://founders.archives.gov/documents/Washington/03-19-02-0517 [Original source: *The Papers of George Washington*, Revolutionary War Series, Vol. 19, 15 January-7 April 1779, Philander D. Chase and William M. Ferraro, eds. Charlottesville, VA: University of Virginia Press, 2009, 524-526], accessed Aug. 11, 2019.

"To George Washington from Colonel John Cadwalader, December 26, 1776," http://founders.archives.gov/documents/Washington/03-07-02-0347 [Original source: *The Papers of George Washington*, Vol. 7, 442-444], accessed Dec. 25, 2019.

"To George Washington from Colonel John Cadwalader, December 27, 1776,", http://founders.archives.gov/documents/Washington/03-07-02-0353 [Original source: *The Papers of George Washington*, Vol. 7, 451-452], accessed Aug. 11, 2019.

"To George Washington from Colonel John Cadwalader, December 28, 1776," http://founders.archives.gov/documents/Washington/03-07-02-0361 [Original source: *The Papers of George Washington*, Vol. 7, 464-465], accessed Aug. 11, 2019.

"To George Washington from Colonel John Cadwalader, December 31, 1776," https://founders.archives.gov/documents/Washington/03-07-02-0386 [Original source: *The Papers of George Washington*, Vol. 7, 491-495], accessed Aug. 11, 2019.

"To George Washington from Colonel Joseph Reed, December 22, 1776," http://founders.archives.gov/documents/Washington/03-07-02-0324 [Original source: *The Papers of George Washington*, Vol. 7, 414-417], accessed Aug. 11, 2019.

"To George Washington from Commodore Esek Hopkins, May 1, 1776," https://founders.archives.gov/documents/Washington/03-04-02-0148 [Original source: *The Papers of George Washington*, Revolutionary War Series, Vol. 4, 1 April-15 June 1776, Philander D. Chase, ed. Charlottesville, VA: University Press of Virginia, 1991, 182-183], accessed Aug. 30, 2019.

"To George Washington from John Hancock, September 10, 1776," https://founders.archives.gov/documents/Washington/03-06-02-0218 [Original source: *The Papers of George Washington*, Vol. 6, 273], accessed Oct. 1, 2019.

"To George Washington from Major General Charles Lee, February 19, 1776," https://founders.archives.gov/documents/Washington/03-03-02-0242 [Original source: *The Papers of George Washington*, Vol. 3, 339-341], accessed Sept. 1, 2019.

"To George Washington from Major General Charles Lee, November 30, 1776," https://founders.archives. gov/documents/Washington/03-07-02-0169 [Original source: *The Papers of George Washington*, Vol. 7, 235-236.], (accessed November 16, 2019).

Founders Online, National Archives, "To George Washington from Major General Israel Putnam, December 12, 1776," https://founders.archives.gov/documents/Washington/03-07-02-0250 [Original source: *The Papers of George Washington*, Vol. 7, 315-317], accessed Nov. 22, 2019.

"To George Washington from Major General John Sullivan, December 13, 1776," https://founders.archives. gov/documents/Washington/03-07-02-0261 [Original source: *The Papers of George Washington*, Vol. 7, 328], accessed Nov. 30, 2019.

"To George Washington from Major General Nathanael Greene, September 5, 1776," https://founders.archives. gov/documents/Washington/03-06-02-0180 [Original source: *The Papers of George Washington*, Vol. 6, 222-224], accessed Sept. 30, 2019.

"To George Washington from Major General Nathanael Greene, November 9, 1776," https://founders.archives. gov/documents/Washington/03-07-02-0085 [Original source: *The Papers of George Washington*, Vol. 7, 119-121], accessed Oct. 23, 2019.

"To George Washington from Major General Nathanael Greene, November 15, 1776," https://founders.archives. gov/documents/Washington/03-07-02-0117 [Original source: *The Papers of George Washington*, Vol. 7, 162], accessed Oct. 13, 2019.

"To George Washington from Robert Morris, December 23-24, 1776," http://founders.archives.gov/documents/ Washington/03-07-02-0328 [Original source: *The Papers of George Washington*, Vol. 7, 420-423], accessed Aug. 11, 2019.

"To John Adams from William Prescott, August 25, 1775," https://founders.archives.gov/documents/ Adams/06-03-02-0070 [Original source: *The Adams Papers, Papers of John Adams*, Vol. 3, May 1775-January 1776, Robert J. Taylor, ed. Cambridge, MA: Harvard University Press, 1979, 124-126], accessed Aug. 11, 2019.

Other Online Collections

Biddle, R. "Selections from the Military Papers of General John Cadwalader." *The Pennsylvania Magazine of History and Biography*, Vol. 32 (January 1, 1908), https://archive.org/stream/jstor-20085424/20085424_djvu. txt, accessed Dec. 25, 2019.

Lacey, John and Armstrong, John. "Memoirs of Brigadier-General John Lacey, of Pennsylvania (continued)." *The Pennsylvania Magazine of History and Biography*, Vol. 26, No. 1 (1902), 101-111, www.jstor.org/ stable/20086016, accessed Nov. 30, 2019.

"Letter from Massachusetts Provincial Congress, May 3, 1775, quoted from, The journals of each Provincial congress of Massachusetts in 1774 and 1775, and of the Committee of safety, with an appendix, containing the proceedings of the county conventions—narratives of the events of the nineteenth of April, 1775— papers relating to Ticonderoga and Crown Point, and other documents, illustrative of the early history of the American revolution. Pub. agreeably to a resolve passed March 10, 1837, under the supervision of William Lincoln," 188, found at https://archive.org/stream/journalsofeachpr00massuoft/journalsofeachpr00massuoft_ djvu.txt, accessed July 28, 2019.

Library of Congress, "Marines' Hymn," https://www.loc.gov/item/ihas.200000011/, accessed Dec. 31, 2019.

"Muster-Rolls of Marines and Artillery Commanded by Capt. Isaac Craig, of Pennsylvania, in 1775 and 1778," *The Pennsylvania Magazine of History and Biography*, Vol. 13 (October 1, 1888), 351, https://archive.org/ details/jstor-20083274/page/n1, accessed July 7, 2019.

National Archives—America's Founding Documents, "The Declaration of Independence: A Transcription," https://www.archives.gov/founding-docs/declaration-transcript, accessed Aug. 11, 2019.

Reed, Joseph. "General Joseph Reed's Narrative of the Movements of the American Army in the Neighborhood of Trenton in the Winter of 1776-77," https://ia801906.us.archive.org/35/items/jstor-20084674/20084674. pdf, accessed Aug. 11, 2019.

Rush, Benjamin. *The Autobiography of Benjamin Rush; His Travels Through Life*. London: Oxford University Press, 1948, https://www.harvardsquarelibrary.org/wp-content/uploads/2017/03/The-Autobiography-of-Benjamin-Rush.pdf, accessed Aug. 11, 2019.

Schlieffen, Bardeleben, Heikennitz, W., Kenn, Jung, Schramm, Wangermann, & Stryker, William. "Report of the Court-Martial for the Trial of the Hessian Officers Captured by Washington at Trenton, December 26, 1776," *The Pennsylvania Magazine of History and Biography*, Vol. 7, No. 1 (1883), 45-49, www.jstor.org/stable/20084591, accessed Nov. 28, 2019.

"Selections from the Military Papers of General John Cadwalader." https://archive.org/stream/jstor-20085424/20085424_djvu.txt, accessed Aug. 11, 2019.

Tustin, Joseph, ed. *A Diary of The American War: A Hessian Journal, Captain Johann Ewald*. New Haven, CT: Yale University Press, 1979, https://archive.org/stream/EwaldsDIARYOFTHEAMERICANWAR/Ewalds%20DIARY%20OF%20THE%20AMERICAN%20WAR_djvu.txt, accessed Aug. 3, 2019.

United States House of Representatives—History, Art, & Archives, "The Continental Congress Declared Independence from Great Britain," https://history.house.gov/Historical-Highlights/1700s/The-Continental-Congress-agreed-to-Decemberlare-independence-from-Great-Britain/, accessed Sept. 1, 2019.

University of Virginia, Washington Papers, "Correspondence between Major General Charles Lee and George Washington, June 1778," http://gwpapers.virginia.edu/resources/topics/major-general-charles-lee/, accessed Aug. 14, 2019.

Northern Illinois Digital Library, "Correspondence and Journals of Samuel B. Webb," https://digital.lib.niu.edu/islandora/object/niu-prairie%3A2069, accessed July 19, 2020.

White, Joseph. *An Narrative of Events, As They Occurred from Time to Time, in the Revolutionary War, with an Account of the Battle of Trenton, Trenton-Bridge, and Princeton, Charlestown, 1833*. https://www.americanheritage.com/content/good-soldier-white, accessed Aug. 11, 2019.

Published Books

Adams, Charles, ed. *The Works of John Adams, Second President of the United States: With a Life of the Author, Notes, and Illustrations*, Vol. 2. Boston: Charles Little and James Brown, 1850.

_____. *The Works of John Adams, Second President of the United States*, Vol. 9. Boston: Little, Brown and Company, 1854.

Anderson, Enoch. *Personal Recollections of Captain Enoch Anderson, an Officer of the Delaware Regiments in the Revolutionary War*. Manchester, MA: Ayer Company Publishers Inc., 1971.

Andrist, Ralph, ed. *The Founding Father: George Washington, A Biography in His Own Words*, 2 Vols. New York: Newsweek, 1972.

Arnold, James, ed. *Americans at War: Eyewitness Accounts from the American Revolution to the 21st Century*, Vol. 1. Santa Barbara, CA: ABC-CLIO, LLC, 2018.

Barber, John & Howe, Henry. *Historical Collections of the State of New Jersey*. New York: S. Tuttle, 1846.

Barnes, George & Owens, John eds. *Private Papers of Earl of Sandwich, First Lord of the Admiralty, 1771-1782*. London: Navy Records Society, 1932-38.

Bolton, Charles, ed. *Letters of Hugh, Earl Percy, from Boston and New York, 1774-1776*. Boston: The Merrymount Press, 1902.

Breck, Samuel & Scudder, Horace, *Recollections of Samuel Breck: With Passages from his Notebooks, 1771-1862*. Carlisle, PA: Applewood Books, 1877.

Brown, Stuart Gerry & Baker, Donald, eds. *The Autobiography of James Monroe*. Syracuse, NY: Syracuse University Press, 1959.

Bruce, Peter, *Memoirs of Peter Henry Bruce, a Military Officer in the Services of Prussia, Russia, and Great Britain*. Dublin: J. and R. Byrn, 1783.

Burgoyne, Bruce, *The Trenton Commanders: Johann Gottlieb Rall and George Washington, as Noted in Hessian Diaries*. Westminster, MD: Heritage Books, 1997.

Butterfield, L. H., ed. *Letters of Benjamin Rush*, Vol. 1. Princeton, NJ: Princeton University Press, 1951.

Chase, Philander, ed. *The Papers of George Washington*, Vol. 7 (October 21, 1776-January 5, 1777). Charlottesville, VA: University Press of Virginia, 1997.

Coghlan, Margaret. *Memoirs of Mrs. Coghlan, Daughter of the Late Major Moncrieffe*. New York: T. H. Morrell, 1864.

Commager, Henry Steele, & Morris, Richard, eds. *The Spirit of Seventy-Six: The Story of the American Revolution as Told by its Participants*. New York: Castle Books, 2002.

Conway, Moncure Daniel, ed. *The Writings of Thomas Paine*, Vol. 1. New York: G. P. Putnam and Sons, 1894.

Cornwallis, Charles, *Correspondence of Charles, First Marquis Cornwallis*. Cambridge, MA: Harvard University Press, 2011.

Dann, John, ed. *The Revolution Remembered: Eyewitness Accounts of the War for Independence*. Chicago: University of Chicago Press, 1980.

Dexter, Franklin, ed. *The Literary Diary of Ezra Stiles, D.D., L.L.D.*, Vol. 1. New York: Charles Scribner's Sons, 1901.

Endicott, Charles, *Account of Leslie's Retreat at the North Bridge in Salem, on Sunday February 26, 1775*. Salem, MA: William Ivers and George Pease, 1856.

Ewald, Johann & Tustin, Joseph eds. *Diary of the American War: A Hessian Journal*. New Haven, CT: Yale University Press, 1979.

Fitzpatrick, John, ed. *The Writings of George Washington: From the Original Manuscript Sources, 1745-1799*, 39 Vols. Washington, D.C.: U.S. Government Printing Office, 1931-44.

Fleming, Thomas, ed. *The Founding Fathers: Benjamin Franklin, A Biography in His Own Words*, Vol. 2. New York: Newsweek, 1972.

Foner, Eric, ed. *Thomas Paine: Collected Writings: Common Sense / The Crisis / Rights of Man / The Age of Reason / Pamphlets, Articles, and Letters*, 2nd edition. New York: Library of America, 1995.

Force, Peter and Clarke, Matthew St. Clair, eds. *American Archives: Consisting of a Collection of Authentick Records, State Papers, Debates, and Letters and Other Notices of Publick Affairs, the Whole Forming a Documentary History of the Origins and Progress of the North American Colonies; of the Causes and Accomplishment of the American Revolution; and of the Constitution of Government for the United States, to the Final Ratification Thereof. In Six Series*. Washington, D.C.: U.S. Congress, 1837-46, 1853.

Ford, Worthington, ed. *Journals of the Continental Congress, 1774-1789*, 34 Vols., Washington, D.C., Government Printing Office, 1904-1937.

_____. *The Writings of George Washington*, Vol. 5 (1776-77), New York: Putnam's Sons, 1890.

French, Allen. *Diary of Captain Fredrick Mackenzie of the British Army*, 2 Vols. Cambridge, MA: Harvard University Press, 1936.

Greene, George Washington. *The Life of Nathanael Greene: Major General in the Army of the Revolution*, Vol. 1. Princeton, NJ: G. P. Putnam and Son, 1867.

Harcourt, Edward, ed. *The Harcourt Papers*, 13 Vols. Oxford: Parker, 1880-1905.

Heckert, C. W. *The German-American Diary: Notes of Related Historical Interest, Including Translated Excerpts from the Wiederholdt Diary, American Revolutionary War*. Buckhannon, WV: McClain Printing Co, 1980.

Hills, George. *History of the Church in Burlington, New Jersey; Comprising the Facts and Incidents of Nearly Two Hundred Years, from Original Contemporary Sources*. Trenton, NJ: William Sharp, 1876.

Izard, Ralph. *Correspondence of Mr. Ralph Izard, of South Carolina: From the Year 1774-1804; With a Short Memoir*, Vol. 1. New York: Charles Francis & Co., 1844.

Johnston, Henry, ed. *Memoir of Colonel Benjamin Tallmadge*. New York: Gliss Press, 1904.

Jones, Edward. *The Loyalists of New Jersey: Their Memorials, Petitions, Claims, Etc., from English Records*. Boston: Gregg Press, 1972.

Lydenberg, Harry. *Archibald Robertson, Lieutenant General Royal Engineers. His Diaries and Sketches in America, 1762-1780*. New York: The New York Public Library, 1930.

Marshall, Douglas, & Peckham, Howard. *Campaigns of the American Revolution: An Atlas of Manuscript Maps*. Ann Arbor, MI: University of Michigan Press, 1976.

Martin Joseph P. *A Narrative of Some of the Adventures, Dangers and Sufferings of A Revolutionary Soldier*. Hallowell, ME: Glazier, Masters, and Co., 1830.

Minutes of the Provincial Council of Pennsylvania, From the Organization to the Termination of the Proprietary Government, Vol. 10. Harrisburg, PA: Theo. Finn and Co., 1852.

Moore, Frank. *Diary of the American Revolution: From Newspapers and Original Documents*, Vol 1. New York: Charles Scribner, 1859.

Morris, Margaret. *Private Journal Kept During a Portion of the Revolutionary War, for the Amusement of a Sister.* Philadelphia: Privately Printed, 1836.

Moultrie, William, *Memoirs of the American Revolution: So Far as it Related to the States of North Carolina, South Carolina, and Georgia*, Vol. 1. New York: David Longworth, 1802.

Niles, Hezekiah, ed. *Principles and Acts of the Revolution in America: or, An Attempt to Collect and Preserve Some of the Speeches, Orations, & Proceedings, with Sketches and Remarks on Men and Things, and other Fugitive or Neglected Pieces, Belonging to the Men of the Revolutionary Period in the United States which Happily Terminated in the Establishment of their Liberties.* Baltimore: William Ogden Niles, 1822.

Peters, Richard, ed. *The Public Statutes at Large of the United States of America; From the Organization of the Government in 1789, to March 3, 1845*, Vol. 1. Boston: Charles C. Little and James Brown, 1846.

Reed, William. *Life and Correspondence of Joseph Reed: Military Secretary of Washington at Cambridge; Adjutant General of the Continental Army; Member of the Congress of the United States; and President of the Executive Council of the State of Pennsylvania*, Vol. 1. Philadelphia: Lindsay and Blakiston, 1847.

Rhode Island Historical Society. *The Letter Book of Esek Hopkins, Commander-in-chief of the United States Navy, 1775-1777.* Providence, RI: E. L. Freeman Company, 1932.

Rodney, Thomas. *Diary of Captain Thomas Rodney, 1776-1777*, Papers of the Historical Society of Delaware, Vol. 8. Wilmington, DE: Historical Society of Delaware, 1888.

Ryan, Dennis, ed. *A Salute to Courage; The American Revolution as Seen Through the Wartime Writings of Officers of the Continental Army and Navy.* New York: Columbia University Press, 1979.

Sands, Robert, ed. *Life and Correspondence of John Paul Jones, including his Narrative of the Campaign of the Liman.* New York: D. Fanshaw, 1880.

Sherburne, Andrew. *Memoirs of Andrew Sherburne: A Pensioner of the Navy of the Revolution.* Providence, RI: M. H. Brown, 1831.

Sedgwick, Theodore. *A Memoir of the Life of William Livingston: Member of Congress in 1774, 1775, and 1776; Delegate to the Federal Convention, 1787; and Governor of the State of New Jersey from 1776 to 1790.* New York: J & J Harper, 1833.

Showman, Richard; Conrad, Dennis; Parks, Roger; & Stevens, Elizabeth, eds. *The Papers of General Nathanael Greene*, 13 Vols. Chapel Hill, NC: University of North Carolina Press, 1976-2005.

Sparks, Jared. *The Writings of George Washington, being his Correspondence, Addresses, Messages, and other Papers, Official and Private, Selected and Published from the Original Manuscripts; with a Life of the Author, Notes, and Illustrations*, Vol. 4. Boston: Russel, Odiorne, and Metcalf, and Hillard, Gray, and Co., 1834.

Stark, Caleb. *Memoir and Official Correspondence of Gen. John Stark, With Notices of Several Other Offices of the Revolution.* Boston: Gregg Press, 1972.

Stiles, T. J., ed. *The American Revolution: First-Person Accounts by the Men Who Shaped Our Nation.* New York: Berkley Publishing Group, 1999.

Wilkinson, James. *Memoirs of My Own Times*, Vol. 1. Philadelphia: Abraham Small, 1816.

Woodward, Ashbel. *Memoir of Colonel Thomas Knowlton of Ashford Connecticut.* Boston: Henry Dutton and Son, 1861.

Young, William, *Journal of Sergeant William Young, 3rd Battalion, Pennsylvania Militia. The Pennsylvania Magazine of History*, Vol. 8, 1884.

Government Documents

Berger, David, *A Concept for Stand-in Forces*, Washington, D.C.: Headquarters, United States Marine Corps, December 2021.

Congress.gov, "H.R.3622 - Goldwater-Nichols Department of Defense Reorganization Act of 1986," https://www.congress.gov/bill/99th-congress/house-bill/3622, accessed Dec. 31, 2019).

Corbett, Art. "Expeditionary Advanced Base Operations (EABO) Handbook," Marine Corps Warfighting Lab (MCWL), Concepts & Plans Division, Quantico, VA: MCWL, 2018, accessed at https://mca-marines.org/wp-content/uploads/Expeditionary-Advanced-Base-Operations-EABO-handbook-1.1.pdf, accessed Dec. 31, 2019.

Department of Defense, "Speech delivered by Deputy Secretary of Defense Gordon R. England, Washington, D.C., Saturday, November 08, 2008," http://archive.defense.gov/Speeches/Speech.aspx?SpeechID=1321, accessed July 12, 2020.

Department of the Navy, Naval History & Heritage Command, "Ship Naming in the United States Navy," https://web.archive.org/web/20150103224426/http://www.history.navy.mil/faqs/faq63-1.htm, accessed July 12, 2019.

Donnelly, John. Historical Division, Headquarters, United States Marine Corps, *An Annotated Bibliography of United States Marine Corps Artillery*. Washington, D.C., 1970.

Headquarters, United States Marine Corps, *Marine Corps Doctrinal Publication 1, Warfighting*. Washington, D.C.: U.S. Government Printing Office, 1997.

Joint Staff, *Joint Publication 1-0, Department of Defense Dictionary of Military and Associated Terms*. Washington, D.C.: U.S. Government Printing Office, 2001 (amended through 2007).

Neller, Robert & Richardson, John. *Littoral Operations in a Contested Environment*. Washington, D.C.: Headquarters, United States Marine Corps, 2017.

Neller, Robert. *The Marine Operating Concept: How an Expeditionary Force Operates in the 21st Century*. Washington, D.C.: Headquarters, United States Marine Corps, September 2016.

United States Congress, Congressional Record. *Proceedings and Debates of the 76th Congress*, 1st Session, Vol. 84, Part 13. Washington, D.C.: U.S. Government Printing Office, 1939.

_____. *Proceedings and Debate of the 90th Congress*, 2nd Session, Vol. 114, Part 23 (Oct. 4-10, 1968). Washington, D.C.: U.S. Government Printing Office, 1968.

United States Marine Corps. *Marine Corps Doctrinal Publication 1-0: Marine Corps Operations*. Washington, D.C.: U.S. Government Printing Office, 2011.

Periodical Collections

Bamford, William. "Bamford's Diary." *Maryland Historical Magazine*, Vol. 28 (1933).

Fitzgerald, John. "Col. John Fitzgerald to General Washington: On the Conway Cabal Against Washington, (Alexandria 17 March 1778)." *The American Catholic Historical Researches*, Vol. 17, No. 3 (July 1900).

Gordon, William. "Letter of the Reverend William Gordon to Samuel Wilson, Jamaica Plain, April 6, 1776." *Proceedings of the Massachusetts Historical Society*, LX.

Lacey, John. "Memoirs of Brigadier-General John Lacey, of Pennsylvania." *The Pennsylvania Magazine of History and Biography*, Vol. 25, No. 1 (1901).

Marsh, Esbon. "The First Session of the Second Continental Congress," *The Historian*, Vol. 3, No. 2 (Spring 1941).

McMichael, James. "Diary of Lieutenant James McMichael of the Pennsylvania Line, 1776-1778." *The Pennsylvania Magazine of History and Biography*, Vol. 26, No. 2 (1892).

Morris, Margaret. "Revolutionary Journal of Margaret Morris." *Bulletin of the Friends' Historical Society of Philadelphia*, Vol. 9, No. 2 (November 1919).

Peale, Charles Willson. "Journal by Charles Willson Peale, December 4, 1776-Jan. 20, 1777." *The Pennsylvania Magazine of History and Biography*, 1914.

Sergeant R___, "Account of Princeton." *The Pennsylvania Magazine of History and Biography*, Vol. 20 (1832), quoted from Commager and Morris, *Spirit of Seventy-Six*.

Sullivan, Thomas. "The Battle of Princeton, (excerpts from the journal of Sergeant Thomas Sullivan of Her Majesty's 49th Regiment of Foot), *The Pennsylvania Magazine of History and Biography*, Vol. 32, No. 1 (1908).

Secondary Sources

Books

Alden, John. *General Gage in America: Being Principally a History of His Role in the American Revolution.* New York: Greenwood Press, 1948.

Allen, Thaddeus. *An Inquiry Into the Views, Services, Principles, and Influences of the Leading Men in the Origination of our Union, and the Formation and Early Administration of the Present Government.* Boston: Saxton and Kelt, 1847.

Allen, Thomas. *George Washington, Spymaster: How the Americans Outspied the British and Won the Revolutionary War.* Washington, D.C.: National Geographic, 2004.

Anderson, Fred. *Crucible of War: The Seven Years' War and the Fate of the Empire in British North America, 1754-1766.* New York: Alfred Knopf, 2000.

Avery, Elroy. *A History of the United States and Its People, From Their Earliest Records to the Present Time*, 16 Vols., Vol. 6. Cleveland: The Burrows Brothers Company, 1904.

Barnes, Ian. *The Historical Atlas of the American Revolution.* New York: Routledge, 2000.

Beck, Derek. *Igniting The American Revolution, 1773-1775.* Naperville, IL: Source Books, 2015.

Belcher, Henry. *The First American Civil War: First Period, 1775-1778*, 2 Vols. London: MacMillan and Co, 1911.

Belsham, William. *History of Great Britain: From the Revolution, 1688, to the Treaty of Amiens, 1802*, 12 Vols., Vol. 6. London: Richard Phillips, 1805.

Bennett, William & Cribb, John. *The American Patriot's Almanac: Daily Readings on America.* Nashville: Thomas Nelson Publishing, 2008.

Betts, William. *The Nine Lives of George Washington.* Bloomington, IN: Universe Books, 2013.

Bill, Alfred. *The Campaign of Princeton, 1776-1777.* Princeton, NJ: Princeton University Press, 1948.

Billias, George. *General John Glover and his Marblehead Mariners.* New York: Henry Holt and Company, 1960.

Bishop, Barry. *Nathan Hale: The Life of a Colonial Freedom Fighter.* Pittsburgh: RoseDog Books, 2013.

Bonk, David. *Trenton and Princeton, 1776-77: Washington Crosses the Delaware.* Oxford: Osprey Books, 2009.

Broadwater, Robert. *American Generals of the Revolutionary War: A Biographical Dictionary.* Jefferson, NC: McFarland and Co., Inc., 2007.

Brooks, Noah. *Henry Knox, A Soldier of the Revolution, Major-General in the Continental Army and Washington's Chief of Artillery.* New York: Cosimo Classics, 2007.

Callahan, North. *George Washington: Soldier and Man.* New York: William Morrow and Company, Inc., 1972.

Carbone, Gerald. *Nathanael Greene: A Biography of the American Revolution.* New York: Palgrave MacMillan, 2008.

Chadwick, Bruce. *The First American Army: The Untold Story of George Washington and the Men Behind America's First Fight for Freedom.* Naperville, IL: Sourcebooks, 2007.

_____. *George Washington's War: The Forging of a Revolutionary Leader and the American Presidency.* Naperville, IL: Sourcebooks, 2004.

Chernow, Ron. *Alexander Hamilton.* New York: Penguin Books, 2004.

_____. *Washington: A Life.* New York: Penguin Books, 2010.

Chenoweth, Avery, & Nihart, Brooke. *Semper Fi: The Definitive Illustrative History of the U.S. Marines.* New York: Fall River Press, 2005.

Chorlton, Thomas. *The First American Republic, 1774-1789: The First Fourteen American Presidents Before Washington.* Bloomington, IN: Author House, 2011.

Clark, George. *A Short History of the United States Navy.* Philadelphia: J. B. Lippincott Company, 1911.

Clary, David. *George Washington's First War: His Early Military Adventures.* New York: Simon and Shuster, 2011.

Coelho, Chris, & Matlack, Timothy. *Scribe of the Declaration of Independence.* Jefferson, NC: McFarland and Co., 2013.

Coggins, Jack. *Ships and Seamen of the American Revolution.* Harrisburg, PA: Stackpole Books, 1969.

Cooper, James Fenimore. *History of the Navy of the United States of America*, abridged in one volume. New York: Stringer and Townsend, 1856.

Crowder, Jack. *African Americans and American Indians in the Revolutionary War.* Jefferson, NC: McFarland & Co., Inc., 2019.

Daughans, Charles. *If By Sea: The Forging of the American Navy-From the Revolution to the War of 1812.* New York: Basic Books, 2008.

Dowart, Jeffery. *Invasion and Insurrection: Security, Defense, and War in the Delaware Valley, 1621-1815.* Newark, NJ: University of Delaware Press, 2008.

Drake, Francis. *Life and Correspondence of Henry Knox.* Cambridge, MA: Wilson and Son, 1873.

Dwyer, William. *The Day Is Ours! An Inside View of the Battles of Trenton and Princeton, November 1776-January 1777.* New Brunswick, NJ: Rutgers University Press, 1998.

Elleman, Bruce & Paine, S.C.M., eds. *Commerce Raiding: Historical Case Studies, 1755-2009.* Newport, RI: Naval War College Press, 2013.

Ellis, Joseph. *Revolutionary Summer: The Birth of American Independence.* New York: Alfred Knopf, 2013.

Encyclopedia Britannica. *The Annals of America*, Vol. 2, 1755-83. Chicago: Encyclopedia Britannica, Inc., 1976.

Engler, Jr., Richard. *The Challenge of Diversity.* New York: Harper & Row, 1964.

English, Frederick. *General Hugh Mercer: Forgotten Hero of the American Revolution.* Princeton, NJ: Princeton Academic Press, 1995.

Estes, Kenneth. *The Marine Officer's Guide*, 5th ed. Annapolis, MD: Naval Institute Press, 1989.

Ferling, John. *A Leap in the Dark: The Struggle to Create the American Republic.* New York: Oxford University Press, 2003.

_____. *Almost a Miracle: The American Victory in the War of Independence.* New York: Oxford University Press, 2007.

_____. *Whirlwind: The American Revolution and the War that Won It.* New York: Bloomsbury Press, 2015.

Field, Cyril. *Britain's Sea Soldiers*, 2 Vols. Liverpool: The Lyceum Press, 1924.

Fischer, David H. *Paul Revere's Ride.* New York: Oxford University Press, 1994.

_____. *Washington's Crossing.* New York: Oxford University Press, 2004.

Fleming, Thomas. *1776.* Boston: New Word City, 2016.

Forbes, Esther. *Paul Revere and The World He Lived In.* New York: American Heritage Library, 1942.

Fredriksen, John. *Revolutionary War Almanac.* New York: Facts on File, Inc., 2006.

Frost, John. *The Book of the Army: Comprising a General Military History of the United States.* New York: D. Appleton, 1845.

Frothingham, Richard. *History of the Siege of Boston and of the Battles of Lexington, Concord, and Bunker Hill.* Boston: Charles C. Little & James Brown, 1851.

Frothingham, Richard. *The Centennial: The Battle of Bunker Hill.* New York: Little, Brown, & Company, 1875.

Fuller, J. F. C. *Decisive Battles of the U.S.A., 1776-1918.* Lincoln, NE: University of Nebraska Press, 1942.

Gimms, Daniel. *The Hessians and the American Revolution: The Whole Story.* Pennsauken, NJ: BookBaby, 2011.

Gove, Philip, ed. *Webster's Third New International Dictionary.* Springfield, MA: Merriam-Webster, Inc., 1986.

Green, Thomas. *Historic Families of Kentucky.* Cincinnati: Robert Clarke & Co., 1899.

Greene, George Washington. *The Life of Nathanael Greene*, 3 Vols. New York: Hurd & Houghton, 1871.

Greene, Jack, & Pole, J. R. *A Companion to the American Revolution.* Oxford: Blackwell Publishers, Ltd., 2000.

Greenwood, Joseph R., ed. *The Revolutionary Service of John Greenwood of Boston and New York, 1775-1783.* New York: De Vinne Press, 1922.

Griffin, Martin. *Catholics and the American Revolution.* Philadelphia: Martin I.J. Griffin, 1909.

_____. *Stephen Moylan, Muster-master General, Secretary and Aide-de-camp to Washington, Quartermaster-general, Colonel of 4th Pennsylvania Light Dragoons and Brigadier-general of the War for American Independence, the First and the Last President of the Friendly Sons of St. Patrick of Philadelphia.* Philadelphia: Martin Griffin, 1909.

Griffin, Samuel. *The War for American Independence: From 1760 to the Surrender at Yorktown in 1781*. Urbana, IL: University of Illinois Press, 1976.

Grimshaw, William. *History of the United States, from Their First Settlement as Colonies, to the Cession of Florida in Eighteen Hundred and Twenty One*. Philadelphia: John Grigg, 1826.

Hacker, Diana. *The Bedford Handbook*, 7th edition. Boston: Bedford/St. Martins, 2006.

Hagan, Kenneth. *This People's Navy: The Making of American Seapower*. New York: The Free Press, 1991.

Hamilton, John. *The Life of Alexander Hamilton*, Vol. 1. New York: Halsted & Voorhies, 1834.

Hannings, Bud. *Chronology of the American Revolution: Military and Political Actions Day by Day*. Jefferson, NC: McFarland and Company, Inc., 2008.

Hart, Gary. *James Monroe: The American Presidents Series: The 5th President, 1817-1825*. New York: Times Books, 2005.

Hazard, Samuel, ed. *The Register of Pennsylvania: Devoted to the Preservation of Facts and Documents, and Every Kind of Useful Information Respecting the State of Pennsylvania*. Philadelphia: W. F. Geddes, 1828.

Heathcote, T. A. *The British Field Marshals: 1736-1997: A Biographical Dictionary*. South Yorkshire, UK: Pen & Sword Books, 2012.

Holmes, Abiel. *The Annals of America: From the Discovery by Columbus in the year 1492 to the year 1826*, 2nd Edition, Vol. 2. Cambridge, MA: Hilliard and Brown, 1829.

Hoock, Holger. *Scars of Independence: America's Violent Birth*. New York: Crown, 2017.

Howarth, Stephen. *To Shining Sea: A History of the United States Navy, 1775-1991*. New York: Random House, 1991.

Hubbard, Robert. *Major General Israel Putnam: Hero of the American Revolution*. Jefferson, NC: McFarland and Company, 2017.

Irving, Washington. *Life of George Washington*, Vol. 2. New York: Putnam & Co, 1859.

Johnston, Henry. *The Battle of Harlem Heights, September 16, 1776*. New York: Macmillan Company, 1897.

Ketchum, Richard. *Decisive Day: The Battle for Bunker Hill*. New York: Henry Holt and Company, 1962.

Ketchum, Richard, ed. *The American Heritage Book of The Revolution*. New York: American Heritage Publishing, 1958.

Kraska, James & Pedrozo, Raul. *International Maritime Security Law*. Leiden, NL: Martinus Nijhoff Publishers, 2013.

Krulak, Victor. *First to Fight*. New York: Pocket Books, 1984.

LaBree, Clifton. *New Hampshire's General John Stark: Live Free or Die: Death Is Not the Worst of Evils*. New Boston, NH: Fading Shadows Imprint, 2014.

Landenburg, Thomas. *The Causes of the American Revolution*. Madison, WI: Science Education Consortium, 1989.

Langguth, A. J. *Patriots: The Men Who Started the American Revolution*. New York: Simon and Shuster, 1988.

Leckie, Robert. *George Washington's War*. New York: Harper Collins Publishers, 1992.

Lefkowitz, Arthur. *Benedict Arnold's Army: The 1775 American Invasion of Canada During the Revolutionary War*. El Dorado Hills, CA: Savas Beatie, 2008.

_____. *Benedict Arnold in the Company of Heroes*. El Dorado Hills, CA: Savas Beatie, 2012.

_____. *George Washington's Indispensable Men: Alexander Hamilton, Tench Tilghman, and the Aides-de-Camp who Helped Win American Independence*. Guilford, CT: Stackpole Books, 2003.

Lengel, Edward. *General George Washington: A Military Life*. New York: Random House, 2005.

Lookingbill, Brad. *American Military History: A Documentary Reader*, 2nd Edition. Hoboken, NJ: John Wiley and Sons, Inc., 2019.

Lossing, Benson. *The Pictorial Field-Book of the Revolution*, 3 Vols., Vol. 2. Gretna, LA: Pelican Publishing Company, 2008.

Lundin, Leonard. *Cockpit of the Revolution: The War for Independence in New Jersey*. Princeton, NJ: Princeton University Press, 1940.

Manstan, Roy & Frese, Frederick. *Turtle: David Bushnell's Revolutionary Vessel.* Yardley, PA: Westholme Publishing, 2010.

Martin, Lain, ed. *The Greatest U.S. Army Stories Ever Told: Unforgettable Stories Of Courage, Honor, and Sacrifice.* Guilford, CT: The Lyons Press, 2006.

Martyn, Charles. *The Life of Artemas Ward: The First Commander-In-Chief of the American Revolution.* New York: Artemas Ward, 1921.

Mays, Terry. *Historical Dictionary of the American Revolution*, 2nd Edition. Lanham, MD: Scarecrow Press, 2010.

McClellan, Edwin. *History of the United States Marine Corps*, Vol. 1. Washington, D.C.: Marine Corps Historical Section, 1931.

McCullough, David. *1776.* New York: Simon and Schuster, 2005.

_____. *John Adams.* New York: Simon and Schuster, 2001.

McGrath, Tim. *Give Me a Fast Ship: The Continental Navy and America's Revolution at Sea.* New York: Penguin Group, 2014.

McNabney, James. *Born in Brotherhood: Revelations About America's Revolutionary Leaders.* Bloomington, IN: Author House, 2006.

Meltzer, Milton. *Benjamin Franklin: The New American.* New York: Franklin Watts, 1988.

Middlekauff, Robert. *The Glorious Cause: The American Revolution, 1763-1789.* New York: Oxford University Press, 2005.

Morgan, George. *The Life of James Monroe.* Boston: Small, Maynard, & Co., 1921.

Miller, John. *Origins of the American Revolution.* Boston: Little, Brown, & Co., 1943.

Millett, Allan and Shulimson, Jack, eds. *Commandants of the Marine Corps.* Annapolis, MD: Naval Institute Press, 2004.

_____. *Semper Fidelis: The History of the United States Marine Corps.* New York: The Free Press, 1980.

Morison, Samuel. *John Paul Jones.* New York: Time Incorporated, 1959.

Morrissey, Brendan. *Monmouth Courthouse 1778*: The Last Great Battle in the North. Oxford: Osprey Books, 2004.

Muehlbauer, Matthew, & Ulbrich, David. *Ways of War: American Military History from the Colonial Era to the 21st Century.* New York, Routledge, 2013.

Murphy, Daniel. *William Washington, American Light Dragoon: A Continental Cavalry Leader in the War of Independence.* Yardley, PA: Westholme, 2014.

Nagy, John. *George Washington's Secret Spy War: The Making of America's First Spymaster.* New York: St. Martin's Press, 2016.

Nelson, James. *Fire and Sword: The Battle of Bunker Hill and the Beginning of the American Revolution.* New York: Thomas Dunne Books, 2011.

Nelson, James. *George Washington's Great Gamble and the Sea Battle that Won the American Revolution.* New York: McGraw Hill, 2010.

Nelson, Paul. *General James Grant: Scottish Soldier and Royal Governor of East Florida.* Gainesville, FL: University Press of Florida, 1993.

Newton, Michael. *Angry Mobs and Founding Fathers: The Fight for Control of the American Revolution.* Phoenix: Eleftheria Publishing, 2011.

O'Donnell, Patrick. *Washington's Immortals: The Untold Story of an Elite Regiment Who Changed the Course of the Revolution.* New York: Grover Press, 2016.

Onderdonk, Henry. *Revolutionary Incidents of Suffolk and Kings Counties: With an Account of the Battle of Long Island and the British Prisons and Prison-Ships at New York.* New York: Leavitt & Co., 1849.

Palmer, Dave. *George Washington and Benedict Arnold: A Tale of Two Patriots.* Washington, D.C.: Regnery Publishing, Inc., 2006.

Paterson, Bentton Rain. *Washington and Cornwallis: The Battle of America, 1775-1783.* Lanham, MD: Taylor Trade Publishing, 2004.

Patton, Robert. *Patriot Pirates: The Privateer War for Freedom and Fortune in the American Revolution*. New York: Vintage Books, 2009.

Pencak, William. *Pennsylvania's Revolution*. University Park, PA: Pennsylvania State University Press, 2010.

Philbrick, Nathaniel. *Bunker Hill: A City, A Siege, A Revolution*. New York: Penguin Books, 2013.

_____. *Valiant Ambition: George Washington, Benedict Arnold, and the Fate of the American Revolution*. New York: Viking, 2016.

Piecuch, Jim. *The Battle of Camden: A Documentary History*. Charleston, SC: The History Press, 2006.

Puls, Mark. *Henry Knox: Visionary General of the American Revolution*. New York: Pallgrave MacMillan, 2008.

Randall, Willard. *Benedict Arnold: Patriot and Traitor*. New York: William Morrow & Co., Inc., 1990.

_____. *Ethan Allen: His Life and Times*. New York: W. W. Norton and Company, 2011.

Rees, James & Spignesi, Stephen. *George Washington's Leadership Lessons: What the Father of Our Country Can Teach Us About Effective Leadership and Character*. Hoboken, NJ: John Wiley and Sons, 2007.

Richards, Henry Melchior Muhlenberg. *The Pennsylvania-German in the Revolutionary War, 1775-1783*. Lancaster, PA: Metalmark Books, 1908.

Ronald, D. A. B. *The Life of John Andre: The Redcoat Who Turned Benedict Arnold*. Philadelphia: Casemate, 2019.

Russell, David. *The American Revolution in the Southern Colonies*. Jefferson, NC: McFarland and Co., Inc., 2000.

Savas, Theodore & Dameron, J. David. *The New American Revolution Handbook*. El Dorado Hills, CA: Savas Beatie, 2010.

Scharf, John. *History of Maryland, 1765-1812*, Vol. 2. Baltimore: John Piet, 1879.

Scharf, Thomas. *History of Delaware*. Philadelphia: L. J. Richards & Co., 1888.

Scheer, George, and Rankin, Hugh. *Rebels and Redcoats*. New York: World Publishing, 1957.

Seymour, Joseph. *The Pennsylvania Associators, 1747-1777*. Yardley, PA: Westholme Publishing, 2012.

Siebert, Wilbur. *The Loyalists of Pennsylvania*. Columbus, OH: Ohio State University Press, 1920.

Siefring, Thomas. *History of the United States Marines*. Secaucus, NJ: Chartwell Books Inc., 1979.

Simmons, Edwin & Moskin, Robert, eds. *The Marines*. Hong Kong: Hugh Lauter Levin Associates, Inc., 1998.

Siry, Steven. *Greene: Revolutionary General*. Washington, D.C.: Potomac Books, 2006.

Smith, Charles. *Marines in the Revolution*. Washington, D.C.: History and Museums Division, Headquarters, U.S. Marine Corps, 1975.

Smith, David. *Whispers Across the Atlantick: General William Howe and the American Revolution*. Oxford: Osprey Publishing, 2017.

Smith, Page. *A New Age Now Begins: A People's History of the American Revolution*. New York: Penguin Books, 1976.

Smith, Page. *John Adams*, 2 Vols. Garden City, NJ: Doubleday & Co., 1962.

Smollett, Tobias, ed. *The Critical Review: Or, Annals of Literature*, Vol. 13, "Steadman's History of the American War." London: Falcon-Court, 1795.

Stedman, Charles. *The History of the Origin, Progress, and Termination of the American War*, 2 Vols. London: J. Murray, 1794.

Stember, Sol. *The Bicentennial Guide to the American Revolution*, Vol. 1. New York: The Saturday Review Press, 1974.

Stephenson, Michael. *Patriot Battles: How the War of Independence was Fought*. New York: Harpers Collins Publishing, 2007.

Strokesbury, James. *A Short History of the American Revolution*. New York: William Morrow & Co., 1991.

Stryker, William. *The Battles of Trenton and Princeton*. Boston: Houghton, Mifflin & Co., 1898.

Sun Tzu, *The Art of War*, translated by S. B. Griffith. New York: Oxford University Press, 1982.

Thomas, Ebenezer. *Reminiscences of the Last 65 years, Commencing with the Battle of Lexington*, 2 Vols., Vol. 1. Hartford, CT: Case, Tiffany, & Burnham, 1840.

Thompson, Parker. *From its European Antecedents to 1791: The United States Army Chaplaincy*. Washington, D.C.: Department of the Army, 1978.

Tonsetic, Robert. *Special Operations During the American Revolution*. Philadelphia: Casemate, 2013.

Tourtellot, Arthur. *Lexington and Concord: The Beginning of the War of the American Revolution*. New York: W. W. Norton & Co., 1959.

Trevelyan, George. *The American Revolution*. New York: David McKay Co., Inc., 1964.

Tuchman, Barbara. *The First Salute: A View of the American Revolution*. New York: Ballantine Books, 1988.

Tucker, Phillip Thomas. *George Washington's Surprise Attack: A New Look at the Battle That Decided the Fate of America*. New York: Skyhorse Publishing, 2016.

Tunis, Edwin. *The Tavern at the Ferry*. Baltimore: John Hopkins University Press, 1973.

Unger, Harlow. *American Tempest: How the Boston Tea Party Sparked a Revolution*. Cambridge, MA: Da Capo Press, 2011.

_____. *Dr. Benjamin Rush: The Founding Father Who Healed a Wounded Nation*. New York: Da Capo Press, 2018.

Upton, Leslie Francis Stokes. *Revolutionary Versus Loyalist: The First American Civil War, 1774-1784*. Waltham, MA: Blaisdell Publishing Company, 1968.

Ward, Christopher. *The War of the Revolution*, Vol. 6. New York: The Macmillan Company, 1952.

Ward, Harry. *Charles Scott and the Spirit of '76*. Charlottesville, VA: University Press of Virginia, 1988.

Weintraub, Stanley. *Iron Tears: America's Battle for Freedom, Britain's Quagmire, 1775-1783*. New York: Free Press, 2005.

Whittmore, Charles. *A General of the Revolution: John Sullivan of New Hampshire*. New York: Columbia University Press, 1961.

Williams, Catherine. *Biography of Revolutionary Heroes; Containing the Life of Brigadier General William Barton and Captain Stephen Olney*. New York: Catherine Williams, 1839.

Periodical articles

Alter, Robert. "Boots for the Battle." *Boy's Life*, December 1964, 17-19, 71-72.

Bauer, Fredrick. "Notes on the Use of the Cavalry in the American Revolution." *The Cavalry Journal*, Vol. 47, No. 1 (1938), 136-143.

Cooper, James Fenimore. "Sketches of Naval Men-John Barry." *Graham's Lady's and Gentleman's Magazine*, Vol. 24 (1844), 267-273.

Daigler, Ken. "George Washington's Attacks on Trenton and Princeton, 1776-77." *The Intelligencer Journal of U.S. Intelligence Studies*, Vol. 25, No. 1 (Spring-Summer 2019), 45-47.

Haven, C. C. "Thirty Days in New Jersey Ninety Years Ago: An Essay Revealing New Facts in Connection with Washington and His Army in 1776 and 1777." *Trenton State Gazette*, 1867, 3-72.

Historical Society of Pennsylvania, "Letters from Robert Morris to John Hancock, written in 1776." *The Bulletin of the Historical Society of Pennsylvania*, Vol. 1 (1845-47), 50-74.

McClellan, Edwin, & Craige, John. "American Marines in the Battles of Trenton and Princeton." *Marine Corps Gazette*, Vol. 6. Issue 3 (September 1921), 279-288.

McClellan, Edwin. "The Navy at the Battles of Trenton and Princeton." *United States Institute Proceedings*, Vol. 49, No. 11, Whole No. 249 (November 1923), 1848-1856.

Porter, William. "A Sketch of the Life of General Andrew Porter." *The Pennsylvania Magazine of History & Biography*, Vol. 4, No. 3 (1880), 261-301.

Van Dyke, John. "An Unwritten Account of a Spy of Washington." *Our Home Magazine*, October 1873.

Wood, Dakota. "Rebuilding America's Military: The United States Marine Corps." The Heritage Foundation's Rebuilding America's Military Project, Special Report, No. 211, Mar. 21, 2019.

Online sites

Abbott, Tim, "'Another Pair Not Fellows'; Adventures in Research and Reinterpreting the American Revolution," http://notfellows.blogspot.com/2015/11/his-enterprising-disposition-and-thirst.html, accessed Dec. 18, 2019.

American Battlefield Trust, "Banastre Tarleton," https://www.battlefields.org/learn/biographies/banastre-tarleton, accessed Nov. 24, 2019.

American Battlefield Trust, "Edward Hand," https://www.battlefields.org/learn/biographies/edward-hand, accessed Sept. 29, 2019.

American Battlefield Trust, "John Cadwalader: Senior Officer of the Philadelphia Associators," https://www. battlefields.org/learn/articles/john-cadwalader, accessed Nov. 21, 2019.

American Battlefield Trust, "Lexington and Concord," https://www.battlefields.org/learn/revolutionary-war/ battles/lexington-and-concord, accessed July 27, 2019).

American Battlefield Trust, "Richard Howe," https://www.battlefields.org/learn/biographies/richard-howe, accessed Sept. 1, 2019.

American Battlefield Trust, "Ten Crucial Days Campaign: December 25, 1776-January 3, 1777," https://www. battlefields.org/learn/topics/ten-crucial-days-campaign, accessed Dec. 29, 2019.

American Battlefield Trust, "Thunder in New Jersey: Washington's Artillery during the Ten Crucial Days," https://www.battlefields.org/learn/articles/thunder-new-jersey-washingtons-artillery-during-ten-crucial-days, accessed July 27, 2019.

American Battlefield Trust, "William Howe," https://www.battlefields.org/learn/biographies/william-howe?, accessed Sept. 1, 2019.

American History Central, "Administration of Justice Act, May 20, 1774," http://www.americanhistorycentral. com/entries/administration-of-justice-act/, accessed July 18, 2019.

American Heritage Magazine, "The Good Soldier White," Vol. 7, Issue 4, 1956, https://www.americanheritage. com/good-soldier-white#3, accessed December 25, 2019.

"Benjamin Rush," https://www.biography.com/people/benjamin-rush-9467074, accessed July 12, 2020.

"Boeing, MV-22 Osprey," https://www.boeing.com/defense/v-22-osprey/, accessed July 14, 2019.

"Boston Tea Party: A Revolutionary Experience," https://www.bostonteapartyship.com/continental-congress, accessed July 14, 2019.

Brooks, Rebecca Beatrice. "The Sons of Liberty: Who Were They and What Did They Do?" https:// historyofmassachusetts.org/the-sons-of-liberty-who-were-they-and-what-did-they-do/, accessed July 14, 2019.

CanadaHistory.com, "Guy Carleton," https://www.canadahistory.com/sections/periods/Colonial/British_ America/Guy_Carleton.html, accessed Aug. 15, 2019.

ConnecticutHistory.org, "Israel Putnam," https://connecticuthistory.org/people/israel-putnam/, accessed Aug. 14, 2019.

ConnecticutHistory.org, 'Thomas Knowlton: A Small Town's National Hero," https://connecticuthistory.org/ thomas-knowlton-a-small-towns-national-hero/, accessed Aug. 14, 2019.

Constitution Society, "The Olive Branch Petition," http://www.constitution.org/1-History/primarysources/olive. html, accessed Aug. 11, 2019.

Dacus, Jeff. "Gunpowder, The Bahamas, and the First Marine Killed in Action," Journal of the American Revolution, https://allthingsliberty.com/2019/05/gunpowder-the-bahamas-and-the-first-marine-killed-in-action/, accessed Aug. 18, 2019.

Dictionary.com, "Keep ones powder dry," https://www.dictionary.com/browse/keep-one-s-powder-dry, accessed Jan. 2, 2020.

Dictionary.com, "plunging fire," https://www.dictionary.com/browse/plunging-fire, accessed Dec. 23, 2019.

Fleming, Thomas, American Heritage, "The Enigma of General Howe," February 1964, https://www. americanheritage.com/content/enigma-general-howe, accessed Sept. 1, 2019.

Fort Montgomery State Historic Site, New York State Parks, Recreation and Historic Preservation, https://parks. ny.gov/historic-sites/28/details.aspx, accessed Aug. 11, 2019.

Frayler, John, "Privateers in the American Revolution," Salem Maritime National Historic Site, https://www.nps. gov/articles/privateers-in-the-american-revolution.htm, accessed Aug.11, 2019.

George Washington's Mount Vernon, "The Battle of Harlem Heights," http://www.mountvernon.org/digital-encyclopedia/article/battle-of-harlem-heights/, accessed July 27, 2019.

George Washington's Mount Vernon, "Washington's Revolutionary War Battles," https://www.mountvernon.org/george-washington/the-revolutionary-war/washingtons-revolutionary-war-battles/, accessed Dec. 18, 2019.

Giffin, Phillip. "Samuel Blachley Webb: Wethersfield Ablest Officer," *Journal of the American Revolution*, https://allthingsliberty.com/2016/09/samuel-blachley-webb-1753-1807/, accessed Dec. 1, 2019.

Historic Ipswhich, "Leslie's Retreat, or how the Revolutionary War almost began in Salem: February 26, 1775," https://historicipswich.org/2014/07/05/leslies-retreat-or-how-the-revolutionary-war-almost-began-in-salem/, accessed Aug. 11, 2019.

History.House.Gov., History, Art, and Archives: United States House of Representatives, "Forrest, Thomas," https://history.house.gov/People/Detail/13327?ret=True, accessed Nov. 16, 2019.

Jamestown-Yorktown Foundation, "The Battle of Great Bridge," https://www.historyisfun.org/blog/the-battle-of-great-bridge/, accessed Aug. 11, 2019.

Johnson, David. "Revolutionary War Weapons: The American Long Rifle," https://warfarehistorynetwork.com/revolutionary-war-weapons-the-american-long-rifle/, accessed Dec. 25, 2019.

Lovell, Louise. *Israel Angell, Colonel of the 2nd Rhode Island Regiment*, New York: G. P. Putnam and Sons, 1921, accessed at https://archive.org/stream/israelangellcolo00love/israelangellcolo00love_djvu.txt, Aug. 11, 2019.

Merriam-Webster, "Enfilading fire," https://www.merriam-webster.com/dictionary/enfilade, accessed Dec. 23, 2019.

Merriam-Webster, "Spoiling attack," https://www.merriam-webster.com/dictionary/spoiling%20attack, accessed Dec. 1, 2019.

Mifflin, Thomas (1744-1800), http://bioguide.congress.gov/scripts/biodisplay.pl?index=m000701, accessed Oct. 20, 2019.

Military Hall of Honor, "William Prescott," https://militaryhallofhonor.com/honoree-record.php?id=2976, accessed Aug. 14, 2019.

National Museum of the United States Army, "Major General Richard Montgomery," https://armyhistory.org/major-general-richard-montgomery/, accessed Aug. 15, 2019.

National Park Foundation, "Moore's Creek National Battlefield," https://www.nationalparks.org/explore-parks/moores-creek-national-battlefield, accessed Aug. 17, 2019.

Navy History and Heritage Command, "John Barry," https://www.history.navy.mil/research/library/research-guides/z-files/zb-files/zb-files-b/barry-john.html, accessed Nov. 21, 2019.

Naval History and Heritage Command, "The Birth of the Navy of the United States," https://www.history.navy.mil/browse-by-topic/commemorations-toolkits/navy-birthday/OriginsNavy/the-birth-of-the-navy-of-the-united-states.html, accessed Aug. 11, 2019.

Nesnay, Mary. "The Stamp Act: A Brief History," *Journal of the American Revolution*, https://allthingsliberty.com/2014/07/the-stamp-act-a-brief-history/, accessed July 15, 2019.

North Carolina Department of Natural and Cultural Resources, "Battle of Moore's Creek Bridge, 1776," https://www.ncdcr.gov/blog/2014/02/27/battle-of-moores-creek-bridge-1776, accessed Aug. 17, 2019.

Pennsylvania Center for the Book, "Samuel Nicholas," https://pabook.libraries.psu.edu/literary-cultural-heritage-map-pa/bios/Nicholas__Samuel, accessed July 7, 2019.

Randall, Willard. "Hamilton Takes Command: In 1775, the 20-year-old Alexander Hamilton took up arms to fight the British," https://www.smithsonianmag.com/history/hamilton-takes-command-74722445/, accessed Dec. 11, 2019.

Reference.com, "How Long Does It Take to Reload a Musket?" https://www.reference.com/world-view/long-reload-musket-f38b9c2f3e79ce7a, accessed Dec. 20, 2019.

Schenawolf, Harry. "Loading and Firing a Brown Bess Musket in the Eighteenth Century," http://www.revolutionarywarjournal.com/brown-bess/, accessed Dec. 22, 2019.

South Carolina Battleground Preservation Trust, "The Revolutionary War In Mount Pleasant, South Carolina," http://scbattlegroundtrust.org/rwmountpleasant/fort-sullivan-(circa-1776).html, accessed Sept. 1, 2019.

The Connecticut Society of The Sons of The American Revolution, "Lt. Col. Thomas Knowlton, Connecticut's Forgotten Hero," https://www.sarconnecticut.org/lt-col-thomas-knowlton-connecticuts-forgotten-hero/ accessed Aug. 11, 2019.

The Gilder Lehrman Institute of American History, "Henry Knox (1750-1806) to Lucy Knox," https://www.gilderlehrman.org/content/lucy-knox-21, accessed Aug. 11, 2019.

The Gilder Lehrman Institute of American History, "Henry Knox to Lucy Knox, Albany, January 5, 1776," https://www.gilderlehrman.org/collection/glc0243700237, accessed Aug. 30, 2019.

Total War Center, "Force Ratios and the 3:1 Rule Debate," http://www.twcenter.net/forums/showthread.php?746807-Force-Ratios-and-the-3-1-Rule-Debate, accessed Aug. 8, 2019.

Ushistory.org, The PA State Navy, http://www.ushistory.org/march/other/pennnavy.htm, accessed Nov. 16, 2019.

Washington's Mount Vernon, "Washington's Triumph at Trenton," https://www.mountvernon.org/george-washington/the-man-the-myth/washington-stories/the-triumph-at-trenton/, accessed Aug. 11, 2019.

Woodford, Shawn, "Comparing the RAND Version of the 3:1 Rule to Real-World Data," posted March 5, 2018 on "Mystics & Statistics: A blog on quantitative historical analysis hosted by The Dupuy Institute," http://www.dupuyinstitute.org/blog/2018/03/05/comparing-the-rand-version-of-the-31-rule-to-real-world-data/, accessed Aug. 8, 2019.

Dissertations and theses

Blanco, Richard, "American Army Hospitals in Pennsylvania During the Revolutionary War," State University of New York, Brockport, 1980, accessed at https://journals.psu.edu/phj/article/view/24277, Dec. 1, 2019.

Pawlikowski, Melissah, "From the Bottom Up: Isaac Craig and the Process of Social and Economic Mobility During the Revolutionary Era," Master's thesis, Duquesne University, 2007, https://dsc.duq.edu/etd/1028, accessed July 14, 2019.

Index

Adams, John, 11n, 24, 29-30, 35, 40, 43, 45, 58, 84, 88, 89, 300

Adams, Samuel, 23-24, 35, 40, 43, 45

Administration of Justice Act, 22

Alexander, Capt. Charles, 155

Alexander, Gen. William (Lord Stirling), 76n, 100, 146, 158, 162, 184, 229; capture of, 103; exchanged prisoner, 119; Brunswick, NJ, 135, 137, 139; French and Indian War (1756-63), 135; Trenton, 147, 182, 187, 190; winter of 1776, 150; the march to Trenton, 199-200, 206; the army forms for battle at Trenton, 208; Trenton, the battle begins, 215; post-Trenton, 225; return to Pennsylvania, 228; pursuing von Donop, 238

Allen, Ethan, 40

Altenbockum, Capt von (British), 211

Amboy, NJ, 135

American Revolution, 17, 21, 26, 52

The American Crisis, 176

Anderson, Capt. Enoch, 139, 147

Anderson, Capt. Richard, 202

Andre, Maj. John (British), 114

Andrews, John, 26

Angell, Maj. Israel, 278

Arnold, Gen. Benedict, xii, 40, 95-96, 114, 178n, 199; use of small personal fleets, 6; Quebec, 60; builds a fleet to block Lake Champlain, 116-117; protected Washington's northern flank, 117; Valcour Island, 117

Article 38, Marine Corps *Manual*, 1

Assunpink Creek, (Second Battle of Trenton), x, xii-xiv, 164, 172, 187, 211, 214-217, 242, 250, 253, 258; Trenton: the battle begins, 218; Second Battle of Trenton, 253; departure from Assunpink Creek, 265; modern *photo*(I) of, 244

Babbidge, James, civilian, 76

Bamford, Capt. William (British), 127

Barrett, Col. James, 31-32

Barry, Capt. John, 84, 145

Beale, Ens. Robert, 254

Biddle, Capt. James, 154

Biesenrodt, Capt. Bernard von (Hessian), 218

Bill of Rights, 23

Birmingham, 206

Block Island, Hopkins's raid upon, 79-81, 85; painting by Waterhouse, 81

Bissel, Israel, 36

British Military Units, Army: 1st Brigade, 29; 4th Brigade, x, 147; 10th Regiment of Foot, 29; 14th Regiment, 69; 16th Light Dragoons, 134, 163; 17th Regiment, x, 267-268, 271-272, 280-282; 40th Regiment, x, 267-268, 271, 282; 42nd Highlander Regiment, 179; 55th Regiment, x, 268, 271, 281-282; 64th Regiment, 28; Duke of York and Albany's Maritime Regiment of Foot, 5; Hessian grenadiers, 98; Hessian jaegers, 98; North American Squadron, 6; Prince of Wales American Regiment, 76n; Rall Regiment, 201, 214-215, 217, 226; Royal Marines, 5; von Knyphausen Regiment, 167-168, 207, 213, 215, 218-219; von Kohler Regiment, 179, 201; von Lossberg Regiment, 168, 184, 200-201, 211, 213-215, 217

British Navy Vessels: HMS *Acteon*, 87; HMS *Asia*, 107; HMS *Bolton*, 79, 87-88; HMS *Boyne*, 6; HMS *Carcass*, bomb ketch, 98; *Carleton*, schooner, 116; HMS *Carysfort*, frigate, 109; HMS *Cerberus*, 41, 47; HMS *Chatham*, 78; HMS *Endeavor*, 69; HMS *Experiment*, 87-88; HMS *Falcon*, 48, 155; HMS *Fowey*, 78; HMS *Friendship*, 87; HMS *Gaspee*, 6; HMS *Glasgow*, 80-82; HMS *Greyhound*, frigate, 98; HMS *Hawke*, 79; HMS *Inflexible*, 116; HMS *Lively*, 48; HMS

About the Author

Major General Jason Q. Bohm is a Marine with more than 30 years of service. An infantryman by trade, he has commanded at every level from platoon commander to commanding general in peacetime and war. Bohm also served in several key staff positions, including as a strategic planner with the Joint Chiefs of Staff, Director of the Marine Corps Expeditionary Warfare School, House Director, Marine Corps Office of Legislative Affairs, U.S. House of Representatives, and Chief of Staff of U.S. Naval Striking and Support Forces, NATO. Bohm has a bachelor's degree in marketing, a master's degree in military studies, and a master's degree in national security studies. Jason has written several articles for the *Marine Corps Gazette* and won various writing awards from the Marine Corps Association. He is the author of *From the Cold War to ISIL: One Marine's Journey* (Naval Institute Press, 2019).